MESTIZO
CHRISTIANITY

MESTIZO CHRISTIANITY

Theology from the Latino Perspective

Arturo J. Bañuelas, editor

ORBIS BOOKS

Maryknoll, New York 10545

Second Printing, February 1999

The Catholic Foreign Mission Society of America (Maryknoll) recruits and trains people for overseas missionary service. Through Orbis Books, Maryknoll aims to foster the international dialogue that is essential to mission. The books published, however, reflect the opinions of their authors and are not meant to represent the official position of the society.

Grateful acknowledgment is made to the following for permission to reprint from previously published material: Abingdon Books (Chapter 14), *Apuntes* (Chapters 8, 12), Fortress Press (Chapter 5), *Journal of Hispanic/Latino Theology* (Chapters 6, 11), *Listening: Journal of Religion and Culture* (Chapters 2, 3, 10), *Missiology* (Chapter 4), *New Theology Review* (Chapter 7), *U.S. Catholic Historian* (Chapter 13).

Queries regarding rights and permissions should be addressed to: Orbis Books, P. O. Box 308, Maryknoll, New York 10545-0308.

Published by Orbis Books, Maryknoll, NY 10545-0308
Manufactured in the United States of America

Cataloging-in-Publication Data is available from the Library of Congress, Washington, D.C.

ISBN 1-57075-032-7

Contents

Introduction

Today God-talk is being expressed from a new historical point of departure and by new protagonists in that history: Latino men and women struggling for life. United States Latino theology was born out of this reality and attempts to critically articulate this experience. In this theology, *mestizaje,* the mixture of human groups, is a core paradigm because Latino history begins in the early sixteenth century with the Spanish conquest and the religious and cultural confluence of the Spaniards, Amerindians, and Africans in the Americas. This paradigm of the mixing of bloods and cultures also marks the birth of *mestizo* Christianity, the experience of God from within *mestizaje* reality. *Mestizo* Christianity is the Latino's heritage. Presently, Latino theology is attempting to elaborate the link between *mestizaje* and God's designs for humanity.

In Latino theology, *mestizaje* is given a broader context than in the traditional understanding of a mixing of cultures, blood, and religious traditions. *Mestizaje* is a dynamic reality: it is the creation of a new race. It contributes to God's designs for a new humanity and thus is a *locus theologicus.* Furthermore, when viewed from the Latino peoples' struggles for survival, *mestizaje* is rooted in resistance against assimilationist tendencies by any oppressive, dominant culture. For this reason, Latino theology affirms *mestizaje* in the Latino's struggles for self-identity and self-determination and links it with God's plans for a new world order. While God-talk and *mestizaje* are linked in the Latino history of salvation, the issue of this relationship continues to be unsettled because *mestizaje* is and will continue to be an unfinished process as the place of origin changes.

As *mestizo* Christians, U.S. Latinos live as outsiders on the fringes of the dominant culture, but at the center as insiders in the diversity of peoples and cultures. Latinos live in the daily reality of mixture and interrelatedness. This creates for them a historical tension of ambiguity as well as an opportunity for evangelical mission. This tension results from the anguish of living as "nobodies" in society. Their sense of mission arises from living at the intersection in which God is bringing about a new humanity. Life is always ambiguous when it is lived at the crossroads, as it moves toward a new *mestizaje* while trying to preserve traditions and roots. This is the nature of living as a bilingual and multicultural *mestizo* Christian. It is living on the border of cultures, where a new *mestizaje* is bred.

1

Mestizo Christians comprise the largest racial group in the United States with varied backgrounds, including Mexicans, Puerto Ricans, Dominicans, Cubans, Central Americans, Andean peoples, and the populations of the borderlands of the Southwest. Although they are diverse peoples of various national origins, social classes, and cultural backgrounds, they share the historical foundational events of conquest and *mestizaje,* beginning in the sixteenth century and continuing in the present. Yet, precisely because of their *mestizaje,* they are relegated to live as strangers in their own land.

The total area where Latinos live in the United States is larger than Europe. Their great numbers make this country the fifth largest Spanish-speaking nation in the world. The facts show, however, that Latinos daily experience life as threatening. Bleak statistics reveal that they are still at the bottom of American society's economic, educational, social and political ladders. Even with the few gains they have made in some of these areas, the vast majority (especially women and children) struggle with the death-dealing forces of racism, sexism, and classism. Primary among these dark forces are the assimilationist ideologies of liberal capitalism, often masquerading as evangelization, that promote the continued historical invalidation of Latino culture and God's historical designs. From this experience springs a new theological movement in the United States.

Latino theology is a culturally contextualized theology for life. It is grounded *desde* ("from within") the daily struggles for survival of Latino communities facing death-dealing obstacles that deprive them of a full life. From the perspective of this reality, Latino theology chooses as its main focus the empowerment of the struggling Latino poor. In taking such a stand it avoids becoming a vehicle that justifies the continued oppression of Latinos.

In terms of content, style, and methodology Latino theology is a vibrant and exciting theological development in the Americas. The core tenet of this theology is that God is doing something unprecedented in the United States: in the midst of death-dealing forces, God is raising up the struggling Latinos as protagonists of the promises for new life. While Latino theology departs from North Atlantic theologies, it is connected to the Western Christian tradition, especially in the movement for the liberation of Latino peoples. In this way also, this new Latino theological voice serves as a corrective to the missionary history of cultural imperialism. No one culture can embrace the fullness of the mystery of God's self-revelation. Latino theology, however, claims that to be faithful to the historical plan of God, it must articulate the actions of God who is fashioning a new people in the Americas from within the struggles of the oppressed Latinos.

This emerging theology does not pretend to be neutral because it is directly engaged in the daily struggles of Latinos for survival. In its methodology a new historical subject is the main spokesperson: the unskilled worker, the single mother on welfare, the migrant, the poet, the prison inmate, the political refugee, the low-paid housekeeper, the *abuelita,* the abandoned children. Latino theology, then, is a reflection of the faith dimension in the Latino struggle for life. From within this perspective, Latino theologians make new claims to their right to tell their own version of salvation history, recognizing the fact that Western theological categories are not adequate in dealing with the complexities of *mestizo* Christianity. In fact, some of these categories have been used to justify the assimilation and ongoing injustice forced upon the Latino communities.

While Latino theology has *mestizaje* as its *locus theologicus,* it is informed also by Latin American liberation theologies, feminist theologies, African-American theologies, the social and behavioral sciences, the teachings of Vatican II, new scripture studies, and the growing ecumenical dialogue among Latino theologians. It should be said from the outset that Latino theology is not the stepchild of any other theological movement, precisely because it is grounded in the daily life-struggles and hopes of Latinos trying to survive in a dominant culture. Latino theology's primary source of reference is the activity of God who, through the liberation of Latinos, is fashioning a new human family.

Latino theologians are a new breed who prefer to situate themselves within the historical becoming of the new *mestizaje.* They not only hold positions in universities, but also teach and pastor in parishes, collaborate with Latinos in all fields of work, lead and organize empowerment groups for men and women, work with *barrio* clubs, assist people with AIDS, and participate in the sanctuary movement. With the faith communities they represent, they raise a voice not heard before, determined to speak the truth about God, defined most faithfully when spoken from within the Latino communities' struggle for life and justice. For this reason, they are not concerned about qualifying their categories to meet the pretended requirements for universality in theology. They know that this claim to universal validity can be a call for neutrality, which in turn results in the dominant culture's dictating the direction of theological discourse. They want to be Latino-specific with global implications for the liberation of all peoples.

With the above as background, this first-of-its kind volume is intended to introduce the reader to a core canon of U.S. Latino theology, with a selective bibliography to serve as a major reference source. The bibliographical material represents some 31 books and 186 articles by 47 authors. Of the writers 12 are women, 35 men, 9 Protestant and 38 Roman Catholic. The majority of these authors belong to The Academy of Catholic Hispanic Theologians in the United States (ACHTUS) or *La Comunidad* of Hispanic American Scholars of Theology and Religion. Among the predominant topics that emerge from surveying the bibliographical material are popular religion, methodology, feminist theology, liturgy, scripture, spirituality, Hispanic culture, mariology, pastoral ministry, catechesis and evangelization, the U.S. Latino presence, ecclesiology, and social ethics.

This volume, *Mestizo Christianity: Theology from the Latino Perspective,* with its fourteen articles by first-generation Latino theologians, is indicative of the vibrancy and creativity of Latino theology in its nascent stages. The first four articles point to a new framework for contextualizing Latino theology and outlining major theological categories and challenges (Elizondo, Segovia, Solivián, Bañuelas). What follows is a second series of four articles that explore the initial methodological considerations of this theology (Goizueta, García, Pineda, Recinos). An article on popular religiosity represents an essential tenet of Latino theology and shows how Latino culture is a bearer of revelation in Christian tradition (Espín). Articles by Latina theologians treat issues of gender that impede liberation and offer strategies for overcoming these obstacles (Isasi-Díaz, Aquino). The article on social ethics presents biblical and theological premises for a social, evangelical spirituality that challenges the social mission of the church (Villafañe). In this same vein, the article on the spirituality of U.S. Latinos argues for an inculturated spirituality currently lacking in the church's evangelization and catechetical efforts (Deck). Finally, from an ecumenical perspective, the volume concludes with a discussion on a new Latino reformation in the Americas (González). These articles, along with the works listed in the bibliography, nurture a hope embodied in the daily struggles of Latinos and present a theological vision taking shape in the historical becoming of a new *mestizaje.*

A special word of appreciation to the faculty at the Jesuit School of Theology at Berkeley, California, for their support during the editing of this book. They were the first to give support to the Academy of Catholic Hispanic Theologians in the United States (ACHTUS), and with its faculty the Jesuit School of Theology continues to be one of the best centers for the promotion of Latino theology in the nation. Thanks also to the Teagle Foundation, Inc., for the grant that made the year of research at Berkeley possible. The foundation's vision to support Hispanic projects has already reaped many benefits.

1

Virgil P. Elizondo

Virgil Elizondo was born of a Mexican American family in San Antonio, Texas. Nationally, he is recognized as the most prominent U.S. Latino Roman Catholic theologian. In 1969 he earned his masters (MA) in pastoral studies from the Ateneo University in Manila, and in 1987 a doctorate (STD/PhD) from the Institut Catholique in Paris. He has been awarded honorary degrees from Siena Heights College and from the Jesuit School of Theology at Berkeley.

After his ordination to the priesthood in 1963, Elizondo served in various parish and diocesan assignments. He was director of religious education for the Archdiocese of San Antonio (1965–1970), and academic dean of Assumption Seminary (1967–1972). He is the founder and first president of the Mexican American Cultural Center and of the Incarnate Word Pastoral Institute. He was the Henry Luce professor of World Christianity at Union Theological Seminary, and visiting professor at Regina Mundi Pontifical Institute in Rome and at Boston College. Presently he is rector of San Antonio's San Fernando Cathedral and executive producer of a live mass in Spanish which is televised internationally to over three million viewers.

Elizondo is considered a pioneer of U.S. Latino/a theology. Among his many contributions, his notion of *mestizaje* plays a significant and an influential role as a point of departure for this emerging U.S. Latino theology. His interpretation of the story of Our Lady of Guadalupe from the *mestizo* perspective is among his most important works. He has authored ten books, co-edited ten volumes in the *Concilium* series, and published over fifty articles.

Elizondo is on the editorial board of the *International Review of Theology: Concilium, Revista latinoamericana de teologia,* the Ecumenical Association of Third World Theologians, the National Committee for the Prevention of Child Abuse, and the Academy of Catholic Hispanic

Theologians in the United States. This Academy named its annual award for theological excellence the "Virgilio Elizondo Award," and he was the first recipient in 1989.

San Fernando Cathedral
115 Main Plaza
San Antonio, Texas 78205
512-227-1297

Mestizaje as a Locus of Theological Reflection

Virgil Elizondo

From the perspective of the millions of Hispanics in the United States, two great events took place in 1971 which have had a tremendous impact on Hispanic ministry in the United States: the birth of the Mexican-American Cultural Center (MACC) and the first publication in Lima, Peru, of Gustavo Gutiérrez's *Teología de Liberación*. Since then, Gustavo and the work of MACC have been intimately interrelated. Both emerge out of the same situation: the need for the church to see the suffering of the poor, to hear their cries, and to enter into their quest for liberation! In a way there was nothing new, Moses had already started the way, Jesus had died for it, and others in time have dedicated their lives to it.

What was radically new about MACC and Gustavo was that in a time when the institutions of the church had generally speaking ignored the cries of the poor or at best had sought to feed them, clothe them, and give them minimal medical aid, this new way was beginning with the poor themselves becoming the active agents of the salvation of all! It was not for the church to go out to the poor to be of service, but for the poor themselves, in response to God's word, to become church and work for the betterment of their own situation. As long as we did it "for the poor," we would maintain them poor! But to empower them so that out of their own poverty they would dare to dream and begin something really new, would indeed be an act of the all-powerful creative Spirit of God.

It has been my privilege to know Gustavo well since 1971. I have been his student, close friend, and collaborator. He has come to MACC every summer. It was here that he learned English and was able to experience the complexities of the U.S. way of life. He formed close friendships with MACC's team, especially our scripture scholars John Linskens and Juan

"*Mestizaje* as a Locus of Theological Reflection," *The Future of Liberation Theology,* ed. Marc Ellis and Otto Maduro (Maryknoll, New York: Orbis Books, 1989), pp. 358–74.

Alfaro, both of whom are continually feeding him good scriptural interpretations and works that can further the biblical understanding of liberation. Everyone at MACC and in the archdiocese of San Antonio loves him and believes in him.

Whether eating, exchanging jokes, discussing scripture, exploring new theological insights or church practices, swimming, or speaking about the issues of the poor in Latin America, the U.S.A., or anywhere in the world, being with Gustavo has always been a memorable experience. Padric O'Hare, formerly of Boston College, says that Gustavo is the only person he has ever met who seems to consciously live in the presence of God every moment of his life. I would certainly concur with that opinion. In the summer of 1985, Archbishop Flores introduced Gustavo to an auditorium full of expectant listeners, saying: "The two people I most admire and respect in this world are Mother Theresa and Father Gustavo for they have both chosen to do the greatest work of all: dedicate their lives to the service of the poor."

The MACC Challenge

The Hispanic Catholics of the United States have experienced a long history of neglect and oppression not only by society at large, but by the very church that is supposed to be our mother. We had somewhat been ministered to but we had never been invited to be active ministers in our own church. The church was so foreign to us that many felt priests were born Irish or Spanish, but it was unthinkable that we would become a priest or a religious.

Quite often we were scolded because we were not what the foreign missioners expected us to be as measured by the standards of the Catholicism of their place of origin. But hardly ever were we confirmed in our faith and helped to grow and develop in our pilgrimage of faith. Yet it was the deep faith and simple home practices of our *abuelitas* and *abuelitos* (grandparents) that sustained us in the faith and maintained us loyal to the Catholic tradition.

Church institutions had been so oppressive to us that when the radical Chicano movements started in the 1960s, the leaders often told priests and religious who tried to join them to get lost. They felt that the only way to help Hispanics get ahead was to get rid of Catholicism. It was painful to hear their insults, but as painful as their accusations were, we had to admit that they were true—if not totally, at least 95 percent of what they were saying against the church was correct. The church had kept us out and had witnessed and by its silence approved the ongoing exploitation and oppression of the Hispanics in the country.

The Chicano movements gave inspiration to the Chicano clergy and later on to all the Hispanic clergy in this country. We began to organize and to work for change within our own church. It was quickly evident that it was not sufficient to simply use Spanish in the liturgy, create our own music, and get more people involved in the work of the church. Much more was needed. We needed both practical know-how so that we could make the structures of our society work in favor of our people and we needed to create a new knowledge about ourselves, our social situation, and our religious beliefs. Until now, others had been telling us who we were. Nobody had bothered to ask us "Who are you?" Until now, all kinds of people had studied us, but no one had even sought to enter into conversation with us so that they might truly understand who we see ourselves to be. This was the very root of our oppressions. We were not allowed to be who we were. We were never allowed to simply say: "I AM."

It was at this moment of the struggle that we met Gustavo and his method of doing theology. It was God-sent! He was conceptualizing and expressing perfectly what we felt had to be done but had no idea of how to do it or even that we were on the right track. From the documents of Vatican II and our own experience of exclusion, we pretty well sensed what had to be done, but it was not yet clear. Reading Gustavo's work was like turning on the light-switch.

The first thing we learned from Gustavo was that theology is so important that we cannot leave it to the theologians alone ... and much less to theologians who are foreigners. Theology cannot be imported and neither can it be developed in isolation from the believing and practicing community. It is a joint enterprise of the believing community, which is seeking the meaning of its faith and the direction of its journey of hope lived in the context of charity. Great theologies were coming out of other parts of the world, but no one could do our theologizing for us. We had both the privilege and the responsibility! What follows is an attempt to do our own interpretation of our Christian existence.

The Human Situation of Mexican-Americans

The ancestors of today's Mexican-Americans have been living in the present-day U.S.A. since the early 1700s. Our group did not cross the border to come to the U.S.A., rather the U.S.A. expanded its borders and we found ourselves to be a part of the U.S.A. Since the early beginnings, many generations have crossed the Rio Grande to come over to the other side of the family lands. Yet we have always been treated as foreigners in our own countryside—exiles who never felt at home. The Mexican-Americans are a people twice conquered, twice colonized, and twice mestized. This is our socio-historical reality!

Mestizaje: The Undefined Identity and Consequent Margination

Mestizaje is simply the mixture of human groups of different makeup determining the color and shape of the eyes, skin pigmentation, and makeup of the bone structure. It is the most common phenomenon in the evolution of the human species. Scientists state that there are few, if any, truly "pure" human groups left in the world and they are the weakest because their genetic pool has been gradually drained. Through mixture, new human groups emerge and the genetic makeup is strengthened. Biologically speaking, *mestizaje* appears to be quite easy and natural, but culturally it is usually feared and threatening. It is so feared that laws and taboos try to prevent it from taking place for it appears as the ultimate threat to the survival of the species itself.

Mestizaje could certainly come in various ways, but it is a fact of history that massive *mestizaje* giving rise to a new people usually takes place through conquest and colonization. This has certainly been the case of the Mexican and the Mexican-American *mestizaje*. The first one came through the Spanish conquest of Mexico beginning in 1519 and the second one started with the Anglo-American invasion of the Mexican northwest beginning in the 1830s. The French biologist Ruffie states that, since the birth of Europe 35,000 years ago, when the invading Cro-Magnons mated with the native Neanderthals, no other event of similar magnitude had taken place until the birth of European-Mexico less than five hundred years ago. I would add that a similar event of equal magnitude is presently taking place in the southwest of the United States—an area larger than Western Europe and populated by several million persons.

Conquest comes through military force and is motivated by economic reasons. Yet, once it has taken place, the conquest is totalitarian. It imposes not only the institutions of the powerful, but also a new worldvision in conflict with the existing one. This imposition disrupts the worldvision of the conquered in such a way that nothing makes sense anymore. In many ways, the ideas, the logic, the wisdom, the art, the customs, the language, and even the religion of the powerful are forced into the life of the conquered. Although the conquered try to resist, the ways and worldvision of the powerful begin to penetrate their minds so that, even if political and economic independence come about, the native culture can never simply return to its preconquest ways.

Yet there is not only the obvious violence of the physical conquest, but the deeper violence of the disruption and attempts to destroy the conquered's inner worldvision, which gives cohesion and meaning to existence. The conquered's fundamental core religious symbols provide the ultimate root of the group's identity because they mediate the absolute. They are the final tangible expressions of the absolute. There is nothing beyond them that can put us in contact with God. They are the ultimate justification of the worldvision of the group and the force that cements all the elements of the life of the group into a cohesive, meaningful, and tangible world order. When such symbols are discredited or destroyed, nothing makes sense anymore. The worldvision moves from order into chaos, from significant mystery into a meaningless confusion.

Hence, the ushering in of new religious symbols, especially when they are symbols of the dominant group, are in effect the ultimate conquest. In a nonviolent way, missioners were the agents of a deeper violence. They attempted to destroy that which even the physical violence of the conquerors could not touch—the soul of the native people. In spite of the missionary's conscious opposition to the cruel and bloody ways of the conquistador, the nonviolent introduction of religious symbols of the Spanish immigrant in effect affirmed and justified the way of the powerful, and discredited and tried to destroy the way of the powerless. This same process has taken place with the predominantly Irish and German clergy and religious, who have ministered to Mexican-American Catholics.

The most devastating thing about the conquest is that it established a relationship so concrete and so permanent that it took on the nature of a metaphysical reality. In many ways, it determines the behavior and the characteristics of the members of each group. It even influences the theological reflection as the members of the conquistador group will appeal to scripture and theology to explain and legitimate the relationship. Martin Marty in his classical book, *The Righteous Empire,* gives an excellent exposition of how theology and biblical studies can be used to legitimize oppression. The powerful now establish their own version of truth as objective truth for everyone and impose it through their various means of power.

The image of the conquistador as "superior" and of the conquered as "inferior" will be imposed and interiorized by all the media of communications: dress, food, manners, language, modes of thinking, art, music, bodily gestures, mannerisms, entertainment, and all the institutions of society, such as the family, economics, school system, politics, and church, and most of all by the religious imagery and mythology. It is now the gods of the powerful who preside over the new world order. The totalitarian image that colonizing Europe established and implanted in the colonized peoples as the universal model for everyone continues to have a determining influence around the world. This "normative image" of Western civilization continues to be reinforced and projected through television and movies, books, periodicals, universities, and the European/U.S.A.-controlled religions. Only the white Western way appears as the truly human way of life; all others continue to be relegated to an inferior status. This is not necessarily a conscious effort, but it takes place all the time.

Yet, in spite of the difficult situation of inequality, the very seeds for the destruction of this dichotomy of colonizer-superior vs. colonized-inferior are physically implanted by the conquistador himself. Through his very bodily intercourse with the women of the conquered group, a new biological-cultural race is born, a race that will be both conquistador and conquered, superior and inferior, at one and the same time: he or she will be a real blood sister/brother of both, without being exclusively either. Furthermore, because the mother is the fundamental transmitter of deep cultural traits, it is the culture of the conquered that will gradually triumph over the culture of the conquistador in providing the dominant and deepest personality characteristics of the new group.

Mestizos are born out of two histories and in them begins a new history. The symbolic and mental structures of both histories begin to intermingle so that out of the new story which begins in the mestizo, new meanings, myths, and symbols will equally emerge. They will be meaningful to the mestizo as the firstborn of a new creation, but will remain incomprehensible to persons who try to understand them through the meanings, mythologies, and symbols of either of the previous histories alone. Yet from birth to maturity, there is a long period of painful search.

The deepest suffering of the mestizo comes from what we might call an "unfinished" identity or better yet an undefined one. One of the core needs of human beings is the existential knowledge that regardless of who I am socially or morally, I AM. The knowledge of fundamental belonging—that is, to be French, American, Mexican, English—is in the present world order one of the deepest needs of persons. When this need is met, it is not even thought about as a need, but when it is missing, it is so confusing and painful that we find it difficult to even conceptualize it or speak about it. We strive "to be like" but we are not sure just which one we should be like. As Mexican-Americans, we strive to find our belonging in Mexico or in the United States—only to discover that we are considered foreign by both. Our Spanish is too anglicized for the Mexicans and our English is too mexicanized for the Anglos.

In the case of Mexico, it was the mestizo image of our Lady of Guadalupe who provided the beginning of the new socio-cultural synthesis. It was not merely an apparition, but the perfect synthesis of the religious iconography of the Iberian peoples with that of native Mexicans into one coherent image. This marks the cultural birth of a new people. Both the parents and the child now have one common symbol of ultimate belonging. For the first time, they can begin to say "we are." As the physical birth of Mexicans had come through the conquest, the cultural birth came through the apparition. It is only after the apparition that those who had wanted to die now wanted to live and to celebrate life. In and through her, new meanings, myths and symbols will begin to emerge that will be truly representative and characteristic of Mexico.

Struggles for Accepting and Belonging

In the first stages of the struggle to belong, the mestizo will try desperately to become like the dominant group, for only they appear to be fully civilized and human. This struggle includes every aspect of life because the whole world structure of the dominant will have been assimilated and made normative for human existence. It equally involves a violent rejection of the way of the conquered because that now appears to be inferior. Only the scholars of the dominant group will appear as credible, only their universities as prestigious, their language as civilized, their medical practices as scientific, and their religion as true religion. The dominated will sometimes attempt to keep some of their original folklore, but, in every other way, they try to become like the dominant.

Some of the well-intentioned and kind of the dominant group will help the brighter and more promising ones (according to their own standard of judgment) to better themselves by "becoming like us." They will privilege them with scholarships to the best universities in Europe or the United States, and help them to learn the European or American way of life and language.

Some of the marginated will make it into the world of the dominant society only to discover that they will never be allowed to belong fully, and furthermore that down deep inside they are still somewhat "other." Yet it is this very pain of not being able to belong fully that also marks the beginning of a new search.

In the first stages of the search, the ones who choose not to join the struggle to become like the dominant ones will tend to reject the world of the dominant in a total way: absolutely nothing good can come out of it. They will not only reject it but will hate it passionately. The only way to treat the dominant ones is to get rid of them. They are the ones who are guilty not only of the individual sin of homicide, but of the collective sin of ethnocide.

Throughout all these struggles, there is something radically new beginning to emerge. Even though the seeds are planted from the very beginning, and biologically this new life begins from the very start, it will take time for the cultural identity to emerge as a distinct identity of its own. This new identity does not try to become like someone else, but it struggles to form its own unique individuality. It accepts from both parent cultures without seeking to be a replica of either. It is like the maturing child who no longer tries to be like the mother or like the father, nor to simply reject both of them, but is simply himself or herself. Through the pains and frustrations of trying to be what we are not, the uniqueness of our own proper identity begins to emerge. It is an exciting moment of the process and usually the most creative stage of the life of the group.

It is at this moment that the quest to know ourselves begins to emerge in a serious way. In the beginning, knowledge of ourselves will be confused because we see ourselves through a type of double image—that is, through the eyes of the two parent groups. As the group develops, its own proper image will begin to emerge and it will be easy to study ourselves more critically. It is this new and more clearly defined self-image of who we are as Mexican-Americans that is presently beginning to take shape. As usual, it is the poets, the artists, and the musicians who are beginning to paint and to sing and to suggest the new identity. It is now the critical thinkers who are coming in and beginning to deepen, to conceptualize, to verbalize, and to communicate the reality of our identity. And it is only now that for the first time we begin to ask ourselves about our Christian identity, about our church and about our religion—What does it really mean? Who are we as Mexican-American Christians?

The Human Situation: Divisions and Collective Self-Protection

When one looks at the history of humanity, then wars, divisions, and family fights appear more natural than do peace, unity, and harmony. This is evident from the global level down to the family cell. It appears more natural for brothers and sisters to fight one another than to love one another. We struggle to protect ourselves against each other and to conquer others before they conquer us. We prepare for peace by preparing for war. Only violent means appear to be able to control or curb violence. Might makes right because power establishes its views as objective truth so as to justify its own position of privilege. The survival of the fittest appears to be the first law of individuals and of society—the survival of the powerful at the cost of the weak.

From this struggle for survival at the cost of others, certain anthropologico-sociological characteristics and behavioral laws appear. The members of the dominant group in power will see themselves as pure, superior, dignified, well-developed, beautiful, and civilized. They see themselves as the model for all others. They see their natural greatness as the source of their great achievements. Even the least among them consider themselves superior to the best of the dominated group.

On the other hand, they look upon the conquered and colonized as impure, inferior, undignified, underdeveloped, ugly, uncivilized, conservative, backward. Their ways are considered childish and their wisdom is looked upon as superstition. Because might is subconsciously assumed to be right, everything about the weak is considered to be wrong and unworthy of being considered human. The conquered are told that they must forget their backward ways if they are to advance and become human. Acculturation to the ways of the dominant, in every respect whatsoever, is equated with human development and liberation.

Even the best among the dominant group find it very difficult to truly accept the other as other: to enjoy their foods, learn from their wisdom, speak their language, dress in their styles, appreciate their art and their music, interpret life through their philosophies, live in their ways, and even worship through their forms of cult. Even though many go out, even heroically, to be of service to the poor and the oppressed, and really love them, there is still an inner fear and rejection of their otherness. The way of the powerful as the normative human way for all persons is so deeply ingrained that it literally takes a dying to oneself to be able to break through the cultural enslavements that keep the dominant from appreciating the inner beauty, the values, the worth, and the dignity of the ways of the conquered.

Because of the image imposed upon them about themselves, some of the conquered will begin to think of themselves as inferior and good for nothing. This develops a type of domesticated, happy-go-lucky, subservient attitude in relation to the dominant. It is a very dehumanizing existence, but the powerless have no choice—either conform to the status assigned by the powerful or be eliminated physically. Law and order, policy and justice, work in favor of the rich against the poor. Whereas the rich tend to be considered innocent until proven guilty, the poor are usually considered guilty until proven innocent. They are blamed for all the problems of society and are considered to be the source of all evil and crime. Thus, the very victims of the institutionalized violence of power are labeled by the establishment as the causes of this violence! The powerful can define the image and status of the oppressed as "guilty of all evil" and force them to live accordingly. The poor and the oppressed thus serve as the scapegoats of the crimes of the establishment, which can continue to think of itself as pure and immaculate. However, as long as the traditions of the oppressed continue, especially their deepest religious traditions, they may be forced to live as dirt, but they cannot be forced to perceive themselves as such. Through their traditions, perfectly understood by them but incomprehensible to foreigners, they continue to perceive themselves as they truly are: free human beings with full human dignity who, although dominated through external powers, nevertheless remain free and independent in the innermost core of their being.

The in-group will defend tradition, law, and order because they are the privileged ones of the establishment. National and personal security will be among the top priorities of this group as it strives to maintain the status quo. For the powerful, tradition protects their position of privilege; for the powerless, their own traditions are the ultimate rejection of the status quo of the dominant—their bodies might be dominated but not their souls.

Tradition functions in a diametrically opposed way for the powerful and for the powerless. For the powerless, tradition is the affirmation of inner freedom, independence, and self-worth. It is the power for the radical transformation of the existing order. For the moment, it might appear as a tranquilizer, but we cannot underestimate its power in keeping a people alive as a people. As long as their traditions are alive, they are assured of life and ultimate liberation. If their traditions disappear, they will no longer have to work for integral liberation, because they will have ceased to exist as a people.

In attempting to analyze the dynamics between the oppressor in-group and the oppressed out-group, three constants seem to function as anthropological laws of human behavior.

When one studies the human story across the ages, the tendency of group inclusion/exclusion—that is, to protect our own by keeping others

out—appears to be one of the most consistent and fundamental anthropological laws of nature. Dominant groups will struggle to maintain outside
influences in a multiplicity of ways, and weaker or dominated ones will
likewise fear and resist any type of intrusion. The purity of the group must
be maintained. Human barriers of race, class, language, family name,
education, economic status, social position, and religion are regularly used
as signals to distinguish "our own" from "the others."

The second tendency that appears as an anthropological law of nature
is: others can be used and enjoyed, but a social distance must be maintained.
Deep friendships might develop and even strong love relationships, but
the social barriers are so deeply interiorized and assimilated that they are
very difficult to do away with. There are not just laws that keep peoples
apart, but the relationship of superior-inferior that is established, projected,
transmitted, assimilated, and even sacralized by religion. This keeps persons from truly appreciating each other as fully equal and from seeing the
true human dignity of one another. Even the best among the dominant
group tend to see and treat the others as inferior and "different." We can
even do good things for the lesser others, but they remain lesser. They
can be exploited legitimately because the culture and the laws of the
dominant sanction the superior-inferior relationship. This gives the "master" the right and the obligation to use and "protect" the lesser ones.

This law of social distance is probably the hardest one to break through
because it is not only enforced by external laws and the economic-political
mechanisms of the land, but it is interiorized in a multiplicity of ways.
For example, in ordinary commercials, we see blacks waiting on whites,
but I have never seen a commercial with a white serving a black. Blacks,
but never racially mixed families, appear in commercials. Brown-skins do
not even appear at all. Social barriers of separability are drilled into a people
through all the media of communication and education. Even religious
education material and religious images in our churches exhibit a definite
racial preference, thus indirectly telling the others that they cannot be
reflected in the sacred.

Finally, the third constant that appears as an anthropological law of
nature is: anyone who threatens to destroy or annul the barriers of separation
will be an outcast—an impure untouchable who must be eliminated.

As should be evident by now, *mestizaje* is feared by established groups
because it is the deepest threat to all the humanly made barriers of separation that consecrate oppression and exploitation. It is a threat to the security
of ultimate human belonging—that is, to the inherited national/cultural
identity that clearly and ultimately defines who I am to myself and to the
world. It is even a deeper threat to established societies because the mestizo
cannot be named with clarity and precision. So much is in the mystery of
a name! I am comfortable when I can name you, for, in many ways, it
indicates that I am somewhat in control of the situation. I may not like
what I know, but at least I have the comfort of knowing what it is. But

there is a nervousness when I do not know who you are—your name and your cultural nationality are so important, for they tell me who you are personally and fundamentally. They give me your immediate and ultimate human identity.

Because of the hyphenated identity, mestizos cannot be named adequately by the categories of analysis of either group. They do not fit into the single history set of norms for testing and identifying persons. This is threatening to both groups—we can name them and even study them, but they cannot name us or even figure out how to really study us. It is threatening for anyone to be in the presence of one who knows us very well even in our innermost being, but we do not know who they are. To be an outside-insider, as the mestizo is, is to have both intimacy and objective distance at one and the same time, for, insofar as we are in Mexico, we are outside the United States; but insofar as we are in the United States, we are distant from Mexico. As such we can see and appreciate the aspects of both, which neither sees of themselves or each other. In this very in-out existence lies the potential for our creativity: to pool the cultural genes and the chromosomes of both so as to create a new one!

The potential for newness will not be actualized automatically. The mestizo can simply become like one of the parent groups and continue to do unto others as they have done unto us. However, they can equally, although with more hidden difficulties than anyone suspects, choose to live out the radical meaning of their new being. This is exciting but difficult because, even though the dominant way may be rejected totally and explicitly, subconsciously the oppressed will strive to become like the oppressor, for they have already assimilated many of the characteristics of the dominant group. Will the group simply obtain power and acceptance by reverting to the ways of the parent group or will they initiate new life? That is the key question.

As a Mexican-American Christian, I am convinced that the full potential of *mestizaje* will be actualized only in and through the way of the Lord, which brings order out of chaos and new life out of death. It is in the Lord's way that the salvific and liberating role of our human mestizo way finds its ultimate identity, meaning, direction, and challenge.

The Concrete-Historical Meaning of God's Saving Way

The Human Identity of the Savior

The racial-cultural identity of a person is the very first and immediate revelation of who one is. We all have stereotype prejudices about certain colors, accents, languages, features, regions, and religions. There is a natural tendency to categorize persons according to our sterotypes of them and to prejudge them as to their human worth and potential even before they have said or done anything. Looks are all-important and they are the first revelation, according to the standards of the world, of the worth and dignity of the person. Persons from the outer regions of any country are usually looked down upon as rustics, whereas those from urban centers look upon themselves as sophisticated.

What was the racial-cultural identity of Jesus? What did others think of when they first saw or heard of him . . . before they even heard him speak or saw his actions? These are all-important questions, for we know from the New Testament itself that it is in the human face and heart of Jesus that God has been self-revealed to us. It is through the full humanity of Jesus that God has allowed us to see God in a human way.

There is no doubt that, during his lifetime, Jesus was regularly known as a Galilean, that most of his disciples were from Galilee, and that most of the things we remember best of his activity took place in Galilee. There is no doubt that Galilee plays a key role in the life and mission of Jesus as presented in the Gospels.

The full human signification of the kenosis of the Son of God becomes evident when we look at the image of Galilee in Jesus' time. First of all, if it had not been for Jesus, Galilee would probably remain an unknown region of the world. Jerusalem, Greece, and Rome were all important with or without Jesus, but not Galilee. It was an outer region, far from the center of Judaism in Jerusalem of Judea and a crossroads of the great caravan routes of the world. It was a region of mixed peoples and languages. In Galilee the Jews were looked down upon and despised by the others as they were in the rest of the world. They were considered to be stubborn, backward, superstitious, clannish, and all the negative stereotypes one could think of. Furthermore, the Jews of Judea looked down upon the Galilean Jews, for they considered them ignorant of the law and the rules of the temple, contaminated in many ways by their daily contacts with pagans, not capable of speaking correct Greek, for their language was being corrupted by admixture with the other languages of the region. In short, their own Jewish relatives despised them as inferior and impure. Because of their mixture with others, they were marginated by their own people. There were no doubts about the cultural *mestizaje* that was taking place and, knowing the ordinary situation of human beings, a certain amount of biological *mestizaje* was equally taking place. Culturally and linguistically speaking, Jesus was certainly a mestizo between Judaism and the other cultures that flourished throughout Galilee. And we know from the early Jewish charges that tried to discredit Jesus that he was even accused of being the bastard son of a Roman soldier named Pantera, which could also be a colloquial term for simply meaning "a Roman," which could have made of him a biological mestizo as well. I am, of course, in no way denying or even questioning that Jesus was conceived by the Holy Spirit. What I am saying is that in his human appearance, as viewed by those who knew him only in a worldly way and not through the eyes of faith, he certainly appeared to be of mixed origins. The New Testament itself gives clear evidence that nothing good was expected to come out of Galilee.

The point of bringing out all this is to appreciate the human beginnings of God's mission. God becomes not just a human being, but the marginated, shamed, and rejected of the world. He comes to initiate a new human unity, but the all-important starting point is among the most segregated and impure of the world. Among those whom the world has thrown out, God will begin the way to final unity. It is among those whom the world labels as "impure" that a new criterion for real purity will emerge.

Because the world expected nothing good to come out of Galilee, God chose it to be the starting point of God's human presence among us. The principle behind the cultural image of the Galilean identity is that God chooses what the world rejects. What is marginal to the world is central to God. It is through those whom the world has made nothing that God will reduce to nothing the power and wisdom of the world. It is through the poor and nonpersons of the world that God continues to reveal God's face and heart in a human way and among them—the Galilees and Galileans of today—salvation continues to begin for all the peoples of the world.

The Cultural Function of His Mission

The mission of Jesus is not some sort of esoteric or aesthetic truth. He comes to live out and proclaim the supreme truth about humanity, which will have immediate and long-term implications in everyday life and in the history of humanity. Those who hear his word and are converted to his way will see themselves and will equally see all others in a radically new way. This new image of self and of others will allow everyone to relate with each other as never before.

Because of his concrete human identity, Jesus had personally suffered the pains of margination and dehumanizing insults. He was concerned with the pains of hunger, sickness, bad reputation, rejection, shame, class struggles, loneliness, and all the real sufferings of humanity. His concern was not abstract, but real and immediate. He spoke with the Samaritan woman, ate with the rich, the tax collectors, and sinners alike. He did not feel repelled by the leper; he enjoyed the company of women and little children. Jesus was truly at home with everyone and it is evident that everyone felt at home with him. This is nowhere more evident than in his ability to enjoy himself at the common table fellowship with everyone without exception.

Out of the cultural suffering of rejection, Jesus offers a new understanding of the kingdom. He did not come to restore the kingdom of David for the Jewish people, but to initiate the reign of God who is the Father of everyone. The innermost identity of Jesus was his life of intimacy with God-Father. It is this living relationship with the Absolute that cuts through and relativizes all human images of importance or nonimportance, dignified or undignified. When we know the ultimate origins of a person—that he is really the son of the king—the superficial appearances are no longer important. It is the ultimate origins and name of a person that give us his true worth. It is precisely this intimacy with God-Father which is the basis of the innermost identity of Jesus, which he offers to all others. It is not the labels that the world places on persons that count, but one's own innermost identity and image of oneself as reflective of the likeness of God. By discovering that God is our real Father we begin to see everything in a new way. No longer will I see others as superior or inferior to me, but as brothers and sisters of the same Father. In this realization is the basis for a totally new value system for humanity. In fidelity to God, Jesus refuses to conform to any human law or tradition that will dehumanize and make appear as inferior any human being whatsoever. The truth of Jesus will upset humankind's criteria of judgment. Because one is, one is a child of God. But precisely because everyone can now belong, those who have set up and guarded the multiple barriers of separation, which allow them to enjoy the privileges of being "in" at the cost of keeping the so-called inferior ones "out," will not only refuse the invitation but will discredit the new way and try to prevent it from coming into existence.

But it is not sufficient to invite the rejected into the kingdom. It is not sufficient to tell the exploited and marginated of society that they are truly free human beings who are equal to all others. One must go to the roots of the human mechanisms, both to the external and the internal structures of society, to make known the segregating and dehumanizing evil that has been institutionalized and is now hidden in the various structures of the group. Jesus makes known that he must go to Jerusalem, the route of the sufferings of his people. Truth in the service of love must bring out clearly the evil hidden in human structures, which passes as good. Such a confusion allows the evils of power to appear as the good of society, to even appear as the sufferings of the marginated, as the causes of all evil. Criminals appear as good; victims appear as criminals. This is the on-going confusion of Babel, which continues to mask and confuse both the evil and the good of the world.

Jesus appears in the New Testament as the aggressive prophet of nonviolent love who refuses to conform to the violence of the structures in full loyalty to the tradition of the God of his people, of the God who sees the suffering, who hears the cries of affliction, and who wills to save. He questions the human traditions that oppress or destroy a people. Jesus must go to Jerusalem because that is the center of institutionalized power. When he arrives he goes to the very core of Judaism: the temple. In Jerusalem we see Jesus who does not hesitate to question the very legitimacy of the structures that were enslaving the masses of the people. The house of the God of compassion and justice had become the place that now legitimized and covered up the evil ways of the establishment. The same story is found in all human institutions. We need institutions in order to live in an orderly and peaceful way. Yet, all institutions have the tendency to become self-serving to the benefit of those in control. They are set up to serve persons, but persons end up serving them. It is this very tendency to absolutize that must be confronted and made known. As institutions, customs, and traditions become absolutized, they function as the idols of the group. Whether we call them God or not, they function as the real gods of the group. To question them is the same as questioning God. And when we challenge them, we will be accused of blasphemy. Yet to the degree that these ways dehumanize or reject any human being, they must be questioned in the name of God. But Jesus does not confront the power of the world with a power of the same order. He does not give in to the ways of humanity. He confronts the power of the world and human violence with a power of an entirely different order: the power of unlimited love, which will not give in to violence to eliminate violence.

The nonviolent way of Jesus worked in a diametrically opposed way to the nonviolent way of the missioners of the power countries. First of all, he begins by assuming the way, the language, and the world vision of the Galileans—the non-persons of the world. The all-powerful God, in becoming a Galilean, converts so as to become the marginated, the rejected, and the nonperson of the world. Secondly, he does not only denounce the accepted practices of the powerful, as good missioners often do, but unlike the average traditional missioner, he even denounces and desacralizes their ultimate authority as enshrined in their religious symbols, for it is the religious symbols of the powerful that ultimately legitimize their way as God's way. Thirdly, the radical difference between the missionary activity of Jesus and that of missioners who are culturally and nationally members of the powerful countries is apparent in the response of the officials.

Official Judaism condemned Jesus and got rid of him. His accusers disowned him to the Romans because he questioned their ultimate authority and the ultimate legitimacy of their structures. The officials of mission-sending countries support and reinforce the missionary endeavor because it in effect affirms and perpetuates the legitimacy of their own world order. In supporting the missions, they affirm their own ultimate authority and the divine legitimacy of their ways. Let me be clear on this point; this is not necessarily done in an intentional or malicious way; in fact, I would say that quite often it is done with the best of intentions; however, the final result remains the same. The Spanish missioners did not hesitate to chastise openly and consistently the crimes and abuses of the conquest; however, they legitimized the way of the conquerors by affirming their ultimate symbol as superior and true in relation to the symbols of ultimate reality of captured peoples.

The way of Jesus to Jerusalem and the cross is the challenging task of those who are on the margins of society. Their temptation will always be to become simply the powerful themselves, as even the disciples wanted to do. But the challenge is to be willing to die so that a new way will truly be ushered in. The authorities kill Jesus but they cannot destroy him. He remains faithful to his way to the very end. He came to reject every type of human rejection and, even when all appear to have rejected him, even his God, he rejects no one. He dies in perfect communion with his people and his God. He came to tear down barriers of separation; and no matter what humanity tried to do to stop him, they were not able to break him down. As he lived his life in communion with everyone—so he died. All had rejected him, but he rejects no one.

God's love in and through Jesus triumphs over all the divisive hatreds and consequent violence of humanity. Jesus passes through death to life. In resurrecting him, God rejects the rejection of humanity, destroys all the charges of illegitimacy and demolishes the idolized structures. In the resurrection, God ratified the entire way and message of Jesus. It is from the resurrection that the entire way of Jesus and every aspect of his life takes on a liberating and salvific signification.

It is in the resurrection that the new life initiated and offered to everyone by Jesus is now fully and definitively present. No human power will be able to destroy it or slow it down. Jesus is the firstborn of the new creation, and in his followers a new human group now begins. It is definitely a new human alternative now present in the history of humanity.

First of all, those who had nothing to offer now have the best thing to offer to everyone: new life. It is the rejected and marginated Galileans who have received the Spirit and, without ceasing to be Galileans, now see themselves in a new way as they begin to initiate the new humanity. Everyone is invited, but it is the very ones who had been excluded who are now doing the inviting. It is obvious from the history of the early church how quickly the new way spread to *all peoples.* It crossed all boundaries of separation. Persons, without ceasing to be who they were culturally, nevertheless saw themselves in such a new way that the ordinary human barriers were no longer obstacles to the new fellowship. It is equally evident that the crossing of cultural boundaries was not easy, for each group had its own unsuspected idols, yet the miracle is that it took place. Cultural-national groups, which had been totally separated, now can come together—no longer Jew or gentile, master or slave, male or female, but all one in Christ. They continued to be who they were, but they lived their nationality and religion in a radically new way. Their identity was affirmed but their exclusiveness was destroyed. This openness led them to discover new values and criteria of judgment . . . from competition to cooperation, from divisions to unity, from strangers to a common family, from a superior or inferior status to common friends and all children of the same father.

The radical all-inclusive way of Christianity started among the rejected and lowly of society. This is the ongoing starting point. In the Spirit, they struggle to build new human alternatives so that others will not have to suffer what they have had to suffer. It is they who first hear the invitation to the new universal family of God, and it is the converted poor and suffering of the world, who see themselves in a new way, who now go out to invite—by deeds and words—all others into the new society. God continues to begin where humanity would never suspect. Out of the Nazareths and Galilees of today, salvation continues to come to the entire world.

The God-Meaning of Our Mexican-American Identity and Mission

"God chose those whom the world considers absurd to shame the wise"
(1 Cor. 1:28)

It is in the light of our faith that we discover our ultimate identity as God's chosen people. It is in the very cultural identity of Jesus the Galilean and in his way from Galilee to Jerusalem that the real ultimate meaning of our own cultural identity and mission to society become clear.

For those who ordinarily have a good sense of belonging, the idea of being chosen is nothing special. But for one who has been consistently ignored or rejected, the idea of being noticed, accepted, and especially chosen is not only good news, but new life. For in being chosen, what was nothing now becomes something, and what was dead now comes to life. In the light of the Judeo-Christian tradition, our experience of rejection and margination is converted from human curse to the very sign of divine predilection. It is evident from the scriptures that God chooses the outcasts of the world not exclusively but definitely in a preferential way. Those whom the world ignores, God loves in a special way. But God does not choose the poor and the lowly just to keep them down and make them feel good in their misery. Such an election would be the very opposite of good news and it would truly be the opium to keep the poor quiet and domesticated. God chooses the poor and the marginated of the world to be the agents of the new creation.

The experience of being wanted *as one is,* of being needed and of being chosen, is a real and profound rebirth. Those who had been made to consider themselves as nothing or as inferior will now begin to appreciate the full stature of being human beings. Out of the new self-image, new powers will be released, which have always been there but have not been able to surface. Through this experience, the sufferings of the past are healed though not forgotten, and they should not be forgotten. For it is precisely out of the condition of suffering that the people are chosen so as to initiate a new way of life where others will not have to suffer what the poor have suffered in the past. When one forgets the experience of suffering, as has happened to many of our migrant groups in this country, such as the Irish in Boston, then they simply inflict the same insults upon others that had previously been inflicted upon them. The greater the suffering and the more vivid the memory of it, the greater the challenge will be to initiate changes so as to eliminate the root causes of the evils which cause the suffering. It is the wounded healer who has not forgotten the pain of the wounds who can be the greatest healer of the illnesses of society.

It is in our very margination from the centers of the various establishments that we live the Galilean identity today. Because we are inside-outsiders, we appreciate more clearly the best of the traditions of both groups, while equally appreciating the worst of the situation of both. It is precisely in this double identity that we in effect have something of unique value to offer both. The very reasons for the margination are the bases of our liberating and salvific potential not only for ourselves but for the others as well. In a privileged way, God is present in the marginated, for distance from the powers of the world is closeness to God. It is consistently in the frontier regions of human belonging that God begins the new creation. The established centers seek stability, but the frontier regions can risk to be pioneers. It is the frontier people who will be the trailblazers of the new societies. "The stone which the builders rejected has become the keystone of the structures. It is the Lord who did this and we find it marvelous to behold" (Matt. 21:42).

"I Have Chosen You To Go and Bear Much Fruit" (John 15:16)

God chooses people not just to make them feel good, but for a mission. "I have chosen you to go out and bear much fruit" (John 15:16). To accept God's election is not empty privilege, but a challenging mission. It is a call to be prophetic both in deeds and in words. It is a call to live a new alternative in the world, to invite others into it, and to challenge with the power of truth the structures of the world that keep the new alternative from becoming a reality.

Our Mexican-American Christian challenge in the world today is not to try to become like someone else—Mexicans or Americans—but to combine both into a new way. It is through the very mechanisms of forging a new and more cosmopolitan identity that new life begins to emerge. It must be worked at critically, persistently, and creatively, for the temptation will always be there to become simply one or the other of the previous models. The temptation will always be there to restore the kingdom rather than to usher in the kingdom of God. In our present powerlessness we may think that this is stupid, but, in our faith, we know that we must take the risks and begin to initiate new ways of life that will eliminate some of the dehumanizing elements of the present one. We know that we will not eliminate them all, nor will this come about easily and without much effort, organization, and frustration, but nevertheless the efforts must be made to introduce new forms and new institutions that will continue some of the best of the past while eliminating some of the worst. We will not build the perfect society, but we must do our part to at least build a better one. We must begin with the grass roots, but we must equally go to the very roots of the problems.

This is our "divine must"! We, too, must harden our faces and go to Jerusalem. We must go to the established centers of power, whether political, economic, educational, or religious, to confront their sacred idols which prevent them from truly serving all the people. It is the idols of society which function in favor of the rich and the powerful, and against the poor and powerless. It is they which mass the hidden viciousness and manipulations of the wise of the world who find many ways of exploiting the poor and the simple of the world.

We really do not have a choice if we want to be disciples following Jesus on his way to the cross. It is this road from Galilee to Jerusalem which has to be continued if evil is to be destroyed, not with new forms of evil, but with the power of truth in the service of love. We have no choice but to speak the truth which brings to light clearly the evil of the world, knowing full well that the powers of darkness will not stop at anything in order to put out the light.

"Your Grief Will Be Turned to Joy" (John 16:20)

It is in our fiestas that our legitimate identity and destiny are experienced. They are not just parties; in fact they are the very opposite. They are the joyful, spontaneous, and collective celebrations of what has already begun in us even if it is not recognized by others or verbalized even by ourselves. It is the celebration of the beginning of the ultimate eschatological identity where there will be differences but not division. It is the celebration of what has already begun in germ but is yet to be totally fulfilled. Yet the fiesta is a foretaste and experience, even if for a brief moment, of the ultimate accomplishment. It is a result of who we are and a cause of what is yet to become. For just as it is true that the celebrations of the people can be used to drug the people and keep them in their misery, it is equally true that the fiestas can be used as rallying moments that not only give the people an experience of togetherness, but can also nourish the movements of liberation. In the fiestas, we rise above our daily living experiences of death to experience life beyond death. They are the moments of life that enable us to survive, to come together, to rally, and to begin anew. The spirit not only to survive but to bring about a new existence can be enkindled in the fiestas so as to ignite the people to action.

Fiestas without prophetic action easily degenerate into empty parties, drunken brawls, or the opium to keep the people in their misery. But prophetic action without festive celebration is equally reduced to dehumanizing hardness. Prophecy is the basis of fiesta, but the fiesta is the spirit of prophecy. It is in the combination of the two that the tradition of faith is both kept alive and transmitted to newcomers. It is through the two of them that the God of history who acts on our behalf, on behalf of the poor and the lowly, continues to be present among us bringing the project of history to completion.

Thus it is precisely through our *fiestas* that we are kept together as a people. It is through them that we have continued to maintain our identity and sense of belonging. They are the deepest celebrations of our existence—meaningful to those who belong and incomprehensible and folkloric to outsiders. They are the lifeline of our tradition and the life sources of our new existence.

Annotated Bibliography—Virgil Elizondo

Christianity and Culture (San Antonio: Mexican American Cultural Center, 1975).

One of Elizondo's first works on the relationship between faith and culture from the Mexican-American perspective. He makes appropriate references to the documents of Vatican II, speaks of the importance of bilingualism in theology, and writes about the anthropological-psychological characteristics of Mexican Americans. This is a primer on the popular religious practices of the Mexican American community.

La Morenita: Evangelizer of the Americas (San Antonio: Mexican American Cultural Center, 1980).

Perhaps his most popular work. Elizondo offers an interpretation of the Guadalupe story from within the Mexican American perspective. Viewed from this perspective, the Guadalupe event is a call for a new evangelization as liberation in the fashioning of a new humanity, which Elizondo views as being born anew since the events at Tepeyac. The first part of the book describes the *mestizaje* account. The second part offers his interpretation of the Guadalupe story and image. In the final section, he presents the evangelical challenge of *La Morenita.*

Galilean Journey: The Mexican American Promise (Maryknoll, New York: Orbis Books, 1983).

This volume coalesces Elizondo's basic theological position, which can be categorized as "faith confronts culture." He argues that the church is experiencing a *kairos* moment grounded on the promise of the Mexican American contribution in fashioning a new historical period in the Western Hemisphere. This perspective is born from the experience of a double conquest of the Mexican American, who, through the resultant *mestizaje,* is now proleptically celebrating an eschatological fiesta: the weaving together of a new universalism in North, Central, and South America.

The first chapters describe Elizondo's now classic and most quoted interpretation of the *mestizaje* and history of the conquests that form the Mexican American world view. This text is a must for any course on Latino theology.

The Future is Mestizo (Bloomington, IN: Meyer Stone Books, 1988).

Since theology must be grounded in faith experience, this work is Elizondo at his best. While the book takes the reader through a journey of the author's personal life as a Mexican American Roman Catholic priest in a WASP-dominated society, the result is a dialogue with Elizondo's claims about a universal *mestizaje* that God is building up from within the Mexican American reality. This work is also a testimony of the enduring faith and hope of Mexican Americans who daily face the challenges of this country's assimilationist efforts.

2

Fernando F. Segovia

Fernando Segovia is a Cuban American. He obtained his masters in theology (MA) from the University of Notre Dame in 1976 and his doctorate in theology (PhD) in 1978. He was teaching assistant and lecturer in the Theology Department at Notre Dame (1973–1977) and became assistant and associate professor of theology at Marquette University (1977–1984). Since that time he has been associate professor and now professor of New Testament and early Christian literature at the Divinity School at Vanderbilt University.

Well known as a specialist in the Johannine literature and biblical hermeneutics, Segovia has published four books and over sixteen articles on the Gospel of John. In the area of U.S. Latino theology he has published three major articles, edited an issue on Hispanic American theology, and is co-editing a work entitled: *Aliens in Jerusalem: Towards a Hispanic American Theology.*

Among his many professional duties, Segovia is associate editor of the *Catholic Biblical Quarterly,* serves on the editorial board of the *Journal of Hispanic/Latino Theology,* chairs the Johannine Literature Section at the Society of Biblical Literature, is president of *La Comunidad* of Hispanic American Scholars of Theology and Religion and was president of the Academy of Catholic Hispanic Theologians in the United States (ACHTUS).

Segovia is married to Dr. Elena Olazagasti-Segovia.

The Divinity School
Vanderbilt University
Nashville, Tennessee 37240
615-322-2776

Two Places and No Place on Which to Stand

Mixture and Otherness in Hispanic American Theology

Fernando F. Segovia

One of the fundamental developments in contemporary theological thinking and biblical interpretation has been to point out and emphasize that neither the task of theologizing nor the task of interpretation occurs in a social vacuum: that both theologian and critic are related in a direct but complex way to the social context or location out of which they come, in which they function, and to which they speak. Indeed, in the last twenty years or so, the myth of a systematic and universal theology, as well as the myth of an objective and universal interpretation, have been exposed as highly uncritical constructs which reflect a very definite, though largely implicit, ideological stance which ultimately involves the universalizing of one position or reading (and hence one social location) over all others, favoring and exalting thereby the one reading or position (and thus social location) in question while bypassing and denigrating all others in the process.[1]

In this regard, the rise of contextual theologies on one hand, and the emergence of a wide variety of critical interpretive approaches on the other, have played a key role. The theological movements—including liberation theologies of the Third World, feminist theology, and minority theologies of the First World—have focused on the role of context in the task of theologizing. The critical currents—involving both literary and social approaches to the biblical texts—have emphasized not only the social location and ideology of the biblical texts but also, and more recently, the social location and ideology of the readers and interpreters of such texts.[2] As a result, the issue of perspective on standpoint has come fully to the fore in both theological and critical disciplines, with a corresponding

"Two Places and No Place on Which to Stand: Mixture and Otherness in Hispanic American Theology," *Listening: Journal of Religion and Culture* 27:1 (Winter 1992), pp. 26–40. Reprinted with permission.

and sustained critical focus on the theologian or interpreter and his or her social location.

To be sure, this issue of perspective and social location was not altogether absent from the traditional theological or interpretive enterprises, though it was never explicitly addressed or analyzed as such: systematic theology always exhibited a profound regard for its own religious or ecclesiastical tradition—that sense of and search for a proper grounding in Catholic, Orthodox, Reformed or Evangelical theology; similarly, historical criticism constantly emphasized the *Sitz im Leben* or historical matrix of the text in question, uniformly conceived in terms of theological content, i.e., how the message or teaching of the text presupposed, reflected, and addressed a particular historico-theological situation or problem at hand.

However, recent theoretical developments have led to a radical expansion of this concept of perspective and social location. In effect, social location is now seen as going well beyond both religious affiliation and historico-theological matrix to include a wide variety of identity factors such as gender, ethnic or racial background, socioeconomic class, sociopolitical status and allegiance, sociocultural conventions, educational levels, and ideological stance. All of these factors are now perceived as shaping or influencing the theological and interpretive tasks, and thus subject to critical attention and analysis. Consequently, neither task is seen as reflecting or yielding a universal perspective, as speaking for and to the world; rather, both tasks are seen as pointing to, and reflecting the richness and dignity of, the local perspective, howsoever defined: as speaking for and to the local context, though also, to be sure, in critical dialogue with all other such voices in the world, and thus as speaking ultimately to the entire world as well.[3]

Hispanic Americans as Social Location

One such configuration of social location, presently giving rise to its own theological and hermeneutical voice, is that of Hispanic Americans, circumscribed both in terms of ethnic background (Hispanic) and sociopolitical status and allegiance (American): individuals of Hispanic descent, associated in one way or another with the Americas, who now live, for any number of reasons, on a permanent basis in the United States.[4] This group further reveals a complex twofold character: on one hand, it is quite distinct and readily identifiable; on the other hand, it is also quite varied and thoroughly diverse. Thus, it would be quite improper to regard it, whether from the outside or the inside, as a monolithic or uniform entity, except for specific and clearly articulated analytic or strategic reasons. In effect, I believe that Hispanic American theology must always be keenly mindful of the many similarities that bring us together, as well as the many differences that set us apart. In other words, I conceive of Hispanic American theology as a rich theological locus or matrix within which a wide variety of vibrant theological currents can be found; a rich theological voice within which a broad variety of distinctive inflections can be perceived.

In what follows, I should like to pursue a number of fundamental similarities and differences to be found within the group as a preliminary step towards a beginning elaboration on my part of an autochthonous, self-conscious, and critical Hispanic American theology and hermeneutic—a theology and a hermeneutic that I see as characterized by a radical sense of mixture and otherness, of *mezcolanza* and *otredad,* both unsettling and liberating at the same time.[5]

Hispanic Americans: Binding Similarities

One finds a very clear and pronounced tendency from outside the group to describe all Hispanic Americans in terms of an undifferentiated and highly uncomplimentary sameness. While we certainly do have many and profound characteristics in common, Hispanic American theology must address and analyze in an open, direct, and critical fashion both the image of the group in the wider society—what is attributed unto us by way of stereotype and prejudice, and the image of the group that we ourselves have—what we consider to be our truly distinctive similarities.

1. A first similarity has to do, therefore, with external perception. There is no doubt that from the outside, from the point of view of the dominant culture, a rather monolithic and highly disparaging perception of Hispanic Americans does prevail.[6] Each and every member of the group has myriad tales to tell in this regard, many of which are remarkably and frighteningly similar. Sad to say, such stories also abound in our churches, our seminaries and divinity schools, our graduate programs in religion—right across the full breadth of the ecclesiastical and theological spectrum, from left to right and right to left.[7]

What is this popular conception of the Hispanic American? I should like to summarize it in what is perhaps its most outrageous and virulent, though not at all uncommon, variation by means of a cumulative series of adjectives with corresponding popular images: (a) lazy, unproductive, unenterprising—the sleeping Mexican with the wide *sombrero,* drinking tequila and whiling away the day against a wall, or a bunch of open-shirted Caribbean men drinking beer and playing dominoes at a local, rundown park; (b) carefree, fun-loving, romantic/sensual—latin-lover types with bushy mustachios and beguiling *señoritas* in bright-colored, low-cut dresses; *maracas*-swinging trios and voluptuous vedettes with plenty of flowers or fruits upon their heads; (c) disorderly, undisciplined, violent—uncontrolled progenitors, breeding like rabbits, and knife-wielding gangs, killing one another like animals; (d) vulgar, unintelligent, unteachable—short, swarthy, and primitive people, with funny broken accents and happily occupying the most menial and servile of occupations.

Aside from the extreme character of such a formulation, the overall perception of the group is clearly that of an inferior, uncivilized, and uneducated people.

In a very real sense, therefore, this is the first and immediate characteristic that unites all Hispanic Americans, regardless of geographical origins, social status, or educational attainment: the perception that the dominant culture has of us; the place to which we have been relegated and consigned; the expectations and possibilities that have been granted unto us.

2. A second similarity has to do with who we are, with our culture, our history, and our language. It is an identity that is inherently and uniquely mixed—we are indeed a hybrid people, a *mestizo* and *mulato* people, whether in biological or cultural terms, or both.[8] It is this identity that has been traditionally celebrated throughout Hispanic America on the 12th of October, a holiday known as the day of *La Raza* (the race).

On the one hand, we are the children of Spain and thus of Europe, Mediterranean and Catholic Europe—deeply rooted in Western civilization as mediated by the language, the history, and the culture of Spain. On the other hand, we are also the children of pre-Columbian America and Africa—deeply rooted as well in other ancient cultures, histories, and languages. Thus, we are neither European nor Amerindian nor African, but rather *criollos,* the native children of the white and the black and the brown, of the conquerors and the conquered, the masters and the slaves, the North and the South.[9] Such *mestizaje* and *mulatez* permeates our art, our music, our language, our food, our religion, our very way of constructing and functioning in the world. Thus, biological and/or cultural miscegenation lies at our very roots and stamps our very praxis, sharply distinguishing us in a society that still thinks of itself by and large, even today, in terms of black and white.[10]

3. A third similarity concerns our sociopolitical status and allegiance, both past and present. On the one hand, we stand in a tradition that has known the political realm at its worst, a long tradition characterized, with very few exceptions, by political oppression and instability—colonial and neocolonial dependency and exploitation; totalitarian and despotic governments, usually centered around the personality cult of singularly unenlightened *caudillos* (national leader; *fürer; duce*); widespread corruption and injustice; and systematic violation of all human rights. It is a tradition at once tragic and hopeful, predestined and changeable, utterly despairing of politics yet firmly committed to life and freedom.

On the other hand, through our permanent presence in the United States, our miscegenation has begun to acquire yet another and radically different dimension: we are now also becoming the children of Europe, Nordic and Protestant Europe, as mediated by the Anglo-Saxon world. Through this tradition we have not only begun to acquire a new language, culture, and history, but have also come to know a very different and much more benign political tradition, marked by freedom and stability—national independence and self-determination; democratic and multiparty governments, with free elections, the right of opposition, and peaceful changes of government; a system of justice based on the rule of law; and widespread respect for human rights.[11] It is a pragmatic and optimistic tradition, where our deep commitment to life and freedom can at least hope to take root and flower.

4. A final similarity concerns our present social conditions in American society. The statistics clearly show that, as a whole, the group is truly marginalized and disadvantaged.[12] It is politically underrepresented and ineffective—an enormous and crippling disadvantage in the American political scene, where lobbying and pressure constitute the very essence of political life; economically hard-pressed, with almost a quarter of its population living in conditions of poverty, as defined by the government, and many others on the borderline; and educationally precarious, with an alarming rate of failure at all levels of the educational system and severe underrepresentation in all skilled or professional lines of occupation.[13] At the same time, recent trends and developments also show the group as a whole becoming increasingly conscious of itself as a group within the society, more and more willing to act together as a united force in the light of similar perceptions and conditions, a growing and extensive interaction at every level of life, and a variety of common goals.[14]

Such fundamental similarities constitute a central part of the Hispanic American reality and experience, and provide a basic point of departure for a Hispanic American theology. We are a people living in two worlds: away from our traditional home, creating and establishing a new home; firmly tied to a rich cultural past, yet ready and struggling to take on yet another dimension of cultural miscegenation; accustomed to intolerable levels of political oppression and instability, searching for a measure of political peace and freedom; rejected and denigrated, poor and ignored in our new home, culture, and country—in the very midst of the land of promise and plenty. We are thus a bicultural people at home in neither world—the permanent "others."

Hispanic Americans: The Unavoidable Differences

Just as one finds a definite tendency from the outside to lump all Hispanic Americans together as one undifferentiated mass, so does one also find a certain tendency from the inside, among Hispanic American theologians themselves, to view the entire group in terms of their own image and likeness.[15] To be sure, these two tendencies are radically distinct: while the former is quite negative in thrust and results, the latter is quite positive and thoroughly well-intentioned. Nevertheless, there are many and profound differences within the group, differences which Hispanic American theology must acknowledge and incorporate, if it is to avoid its own version of the "melting pot" theory.[16]

1. A first difference has to do with our sociocultural identity. While we are the children of biological and/or cultural miscegenation, the nature of the mixture in question differs considerably from area to area and country to country. It should be pointed out in this regard that no one group feels fully comfortable with the title "Hispanic Americans" or any other such nomenclature. On one hand, such appellations are not of our own making, but are rather given unto us. On the other hand, we are all used to identifying ourselves by country of origin, e.g., Mexicans, Dominicans, Puerto Ricans, Cubans, etc. Each geographical area, as well as each country within each area, has its own distinctive history, culture, conventions, and mixture.

It would be foolish to pretend, therefore, that the Mexican tradition is parallel to the Caribbean, or that the tradition of the upper Andes, of Peru and Ecuador, corresponds to that of the lower Andes, of Chile and Argentina. Similarly, it would be foolish to pretend that all Caribbean peoples share the very same tradition, be they Cubans, Dominicans, or Puerto Ricans. Such diversity of traditions lends enormous richness to our theological voice and should not be submerged.

2. A second difference concerns the nature of, and rationale for, our present socio-political status and allegiance. One finds among Hispanic Americans many who are first-generation immigrants, who have come to this country for political and/or economic reasons—for this group, exile tends to override minority status as the fundamental reality. Many others are the children, immediate or distant, of immigrants—for this group, minority status tends to be the predominant reality. And there are many, who, to the great surprise and amazement of the dominant culture, are not immigrants at all, but rather acquired subjects through expansionism and annexation—for this group, minority status is sharpened by a history of previous or ongoing colonialism as the fundamental reality.[17]

Again, it would be foolish to pretend that the most recent experience of Nicaraguans, Guatemalans, or Salvadoreans fleeing for their lives in the midst of civil war is similar to that of the great migration of Puerto Rican families to the cities of the Northeast in the 1940s and 50s, or that the massive exile of Cubans in the 1960s and 70s is similar to the situation of Mexican Americans born in the borderlands of the Southwest, or Puerto Ricans living on the island. Such experiences provide the many hues and tones of our theological voice and should not be ignored.

3. A third difference has to do with our socioreligious affiliation. While traditionally, to be sure, Roman Catholicism, in any of its various forms and expressions within a broad syncretistic framework, has been the basic religious matrix for the vast majority of Hispanic Americans, such is no longer the case; indeed, to the great alarm of the Catholic clergy and episcopacy, recent years have seen a phenomenal growth, both here and in Latin America, of the Protestant churches. From an ecclesiastical point of view, therefore, the group is not only extremely diverse, but also (and regrettably), minimally ecumenical.

Again, it would be foolish to pretend that the world of Roman Catholic Hispanics, deeply steeped in popular religiosity, corresponds to that of Protestant Hispanics, for whom the Bible constitutes the guiding light, or that the vision of Hispanic Protestants in the mainline churches is the same as that of Hispanic Protestants in evangelical or pentecostal churches. Such perspectives provide the many subtle and not-so-subtle colors of our theological voice and should not be overlooked.

Such fundamental differences also constitute a central part of the Hispanic American reality and experience, and provide a further point of departure for a Hispanic American theology. Thus again, we are a people who live in two worlds, but find ourselves at home in neither one. As such, however, we share a world of the past, but we do so with many homes, many mixtures, many traditions, and many conceptions of reality. We further share a world of the present, but again, we do so with many faces, many histories, and many visions of God and the world. We are thus not only a bicultural people but a multicultural people, the permanent others who are also in various respects others to one another.

A Hispanic American Theological Perspective

Out of this rich, complex, and rapidly growing social configuration, a strong theological voice has begun to emerge in recent years, a voice that I like to describe, in deliberately ironic terms, as a manifest destiny—self-confident, vehement, and unstoppable. In keeping with the larger theological and hermeneutical developments outlined above, it is a voice in search of freedom, independence, and autonomy; a voice that seeks to speak in its own terms and with its own visions in mind; a voice that wishes to lay claim to its own reality and experience, give expression to its own view of God and the world, and chart its own future.[18]

In what follows, I should like to articulate some of the fundamental lines and contours of a Hispanic American theology, as viewed from my own angle of vision within the Hispanic American reality and experience—a first-generation immigrant of Caribbean descent, specifically from the Cuban experience of political exile, and grounded in a Roman Catholicism much more at home in popular religiosity than in a historically intransigent and politically retrograde institutional church. The theology that I envision is a theology of mixture and otherness—of *mezcolanza* and *otredad*.

1. Such a theology cannot but be a theology of struggle, liberation, and self-determination.[19] Given the overwhelming cultural barriers faced by all members of the group (the dominant perception of an inferior, uncivilized, and uneducated people), and the enormous social barriers faced by a vast majority of the group (e.g., political, socioeconomic, and educational), such a theology inevitably involves a path of struggle, liberation, and self-determination. The theology of mixture and otherness is a theology

that is very much on the way—from exclusion to inclusion, from passivity to action, from silence to speech, from marginalization as an inferior other to an autochthonous, self-conscious, and critical irruption of an other that does not regard or present itself as superior—that would be a tragic mistake, in the divisive tradition of colonialism[20]—but rather as an equal.

First, such a theology must engage in an active and sustained struggle against the reigning social perceptions and conditions, exposing them for what they are, their rationales and consequences, openly and without fear. This is a struggle that must also be waged in ecclesiastical and theological circles. As such, it is a theology that demands conscientization, education, and sophistication. Second, it must have liberation in mind, a compelling and eschatological view of a different world with different possibilities and alternatives, a world in which human dignity, respect, and rights prevail. This concept of liberation must be extended as well to the ecclesiastical and theological realms. As such, it is a theology that demands commitment, strategy, and *savoir-faire*. Third, it must strive for self-determination in the retrieval and retelling of its own history, in the articulation of its own view of reality, and in the expression of its own future dreams and visions. This sense of self-determination is likewise imperative in all theological and ecclesiastical circles. As such, it is a theology that demands self-confidence, self-definition, and self-direction.

These three essential components of the Hispanic American theology envisioned—struggle, liberation, and self-determination—I do not see at all as separate or sequential but rather as thoroughly interrelated and interdependent, though any one element may predominate at any one time, depending on the circumstances and the strategic aims in question.

2. Such a theology must be ultimately and radically grounded in our profound sense of otherness, our twofold experience of living in two worlds but at home in neither one, and always playing the role of others. This experience is both unsettling and liberating.

The experience is quite unsettling insofar as we find no true and permanent home anywhere—having left our traditional home, we find that our present home is alien, invariably disdainful and hostile; leaving our present home, we find that our traditional home is also alien, largely uncomprehending and unsympathetic. We no longer fit where we came from, and we certainly do not fit where we are. Both our present and former compatriots regard us askance, as strangers, though a major difference is to be noted in this regard: while the latter do so, for the most part, benignly; the former, almost without exception, harshly. The experience is also quite liberating insofar as we perceive immediately the extent to which all reality has a social exterior, scaffolding, and foundation. We function relatively well in our traditional homes: we know its traditions and conventions; we also function more or less well in our present home: we have also come to know its conventions and traditions. We know what makes each world move, and we find that we can go from the one to the other and back again—in an endless process of social translation and retranslation—rather easily. We can thus compare and contrast such worlds: the things people do, the reasons why they do them, the overall framework that underlies and sustains such actions and rationales. We know, therefore, that we can to some extent pick and choose, and this forbidden knowledge gives us the rare ability to offer a fundamental critique of both worlds, an informed critique from the inside.

Consequently, the theology I envision is a theology that must not eschew otherness and alienation, but rather use it as a source of identity and affirmation, comfort and understanding, autonomy and criticism.

3. Such a theology must be ultimately and radically grounded as well in our biological and cultural mixture, in our own *mestizaje* and *mulatez,* in our own expansive and expanding *raza.* In a society ruled, on both sides, by a seemingly intractable white-and-black mentality, a Hispanic American theology must fully acknowledge mixture and rejoice in diversity. We, like few other people in this world, are not only bicultural but also multicultural. We can take delight in reading, as our very own, Cervantes, Guillén, and Asturias—and now Shakespeare, Dickens, and Whitman; in listening to a *zarzuela,* a tango, a corrido, or a mambo—a musical comedy, a country ballad, or a Negro spiritual; in gazing upon a Velázquez, an Arawak petroglyph, or a Mayan or Aztec figurine—a Reynolds or a Benton; in visiting Toledo, Teotihuacán, or Macchu Picchu—Cambridge or Williamsburg.

As such, the theology I envision can play the very important role of self-conscious bridge or translator between North and South, first world and third world, English and Spanish, white and every other color under the sun. First and foremost, such a theology must be imbued with a deep sense of respect for the "other," moving beyond paralyzing stereotypes to understand other theological voices in their own terms and visions. Given its own perception as primitive and inconsequential, it must go out of its way to acknowledge and understand the identity and dignity of other theological voices. Second, it must go beyond an informed understanding of the other to a proper conversation with the other. Given its own tradition as mixed and marginalized, it must avoid provincialism and engage in global dialogue—giving and taking, sharing and appropriating, enlightening and being enlightened. Third, it must go beyond proper conversation with the other to critical exchange with that other. Given its own history of domination and sense of self-determination, it must be ready to offer and accept critique, straightforwardly and to the point, kindly but firmly.

In a world of increasing and irreversible theological pluralization and globalism, such a theology can indeed play a major and constructive role. It has many skins, many faces, many tongues, many mixtures. It knows them from within and without, and it is not ashamed of any of its components. It is a theology that cannot allow itself to override the other as it itself was overridden, or to shun mixture as it itself was shunned; its mission is to respect and affirm both itself and the other.

4. Again, such a theology must be profoundly critical: it must constantly engage in critical exchange with other theological voices, with its own theological ancestors, and with itself, in all its many forms and variations. Given its sense of mixture and otherness, it is ideally suited for this task—it must regard all "reality" as both nature and construction, life and interpretation, with an underlying ideological basis and program, and hence subject to analysis, critique, and change. Given its sense of origins, not only in a historical tradition of violence and injustice, but also in an ongoing context of marginalization and discrimination, it must develop a highly refined hermeneutics of suspicion at its very core, with a healthy and instinctive distrust of power and authority, a questioning of everything and everyone. Given its sense of silence and passivity, of expected docility and gentleness, it must express such suspicion and critique loudly and without cease. It is a theology that must embrace criticism as a vocation, and proceed to exercise it with aplomb and without reservations.

Such a theology cannot spare criticism with regard to other theological voices, even emerging and allied voices: to do so would be to surrender its own sense of self-determination and autonomy—and ultimately underestimate and compromise all other voices as well. It certainly cannot spare criticism vis-à-vis its theological progenitors, whether by blood or adoption: to do so would be to perpetuate and foster the long tradition of colonialism and paternalism. And by no means can it afford to spare itself: to do so would be to yield to a new romanticism or even a new imperialism. Such a theology must be firmly grounded on the principle that the moment criticism is surrendered, the path to authoritarianism—to abuse, oppression, and injustice—becomes wide open.

5. Finally, such a theology must be a theology of and for life, a theology with an undifferentiated and fully intertwined realized and future eschatology, an unwavering commitment to the world with a driving vision of a different and better world, and a profound sense of joy in the midst of anguish. Born in violence and oppression, injustice and repression, such a theology must opt for a radically different future, and an enjoyment of such a future in the present to the extent that it can, be it by way of humor, *joie de vivre,* and/or resistance. Accustomed to paternalism and patronizing, it must opt for a sound and healthy critique, a criticism that follows the path of construction rather destruction, unless the latter becomes absolutely necessary, as it sometimes does. Conceived in mixture, it must opt for the immense richness and diversity of life, not overwhelming the other, as it too was overwhelmed, but rather affirming the other as other, as it too struggles for such affirmation and dignity.

In conclusion, the theology I envision is a theology that, because of its very roots, cannot hide or disguise or reject mixture, for it finds that *mezcolanza* is life and gives life; a theology that, given its very reality and experience, cannot bypass, assimilate, or annihilate the other, for again it finds that *otredad* also is life and gives life. Just as Hispanic American theology finds itself but at its very beginnings, so have I but barely begun in this study to outline the fundamental foundations and contours of this theology of mixture and otherness. The task ahead—the manifest destiny of struggle, liberation, and self-determination—remains enormously demanding, but also supremely satisfying and life-giving.

Notes

1. It is proper to speak, therefore, of an implicit but profound and far-reaching "colonialism" in the realms of theology and interpretation, a colonialism consisting of the Euro-American or North Atlantic "colonizers" and the "colonized" of the third world or within the first world itself, who make up the rest of the Christian world. Within such a system, the true message of Christianity, properly interpreted and systematized, has to be imparted by the "civilized" or "missionary" churches to the "native" or "mission" churches, in order to avoid any sort of local and sullying contact.

2. While the social methodologies (e.g., sectarian studies; millenarianism; cultural anthropology) have emphasized above all the social location and ideology of texts, with minimal attention given to the social location and ideology of the readers of these texts, the literary methodologies have variously focused—in a roughly sequential manner—on texts as rhetorical and ideological products in their own right (e.g., narratology; rhetorical criticism), on the complex act of reading and interpretation (e.g., reader response criticism of the text-dominant variety), and on the social location and ideologies of contemporary readers of texts (e.g., neo-marxist analysis; reader response criticism of the reader dominant variety).

3. Given the dominant system of theological and interpretive colonialism, it is proper to speak as well of a veritable rebellion or "war of independence" on the part of the "colonized," involving: (a) a thorough rejection of the claim of the "colonizers" to speak for all peoples with their own words and visions; (b) a radical claim on the part of the "colonized" to speak for themselves in their own visions and words; and (c) a sharp and painful reminder from the "colonized" to the "colonizer" that their visions and words are as concrete and local as any other.

4. For a fuller explanation of this definition and the problems inherent in any definition of the group, see my "Hispanic American Theology and the Bible: Effective Weapon and Faithful Ally," in *We Are A People! Initiative in Hispanic American Theology* (ed. R. S. Goizueta; Minneapolis: Fortress Press, 1992).

5. I am deliberately using the term *mezcolanza* rather than *mezcla* as a translation for "mixture" both because of its much more attractive character and its traditionally pejorative connotations (see María Moliner, *Diccionario de uso del español* [2 vols.; Biblioteca Románica Hispánica; Madrid: Editorial Gredos, 1975] 2:408). The term *otredad* is a neologism, to be preferred to the perhaps more acceptable form, *el otro*, given the masculine gender of the latter term.

6. See in this regard the most revealing results of a recent survey on the relative social standing of the different ethnic groups in the country (T. Lewin, "Study Points to Increase in Tolerance of Ethnicity," *The New York Times* 8 January 1992:

A10). Out of thirty-seven such groups, including a fictitious group called the "Wisians," the last seven categories included, in order: Latin Americans; American Indians; Negroes; "Wisians"!; Mexicans; Puerto Ricans; and Gypsies.

7. Given the system of theological and interpretive colonialism, such an attitude should not be at all unexpected or surprising. It is a universal feature of the "colonizers" to dehumanize, to underestimate and denigrate, the "colonized"; otherwise, the entire system collapses from within. A regular feature of such "colonialism" in our theological institutions of learning is the comment, "You do not look Hispanic" (i.e., you do not fit your assigned place and stereotype); whether the answer expected is a "Thank you" or an "I'm sorry," I have not yet been able to figure out. As I myself can attest from first-hand experience, prejudice and discrimination are indeed alive and well in the more liberal institutions; however, such discrimination and prejudice are very subtle indeed, and extremely resistant to change.

8. Given the traditional understanding of *mestizo* and *mestizaje* as the mixture of European and Amerindian and of *mulato* and *mulatez* as the mixture of European and African, I do not like to use one term or the other. Thus, to refer to the mixture as such, which includes the union of Amerindian and African (*zambo*), I prefer to use such terms as miscegenation or hybridization. All of the possible mixtures were elaborately catalogued and named in the course of the colonial period; such mixtures were brought to the canvas in a most revealing series of family portraits painted in the 1760s by the Mexican artist, Miguel Cabrera.

9. The term *criollo* has various connotations: (a) the children of Europeans born outside of Europe; (b) the children of Spaniards born in Hispanic America, the descendants of Spaniards in Hispanic America, or what is native to Hispanic America; (c) children of Africans born outside Africa. See M. Moliner, *Diccionario,* 1:803. I am using it in a very broad sense, along the lines of the third meaning of (b), with reference to all those born in Hispanic America, regardless of origins or mixtures.

10. The claim is not that miscegenation has always been appreciated or even acknowledged, that racism is not present in our midst. The claim is that—whether we like it or not, whether we admit it or deny it, whether we embrace it or excoriate it—we are mixed to the core. I am reminded in this regard of a delicious and very ironic Caribbean song, entitled, "*Y tu abuela a'onde etá*" ("And where is your grandmother?"), involving an aspiring family that tries to hide a darker-than-tolerated grandmother in the kitchen of the house, while the chorus—the eyes of the neighbors—repeatedly asks, "and, by the way, where is your grandmother?" The song not only reveals the racism of our own societies, though very different from that experienced in U.S. society, but also the mixed nature of our people, further conveyed by the untranslatable aphorism, "*El que no tiene de dinga, tiene de mandinga.*" If not from a biological point of view, then certainly from a cultural point of view, both saying and song hold true for us all. For the song itself, see the CD album entitled, "*Estampas de Luis Carbonell*" (Kubaney, CDK-165).

11. Such a contrast should not be seen in either/or terms. It does not take Hispanic Americans long to realize that the picture of the country traditionally exported abroad is only relatively true—not infrequently, freedom is curtailed, the democratic system compromised, injustice and corruption overlooked, and human rights violated. The streets are neither paved with gold, nor do the poor,

huddled masses receive all that warm a welcome. Relatively speaking, however, the contrast does remain a significant one indeed. This contrast also has a much darker and troubling side as well, as Hispanic Americans begin to realize that their new country has been responsible, many times and in many ways, for the subversion of freedom, its process and its hopes, and for the propagation of injustice in their respective homelands—in direct opposition to the values and ideals of the country.

12. The claim is not that there are no differences in social status or economic class among Hispanic Americans, but that the group as a whole shows a considerable lag with respect to the rest of the population, even among those who are citizens of the country by birth.

13. On political power, see, e.g., David González, "Hispanic Voters Struggle to Find the Strength in Their Numbers," *The New York Times* 26 May 1991; on economic distress, see, e.g., Felicity Barringer, "Hispanic Americans Gain but Still Lag Economically, Report Says," *The New York Times* 11 April 1991; on educational problems, see, e.g., Karen de Will, "Rising Segregation is Found for Hispanic Students," *The New York Times* 9 January 1992: A9.

14. Such developments are at work as well in theological circles. For example, an ecumenical theological organization (La Comunidad of Hispanic American Scholars and Teachers of Religion), associated with the American Academy of Religion, has been formed, facilitating a much-needed forum for discussion and interaction. Similarly, in the fall of 1991, a highly successful ecumenical conference on Hispanic Theology took place at Auburn Seminary in New York City ("Faith Doing Justice: An Ecumenical Conference on Hispanic Theology"), the first of many envisioned for the future.

15. See, e.g., A. M. Isasi-Diaz, *Hispanic Women: Prophetic Voice in the Church* (San Francisco: Harper & Row, 1988)—a view of Hispanic women largely in terms of Catholic women; H. Recinos, *Hear the Cry! A Latino Pastor Challenges the Church* (Louisville: Westminster/John Knox Press, 1989)—a view of the Hispanic American reality largely in terms of the *barrio,* grounded in the Puerto Rican experience in the cities of the Northeast; J. González, *Mañana: Theology from a Hispanic Perspective* (Nashville: Abingdon, 1989)—a view of the Hispanic American reality largely in terms of exile. Though in all cases explicit allowance is made for differences, nevertheless one reality, that of the author, tends to become representative of or paradigmatic for the others. On this point, see the sharp comments by J. Quiñonez-Ortiz, "The Mestizo Journey: Challenges for Hispanic Theology," *Apuntes* 11 (1991) 62–72.

16. The claim is not that division and separatism should be preserved and fostered, whether within the group itself or in the country at large. Such a strategy would be absurd, not only unattainable, but also highly counterproductive. First, we already come, each and every one of us, from a tradition of mixture. Second, we have established a permanent presence in the country. Third, we can only find the social and political strength we need in union and numbers. The claim is rather one of enlightened integration, whereby we do not lose an essential part of our identity in and through such a mixture. The aim should be a respectful and liberating mixture—enriching for each group, for Hispanic Americans as a whole, and for the country at large.

17. From a legal point of view, therefore, Hispanic Americans include born citizens, naturalized citizens, legal residents, and illegal residents. There are also

many Hispanic temporary workers, both legal and illegal, but, given the absence of a permanent association with the country, this group does not qualify as Hispanic American.

18. In terms of the traditional system of theological and interpretive colonialism, it is proper to speak further of an ongoing process of "decolonization," a process in which the voice and vision of the newly independent begin to take shape with a view towards autonomous self-definition and self-direction. This process involves of necessity a radical critique of the "colonizers," of the theological "masters," much to their surprise and consternation.

19. For liberation as a fundamental characteristic of Hispanic American theology, see my "A New Manifest Destiny: The Emerging Theological Voice of Hispanic Americans," *Religious Studies Review* 17 (1991) 101–109; for liberation as a fundamental characteristic of Hispanic American hermeneutics, see my "Hispanic American Theology and the Bible: Effective Weapon and Faithful Ally" (see n. 4 above).

20. See in this regard Edward W. Said, "Yeats and Decolonization," in *Nationalism, Colonialism, and Literature* (S. Deane, ed.; Minneapolis: University of Minnesota Press, 1990) 69–95.

Annotated Bibliography—Fernando F. Segovia

"Hispanic American Theology and the Bible: Effective Weapon and Faithful Ally," in *We Are a People! Initiatives in Hispanic American Theology,* Roberto Goizueta, ed. (Minneapolis: Fortress Press, 1992), pp. 21–49.

Using contemporary hermeneutical approaches, the author studies four Latino/a theologians' use of the Bible: Ada María Isasi-Díaz's *mujerista* theology, Harold Recinos's *barrio* theology, Virgil Elizondo's *mestizaje* theology, and Justo González's *mañana* theology. In his attempt to be inclusive of the social location of the majority of Latinos in the country, he studies the work of a Catholic Latina theologian, a Puerto Rican United Methodist minister working in the barrio, a Mexican American priest in the Southwest, and a Cuban American United Methodist minister whose work promotes an ecumenical reformation.

Segovia outlines and compares these authors' similarities and differences in their use of the Bible. He concludes that these authors understand the Bible as liberative when read from the distinct social context and perspective of Hispanic Americans. He further argues that these writers see the Bible as both an effective weapon in the struggle against marginalization and discrimination and a faithful ally in the struggle for liberation.

"A New Manifest Destiny: The Emerging Theological Voice of Hispanic Americans," *Religious Studies Review* 17:2 (April 1991) pp. 102–109.

In this article Segovia reviews seven works by leading Catholic and Protestant Latino/a theologians published between 1983 and 1990. His selection is characteristic of the major voices in emerging U.S. Latino theology. The theologians he surveys focus on such topics as *mestizaje,* a Chicano theology of liberation, *mujerista* theology, evangelization among Hispanics in the United States, theology of the *barrio,* the theological education of Hispanics, and a rereading "in Spanish" of the scriptures and theology.

Segovia finds that Latino theology is retelling the story of an often neglected voice in history, that Hispanic Americans want to enlighten and broaden in a critical way the very provincial Euro-American tribalism of our churches, and that this theology has an underlying thrust of mission directed toward the dominant culture. He concludes that the emerging Latino theological movement is a new manifest destiny which represents a significant contribution to the theological landscape.

3

Samuel Soliván-Román

Samuel Soliván was born in the Bronx, New York. Originally ordained for Gethsemani Pentecostal Church in New York in 1970, he transferred ordination to The Assemblies of God, Spanish Eastern District. He received his masters in divinity (MDiv) from Western Theological Seminary, Holland, Michigan in 1976, his masters in sacred theology (STM) in 1977, and his doctorate (PhD) in 1993 in systematic theology, both from Union Theological Seminary, New York.

As a minister of his church, Reverend Soliván has been a pastor, director, and administrator of various church projects, missionary to Venezuela, lecturer and evangelist. As a professor, he has been adjunct faculty at New York Theological Seminary, at Gordon-Conwell Seminary in Boston, at *Seminario Teologico Distrito Hispano Del Este* in New York, and professor of theology at New York Seminary (1981–1989). Presently he is associate professor of Christian theology at Andover Newton Theological School in Boston, Massachusetts.

In his writings and lectures, Soliván focuses on the issues of present-day Pentecostalism from the U.S. Latino perspective, and U.S. Latino theology from within the Pentecostal tradition. He is among the first U.S. Latino Protestant theologians to bridge the ecumenical discussion in Latino theology. His professional associations include the American Academy of Religion, Hispanic Educators, *La Comunidad* of Hispanic American Scholars of Theology and Religion, and (associate of) the Academy of Catholic Hispanic Theologians of the United States. He also serves on the editorial board of the *Journal of Hispanic/Latino Theology.*

Soliván is married to Irene Marrero, and they have four children.

Andover Newton Theological School
125 Herrick Circle
Newton Centre, MA 02159
617-964-1100
Fax 617-965-9756

The Need for a North American Hispanic Theology

Samuel Soliván-Román

The following seven considerations point to the need for Hispanic American scholars to develop a theology that will inform and articulate the Christian faith from a Hispanic perspective, a perspective which informs our lives in its many diverse expressions, corresponding to our particular Hispanic heritages, such as the Mexican American, Puerto Rican, Cuban, and others. Indeed, the need for a North American Hispanic theology is an urgent one.

A Biblically Grounded Faith Requires It

The witness of the Scriptures calls for an affirmation of our ethnic and cultural identities as expressions of grace. If one believes that God is a just and loving God, that God created all peoples as equals, then we are called to celebrate our commonness as well as our particularity. Our particularity is expressed in our color, language, and culture.

A Hispanic American theology seeks to reflect critically and consciously from the perspective of our *mestizaje*.[1] Our culture and language, our history and experience as North American Hispanics serve as important sources for doing theology. The experience of living in the "belly of the beast," of knowing hunger in the land of good and plenty, of being poor on the streets of gold provides a different perspective and a different set of questions about who God is and what God is doing in the world.

Our color in its full spectrum from black to white, our language, our cultural heritage—drawn from the blood of our Spanish, African, Amerindian, and Anglo-American parents—are affirmed as gifts of grace and expressions of divine providence. This affirmation does not annul our critique of the history of oppression which accompanies the diverse compo-

"The Need for a North American Hispanic Theology," *Listening: Journal of Religion and Culture* 27:1 (Winter 1992), pp. 17–25. Reprinted with permission.

nents of our heritage. We recognize the oppressive history of the Spanish empire and the contemporary history of our Anglo-American heritage, yet in a spirit of confession and repentance we move beyond it to a place of affirmation and transformation. This historical consciousness of the oppressive character of our forebears will serve as a warning for our own praxis.

In appropriating our language and culture as creative sources for doing and thinking theologically, we also affirm the liberating power of the life, death, and resurrection of Jesus the Christ. It is in the power of our resurrected Lord that we dare to revive the use of our languages, both Spanish and English. No longer must we choose between them. No longer must we be forced to deny part of who we are. As Hispanic Americans we affirm the biblical disclosure of grace in our persons, language, and culture as we dare to appropriate them for the sacred task of proclaiming the Good News of the Gospel.

The New Testament, as well as the Old Testament, clearly call us to assume responsibility for making known the Good News. Each is called to do so in light of his or her context. In the Gospels we are commanded to make disciples of all nations (Matthew 28:19–20). In the book of Acts, we find that the Holy Spirit addresses the diverse crowd on the Day of Pentecost in their own tongues (*dialectos*), respecting the particularity of their cultures and languages (Acts 2:1–11). This cultural glossolalia is a call for all to assume responsibility for the proclamation of the Gospel. All are called upon to give reason for the hope that is in them (1 Peter 3:15).

The Nature and Task of Theology Requires It

Theological developments of the past twenty years—precipitated by the theologians of liberation who have pointed to the theological necessity of theology as a local, contextual task with global implications—summon us to take as our point of departure our North American setting as mediated by our Hispanic experience. It is this *locus teologicus* which serves as the matrix through which questions posed are understood and addressed.

As our Anglo-European brothers and sisters have over the past centuries produced biblical commentaries and other theological works, as our fore-parents in Spain and Africa also assumed responsibility for an apology of the faith, so too, we, their heirs, as Hispanic Americans, commit ourselves to the task of making sense of the Gospel in light of who and where we are. No longer will we be content to be the recipients of the contributions of others. We are thankful for their contributions, yet we are called upon to contribute, not only for the benefit of our own Hispanic community, but also for the benefit of all other communities.

Hispanic American theology, if it is to be authentic, must hold itself accountable to the mestizo composition of the Hispanic American communities. This does not exclude other Hispanic people. Every theologian reflects from a given, particular cosmovision. It is that place which informs both one's questions and answers. It serves as the subjective matrix through which one's perceptions and opinions are shaped.

As Hispanic American theologians aware of the subjectivity of our task, we engage in it unapologetically. Yet critical of the inherent dangers of subjectivism or reductionism, we dare engage in the theological arena subject to both an internal and an external critique of our community and the theological guilds. We do so believing that a Hispanic American perspective will yield benefits and insights which will enrich and empower our respective communities and the church at large.

The Mission of the Church Requires It

In an era critical of the missionary enterprise as an extension of Anglo values and exploitation,[2] the contributions made by Hispanic Americans to the theological formulations of missionary proposals (as in the works of our beloved *compañero,* Orlando Costas[3]) serve as a corrective to a missionary history of cultural imperialism.

The contribution of Hispanics to the missionary enterprise can inform and enrich the mission of the church in several ways: first, it can lend to the missionary task a different perspective than that which usually informs it. Hispanic Americans bring to the missionary task the experience of being the immediate past receptors of missions. This is important in that both the positive and negative aspects of that missionary enterprise are still available for correction and reinterpretation.

Second, Hispanics come with a missionary vision which is informed by the life of the church of the poor in North America. Yet we have also learned from the dangers of a missionary theology that failed to distinguish between the Gospel and cultural imperialism. Our experience as a boundary people, between cultures and languages, can be helpful in reshaping the missionary enterprise as an instrument of cultural pluralism.

Third, the presence of Hispanic Americans can serve to facilitate a constructive and non-competitive relationship between the church groups involved in mission work in the Spanish-speaking world. Our common linkages of culture, language, history, and relative social class can be instructive in forging a healthy partnership.

Fourth, another benefit of Hispanic presence in the missionary enterprise is that it will serve to increase both the ecumenical as well as the ethnic composition of the global missionary work, which has been dominated by Anglo-Nordic people.

Fifth, a further benefit of Hispanic involvement in the global mission of the church is that it will remind the Hispanic church that it, too, must be open to other voices and perspectives as it seeks to be faithful. Both the work with, and the exposure to, other peoples and experiences will enrich our own, and further sensitize us to the vast diversity of which we are only a small part.

Hispanic Americans can serve a creative role as the intermediaries between the Mission Boards of the North American church and our Latin American brothers and sisters. Hispanic American reflections on the issues of global mission of the church will lend integrity to the mission, and will provide for a perspective of those who live on the boundaries between third-world and first-world peoples.

The Hispanic American Sociopolitical Reality Requires It

The 1980 census projections indicate that by the year 2000 Hispanic Americans will comprise the largest minority group in the United States. The Spanish language is already the second most spoken language in the United States. In light of these and other factors, our Hispanic communities are in need of a voice in the church, a voice which will inform not only its religious life, but also its daily confrontations with the institutions that oppress them. There is a need for a theology which takes their predicament seriously, that proposes adequate responses to their condition by utilizing those strategies and resources which emerge from our own communities.

A Hispanic American theology which seeks to be responsive to our communities must be ecumenical, bilingual, and multicultural. It must possess a comprehensive understanding of the nature of sin both at its systemic and personal levels. It should seek to be informed by, as well as to inform, the popular spirituality of the people. The theological agenda must not only be responsive to the questions of theodicy with which our sisters and brothers are faced daily, but must also provide the insights for engagement with the institutions both of church and state.

The political agendas of our communities are in need of the contribution and support of our churches. Yet, the present theological models, on one hand conservative and reactionary in nature, and on the other liberal and patronizing, continue to undermine our efforts at proper political engagement. A Hispanic American theology is needed to propose a hermeneutical scheme and an exegetical rationale that take our people's religiosity and marginalization as the starting point for a hermeneutic of engagement and transformation. It must be a theology that retains the tension between the Reign of God now and the Reign of God to come, a theology that is neither reductionist nor simplistic.

In light of these comments, a Hispanic theology will require that the following theological and doctrinal themes be addressed or further developed. From a Pentecostal perspective, a fundamental hermeneutical shift must accompany it if other doctrinal themes are to be modified or enlarged to meet the present challenges faced by the Hispanic church.

First, a different hermeneutical approach must be utilized for doing theology. The present approach assumes and works off a bifurcation between the sacred and the profane. It maintains a polarization between the life of faith and the life of politics. This must be overcome with a more biblically faithful approach of a wholistic hermeneutic which brings together these two realities and places them in conversion and mutual critique. The separation of these two vital spheres has resulted in a theological schizophrenia which has served to disempower Hispanic sociopolitical engagement in our communities. It reduces the realm of the Lordship of Christ and the work of the Holy Spirit. It also betrays the claim that we trust fully in the leading of the Holy Spirit. This new hermeneutical approach must bring together the best of the insights of liberation hermeneutics, i.e., a new starting point and praxis, and the best of an Evangelical understanding of the authority of Scripture. It must seek to maintain a creative and liberating tension between these two different, and at times, conflicting approaches. This new hermeneutic, already evident in the work of some Hispanic theologians, is an important precondition for a wholistic Hispanic spirituality.[4]

A second doctrinal theme that needs to be reconsidered is the doctrine of sin. Both Catholic and Protestant theologies, in their conservative expressions, have placed the emphasis on the individual nature of sin. Since Vatican II and the contribution of liberation theologians, there has been a significant shift in emphasis towards the systemic nature and expression of sin. A similar shift has not occurred in the Evangelical Protestant community, much less in the Hispanic Pentecostal community. A broader conceptualization of sin is essential for addressing the sociopolitical realities which the Hispanic churches face. Sin as a strictly personal matter is inadequate for addressing our modern world, and incomplete in representing the biblical understanding of sin. The work of Walter Wink is especially helpful in this area,[5] as is Reinhold Niebuhr's *The Nature and Destiny of Man.*[6] This broader understanding of sin and its serious consequences on our daily lives, as it is informed by the sociopolitical and biblical witness of our times, will enhance our ability to understand and engage in an overcoming of the powers of evil that serve to bring suffering and pain to all. The immediate benefits of this approach will be an understanding of the interrelationship between the sacred and the profane in the daily task of ministry, as well as the wholistic analysis and response that suffering will require. Spiritual or sociopolitical solutions alone are inadequate.

A third doctrinal theme important for addressing our sociopolitical reality as a Hispanic Church is that of eschatology. An important aspect of this issue is how we understand the relationship between Christ or our faith and our cultural milieu. At present, Hispanic eschatology in general—and Pentecostal in particular—may be characterized as premillennial and pretribulationist. This has resulted in an orientation towards the present which tends to be fatalistic and therefore unresponsive. This eschatological posture has led to a practical theology which is disengaged from the sociopolitical challenges of the present, and finds refuge in an escapism of religiosity and spiritual experience. A Hispanic theology must engage in the construction of a new eschatological vision which affirms, on one hand, the work of the Holy Spirit in the world establishing God's reign, and, on the other, the important role we play in contributing to the building of God's reign. This new eschatological vision must not reduce the task of the building of God's reign either to pietist quietism or revolutionary activism. Both are required. This eschatological posture will require saints who know not only how to pray but also what to pray for, and prophets who not only denounce but also announce and pray.

The Future of Hispanic American Leadership Requires It

For far too long our churches have had to depend on their leaders being taught by non-Hispanics. The resources available to most of our congregations are translated either from English or another foreign language. Sunday School, teacher-training materials, and most other aspects of leadership formation in our churches have been defined by, and confined to, materials incongruent with Hispanic Americans' needs and experiences. This has resulted in the formation of many Hispanic leaders, pastors, deacons, etc., who hold to values and beliefs that are detrimental to the well-being of the Hispanic community. Such a situation fosters the decay of self-esteem, and offers a poor model for indigenous Hispanic leadership.

There is an urgent need for a theology that will inform our Christian educators, biblical scholars, and local leaders; a theology which can serve to correlate their daily experience with the claims of the Gospel; a theology that restores the self-worth of our people and empowers them to affirm their Hispanic identity. The future of Hispanic American Christian leadership for the second millennium will continue to be defined by mainstream conservative religion unless a Hispanic American alternative is available to our churches.

The Ecumenical Character of the Church Requires It

In the midst of the excitement about the globalization of theology presently sweeping the American seminaries, it is important to address the particular nature of all theological discourse. If the move toward the globalization of theology is not cemented in the development and affirmation of local theologies, the integrity of the global project is undermined. What lends strength and integrity to the globalization of theology is the strength and integrity of the local theologies represented around the table of the dialogue.

A fundamental premise of the globalization of theology is the ecumenical base of its theological assumptions. This basic premise places upon us in the Hispanic American community the responsibility of contributing to such an endeavor in a responsible manner, not just as spectators but as full participants. This will require of us the articulation of our theological positions as representatives of Hispanic American concerns. The absence of a Hispanic American theological expression reduces our presence at such a dialogue simply to a perfunctory rather than contributive role.

If we, as Hispanic Americans, take seriously the ecumenical character of the church, we too must be prepared to enter into that circle of engagement with some theological assertions which correspond to the vision and contribution of our Hispanic community to the well-being of the whole people of God.

The Self-Esteem of the Hispanic Community Requires It

Hispanic Americans are frequently caricatured as the lazy Mexican sleeping under his sombrero—dependent, always looking for a handout. The modern version of this caricature is that of Hispanics in welfare programs and standing in line to receive the leftovers of educational aid in our universities and seminaries. Our theology is seen as dependent upon and shaped by others. We are perceived as theological ventriloquists. The voice that is heard is not ours but someone else's.

Our self-esteem as a people requires that we, too, contribute to the theological *sancocho* (stew) that is being cooked. If we are to affirm our honor, we must demonstrate through our contribution to the whole that the almighty God has also been gracious with us. We, too, are given insight by the same Spirit. We, too, have been given a prophetic word for our times. A Hispanic American theology will serve to encourage others in our churches and seminaries to share their insights on the questions of the day. It can empower us to join in the ongoing dialogue for solutions to the challenges we face as a Christian community in a pluralistic world.

Notes

1. Virgil Elizondo, *Galilean Journey: The Mexican American Promise* (Maryknoll: Orbis Books, 1985).

2. See, e.g., Enrique Dussel, *Historia de la Iglesia en América Latina: Coloniaje y Liberación 1494–1973* (Barcelona: Editorial Nova Terra, 1974); Luis Rivera Pagán, *Evangelización y violencia: La conquista de América* (San Juan: Editorial Gemí, 1991); Orlando Costas, *Theology of the Crossroads in Contemporary Latin America* (Amsterdam: Rodopi, 1976) and *Christ Outside the Gate: Missions Beyond Christendom* (Maryknoll: Orbis Books, 1982); David J. Bosch. *Transforming Mission: Paradigm Shifts in Theology of Mission* (Maryknoll: Orbis Books, 1991).

3. In addition to the writings mentioned in n.2 above, see also his *The Church and Its Mission: A Shattering Critique from the Third World* (Wheaton: Tyndale House, 1974) and *Liberating News: A Theology of Contextual Evangelization* (Grand Rapids: Wm. B. Eerdmans, 1989).

4. See, e.g., the works of Orlando Costas, Justo I., González, René Padilla, José Míguez Bonino, and Eldín Villafañe.

5. W. Wink, *Naming the Power: The Language of Power in the New Testament* (Philadelphia: Fortress Press, 1984).

6. R. Niebuhr, *Nature and Destiny of Man* (New York: Scribner's, 1941).

4

Arturo J. Bañuelas

Arturo Bañuelas was born in Pecos, Texas, a third-generation Chicano. He obtained his masters of divinity (MDiv) in 1976 from Notre Dame Seminary in New Orleans where he completed course work for a masters in sacred theology (STM). In 1986 he earned a licentiate (STL) and in 1988 a doctorate (STD) in fundamental theology from the Gregorian University in Rome. He is a native priest of the Diocese of El Paso, Texas.

In his ministry assignments Bañuelas has served as pastor, co-founder of the diocesan Ministry to Divorced and Separated, and the Diocesan Commission for Evangelization for Hispanics, administrative assistant to the bishop and co-director of the Permanent Deacon Program. In 1988 he became founding director of Tepeyac Institute, a diocesan lay ministry formation center.

In his works and lectures, Bañuelas focuses on documenting U.S. Latino theology, the relationship between faith and politics, ministry in the Hispanic communities, inculturation from within the Latino perspective, and Latin American theology. In 1991 he taught a first of its kind in the nation course on U.S. Latino theology at the Jesuit School of Theology at Berkeley. Since then he has written on this theology and compiled a first working bibliography of over 250 references.

In 1991 he was visiting Hispanic professor at the Jesuit School of Theology, and has taught at the Pastoral Institute, Incarnate Word College, at the Mexican American Cultural Center, the Oblate School of Theology, and lectured at Catholic Theological Union and at Loyola University in Chicago as part of their Pastoral Institute. Presently he directs and teaches at the Tepeyac Institute in El Paso, Texas.

Bañuelas is co-founder of the Academy of Catholic Hispanic Theologians in the United States and was elected its president in 1991. He is also a member of *La Comunidad* of Hispanic American Scholars of Theology and Religion, the Catholic Theological Society of America, and the

Ecumenical Association of Third World Theologians. He also serves on the editorial board for the *Journal of Hispanic/Latino Theology*. In 1992 he was awarded the "Virgilio Elizondo Award" by the Academy of Catholic Hispanic Theologians of the United States and the Jesuit School of Theology at Berkeley awarded him the 1994 Visiting Hispanic Research Scholar grant.

Tepeyac Institute
499 St. Matthew
El Paso, Texas 79907
915-595-5020/915-772-3226

U.S. Hispanic Theology

An Initial Assessment

Arturo J. Bañuelas

As the peoples of the Americas focus on the five centuries of Christian presence in our lands and debate whether to celebrate, commemorate, or obliterate the memory of this historical moment, a new theological voice is now being heard in the Americas. It was inevitable given the 500 years that continue to forge a rich historical, cultural, political, and religious tapestry called Hispanic America. This era is witnessing the emergence of what we can properly call a U.S. Hispanic Theology. Viewed from the perspective of Christianity in the Americas, this theology is not a sub-theology of North Atlantic theology, nor simply a translation of Latin American Liberation Theology.

The years 1968 through 1969 mark decisive moments for theology in general and for U.S. Hispanic Theology in particular. In 1968 Gustavo Gutiérrez published his famous *Hacia un teología de la liberación,* and Virgilio Elizondo his "Educación religiosa para el Mexico-Norteamericano." In 1969 James Cone published his *Black Theology of Liberation.* Since then the confluence of these new theological stands have occasioned paradigm shifts in theology that have altered the theological landscape worldwide.

First Generation U.S. Hispanic Theologians

Since the late 1960s, the first generation of U.S. Hispanic theologians has continued to produce creative, original, and insightful reflections, with the late 1980s being the most productive years of publication. This article will focus on some of the leading first-generation exponents of U.S. Hispanic Theology. Recent writings indicate that the number of U.S. Hispanic theologians is increasing. The list includes Gilbert Romero, Harold

"U.S. Hispanic Theology: An Initial Assessment," *Missiology* 20:2 (April 1992), pp. 275–300. Reprinted with permission.

Recinos, Sixto García, Juan José Huitrado-Hizo, Dolorita Martínez, Clemente Barron, Jaime Vidal, Arturo Pérez, Ana María Pineda, Gary Riebe-Estrella, Marina Herrera, Jeanette Rodríguez-Holguin, Fernando Segovia, Rosendo Urrabazo, and Dominga Zapata.

In this article I will present leading exponents of U.S. Hispanic Theology, including major themes and shared characteristics derived from the works of these theologians, and offer a brief assessment of U.S. Hispanic Theology in its present stage of development.

Virgilio Elizondo—Mestizaje

Virgilio Elizondo is the most prominent U.S. Hispanic theologian. What Gustavo Gutiérrez is to Liberation Theology, Elizondo is to U.S. Hispanic Theology. He is presently rector of San Fernando Cathedral in San Antonio, Texas, his native city. He is also the founder of the Mexican-American Cultural Center (MACC) in that city, a center for theological, pastoral, and Spanish language studies.

With eight books, two co-authored books, and over 40 articles, Elizondo has written more extensively than any other U.S. Hispanic Catholic theologian (1968–1989). His work *The Galilean Journey: The Mexican American Promise* (1983) is his most characteristic volume and will be the focus of this review. This book coalesces Elizondo's basic theological positions which can be categorized as "faith confronts culture." Paradoxically, since faith and culture are both dynamic realities, culture also confronts faith, but this categorization emphasizes culture as a dominant element in Elizondo's theological reflection. In particular, Elizondo's works center around a conquest/fiesta axis which leads him to claim that the church is experiencing a *kairos* moment grounded on the promise of the Mexican-American contribution in fashioning a new historical period in the Western Hemisphere. For Elizondo, a new experience of God is being made manifest from the perspective of the Mexican-American. This perspective is born from the experience of the double conquest of the Mexican-American, who through the resultant *mestizaje,* is now proleptically celebrating an eschatological fiesta: the weaving together of a new universalism in North, Central, and South America.

In *The Galilean Journey,* Elizondo begins with the historical-cultural reading of the Mexican-American faith experience. His contention is that the cultural conditioning of a people is not just an aid to the proclamation of the gospel, but the medium through which God chooses to reveal himself. In the second part of the book, Elizondo examines a cultural rereading of the gospel from within the Mexican-American journey of oppression to liberation. This leads to his claim that the foundational relationship between Christian faith and the cultural milieu is the very essence of the way of Jesus. In the final section he examines the Mexican-American experience from the faith perspective: a gospel rereading of our culture creatively portraying the *mestizaje* as festive prophecy proclaiming the birth of a new Christian universalism.

The first part, Elizondo's major contribution to many discussions on Hispanic theology, outlines a basic thesis of his work—a double, violent conquest produced a *mestizaje* which in turn God chose as axis for forging a new humanity. Beginning with the Iberian Catholic conquest in the sixteenth century, and then the Nordic Protestant conquest of the nineteenth century, Elizondo formulates his fundamental tenet of the *mestizaje*. Its uniqueness consists in the fact that never before in human history has such a particular biological mixture, clash, and confluence of world views occurred. They converge at Tepeyac with the apparition of *Nuestra Señora de Guadalupe* who became an icon for the Mexican-American as well as for the Mexican.[1] This clash and blending of bloods, faiths, and worldviews foundationally characterizes the birth of a new people and Elizondo's theological premise for the promise of the Mexican-American in God's unfolding historical plan of liberation. What the Exodus was for the Hebrews as a foundational event, Tepeyac is for the Mexican-Americans. Using his principles of the dynamics of *mestizaje,* he shows how Mexican-Americans are a doubly marginalized and rejected people by reason of their participation in two different, distinct cultural groups, never fully accepted by either. The deeply religious nature of the rejected *mestizo* has survived and resisted assimilation through its unique form of faith, vividly expressed in symbols of identity and belonging (*posadas,* etc.), of struggle and suffering (Good Friday), and of new creation (Guadalupe, baptism). What becomes characteristic of U.S. Hispanic Theology beginning with Elizondo is the interpretation and relationship of the identity of Mexican-Americans through the symbols of their faith and struggles.

The second part of this volume argues that in Jesus' socio-historical situation one can find a clue to the all-important role of God's saving plan for humanity, which for the Mexican-Americans holds a special promise. The cultural and historical situation of Jesus the Galilean shows noticeable parallels to the Mexican-American situation in the United States. Elizondo offers a distinct Hispanic perspective on Jesus as a *mestizo.*

Galileans were rejected and despised by the Judean Jews because of their racial mixture and Galilee's distance from the temple in Jerusalem. As such their situation parallels that of the American Southwest, a land of rejected *mestizos.* Jesus entered human history and ministered at the margins of society and became himself the one rejected by the Judean Jews. It is from this socio-historical context that Elizondo interprets how the mission of the Mexican-Americans resonates with Jesus' gospel mission. To accomplish his saving work, Jesus the Galilean, living in the margins, confronted Jerusalem, the center of power. He went to Jerusalem to overthrow the religious, political, and intellectual absolutism that builds boundaries of oppression. Jesus destroyed the barriers between people as well as those between people and God. The confrontation was a liberating process of going beyond boundaries into the kingdom where all are welcomed as brothers and sisters.

The third part completes the pattern of the conquest/fiesta axis, explained through the process of going from Galilee to Jerusalem to a new Christian universalism. The *mestizo's* condition of double rejection is a sign of divine election: What the world rejects, God chooses as his very own. It is precisely in this double identity, double rejection that Mexican-Americans have something of value to offer. As *mestizos,* doubly rejected, God has elected them as agents for a new humanity. Their very reasons for marginalization are the bases of their liberating and salvific efforts, not only for themselves, but for others as well. This Christian pedagogy of the oppressed underlies the mission of the church, the *mestizo* par excellence, in that it strives to bring about a new synthesis of the earthly and the heavenly and, thus, has alternatives to offer humanity. Mexican-Americans need to confront racism and liberal capitalism to forge a new, more global, and Spirit-imbued identity so that new life will begin to unfold. Ultimately, Mexican-Americans must reject rejection and confront the barriers within and without with a love that accepts all people as they are into the table fellowship. It is in this sense that *mestizaje* is seen as festive prophecy. "*Mestizaje* is the beginning of a new Christian universalism. The depth of joy present in the mestizo celebration is indicative of the eschatological mestizo identity: they are the ones in whom the fullness of the kingdom has already begun, the new universalism that by-passes human segregative barriers" (Elizondo 1983:124). In the end, Elizondo has added a further clarification to the Latin American concept of liberation in answering the question about the relationship between spiritual redemption and social emancipation: acceptance of the rejected in their giftedness forges a new *mestizaje,* a manifestation of God's liberative action in history.

Elizondo's work marks both a continuity and discontinuity with Latin American Liberation Theologies, thus showing a distinctive U.S. Hispanic character. The use of social analysis, theology as a second act, the victims of oppression as the central datum of theology, and the rereading of the gospels from the perspective of the oppressed are noted Latin American influences in Elizondo's work. However, unlike the Liberation Theologies which emphasize the political dimension, Elizondo emphasizes the historico-cultural one. Both correctly point out the importance of the political dimension as a corrective to any spiritualization or idealization of theology and assert that there is a hierarchy of factors in all oppression. Viewed from the perspective of *mestizaje,* the historico-cultural dimension takes precedence for Elizondo. This does not mean that he ignores the political dimension, but further elaboration would help show how acceptance of the other is integrally linked to new structures and public policies that promote the new universalism.

Elizondo's work is a solid, creative, and insightful voice from within the Mexican-American reality. Of major significance for U.S. Hispanic

Theology is Elizondo's description of the symbols of identity and belonging, of suffering, and of new creation in their relationship to the affirmation of the liberative process of the Mexican-American. This link between faith and culture is significant, given that Mexican-Americans are a people made to feel like foreigners in their own land, a people who are not at home with their self-image, a people who live in a constant state of dilemma and of confusion by reason of their participation in two different cultures—yet are rejected by both. Elizondo has done a great service in the difficult task of pioneering a theological reflection from within the honest reality of a people who have historically lived with a mentality of vanquishment. He has challenged all to accept the Mexican-American experience of God as a privileged and gifted situation from which to discover God's liberative plan.

Elizondo is the first to articulate skillfully *"mestizaje"* as the Hispanic *locus theologicus* used by other U.S. Hispanic theologians. His interpretation of the conquest and the convergence of worlds at Tepeyac has become an assumed tenet of U.S. Hispanic Theology. Even Cuban-American theologians, for whom Our Lady of Charity and not Guadalupe is the central marian symbol, now accept Guadalupe as somehow normative for U.S. Hispanic Theology. However, Elizondo uses *mestizaje* to elucidate the reality of Mexican-Americans, the Roman Catholic Church, and the Tepeyac event. On the one hand, this relationship makes the symbol confessional in his theology. On the other, it calls for a more categorical clarification of this connection. For example, does this mean that if a Mexican-American becomes a non-Catholic, he or she is committing cultural suicide?

His emphasis on the historical Jesus, together with his creative perspective paralleling Jesus' Galilean journey with the mission of Mexican-Americans, provides a challenging pastoral perspective. His work gives credibility to an understanding of revelation in Hispanic popular traditions, songs, and religious symbols as *loci theologici* within which the people speak of God's actions in history today. Elizondo's theological program of "faith confronts culture" asks the key theological question: What is the relationship between self-identity as Mexican-Americans and God's plan of salvation? Here Elizondo unfolds a vision of a new Christian universalism. *Mestizos* must reject rejection and confront all barriers of exclusion leading to a new creation where all share at the festive table of fellowship as brothers and sisters. This mission is grounded in the privileged position *mestizos* are called to perform as a bridge people in the Americas, since they form part of both North and Latin America. This Mexican-American promise further highlights Elizondo's insistence that the victims of oppression are bearers of good news. He artfully articulates this conviction throughout his works. His notion of *fiesta* as celebration of human possibilities for a new humanity highlights a characteristic element of his understanding of the Mexican-American perspective on historical-cultural reality, a perspective forged in the context of the ongoing racism of Euro-American society.

Finally, there is a presumption in this major work by Elizondo: that Mexican-Americans, predominantly Roman Catholic, simply by being doubly rejected *will accept* their divine election and mission to forge a new Christian universalism. Social historical conditioning will continue to be a medium for God's judgment on history. The history of Mexican-American oppression also reveals that this medium brings with it negative manifestations of the very obstacles *mestizaje* is called to overcome. Elizondo's important theological contributions, especially elaborated in this classic volume, will continue to be essential reference for years to come.

Justo L. González—The Coming of the New Reformation—Mañana

Justo L. González, the most prominent U.S. Hispanic Protestant theologian, is a respected author and co-author of 43 books and over 200 articles (González 1990).[2] He is also the editor of *Apuntes,* the only U.S. Hispanic theological journal in the country, and is presently Adjunct Professor of Theology at Columbia Theological Seminary in Decatur, Georgia.

In his most recent major work, *Mañana: Christian Theology from a Hispanic Perspective* (1990), González proposes a rereading of the Christian tradition from the *mañana* perspective of the Hispanic hopes for the coming reign of God. In this provocative work, he outlines his claims for a new twentieth-century reformation era in which a new way of doing theology is emerging specifically from a minority Hispanic ecumenical perspective.

1. Hispanic Minority Perspective

In the first two chapters of this work, González describes the unique historical cultural context which forms the genesis of the book's minority perspective and methodology. Rejecting any claims of objectivity in his theology, he exposes his biased position as a theologian stemming from his minority perspective, first that of being Protestant in Catholic Latin America and later an ethnic minority in the United States. This context provides the setting for a rereading of the Christian tradition in light of the Hispanic experience of oppression.

Unlike the strong individualism of Western theology, González's methodology is grounded in a communal enterprise of a believing, practicing community. He calls it the *fuenteovejuna* theology, *"todos a una"*—after a story in Spain of a town by this name which assumed a collective identity (1990:28–30). A major consideration in his methodology is the Hispanic historical context which indicates that Hispanics are a people in exile and, therefore, live in ambiguity. Nonetheless, he argues, it is precisely as strangers in their own land that Hispanics can make a meaningful contribution as pilgrims living out of their *mañana* hopes.

2. New Reformation of the Twentieth Century

In the third and fourth chapters, González outlines his insightful and provocative claim that U.S. Hispanic Theology, still in its nascent stages, is a significant element of an emerging new reformation period in the twentieth century. He constructs his vision of this reformation era on his claims that the churches are experiencing the end of the Constantinian era during which the church existed in politically and socially advantageous conditions, the failure of the North Atlantic countries to usher forth promised prosperity, and the growing self-consciousness of ethnic minorities. In his view, key indicators that support the macro-events ushering forth this reformation are evident: First, the voices of the poor are now an important theological datum. Second, a new biblical hermeneutic is emerging in the post-Constantinian era, leading to a deeper understanding of the biblical message. Third, the nature of truth is now being understood in relationship to orthopraxis and not simply in metaphysical terms. Fourth, this reformation will be radically ecumenical. Fifth, theology is shifting toward a more historically concrete perspective that questions the philosophical universality of theology based on the present unjust distribution of power, i.e., theology must now correspond to the struggles of Hispanics in its claims for universality. What is distinctive about González's vision of a new reformation is his ecumenically Hispanic minority perspective point of departure and how it significantly embraces not only Hispanic concerns, but also those of other struggling minorities who seemingly are already ushering forth this new reformation.

In describing the role of the Hispanics in this reformation, González grounds himself in the unique historical cultural roots at the birth of *mestizo* Christianity. Standing within this tradition, he provocatively asserts that "the Spanish American Roman Catholic Church is part of the common background of all Hispanics," although many are now Protestant (1990:55). This represents a dramatic rereading of Protestantism, often viewed simply from the Nordic European cultural perspective which neglects the context of the religious-cultural ethos that formed the Hispanic psyche and identity. Furthermore, for a Hispanic Methodist, such as González, to affirm that the Guadalupe event "is indeed part of the gospel message" is an indication not only of the radically ecumenical thrust of this work, but also of the new expressions of reformation *mestizo* Christianity that are being born and developing in the Americas. Ultimately, he argues, because this reformation is arising on the periphery of Christianity, it will contribute greatly to the Western expressions of Christianity which are too often considered normative in theology.

3. Rereading Christian Tradition: A Hispanic Minority Ecumenical Perspective

In the last five chapters, González systematically investigates the doctrinal implications of this new reformation, drawing on his vast background

of patristic studies. His rereading of early Christian theology, when viewed
from the minority Hispanic ecumenical perspective, shows that sociopolitical hidden agendas colored many of the initial doctrinal formulations. He
mounts a convincing challenge to the traditional view of these teachings.

González begins with an attempt to reread Scripture from his unique
point of reference. The Bible must be read "in Spanish," he maintains, in
other words from a Hispanic minority ecumenical perspective. This will
reveal that the Bible carries with it a political agenda. With his proposed
grammar for a new reading of the Bible, González concludes that the
Bible deals with issues of power and powerlessness, that generally it was
intended to be read communally not privately, that its availability to the
poor and simple points to a privileged hermeneutic for biblical interpretation, and that it should be allowed to interpret us and our situation and
not vice versa. He is not arguing against the use of biblical scholarship:
rather, from the perspective of reading the Bible "in Spanish," he is offering
a corrective to many fundamentalist and liberal readings of Scripture
that often fail to show how the Bible teaches Christians to address their
situations meaningfully.

Next, González investigates fundamental tenets of faith. In his typical
scholarly fashion, he focuses on major themes dealing with God-talk, the
Trinity, Creation, Christian anthropology, and Christology. In his rereading
of these themes, González creatively uncovers the hidden agendas of a
theology of the status quo which has formed part of Christian theology
since its early development codified in council documents, dogmas, and
doctrines. Challenging early classical interpretations of key church teachings, he concludes that, since their initial formulation, these teachings have
procured a sociopolitical content.

Language about God, González argues, did not evolve as a politically
neutral notion: prototype God-talk has been linked with the vested interests
of the ruling classes. When Christians began interpreting their God in
Platonic terms, the status quo was sacralized, benefiting the ideology of
the powerful. Changelessness became a divine characteristic justifying the
notion of an aristocratic idea of God which would support the privileges
of the higher classes. Just as idols serve a socioeconomic function,
according to González, God-talk must be questioned from the perspectives
of the interests these notions of God serve.

In his survey of the doctrine on the Trinity, González concludes that it
too contains political overtones. The trinitarian formulations, he asserts,
were also debates about the connection between people's social and economic doctrines and their notion of God. In other words, people's notions
about the Trinity have had drastic consequences for the manner in which
we are to order our society and economic relations within it. To counter
a status quo notion of God, González proposes the notion of a "minority
God," who speaks Spanish and who joins the dispossessed in their struggles, marching them to victory. This notion is based on a "life of sharing,"

and has enormous liberating and subversive powers which challenge any oppressive quality about the Trinity used throughout the centuries to justify a theology of the status quo.

For González, the issues surrounding the doctrine of Creation are particularly relevant to the Hispanic experience and theology. He demonstrates how the doctrine on Creation is more than a statement about origins and the future life. Principally, he proposes that it is an assertion about the positive value of the present reality and, above all, about present responsibility for that reality. Nonetheless, those with vested interest in the status quo have used this doctrine to justify popular versions of the theory of evolution that claim that the ultimate rule of Creation is the survival of the fittest. González contends that this abusive interpretation of this doctrine should extend beyond biological theory which upholds the justification of social policy that accepts the process whereby the powerful oppress the powerless to an evolutionary process of creating a better world.

In regards to the doctrine on what it means to be human, González insists that the discussion should be posed in praxiological terms rather than ontological terms to underscore his consistent claim of these doctrines' sociopolitical content and how they have been used to justify oppression. His discussion of the doctrine of being human goes beyond any explanation of the traditional categories of body and soul. He argues, for example, that the hierarchical understanding of human nature, the spiritual "higher" nature versus the material "lower" nature, was used as the basis for the medieval claim that the church had greater authority than the state. Furthermore, this understanding of this doctrine continues to influence a similarly hierarchical understanding of society. Specifically, he sees this hierarchical ordering of the body and soul as having inherent racist and sexist notions in our society. He contends that a better understanding of human nature will come from within the perspectives of those darker-skinned, oppressed people with dirt under their fingernails, whose woeful bodily existence questions any theory of human nature that justifies the present ordering in society. Additionally, on an ecological note, González maintains that the Greek dualism that leads to the separation of body and soul has also led to a devaluation of our relationship to the earth.

Even the doctrine of the Incarnation, according to González, has been used to reinforce attitudes that lie at the root of oppression of Hispanics. The politicization of this doctrine led to the "Constantinization" of God. The theologians of the status quo expounded a static notion of God in metaphysical terms that dehistoricized the biblical notion of the God actively engaged in human affairs. However, Jesus' Incarnation, "the carpenter from Galilee who was called the Christ," was the stumbling block to the form of Constantinian theology about God, and therefore, it is from this perspective of this Incarnation that we know who God is and what it means to be human. For González, the way to interpret the doctrine of the Incarnation does not center around abstract arguments on the doctrine, but on concrete concerns about "how we can get on with the business of being human in the midst of an oppressive society."

4. *Mañana* People

In his concluding chapter, González masterfully captures the Hispanic sense of a people of the reign of God as a *mañana* people. This term has often been understood in derogatory and stereotypical ways to refer to Hispanics as carefree, irresponsible people who always put things off until tomorrow. González, who understands the core Hispanic psyche and identity, turns this negative notion around and talks about an understanding of *mañana* at the heart of Hispanic spirituality. The church, he explains, must be a *mañana* people in pilgrimage to the reign of God. To live out a *mañana* spirituality is a call to a radical questioning of today, living already out of a time in which God is about to do something new. *Mañana* is already here, lived in the promise of God's faithfulness. It is to live in the eschatological tension of the already and the not yet of the coming reign of God.

González's work admirably fulfills the requirements of a much-needed scholarly exploration of theology from within his unique minority ecumenical Hispanic perspective. Of particular importance for U.S. Hispanic Theology is his vision of an emerging new reformation arising from the periphery in which Hispanics play a determining role. His exploration into the early formulations of fundamental Christian teachings mounts a convincing challenge to the traditional view of these doctrines. He elucidates clearly the theological polarity between a theology of the status quo and the affirmation of the life of the oppressed Hispanics as codified for centuries in the formulations of Christian doctrine—under the guise of Christian theology. González's dissatisfaction with the classical understanding of these early formulations calls into question abstract ivory-tower theological methodologies which ultimately end up supporting the interests of the ruling status quo.

González offers a solid alternative to any naive attempt at doing theology. For him, the real issue is not theology, but rather a new reformation era in which the issue is the liberation of the poor. His work transcends ancient quarrels and present differences among divided Christians and paves the way for a challenging dialogue with fresh perspectives and categories still neglected in ecumenical discussions. While questioning assimilationist and evangelical efforts in ministry and theological methodologies, González has begun a unique systematic approach that understands the minority Hispanic perspective as a contribution to theology.

Even though González demonstrates an impressive mastery over his subject, there are several issues in his work in need of further elaboration. How is reading the Bible "in Spanish" in fact a hermeneutical advantage? What guarantees this Hispanic perspective its redemptive qualities? Furthermore, González's reliance on Karl Barth as a principal supportive reference, at times, stands in contrast to his point of departure. Barth is an exponent of the very theology González challenges. When discussing the doctrine of the Incarnation, González deviates from the book's methodological premises and upholds that only Scripture is the point of departure for Christology (González 1990:151). These few points notwithstanding, González's pioneering work is a benchmark of U.S. Hispanic Theology.

Allan Figueroa Deck—Evangelization of Cultures: Hispanics Facing Modernity

The third theologian I will present is Jesuit priest Allan Figueroa Deck, professor at the Jesuit School of Theology at Berkeley in California. He is the author of two books and 21 articles. An early publication, "A Christian Perspective on the Reality of Illegal Immigration," won the O'Grady Award of the National Conference of Catholic Charities for the best article on Catholic social teaching in 1978. His most recent book, and the principal source I will use in this presentation, *The Second Wave: Hispanic Ministry and the Evangelization of Cultures,* won the Paulist Press Publisher's Award for 1990 (Deck 1989). To my knowledge, Deck is the first Hispanic theologian to receive this distinction.

The central focus of Deck's work is the evangelization of the North American culture in dialogue with immigrant Hispanics facing a modern (postmodern) U.S. culture. He begins with the premise that the "second wave," the migration of millions of Latin American and Asian-Pacific peoples to the United States since the Second World War, constitutes a dramatic new challenge, not only to the survival of the Hispanic culture, but directly to the credibility of the church's evangelization mission. Deck, in this important work, tackles an old problem with renewed vigor to provide a vision for a credible pastoral response to the challenge of the Hispanic presence within the North American milieu during a rapidly changing period approaching the twenty-first century. Given the fact that Hispanics of the "second wave" represent the emerging dominant ethnic group in the U.S. Catholic Church, this timely work is written with a sense of urgency and a challenging pastoral thrust. Based on the conviction that effective church ministry must include the positive recognition of the Hispanic ethos and religiosity and the conversion of oppressive values of Western culture, Deck proposes a synthesis not yet achieved by the church at large when dealing with the question of Hispanic ministry. Although he grounds himself on the perspective of Hispanics of Mexican origin in California, many of his arguments are valid for a broader dialogue dealing with Hispanic issues in the church throughout the country.

The Second Wave is developed from the twofold perspective of addressing the Hispanic socio-historical reality and the church's pastoral-theological response to that reality as it attempts to evangelize within a changing North American context. The first chapter includes Deck's analysis of the demographic and social scientific interpretation of the Hispanic reality in general and of California in particular. Given the dearth of data on this topic, he has shed new light that cannot not be ignored when dealing with the Hispanic situation in the United States. For example, his analysis categorizes immigration as internal migration (there was an established Hispanic presence before borders were set) and as a type of revolving-door situation that challenges a nation caught up with a false sense of cultural pluralism and set on assimilation policies. The second chapter highlights significant factors that make up the historico-cultural background of Hispanics of Mexican origin in California. In this chapter, divided into five sections, he presents a concise background of key historical periods that span from the Hispanic's pre-Columbian heritage to after the 1846 Mexican-American War.

The last three chapters, which form the heart of the book, proceed to provide a creative chronicle of the pastoral practices of Hispanic ministry in California. Included here is his central assertion of the need for a dual socio-cultural analysis to develop a critical sense of the U.S. dominant culture as well as the dependent Hispanic culture in light of the church's evangelization mission. He concludes with proposals for pastoral praxis in view of findings in the previous chapters.

The merit of this work goes well beyond fulfilling the requirements set out in the title. From the perspective of U.S. Hispanic Theology, the deeper scope of this volume is the initial task of elaborating critical socio-historical and cultural dynamics at the core of what Hispanics call the Euro-American conquest of the Western half of the country. For pastoral agents who maintain that the conquest is past history, and for those who refuse to recognize the oppressive undercurrents still at work even within the church, this work is a bold challenge. Furthermore, from a liberationist perspective, Deck brings to the forefront of theology in the United States how the poor are a significant point of departure for the evangelization of the rich. While Deck does not call his work specifically a theology, his praxiological thrust aims at rooting the Christian tradition within the broader realities of the ongoing clash and struggles between a traditional Hispanic popular Catholicism and a North American middle class urban culture with Protestant origins. It is from this complex situation that the church will find a clue for forging a vision of being Catholic and North American as it enters the twenty-first century.

To sustain his thesis, Deck advocates eight mutually related pastoral objectives that range from empowerment of lay leaders to *pastoral de conjunto* and, thus, continues to fuel the unprecedented discussion on a proper response to the challenging Hispanic presence in North America. What is provocative about his arguments is the implied notion that inculturation in pastoral praxis is linked to liberation only when pastoral agents in the United States recognize their inherently modern presuppositions when dealing with historico-culturally premodern Hispanics. Failure to recognize this dichotomy will serve only to further ideologies of assimilation, masquerading as evangelization among Hispanics.

Other merits of this work include the author's use of social analysis in interpreting Hispanic data. His familiarity with the California pastoral reality is evident and impressive. However, since the pastoral profile throughout is necessarily tilted toward the Hispanic context, the postmodern North American reality is given only cursory examination. Although his project is not primarily to examine definitively all the historical factors of the Hispanic social and pastoral context, and the book has as its point of departure the Californian of Mexican origin, perhaps the prophetic voice of Cesar Chavez and the use of more recent authoritative studies of the borderlands experience (Oscar Martinez, Raul Fernandez) would make a good book even better.

The appearance of Deck's work is quite timely in the ongoing endeavor to theologize from within a particular context. For Deck, part of the context includes the North American postmodern reality. Here he has gone beyond other Hispanic voices in articulating a unique and a fundamental issue that needs to be broached by U.S. Hispanic Theology. Five centuries of history show that Hispanics differ in assimilation patterns from other minority groups within the broader dominant North American culture. This is due largely to the fact that, in one sense, Hispanics view themselves as a minority within the North Atlantic reality; but, in another sense, they view themselves as a majority within the Western Hemisphere in terms of faith, culture, and language. Deck's insightful work shows how this paradox can actually serve in the church's evangelical mission by relativizing the cultural absolutisms of both Anglo and Hispanic America. Furthermore, this situation not only underscores the urgency of Deck's praxiological vision, but also radically decries any effort at absolutizing any culture by neglecting to investigate its oppressive presuppositions. Along this vein, there is an assumption throughout this work that Hispanic popular Catholicism stands as a corrective to the crisis situation of postmodernity within the North American context. The validity of this assumption will be established by how seriously pastoral agents heed Deck's challenge for the liberative evangelization of cultures.

From the view of U.S. Hispanic Theology, this work rightly calls for a purification and a critical study of the Hispanic reality, while at the same time calling for a respectful and affirming understanding of a tradition that has nurtured a unique religious experience, now finding articulation by its own theologians. Altogether, it is a valuable work with an even wider scope than its subtitle suggests.

Ada María Isasi-Díaz and Yolanda Tarango—Mujerista Theology

The first volume from a Hispanic feminist perspective, entitled *Hispanic Women: Prophetic Voice in the Church,* is co-authored by Ada María Isasi-

Díaz and Yolanda Tarango (Isasi-Díaz and Tarango 1988). Isasi-Díaz is Cuban-American, presently Assistant Professor of Theology and Ethics at Drew University, Madison, New Jersey; Yolanda Tarango, a Mexican-American, is national coordinator of La Hermanas, a national organization of Hispanic women. Isasi-Díaz's other works include co-authorship of three books and 11 articles, some of which have been included as chapters in five different books (Isasi-Díaz 1986, 1989).

This five-chapter work is an exercise in Liberation Theology from the viewpoint of Hispanic women's struggles to survive. Appropriately, they prefer to call their work *mujerista* theology to characterize better a reflection from the self-determined Hispanic women's viewpoint. Accordingly, the volume interconnects *mujerista,* liberation, and cultural dimensions from the perspective of the lived experiences of Hispanic women.

The first three chapters outline a basic framework for Hispanic women's Liberation Theology. In the first chapter, Isasi-Díaz and Tarango describe their work's *locus theologicus* as Hispanic women's cultural-historical reality, the *mestizaje.* Specifically, they refer to Roman Catholic Mexican-Americans, Puerto Ricans, and Cubans. Prescinding from the presupposition of questions of survival of Hispanic women, the theological process entails a threefold commitment: (1) to do theology, (2) from a specific perspective, (3) as a communal process. From within the *mujerista* perspective, Hispanic women's struggles are also theological questions—women made in the image of God, from within their lived reality struggle to become fully human.

The second chapter employs interviews with seven Hispanic women, focusing on their experience of the divine and sums up their recurring themes into three categories: as *promesas, sentir-sentimiento,* and church and/or priests. Interpreting the interviews, Isasi-Díaz and Tarango determine that Hispanic women have a deep sense of being church, even though this does not necessarily mean participation in the institutional church. This conclusion can easily be validated, for Hispanics talk about being Catholic or refer to *la iglesia* to characterize a reality that goes beyond describing the institutional church. The content of the interviews also reveals that Hispanic women draw on their religious impulse as a source, as if drawing from a biblical tradition, when speaking about their religious sense of faith. Hispanic women, the authors contend, have a more holistic sense in religious experience. In other words, to believe, to feel, to understand are all one and the same thing.

The third proceeds to describe the sources of Hispanic women's Liberation Theology from three perspectives: existential, religious, and cultural. The existential view refers to Hispanic women's main preoccupation with cultural, physical, psychological, and economic survival. The religious view refers to the major motivations that lead to self-determination which to some extent are embedded in the popular religiosity lived daily by Hispanic women. Cultural perspective refers to the link between the religious dimension and Hispanic women's self-understanding. From describing these sources, the writers conclude that the importance of Hispanic women's Liberation Theology lies in its being an intrinsic element in the process of creating a Hispanic women's culture and an articulation of the new reality being birthed.

The fourth chapter proceeds with a return to the interviewees to discern from them ethical understandings. The authors assert that Hispanic women view moral good as having to do with obligations for the good of others, basically their community and family. In regards to evil, Hispanic women refer to it as social evil. Moreover, as the findings suggest, an adequate social ethic from the *mujerista* perspective claims that Hispanic women are responsible for both interpersonal and social life and, thus, have an active role to play in social transformation.

The final chapter is an elaboration of Isasi-Díaz and Tarango's specific methodology and proposed task for a Hispanic women's Liberation Theology. The methodology is described as dialogic, referring to a relation of empathy between two poles that are engaged in a joint search, and it involves an ongoing process of conscientization intrinsic to being agents of one's own history. Furthermore, this process of critical consciousness involves four interrelated and interdependent moments: telling stories, analyzing, liturgizing, and strategizing. In addition, the task is to further the liberation of Hispanic women from socio-economic and political oppression, from the historical constraints that do not allow them to determine their own future, and finally from sin. They envision their methodology as subversive praxis since the goal of Hispanic women is not simply equality, or accommodation to church or academic structures. The goal is all that leads to self-determination.

The strength of this volume lies in its capacity to address a complex situation of Hispanic women proceeding from a sophisticated methodology and in the combined voices of Hispanic women who lay the groundwork for a Hispanic women's Liberation Theology. Their claims are thought-provoking. As a first work addressing the situation of U.S. Hispanic women, it is most welcomed. Consistent with other U.S. Hispanic voices, this significant work asks why there is oppression; but it does so from within the particular reality of Hispanic women's struggles to survive. This work creatively draws from Hispanics' own historical experience, from within their own religious impulse. Again, as in other works by U.S. Hispanic theologians, the voice of the neglected is heard: but in this particular volume the methodology and task of Hispanic women's Liberation Theology proclaims that it will no longer be silent. In their work these two authors have successfully shown the productive nature of the communal theological process, *teología de conjunto,* in critically reappropriating Hispanic women's religious experience. This volume is at its best in the way it interconnects feminist, liberation, and cultural dimensions in the lived experience of Hispanic women as a context within which to theologize. This book does not place blame on any particular culture for its Hispanic women's struggles. Instead it calls Hispanic women to self-determination within the overall gospel mandate of liberation for all humanity. Even though the women in the interviews had varying views about the church, Hispanic women's Liberation Theology considers the church as an important instrument of Hispanic women's motivations for self-determination. This in part helps to explain why the persons interviewed were Roman Catholic, yet a broader scope including non-Catholics would help avoid the charge of being ecclesiocentric.

It is interesting to note that in Afro-American and Latin American Liberation Theologies women's voices lagged behind. *Hispanic Women* is among the first to be published alongside other U.S. Hispanic voices and, thus, as a partner will impact the direction of U.S. Hispanic Theology from its inception.

Orlando Espín—Popular Religiosity

Orlando Espín is a Cuban-American, presently Associate Professor of Theology at the University of San Diego in California. Espín and seminary professor Sixto García began publishing their theological reflections together, a striking example of what has emerged as a cooperative style and method of doing U.S. Hispanic Theology, called *teología de conjunto*.[3] Espín has published nine articles, two chapters in books, and has a book in preparation on the subject of popular Catholicism and grace (Espín 1984, 1988, 1989). The primary focus of much of his writings centers on the theology implicit in Hispanic popular religiosity in the United States. Convincingly, Espín demonstrates that a U.S. Hispanic Theology can not be a mere theological transplant of North Atlantic or Latin American theologies. It must be born out of the life and faith experiences of Hispanic-Americans in the United States. For Espín this means retrieving data from popular religiosity, the privileged locus for Hispanic self-disclosure. In a systematic fashion, Espín argues that popular religiosity can be theologically understood as a cultural expression of the *sensus fidelium* with all that this understanding implies for the theology of tradition in the Roman Catholic Church. He effectively employs the dominant symbols of Mary and Christ in the Hispanic tradition as two prime examples of bearers of the *sensus fidelium*. In his characteristically systematic fashion, Espín elaborates a basic tenet of his work that popular religiosity is the main vehicle for evangelization and guardian of Hispanic culture.

From the perspective of U.S. Hispanic Theology, Espín has contributed greatly in demonstrating the important link between the church's tradition and popular religiosity, first as a way to retrieve the experienced doctrine from within an intuitively contemplated Hispanic tradition, and secondly, as a privileged place for doing theology. Espín's initial work is already a serious indication of a significant and leading voice in shaping the emerging reflections of U.S. Hispanic theologies.

Roberto Goizueta—Theory-Praxis-Aesthetic

Roberto Goizueta, also a Cuban-American, is presently Professor of Fundamental Theology at Emory University in Atlanta, Georgia. While he has published one book and some 11 articles, it is principally in his recent works (1992a, 1992b, 1992c) that he deals specifically with issues directly related to U.S. Hispanic Theology. Popular religiosity is a major factor also in Goizueta's recent work. His perspective on popular religiosity differs from those mentioned above in that he relates it to the empowerment of victims. He argues that theologizing from within the struggle of solidarity with the marginalized Hispanics will unmask the cultural presuppositions underlying Euro-American notions of empowerment and pluralistic participation which parade as honest interpretations of reality, but, in effect, condone oppression. From this perspective, popular religiosity is a source of liberative self-empowerment.

Presently Goizueta is working on a book entitled "Foundations of Theology: An Hispanic-American Perspective." A principal thesis of this work is the importance of the aesthetic dimension of praxis as the ground for theology, most evident in popular religiosity. His contention is that Hispanic popular religiosity embodies the dialectical unity of reason, justice, and beauty as mutually implicit dimensions of Christian faith. In so doing, it offers a radical critique of mainline North American Christianity, at the same time suggesting possible avenues for the latter's renewal and transformation. This promising work will undoubtedly have a major impact as an indispensable source of reference on any discussion of U.S. Hispanic Theologies.

Pilar Aquino—Perspectivas desde la Mujer Latinoamericana

María del Pilar Aquino has the distinction of being the first woman to obtain a doctorate in theology from the Pontifical University of Salamanca, Spain. She is presently professor at Mount St. Mary's College in Los Angeles, California. Aquino thus far has published 11 articles and is presently awaiting publication of her work on Liberation Theology from the perspective of the oppressed Latina women. This work is a systematic presentation of the unique categories that emerge when one theologizes from the perspective of the Latin American woman (Aquino 1980, 1988, 1990). She identifies sexist, racist, and classist presuppositions inherent in some theological discourses, even those claiming to be Liberation Theologies. The extensive use of resources and copious endnotes attest to the profound and solid scholarship of this work. In this massive volume, Aquino identifies women's reflective processes as a way to speak about a new manner of self-understanding, to understand and verbalize revelation, to discern daily and global reality, and to experience a new woman-man relationship that opens up into a new spirituality from within the perspective of "woman as woman." This valuable work will bring systematically presented, fresh insights from the perspective of oppressed women. Aquino, with her work, affirms the hopes of a promising future for the emerging U.S. Hispanic theologies.

Shared Characteristics

Born Out of Conquest

U.S. Hispanic Theology was born out of conquest experiences, the sixteenth-century Spanish invasion and the nineteenth-century Nordic assaults. As foundational events, the conquests account for the violent forging of a new biological person with the mixture of Iberian and Amerindian bloods and a coerced marriage of two strongly religious traditions, medieval European Catholicism and ancient Amerindian religion. Their convergence at Tepeyac distinctively marks the genesis of the *mestizaje*. As a consequence of the double conquests, the *mestizo* peoples were subjugated to live as foreigners in their own land. In U.S. Hispanic Theology, oppression, as a theological datum, is first characterized as the experience of not being valued and accepted for who people are.

Popular Religiosity

Popular religiosity is a major characteristic in U.S. Hispanic Theology in which theologians ask the question: What is the relationship between our self-determination as a *mestizo* people and God's saving plan? The answer affirms popular religiosity as the *locus theologicus* of U.S. Hispanic Theology, because Hispanic people's identity is tied to their symbols of faith and struggles for liberation. This also explains why the historico-cultural dimension is dominant in the works of U.S. Hispanic theologians, unlike liberation theologians who stress the political dimension.

Because of the rich variety of cultures that form the Hispanic-American context, self-descriptive terms such as "Hispanic" or "Latino" are problematic. Nonetheless, popular religiosity emerges as a common element embedded in these cultures. Dominant North Atlantic theology has generally regarded popular religion as a primitive form of religious expression needing to be evangelized. U.S. Hispanic Theology, on the other hand, recognizes popular religiosity as a Hispanic intuitive, contemplative tradition; a credible medium of Hispanic people's experience of the *mysterium tremendum;* and a positive reservoir of values for self-determination. They see that popular religiosity also plays a significant role in the lives of Hispanics as a reservoir of liberative values, an empowerment of victims, a guardian of Hispanic culture, a vehicle of evangelization, and also as a corrective to certain dominant values in postmodern North America. Undoubtedly, the debate on popular religion will continue for decades to come. However, U.S. Hispanic theologians affirm its validity as a new dimension in theology.

Pastoral de Conjunto

U.S. Hispanic theologies are the result of a process called *pastoral de conjunto*. This process implies a method that stresses direct involvement and analysis of reality as necessary first steps to the author's option to theologize from within the Hispanic social and pastoral context. *Pastoral de conjunto* assures that Hispanic theologizing is grounded in human experience, especially the experience of oppression. U.S. Hispanic Theology attempts to give a voice to the voiceless. As members of the community, in the *pastoral de conjunto* process theologians also see themselves as *mestizos,* articulating their own theology. This process calls for a new kind of theologian with a new type of consciousness and commitment, so that theology will not emanate from ivory-tower abstract positions, but from engagement with other Hispanos articulating their struggles and hopes for liberation. Immersed in the Hispanic reality of oppression, these theologians understand how their cultural bias influences their theological presuppositions. They admit the non-neutrality of their theology since their common project, their *teología de conjunto,* is the liberation of Hispanics as part of God's salvific plan for a new humanity.

Guadalupe

The symbol of Mary, especially *Nuestra Señora de Guadalupe,* plays a fundamental role in U.S. Hispanic Theology as a cryptogram that retrieves liberative values and culturally affirms Hispanics. Instead of the Exodus biblical account, the occurrences at Tepeyac are the foundational paradigmatic events for U.S. Hispanic Theology. Since suffering and conquest continue to color Hispanic history, Guadalupe emerges as the symbol and the justification for a rereading and remaking of that history, because she is a member of the conquered race and a mother who mediates the promise of new life. This multivalent Marian symbol both affirms Hispanic cultural identity and provokes the Latino's evangelical mission of liberative praxis. The image of Guadalupe announces a season of advent of God's saving activity in history, as seen in the contributions of the victims who struggle to fashion a new humanity.

Social Analysis

U.S. Hispanic theologians use social analysis as a tool to inform their theology. This helps assure that their reflections remain relevant to the concrete Hispanic reality. Social analysis is instrumental in unraveling the dynamics of oppression, assimilation, racism, sexism, exploitation, and violence in order to explore an appropriate theological interpretation. For example, grace is described in relationship to becoming fully human, and sin is depicted as being both a social and a personal evil. Analysis of the historical Hispanic reality from the conquest to the present is crucial to identify the obstacles operative in all efforts for liberation.

Subversive Theology

U.S. Hispanic Theology is subversive theology. For centuries, the history of Hispanic cultures has been written by a Euro-American hand. In recent history, Hispanics have begun to write their own history in collaboration with their own theologians. This retelling and rewriting of the Hispanic story has led to a new collective identity. Since the *mestizo* story is one of suffering and conquest, it has also enkindled a subversive spirit. On the one hand, this rebellious spirit makes demands of Hispanics to become conscious of the reasons for their oppression, and, on the other hand, it inspires them to enunciate their hopes for liberation.

As subversive theology, U.S. Hispanic Theology challenges the absolutizing of any culture as normative, providing further evidence that no one culture can exhaustively embody the gospel or Christian way of life. As subversive theology, it offers a critique from the *mestizaje* context so that theology does not develop into a tool of oppression by justifying the status quo. U.S. Hispanic Theology takes a countercultural prophetic stance. As long as there are unjust barriers of pervasive discrimination and oppression, God's plan is incomplete. Furthermore, as subversive theology, it challenges pastoral agents to investigate their theological presuppositions as a way to critique any efforts in ministry to perpetuate cultural assimilation, paternalism, and underlying attitudes of superiority often masquerading as evangelization.

Survival

Survival is a constant motif in U.S. Hispanic Theology. *La vida es la lucha* (life is the struggle) (Isasi-Díaz) is a dictum of U.S. Hispanic Theology. It is from the efforts to survive these struggles that Hispanics find hope in the historical fulfillment of God's intentions. With this hope, Hispanics are becoming protagonists of their own history. They are calling for their own self-determination as their right, not as charity or as a goodwill gesture (Goizueta). These theologians denounce as false and non-Christian the life-styles and gods who justify the continued conquest. Christianity can no longer serve the god of the conquistadores or the ideologies and policies of Manifest Destiny that insist on keeping people from being free, fed, and housed in the land of plenty. In their struggles,

Hispanics proclaim that the glory of the true God is best recognized in all that favors the conquered toward fuller life and acceptance.

Since Hispanics are still at the bottom of the economic and political ladder, the issues of survival put into question and judge as false all theologies and spiritualities that consider themselves apolitical. Such theologies epitomize an evasive spiritualism that, in effect, sides with the oppressors to justify their tyrannical positions, which, ultimately, are nothing less than historical obstacles to the reign of God. Hispanics' struggles to survive as children of God make those entrenched in neutrality uncomfortable while others continue to suffer.

Border Theology

U.S. Hispanic Theology is border theology articulated from the unique historical and religious character of the *mestizaje,* that of being a bridge people between North and South America. This role has as its task the elimination of all cultural, political, sexual, and economic boundaries to pave the way for the fashioning of a new historical project that subsists in the unfolding of God's reign. As border theology, U.S. Hispanic Theology brings to the forefront the biblical question, "Who is my neighbor?" (Luke 10:25). As *mestizos,* we can turn to all the peoples in the Americas and reply that our neighbor is literally next door. The *mestizo* partial mixture of races is a foretaste of a possible new universal humanity without boundaries. As a border people, Hispanics understand the Latin and North American traditions as insiders *and* as outsiders. They live within the constant tension of the Hispanic holistic worldview and the Anglo ontological individualism. From this gifted perspective, U.S. Hispanic Theology can challenge stereo-types throughout the Americas. The *mestizo* presence in both North and Latin America is a call for solidarity at the historical juncture where God is raising up a new historical moment. For many, the unique *mestizo* border reality is a *kairos,* a moment of grace and opportunity experienced in the decisive action to act as bridge people between the Americas.

Mujerista Theology

U.S. Hispanic Theology is informed by *mujerista* theology, although not all theology done by Hispanic women claims to be *mujerista.* Unlike the Afro-American and Latin American theologies of liberation, among the first proponents of U.S. Hispanic Theology are included Hispanic women's prophetic voices. This undoubtedly colors and broadens the sources of reflection used in the emerging U.S. Hispanic Theology. *Mujerista* theology emphasizes the importance of self-determination in the act of self-identification from the perspective of the oppressed *mujer Hispana.* These Hispanic women's voices present a constant challenge to U.S. His-

panic Theology to respond to matters of women's survival issues as a way
to remain faithful to the Word of God. Because *mujerista* theology of
liberation relates the various levels of transformation which include psychological, physical, political, and spiritual in Hispanic women's daily
experience, it challenges women to move from a situation of inferiority
as an oppressed community to communities that influence the horizons
of liberation in the self-realization of all persons. Additionally, *mujerista*
theology with its strong communal thrust further reinforces U.S. Hispanic
Theology's methodology of *pastoral de conjunto.*

Passionate Theology

U.S. Hispanic Theology is passionate theology. These theologians are
recovering an intuitive, contemplative dimension in the Hispanic way of
talking about God. They understand praxis as having an inherently aesthetic
or affective dimension. It is, above all, in popular religiosity that the unity
of theory-praxis-affect is revealed as foundational in Hispanic culture and,
thus, Hispanic theology (Goizueta). As passionate theology, it retrieves
genuine values from the Hispanic Christian tradition that have been ignored
in the West's appropriation of Christianity.

Church as Instrument of Liberation for Hispanics

Despite the church's dismal record in dealing with U.S. Hispanics, these
theologians consider the church as having a crucial role in Hispanics'
struggles for liberation. Since *mestizaje* was founded and nurtured in
historico-cultural and ecclesial contexts, there is an intrinsic link between
faith and culture for Hispanics. Viewed from the perspective of the Hispanic
poor, this link reveals the history of the church as a history of suffering
and continued conquest. Dominant North Atlantic theology has not
expressed the faith of this suffering majority of Christians who form the
greater part of the Americas.

U.S. Hispanic Theology seeks to reform the church's pastoral practices
by making the suffering poor the primary subjects of its liberating mission.
Hispanic theologians do not ask the church to join the struggle against an
evil pagan world, but rather against oppressors (sometimes Christians),
and even against the church itself when it neglects Hispanics and blesses
those pastoral agents who instead of evangelization promote assimilation.

What is militant about U.S. Hispanic Theology is not its criticisms about
the church, but its insistence on fidelity to church tradition from the
perspectives of *mestizo* struggles for self-determination and cultural affirmation. For Hispanics, the church's efforts at inculturation and liberation
become two names for a similar process. These theologians see their task
not as one of updating the truth of faith, but of articulating the present
mestizo reality so that they can stand in a critical, yet creative, relationship

to that church tradition. U.S. Hispanic Theology asks the church to be engaged in the survival struggles for a more humane and just world by reading (rereading) the gospel from the perspective of the immigrant, the *mujeristas,* the refugee, the migrant, the border, and from the Hispanic's popular religious traditions. A result of this process will be a change in the church's pastoral attitude from seeing Hispanics as a problem to be solved to one that will insure that the gospel is made incarnate and liberative within the distinctive shapes of all cultures.

Fiesta as Eschatological Hope

In U.S. Hispanic Theology *fiesta* is more than simply a party. It is a celebration of eschatological hope. It proclaims who we are as *mestizos* and offers the possibility of a new universalism already beginning in a people who through rejection and struggles continue to proclaim *que la vida es lucha, pero con victoria* (that life is a struggle, but with victory). *Fiesta* prophetically announces in festive form the table being readied for the day all peoples can be as one.

Assessments

Finally, I will close with some general assessments on this initial stage of development of U.S. Hispanic Theology from the material presented above. U.S. Hispanic Theology is in its embryonic stages and it is too early to tell where it will go. However, this first generation of U.S. Hispanic theologians already offers serious challenges and creative approaches. I offer the following comments in support of an ongoing critical discussion and thematization of U.S. Hispanic Theology.

Pastoral de Conjunto: Voiceless as Subjects, Not Objects of Theology

In its attempts to do theology from within human praxis, U.S. Hispanic Theology is caught in a precarious situation. On the one hand, it has to resist the temptation of facile synthesis and abstract theorizing; on the other hand, it has to avoid falling into uncritical pastoral praxis. There is a further problem, I see, in the types of instruments that are used in the various approaches of a *pastoral de conjunto.* The better instruments are those that help people go beyond simply reporting from interviews or planning sessions. Listening to the voices of the poor requires an approach that will enter their reality with sensitivity so as to savor a new expression at times difficult to summarize in a report.

U.S. Hispanic theologians must continue to develop a rigorous and critical reflection level in their theologies, yet not lose sight of the fact that the Hispanic poor are the primary subjects of their theology and also their main audience. If this perspective is lost, then *pastoral de conjunto* will turn the voices of the poor into objects of their theologies and risk losing its liberative intent.

Cultural Linguistic Dimension of Oppression

The importance of the linguistic element, specifically the Spanish language, in the historico-cultural character of U.S. Hispanic Theology needs to be given more significant attention. There are several reasons for this importance.

Spanish is the dominant language of Hispanics. Furthermore, the facts show that the United States is now the fifth largest Spanish-speaking nation in the world, and the majority of those who speak Spanish are Roman Catholic. Viewed from the perspective of the Western Hemisphere, Spanish is the language spoken by the majority of the victims of oppression that constitute the history of suffering Christianity in the Americas. Spanish affirms the Hispanic reality and is the door into a particular worldview. For the pastoral agent, Spanish is most important because it is intrinsically linked to the religio-psyche of the people.

The implications for the use of Spanish in theology and pastoral ministry are enormous. If U.S. Hispanic Theology is going to retrieve the storehouse of liberative values inherent in popular religiosity, a core characteristic of its theology, the Spanish language, is an essential element of this exercise. *Mañanitas* to Guadalupe on the twelfth of December are just not the same if they are sung in another language. Translations limp in their attempts to convey *el sentido Hispano*—the Hispanic sense of life.

This is not to deny the importance of English for Hispanic-Americans. For Hispanics as a bridge people, English will always be important. However, English must be at the service of bridge building between peoples and not be imposed on Hispanics as a tool of assimilation.

Ecclesiocentrism

U.S. Hispanic Theology is ecclesiocentric. To some extent this is understandable since the Hispanic perspective is necessarily grounded on a historically strong Catholic tradition. Justo González's work is a notable exception. However, a consistent *mestizaje* dimension in this emerging theology calls for continued multidimensional, cross-cultural consciousness inclusive of the various religious denominations. In its critical reflection, this theology must include a more ecumenical and global dimension. U.S. Hispanic Theology is another indication that the coming of the world church is certain and that the globalization of Christianity is an inevitable reality. Critical dialogue with other theological perspectives, liberation movements, and religions will serve to help U.S. Hispanic Theology assess its faithfulness to its own church tradition.

Theology of Ministry from the Underside of History

Since Vatican II, the role of the laity has been greatly emphasized in the church. Certain theologies of the laity are evolving that need further evaluation from the perspective of the Hispanic experience of ministry. Pastoral plans for the development of ministry many times began with the assumption that there is a lack of ministers in the Hispanic church. Pastoral agents assume that little if any ministry is happening in their communities simply because these ministries are not listed on the parish roster. Viewed from the Hispanic reality, this is a false and demeaning assumption.

The Hispanic church developed in spite of the scarcity of priests. In many cases where there were priests, they were foreign-born and resisted inculturation into the U.S. Hispanic context. Thus, from the early beginnings of the Hispanic church, a certain structure of ministry has evolved, usually at the margins of the institutional church. Hispanics developed a variety of ministries for people that include catechists, sacristans who acted as parish administrators, *rezadores* who led the special prayers at funerals or other moments of family crisis, spiritual directors, *mayordomos* who performed the duties of a ministry council and took responsibility for the parish finances, and marriage preparation catechists, to mention a few. More investigation needs to be done on this solid ministerial heritage. Otherwise, in the name of a modern theology of ministry or in the name of Westernization and Romanization, the resultant theology of ministry would become yet another attempt to eradicate and invalidate a rich and long-standing ministerial tradition from the underside of history and still on the fringes of the institutional church.

Retrieving the Contemplative, Mystical Dimension and Liturgy

Generally speaking, popular religiosity in North Atlantic theologies has been relegated to a secondary position. U.S. Hispanic Theology has made an excellent beginning in an attempt to retrieve the intuitive, and in this sense contemplative and even mystical, dimension of the Hispanic religious experience. For Hispanics, popular religiosity is a valid liturgical expression and avenue of communication with God. This is why U.S. Hispanic theologians need to dig deeper still and specifically relate their findings to the church's liturgical tradition. This will enhance the church's liturgy with renewed vibrancy and will critique false cultural adaptations (e.g., decorating the altar with *serapes*) presently going on in many parishes with a Hispanic population.

Political Strategy: Identifying False Alliances

U.S. Hispanic theologians stress the historico-cultural dimension of Hispanic reality as a core tenet of their theology. This does not mean that they deny or neglect the importance of the political dimension. In fact, it is evident that they strongly assume it. On the other hand, theologies of liberation which stress the political dimension usually simply assume the historical-cultural dimension. All of these theologies espouse integral liberation from oppression in all its dimensions. In my estimation, these theologies need to continue to investigate the dynamics of oppression at work within both the political and the historical-cultural dimensions in view of the liberation process. In this regard, U.S. Hispanic Theology needs to stress more the socio-political element. It needs to focus more on a social and political analysis to pinpoint the dynamics of oppression in the Hispanic reality. The anti-reign is well organized around a political strategy. Transforming the structures of oppression is fundamentally a matter of politics. The question of the relationship of these dimensions as theological data and the use of serious social analysis will continue to play major roles in this developing theology.

U.S. Hispanic Theology asks: Whose God are we worshiping? A credible answer can be given in the process of identifying the destructive forces that continue to bring oppression to peoples. Many times this oppression is carried out by well-intentioned persons steeped in false ideologies. These theologians need to continue to speak out loudly and to name the culprits: colonialism, assimilationist tendencies, racism, liberal capitalism, political corruption, machismo, and sexism, to mention a few. Their commitment to the liberation of Hispanic peoples will provide them with the proper position from which to be able to critically unmask false alliances, oppressive lifestyles, and erroneous theological presuppositions.

Conclusion

Even though U.S. Hispanic Theology is in its nascent stages, these theologians write with maturity and depth. Their shared themes are accentuated by a sense of urgency because of the lived experience of suffering and oppression of Hispanics. This theology is linked to the struggling existence of the Hispanic peoples. For this reason, U.S. Hispanic theologians are emerging as an important voice alongside those struggling to remain faithful to the gospel from within the Hispanic reality. With the advent of the 500th anniversary of the first preaching of the good news in the Americas, U.S. Hispanic Theology will be able to contribute decisively to the fashioning of a new *mestizaje*—a genuine reign of God.

Notes

1. Elizondo develops this *mestizaje* in greater detail in his work *La Morenita: Evangelizer of the Americas* (1980).

2. Justo González authored the three-volume *History of Christian Thought* (1970) and *Christian Thought Revisited* (1989).

3. In this brief exposé, I am also drawing from Espín's works: "Grace and Humanness: A Hispanic Perspective," to appear in R. S. Goizueta, ed. *We Are a People: Initiatives in Hispanic American Theology*, 1992; and from "Tradition and Popular Religion: An Understanding of *sensus fidelium*," to appear in A. F. Deck, ed. *Frontiers of U.S. Hispanic Theology*, 1992.

References Cited

Aquino, María del Pilar
    1980 "Presencia de la mujer en la tradición profética." *Servir* 5(20):535–558.
    1988 "Women's Participation in the Church: A Catholic Perspective." In *With Passion and Compassion: Third World Women Doing Theology*. V. Fabella and M. A. Oduyoye, eds. Pp. 159–164. Maryknoll, NY: Orbis Books.
    1990 "Teologia latinoamericana de la liberación desde la perspectiva de la mujer." Ph.D. dissertation, Pontifical University of Salamanca, Spain.
Cone, James
    1970[1969] *Black Theology of Liberation*. Philadelphia, PA: J. B. Lippincott Company.
Deck, Allan Figueroa
    1978 "A Christian Perspective on the Reality of Illegal Immigration." *Social Thought* Fall: 39–53.
    1989 *The Second Wave: Hispanic Ministry and the Evangelization of Cultures*. Mahwah, NJ: Paulist Press.
Elizondo, Virgilio
    1968 "Educación religiosa para el Mexico-Norteamericano." *Catequesis Latino-americana*.
    1975 *Christianity and Culture*. Huntington, IN: Our Sunday Visitor.
    1978 *Morenita: The Dialectic of Birth and Gospel*, San Antonio, TX: MACC.
    1980 *La Morenita: Evangelizer of the Americas*. San Antonio, TX: MACC.
    1983 *The Galilean Journey: The Mexican American Promise*. Maryknoll, NY: Orbis Books.
    1988 *The Future Is Mestizo: Life Where Cultures Meet*. New York: Meyer-Stone.
    1989 "*Mestizaje* as *Locus* of Theological Reflection." In *The Future of Liberation Theology*. Marc Ellis and Otto Maduro, eds. Pp. 358–374. Maryknoll, NY: Orbis Books.
Espín, Orlando
    1984 "Religiosidad popular: Un aporte para su definición y hermenéutica." *Estudios Sociales* 18(44):41–56.d 1988 "Sources of Hispanic Theology." *Proceedings of the Forty-Third Annual Convention, CTSA* 43:122–125.
    1989 "Lilies of the Field: A Hispanic Theology of Providence and Human Responsibility." *Proceedings of the Forty-Fourth Annual Convention, CTSA* 44:70–90.
    1992a "Grace and Humanness: A Hispanic Perspective." In *We Are a People: Initiatives in Hispanic American Theology*. R. S. Goizueta, ed.
    1992b "Tradition and Popular Religion: An Understanding of *sensus fidelium*." In *Frontiers of U.S. Hispanic Theology*. Allen F. Deck, ed. Maryknoll, NY: Orbis Books, 1992.

Espín, Orlando, and Sixto J. Garcia
    1987 "Hispanic-American Theology." *Proceedings of the Forty-Second Annual Convention, CTSA* 42:114–119.
Goizueta, Roberto
    1992a "The Challenge of Pluralism: Particularity and Universality in the Church of the Third Millennium." In *Frontiers of a United States Hispanic Theology.* Allan F. Deck, ed. Maryknoll, NY: Orbis Books, 1992.
    1992b "The Church and Hispanics in the United States: From Empowerment to Solidarity." In *"That They Might Live": Power, Empowerment and Leadership in the Church.* Michael Downey, ed.
    1992c "The History of Suffering as *Locus Theologicus:* Implications for U.S. Hispanic Theology." In *Voices from the Third World: Journal of the Ecumenical Association of Third World Theologians.*
González, Justo L.
    1970–1979 *History of Christian Thought.* 3 vols. Nashville, TN: Abingdon.
    1989 *Christian Thought Revisited: Three Types of Theology.* Nashville, TN: Abingdon.
    1990 *Mañana: Christian Theology from a Hispanic Perspective.* Nashville, TN: Abingdon.
Gutiérrez, Gustavo
    1968 *Hacia un teología de la liberación lineas pastorales de la iglesia en América Latina.* Lima, Peru: CEP.
Isasi-Díaz, Ada María
    1986 "*Apuntes* for a Hispanic Women's Theology of Liberation." *Apuntes* Fall: 61–71.
    1989 "Mujeristas: A Name of Our Own." In *The Future of Liberation Theology.* Marc Ellis and Otto Maduro, eds. Pp. 410–419. Maryknoll, NY: Orbis Books.
Isasi-Díaz, Ada María, and Yolanda Tarango
    1988 *Hispanic Women: Prophetic Voice in the Church.* San Francisco, CA: Harper and Row.

5

Roberto S. Goizueta

Roberto Goizueta was born in La Habana, Cuba. He obtained his masters in theology (MA) from Marquette University in 1982 and his doctorate in religious studies (PhD) in 1984. He began teaching as instructor and assistant professor at Loyola University, New Orleans, Louisiana (1983–1986), was program director, adjunct professor and co-director at the Aquinas Center of Theology at Emory University in Atlanta, Georgia (1986–1992). Currently he is associate professor at Loyola University of Chicago.

Recognized nationally as a leading Latino theologian, Goizueta's published works and lectures deal with the key issues of theological methodology, the liberative context for doing theology from within the Latino perspective, the aesthetic dimension in theology and salient theological challenges to North Atlantic theologies. In the area of U.S. Latino theology, he has edited an important volume, *We Are a People! Initiatives in Hispanic-American Theology* (1992), published nine articles, and has lectured extensively around the country. His forthcoming book is entitled: *Caminemos con Jesús: Liberation and Aesthetics: Toward a Hispanic/Latino Theology of Accompaniment.*

As a founding member of the Academy of Catholic Hispanic Theologians, Goizueta has also served as a board member and as its president (1990–91). He is also a member of *La Comunidad* of Hispanic American Scholars of Theology and Religion, the American Academy of Religion and the Ecumenical Association of Third World Theologians. Presently he is also associate editor of the *Journal of Hispanic/Latino Theology.*

Goizueta is married and has two children.

Department of Theology
Loyola University of Chicago
6525 N. Sheridan Rd.
Chicago, Illinois 60626
312-508-2366

Rediscovering Praxis

The Significance of U.S. Hispanic Experience for
Theological Method

Roberto S. Goizueta

As U.S. Hispanic theologians attempt to develop a theological reflection born out of the historical experience of our communities, we are confronted with the question, What are we doing when we ground our reflection in that experience? Implicit in the question of theological context, or sources, is the question of theological method: What is the relationship between the *locus theologicus* (the context of theological reflection) and the theological enterprise itself? Insofar as U.S. Hispanic theologians seek to articulate a *teología de conjunto,* the question of methodology is fundamental and, thus, must be addressed explicitly if we are to be faithful to our explicit intent. At its core, the methodological question is that of the relationship between praxis and theory. This question has been particularly central to the development of liberation theologies insofar as these have sought to affirm the foundational significance of praxis over against modern Western conceptualism and rationalism.[1]

Informed by the insights of Latin American liberation theologians, U.S. Hispanic theologians likewise affirm the foundational import of praxis. At the same time, however, we recognize that any uncritical assimilation of Latin American liberation theology would represent a betrayal of the very methodology that we affirm; the uncritical assimilation of any theological model would represent a failure to ground our reflection in the experience of our own communities, the communities of Hispanics living in the United States. As U.S. Hispanic *theologians,* we seek to learn from other theologians; as *U.S. Hispanic* theologians, we seek to redefine the theological task by locating it within the praxis of U.S. Hispanic communities—thereby redefining praxis itself as the foundation of theology.

It is equally clear that an uncritical repudiation of modern Western theological movements would, likewise, represent an infidelity to the praxis of our communities inasmuch as, for better or worse, these communities participate in modern Western history—even if principally as the bearers of its dehumanizing consequences. Any uncritical rejection of Western theology would imply a concomitant rejection of our historical praxis as *U.S.* Hispanics. The task confronting us, therefore, is one of neither assimilation nor repudiation; it is, rather, a task of critical appropriation. Such a task requires that we approach and critique traditional theological sources and methods, whether European or Latin American, from the perspective of U.S. Hispanics in order to be able to articulate the significance of that perspective for the life of our communities, the church, and society.

To suggest possible ways in which the U.S. Hispanic experience might contribute to an understanding of praxis and, hence, theological method, we will (1) examine critically, if briefly, the modern Western notion of praxis; (2) trace the emergence of that notion by examining the interpretations of praxis that have exerted the greatest influence on Western thought; (3) examine the notion and role of praxis as reinterpreted within Latin American liberation theology; (4) suggest how U.S. Hispanic theologians might learn from (1), (2), and (3) while at the same time moving beyond these, thereby contributing to the theological task of the church and the academy; and, finally, (5) explore how the U.S. Hispanic experience might contribute to an understanding of the relationship between praxis and theory.

The History of Praxis

Aristotle, Marx, and Liberation Theology

That the notion of praxis has a long history is a fact that has all too often been ignored in the midst of contemporary debate about the primacy of praxis in the theological enterprise and, indeed, in the everyday life of the Christian. If U.S. Hispanic theologians are to make a significant contribution to this debate about the nature of not only Christian theology, but also Christian faith (for example, orthodoxy vis-à-vis orthopraxis), a critical retrieval of that history will facilitate such a contribution by revealing the lacunae and distortions in the contemporary debate and suggesting ways in which we might help address these. With its own roots in communities still influenced by premodern cultures, our theological reflection may then be able to effect a critical retrieval of premodern Western notions of praxis, which have been distorted by modern Cartesian epistemologies. At the same time, as rooted in premodern cultures marginalized by Western imperialism, the historical praxis of our communities would provide a critique of premodern Western notions of praxis that do not attend to the demands of social transformation.

By virtue of its manifold meanings and etymological history, the term *praxis* is much more multivalent than is indicated by its usage in many contemporary contexts, where the word is often employed as a synonym for "practice." Indeed, as Hans-Georg Gadamer, Jürgen Habermas, Richard Bernstein, Matthew Lamb, and others have observed, the modern notion of practice is itself reductionist, and hence distorted.[2] Gadamer, for example, writes that "the concept of '*praxis*' which has developed in the last two centuries is an awful deformation of what practice really is. In all the debates of the last century practice was understood as application of science to technical tasks. . . . It degrades practical reason to technical control."[3] Lamb contends that, in the context of the natural sciences' epistemological hegemony, "modern notions of praxis all tend either to connote or explicitly invoke *movement*. . . . In such a context the call to praxis could mean no more than a call to practicality . . . for if all human activity is basically just another species of movement, then being practical means learning the skills and techniques of control."[4] Among the key historical factors influencing this process of distortion has been the intellectual hegemony exercised by Cartesian and scientific epistemological paradigms. If praxis is but the action of a Cartesian ego upon an external object (for example, another human "individual"), an action that implies movement, praxis is reduced to mere technique; that is, praxis is defined as the subject's control and manipulation of the external object in order to achieve some predetermined end.[5]

Yet the reduction of praxis to practice remains incomplete, and thus ambiguous, insofar as the effects of praxis are understood to be not only external, with respect to the object being controlled or manipulated, but also internal, with respect to the subject. That is, the subject's praxis in the world is seen as contributing to the empowerment and liberation of the subject. The modern notion of praxis suffers from this ambiguity between the external, or technical, and internal, or humanistic, ends of human praxis.[6]

The unintended, destructive consequences of so many modern ideologies derive precisely from a failure to attend adequately to this ambiguity. Lured by the humanistic claims of praxis as an instrument for empowerment and liberation, Marxists and others have not been sufficiently attentive to the ambiguities present in this instrumentalization of praxis—however noble the ends that are sought. Whatever our ends, the instruments we employ (in this case, human praxis and, hence, human beings) always remain ambiguous because all instruments, insofar as they utilize the external environment in order to achieve those ends, necessarily involve manipulation and control—that is, coercion. To ignore this ambiguity is to undermine precisely those ends that we seek.

The identification of praxis with practice, and practice with technique, reveals a contradiction internal to modern praxis-based theories of change, for these predicate the achievement of human freedom on the application of techniques and strategies to the social world, which, of course, includes human beings. The human person becomes an object to be utilized, through praxis, to achieve a higher end, even if that end is the supposed transformation or liberation of the person himself or herself. Moreover, even when the person is perceived as his or her own agent of liberation, praxis becomes the means whereby the concrete, historical person in the present recreates himself or herself (that is, "works upon" himself or herself as if upon an object), thereby achieving self-esteem, self-worth, and liberation. Concrete persons then derive their value from their ability to turn themselves into instruments of their own liberation, or to make the present (historical praxis) an instrument for creating the future; this implies a process of self-objectification. While the process of human growth and development is always important, one must not lose sight of the tendency therein to devalue present, concrete life, however ugly, by perceiving it as simply the raw material to be used in the creation of the future "new person." To the extent that the present is thus instrumentalized, concrete, historical praxis is subordinated to a conceptual reality, whether "the Future" or "the New Person." Human life, or praxis, is sacrificed to the concept.

Consequently, the modern tendency to identify praxis with technique has led to an identification of knowledge itself—*all* knowledge—with the conceptual, empiricist, and technological; in other words, the reduction of knowledge to what can be observed, measured, quantified, and thus brought under our control. Any aspect of life that is not thus observable, measurable, or quantifiable is deemed impractical and thus irrelevant and meaningless. Value is identified with practicality, and practicality is, in turn, defined in terms of quantifiable criteria.[7]

The danger of falling prey to such reductionism can only be averted if the external, objectivizing, and transformative ends of praxis are grounded in concrete human praxis *as an end in itself.* To correct the modern distortions, numerous scholars have essayed a critical retrieval of the premodern, Aristotelian notion of praxis.[8] Aristotle uses the term *praxis* to denote all human activity whose end is internal rather than external to itself. He thus distinguishes praxis, activity that is an end in itself, from *poiesis,* activity that seeks some end external to the performance itself, and distinguishes both of these from *theoria.* The paradigmatic examples of praxis are political activity and moral conduct. The difference between praxis and poiesis may be rendered as that between doing and making, where the former is its own reward while the latter seeks its reward in the results of the performance; the end of praxis is the praxis itself, whereas the end of poiesis is the result left over after one has completed the task.[9] Given this distinction, the fundamental form of praxis is nothing other than life, or living, itself; in the *Politics*, Aristotle avers that "life is action [praxis] and not production [poiesis]."[10]

The distinction becomes blurred, however, in the (much later) Marxian notion of praxis. If Aristotle identifies human life with praxis, inasmuch as life is always an end in itself, Marx identifies human life with productive labor, for it is through labor that we actualize, or "produce," ourselves as persons: "Conscious life-activity directly distinguishes man from animal life-activity. . . . In creating an objective world by his practical activity, in working-up inorganic nature, man proves himself a conscious species being."[11] What defines human praxis, or "conscious life-activity," is its productive capacity; the person becomes a person (praxis) by his or her ability to "create an objective world" (poiesis).[12] Praxis is thus reduced to poiesis. Indeed, Marx's fundamental criticism of capitalism is precisely that, in capitalism, productive labor is seen as merely a means to an end (survival), whereas, for Marx, human productive labor (poiesis) is "life-activity" itself (praxis)—that which defines the human as human. For Marx, praxis is predicated on, and thus subordinated to, poiesis. This anthropology underlies Marx's historical materialism: the mode of production is the engine of history.[13]

Alienation results when productive labor, through which humankind produces itself, is no longer viewed as an end in itself, but as merely a means to an external end (which, of course, is exactly how Aristotle saw it). Our labor is what distinguishes us from animals; it is in our work that we should experience ourselves as most human. The problem with capitalism, argues Marx, is that it fails to account for the fact that human productive activity is not only a means to life but is, in fact, the very meaning of life itself—at least human life.[14]

This close identification of human activity with productive activity leads to a blurring of the distinction between praxis and poiesis. What Aristotle had conceived as but a means becomes, with Marx and, especially, so-called orthodox Marxism, an end in itself—indeed, the privileged characteristic that defines our existence as human. If part of the Marxian legacy is the important recognition of productive activity as constitutive of the human, an equally significant part of that legacy is the attenuation of the Aristotelian distinction between human activity and productive activity. The historical transition from the premodern, Aristotelian notion of praxis to the modern, Marxian notion of praxis is outlined by Clodovis Boff in his book *Theology and Praxis:*

> Aristotle sees a neat distinction between *praxis* and *poiesis*. Praxis is a form of activity characterized by its immanence: its development is its own end. . . . As for the second form of activity (*operatio-poiesis*) . . . we have a *transitive* activity: its finality is something other than itself. . . . In current usage, "praxis" means both types of activity discerned by Aristotle. . . . Primarily owing to the ideological

and historical pressure of Marxism, praxis is no longer understood as its own end, *Selbstzweck,* self-finalized activity—but on the contrary, as the production of an external result. Praxis is action resulting in an effect of transformation. . . . The semantic reverse of the term is total, then.[15]

What Marx—like all modernity—failed to appreciate is the ambiguity inherent in any notion of human praxis that defines it in terms of production, even if what is being produced is "the just person" or "the just society." Production necessarily involves manipulation and coercion, and these are, at best, ambiguous instruments of liberation. Recent centuries are strewn with the victims of nations and leaders who, inspired by a Rousseauian magnanimity, have insisted on forcing people to be free. Marx's antidote to the instrumentalization of human life that he identifies with modern capitalist society is thus . . . instrumentalization, albeit toward an ostensibly more noble end. If, in capitalism, the life of the worker becomes an object to be manipulated in the service of the commodity, in Marxism the life of the worker becomes an object to be manipulated—even if by the worker himself or herself—in the service of the future "New Person": "his own life is an object for him."[16] What neither ideology appreciates is that to make life an object to be worked upon is to instrumentalize life and thus, inevitably, to kill life.

Any notion of praxis that subordinates the concrete present to the hoped-for future undermines not only the present but that future as well. The fall of the Berlin Wall in the socialist East and the environmental crisis, urban crisis, drug epidemic, and moral breakdown in the capitalist West serve as reminders that the attempt to make the concrete present the instrument for achieving a hoped-for idyllic future will always be self-defeating.

Latin American liberation theology emerges from the underside of modernity to critique its dark side, the consequences of which the people of Latin America continue to bear. At the same time, liberation theology inherits some of the ambiguities latent in modern views of praxis, particularly insofar as liberation theologians are influenced by the Marxian notion of praxis. In the formative writings of the liberation theology movement, the notion of praxis is sometimes given several meanings, often overlapping ones. In its broadest sense, the term refers to historical praxis, which Gustavo Gutiérrez defines as simply a person's "active presence in history."[17] A second, more specific meaning is that of Christian praxis, the specifically Christian way of being actively present in history through commitment and prayer, action and contemplation.[18] In its third, most particular sense, the term specifies, with greater concreteness, just what Christian commitment and prayer entail, namely, liberating praxis: "The praxis on which liberation theology reflects is a praxis of solidarity in the interests of liberation and is inspired by the gospel. . . . Consequently, a praxis motivated by evangelical values embraces to some extent every effort to bring about authentic fellowship and authentic justice. . . . This liberating praxis endeavors to transform history in the light of the reign of God."[19]

The significance of this methodological emphasis on transformation as foundational for theology cannot be overestimated; it is perhaps the most important contribution of liberation theology. Yet the term liberating praxis itself contains an ambiguity: Is liberation a concomitant or a goal of praxis? If the former is true, then praxis is its own end: one becomes free in the very act or process of transforming history. If the latter is true, then the end of praxis is external to the praxis itself: one becomes free *after* one has transformed history. The first understanding of praxis tends toward a more Aristotelian view, whereas the latter tends toward a more Marxian view.[20] Both of these views can be found in the writings of liberation theologians and in the liberation theology movement itself: (the former in the emphasis on the self-empowerment of the poor as the subjects of social transformation, and the latter in the very call for social transformation). Yet the relationship between these two dimensions of praxis—praxis as *intrinsically* liberative and praxis as yielding a liberative *result*—needs to be addressed more systematically.[21]

Contributions of U.S. Hispanic Experience

As critical reflection on praxis, the theology being developed by U.S. Hispanics is informed by the methodology of Latin American liberation theology. At the same time, however, a genuine fidelity to this methodology will imply that the content of our theological reflection will differ from its Latin American counterpart; that is, because the historical praxis of U.S. Hispanic communities is different (even if similar in important ways), that praxis will yield a different understanding of the community's faith. More specifically, the concrete historicity of U.S. Hispanic communities will furnish new insights into the very meaning of historicity, or praxis, itself.

These new insights (or, perhaps more correctly, new emphases) which, while present in some liberation theology, have taken on a new centrality in the theological reflection of U.S. Hispanics, offer us a way of addressing the ambiguities and contradictions latent in the modern notions of praxis to which we, as theologians, are heirs. That U.S. Hispanic praxis offers us resources for addressing those ambiguities is evident, above all, in the centrality accorded popular religiosity as a principal expression of the historical praxis of our communities.[22] By emphasizing the popular religious character of historical praxis, U.S. Hispanic theologians are emphasizing the inherently communal and aesthetic character of praxis, without, on the other hand, depreciating its transformative character.

Virgilio Elizondo, Orlando Espín, Sixto García, and other U.S. Hispanic
theologians have observed that the popular religiosity of U.S. Hispanics
is, for us, a principal way of being in the world.[23] Even though not all
Latinos and Latinas are regularly involved in the performance of religious
devotions, or are even believers, all share a common *manera de ser,*
or way of being, which both presupposes and affirms relationality and
sacramentality as fundamental realities definitive of human praxis. This
way of being then finds ritual expression not only in popular religious
devotions but in everyday language as well. Espín and García refer, for
instance, to the popular religious character of wisdom phrases, such as *si
Dios quiere* ("if God wills it"), *Jesús, María y José!,* or *Dios sabe lo que
hace* ("God knows what God is doing").[24] These and other such exclama-
tory and aphoristic sayings are an inextricable part of U.S. Hispanic culture
in a way that similar sayings in Anglo American culture are not; indeed,
such ritualistic invocations of the deity would often be deemed unseemly,
if not blasphemous, by the dominant culture. In short, popular religiosity
is but the expression, in symbol and ritual, of the historical praxis of our
U.S. Hispanic communities.

What popular religiosity expresses, above all, is the communal and
aesthetic character of praxis. In its most basic sense, popular religiosity
is the affirmation of an essential social and cosmic solidarity as intrinsic
and foundational to human praxis; conversely, injustice, alienation, and
oppression are distortions of praxis. The fundamental goal of popular
religiosity is the practical, performative, and participatory affirmation of
community as the foundation of all human activity. That community
includes not only our contemporaries but also past and future generations;
it likewise includes God and the saints. The principal metaphor for this
community is the family.[25]

The community implicit in praxis is not, however, the modern Western
community, understood as a voluntary association of atomic individuals;
rather it is an organic reality in which the relationship between persons
is not only extrinsic but, at a more fundamental level, intrinsic as well.
In and through praxis, the intrinsic unity of person, community, and God
is affirmed. In the praxis of the modern Western subject, the subject has
ontological priority, for he or she chooses community; in the praxis of
U.S. Hispanics, community has ontological priority, for it gives birth to
subjectivity. Virgilio Elizondo describes the difference between these two
views of community:

> For our native forefathers, it was not the individuals who by coming
> together made up the community, but rather it was the community
> which had been developing since the Lord and Lady of creation
> allowed man and woman to descend unto earth through the many
> generations of their ancestors which actually brought the individual
> person into existence. . . . Thus it was the community which called

forth the individuality of the person. The unique way in which the
person embodied the ways and traditions of the group determined
his/her individuality. It was the community which made the individual
person: it accepted to make him/her at baptism, it called him/her
into existence through the educational process of the group and
sustained him/her in existence through the various closely-knit systems of inter-relationships not only with the various members of the
clan, but also with all of nature and even with the astral world.[26]

The modern Western subject forges a self-identity by distancing himself
or herself from community (for example, family) and tradition in order
to achieve autonomy and independence; the U.S. Hispanic, on the other
hand, derives his or her identity from that very community, which remains
an important part of self-identity even if the person should physically
leave the formative community.[27]

The essential goal of popular religious praxis is the affirmation and
perpetuation of these ontological bonds. Popular religiosity represents the
practical affirmation of the interpersonal bonds existing among persons,
Christ, Mary, and the saints, all of whom are treated not as "powerful,
sacred entities" but as "members of the family."[28] If popular religious
praxis is perceived through Western, Enlightenment lenses as a superstitious attempt at spiritual manipulation, for U.S. Hispanics it is, at bottom,
simply a practical or performative reaffirmation of the intrinsic value of
these relationships. Elizondo describes the organic cosmovision underlying
the Mexican symbol of Tonantzín, which eventually developed into the
Christian symbol of Guadalupe: the cosmic force represented by Tonantzín
"acted as a sort of collective soul which thereby brought about the intrinsic
unity of everything which is. . . . *Nothing is unrelated*. . . . We do not find
ourselves in the presence of 'large chains of rationalizations,' but in a
reciprocal and continuous implication of the diverse aspects of a single
totality."[29] Popular religiosity, then, "is the way in which masses of the
people express their communion with the ultimate, and through this communion find meaning and strength in their lives."[30] In other words, the
end of popular religiosity is this interpersonal relationship itself.

The possibility and, indeed, the obligation of social transformation arises
out of this internal end of praxis. Insofar as human praxis reveals the
ontological priority of community as intrinsic to historical praxis, it also
implies an ethical-political obligation to struggle against every obstacle
to such community.[31] The demand for social transformation is not extrinsic
to personal praxis; that is, such a demand does not presuppose an isolated
subject who is confronted by community and society with their ethical-
political demands. On the contrary, those demands are intrinsic to praxis
since they are already presupposed in the very constitution of the person,
who is always inherently and unavoidably social by nature. The intrinsic
communal character of praxis grounds and makes possible its extrinsic

ethical-political orientation.[32] To say that the marginalized (for example, U.S. Hispanics) have an epistemological privilege is to say that the experience of alienation, injustice, and oppression is the lens through which these are revealed as distortions of a fundamentally organic reality. The poor can continue to celebrate life in the midst of the struggle against death precisely because that struggle is what reveals the illusory nature of death's claims to ultimacy—in the same way as the passion and crucifixion of Jesus reveal the illusory nature of the principalities' and powers' claims to ultimacy.

From the perspective of the U.S. Hispanic experience praxis is revealed as not only inherently communal but also inherently celebratory, or aesthetic. The centrality of music, dance, and ritual in Hispanic life reveals the aesthetic sense underlying that life. Insofar as praxis is an affirmation of community, it is an affirmation of community as the highest form of beauty. Popular religiosity reveals praxis as communal, aesthetic performance.[33] Again, the fundamental end of praxis is not extrinsic but intrinsic, since that end is the practical, performative affirmation of the essential beauty of community in cosmos and history. Beauty is an end in itself; to instrumentalize beauty is to destroy it.

Like the ontological priority of community, however, the ontological priority of beauty has important and necessary ethical-political implications, which are revealed by the experience of suffering. The experience and memories of suffering preclude a sentimentalized aesthetics. Sociohistorical nonidentity mediates aesthetic nonidentity; the historical praxis of the oppressed mediates aesthetic praxis. Consequently, the memories of suffering expressed in U.S. Hispanic popular religiosity—the memories of a vanquished people—prevent us from romanticizing popular religious devotions, music, and ritual, as so often occurs when these are portrayed in the communications media of the dominant culture.

Popular religiosity is an anamnestic performance, or praxis, that, in reenacting the suffering of our people, simultaneously reminds us that that suffering is not the last word. It is no coincidence that the Crucified Jesus and the Virgin Mary are so central to U.S. Hispanic popular religiosity. By identifying with the anguish of the Crucified, we recall the anguish of our people, which, like the cross, is the seedbed of our liberation. By identifying with Mary, especially in her various patronal manifestations, we likewise recall her special concern for the downtrodden, reflected in the fact that those whom she chooses as her messengers are usually poor people of indigenous, mestizo, or mulatto background. When we look at Mary, we see the visage of our people. According to Elizondo, " 'La Virgen de Tepeyac' is the very core to understanding the struggle of the contemporary Mexican, born out of the violent intercourse of Spain and Mexico—of the Old World father and the New World mother. Each generation of Mexicans has been able to see mirrored in the *tilma* [cloak] the reflections of its sufferings, struggles, life, and ideals."[34] Describing the cultural and religious syncretism that gives rise to the Cuban symbol of *Nuestra Señora de la Caridad del Cobre* (Our Lady of Charity), José Juan Arrom writes that "in this synthesis of creeds and hopes beats the soul of the Cuban people."[35] Like Mary, we suffer at the foot of the cross and, like Mary, are emboldened by the news that "he is risen." Our anamnestic solidarity with Jesus and Mary is thus, at the same time, the source of the hope that compels us to struggle for justice.

Insofar as popular religiosity has a subversive character, then, such an orientation toward the subversion of social forces of oppression is derived from its character as communal and aesthetic praxis. By affirming community in the face of oppression, and the beauty of creation in the face of de-creation and destruction, popular religious praxis becomes, indirectly, a crucial source of empowerment and liberation. When popular religiosity is used as a tool of liberation, the praxis of our communities is instrumentalized—that is, *we* are instrumentalized and, indeed, encouraged to view ourselves as instruments of some grand historical design. Such a distortion can only lead to new forms of oppression as the vibrant life (praxis) of our people, expressed in our popular religiosity, is no longer enjoyed as an end in itself, which engenders self-esteem and hope; that life becomes, instead, an object to be manipulated in the service of a presumably higher end. Concrete life is sacrificed to a conceptual future.

The Rationality of U.S. Hispanic Praxis

To assert that the extrinsic ends of praxis must be grounded in its intrinsic ends is not to imply, however, that reflection is to be depreciated. Indeed, the fact that praxis is always *historical* praxis implies that reflection is itself intrinsic to praxis as surely as the mind is intrinsic to the person. As Ada María Isasi-Díaz and Yolanda Tarango point out, "praxis is not reflection that follows action or is 'at the service of action.' Both action and reflection become inseparable moments in praxis. . . . To bring reflection to bear upon action—that is praxis."[36]

One of the most pernicious legacies of Cartesian and Kantian epistemological paradigms has been the tendency to divorce praxis from theory. Theory is then perceived to be inherently impractical, and praxis is perceived to be inherently irrational. Within the modern paradigm, the only solution to such a dichotomy—the only way to make theory "practical" and praxis "rational"—is to reduce praxis to an instrument of theory. Among the consequences of this radical split has been the dichotomy between the natural sciences, characterized as empiricist, positivist, and instrumentalist, and the human sciences, characterized as humanistic. Moreover, this dichotomy internally divides the various disciplines themselves, so that, for instance, empiricist and functionalist schools in the social sciences are perennially at odds with schools of critical theory. In the former, only theory that is practical, measurable, and verifiable with scientific certainty will be considered genuine knowledge; all other theory—including the insights of poets, philosophers, and theologians—is dismissed as mere speculation. Likewise, only praxis that is practical, measurable, and scientifically verifiable is to be taken seriously; all other praxis, such as popular religiosity, is to be discounted as irrelevant.[37]

The internal logic of this modern dilemma must ultimately lead, however, to the rejection of *all* knowledge (to wit, postmodern deconstruction), since even technical knowledge is, after all, useless until it is actually put into practice; in itself, all knowledge is useless. The logical outcome of the modern dichotomy is thus a radical suspicion of all theory, whether in the natural sciences or the humanistic sciences, since all theory is seen as, by its very nature, removed from reality. The postmodern repudiation of reason is but the logical outcome of the modern worship of reason.[38]

As U.S. Hispanic theologians attempt to articulate the significance of praxis for our theological reflection, we find ourselves caught in the middle of this epistemological crisis. Committed to doing theology from within a self-conscious solidarity with the historical struggles of U.S. Hispanic communities, ours is a praxis-based theology. We reject conceptualist theologies that remain inattentive to their historicity. Yet given the contemporary intellectual climate, where the only alternatives appear to be either the enshrinement of conceptualist, instrumentalist reason (modernity) or the repudiation of all reason (poststructuralist postmodernism), we should not allow ourselves to accept these as the only viable alternatives.[39] As U.S. Hispanics confront the modern rationalist ideologies that have repressed and suppressed our historical praxis for so long, the temptation will be to identify with that praxis over against the rationalism that has for so long served the interests of the dominant society. The danger is that, in an intellectual and social ambience where rationalism is identified not with an ahistorical, conceptualist reason, but with reason itself, we will allow our rejection of rationalism to become a rejection of reason and the intellectual enterprise as such. Our commitment to praxis would then no longer ground our theological reflection, but would instead replace theological reflection. Nothing could undermine the cause of U.S. Hispanics more than an uncritical (even if unwitting) assimilation of the modern Western epistemological dilemma.

If U.S. Hispanic praxis reveals the inherently communal and aesthetic character of praxis, this insight does not diminish the significance of the intellectual enterprise. On the contrary, as we uncover the foundational import of community and beauty, we likewise expand the scope of reason to include these: the recovery of community and beauty as intrinsic to human praxis is a supremely rational endeavor.[40] To ground theory in praxis is to opt for reason, though, of course, not the ahistorical, conceptualist, and instrumentalist reason of modernity. It is this latter that is revealed as utterly irrational in the face of the human and ecological carnage that modern ideologies have left in their wake.

For U.S. Hispanics to overlook the inherent rationality or reasonableness of communal and aesthetic praxis, and the consequent ethical-political exigencies, would be to fall prey to the very epistemological dichotomy that continues to legitimate the oppression of our communities. In the context of that dichotomy, Hispanic culture has been portrayed as a culture of the body, of feelings, of sensuality, and hence of praxis, in contrast to the dominant Anglo American culture, which is assumed to be a culture of the mind, of reason, of science, and hence of theory. Caught in this modern dichotomy, Hispanic culture is simultaneously idealized and marginalized: the same sense of community and beauty for which our culture is rightly admired becomes the justification for its denigration and marginalization, since the commitment to community and beauty is perceived as irrational in a world dominated by individualist, rationalist, and scientific epistemological paradigms. The result is, at best, a patronizing condescension toward Latinos and Latinas. As Isasi-Díaz has pointed out, "this society deals with you [Hispanics] the way they do with a circus: they love our mariachis, salsa, *arroz con pollo, bacaladitos,* margaritas—we can really entertain them."[41]

Postmodern paradigms offer little more hope. Despite the understandable lure of postmodern retrievals of otherness, social situation, and aesthetics, postmodernism remains beholden to modern epistemological dualism insofar as, in postmodernism, the retrieval of otherness, social situation, and aesthetics is interpreted as a leap into irrationality. For example, if modernity derides popular religiosity as superstitious irrationality, postmodernity idealizes it as such. In both cases, we are denied our humanity by being reduced to what is but one part of our humanity, namely our affect, which is in turn pitted against intellect, as if affect and intellect were mutually contradictory. Within the context of either modernity or postmodernity, the possibility that a Latino or Latina might possess an intellect is unthinkable. For white male Anglos in the academic world, the option for irrationality may seem quite liberating; for Latinos and Latinas it can only perpetuate and reinforce the continued oppression of our people. Members of the dominant culture can afford to opt for irrationality only because their culture is already implicitly deemed to be rational. Hispanics who proclaim the death of reason, however, will be perceived as simply corroborating the dominant culture's view of Hispanic culture as, indeed, representing the death of reason insofar as that culture emphasizes (irrational) affect.[42]

By grounding our theology in the praxis of U.S. Hispanic communities, U.S. Hispanic theologians seek to articulate the profound rationality of that praxis, including its communal and aesthetic dimensions. Consequently, we affirm reason and the possibility of rational discourse, but we reject the modern/postmodern dichotomy between praxis and theory. We affirm social situatedness, but we reject the assertion that social situation implies the death of the subject. Modernity proclaims the emergence of the individual, rational subject in the face of a pejoratively irrational community and tradition (understood as intergenerational community); postmodernity proclaims the death of the individual, rational subject in the face of an admirably irrational intersubjectivity. Against both modernity and postmodernity, U.S. Hispanics proclaim that community, or solidarity, is the very basis and ontological precondition for the emergence of the individual, rational subject.

In important ways, the challenge that all U.S. Hispanics represent for modern/postmodern dualisms is even more acutely visible in the experience of U.S. Hispanic women. If Hispanics have traditionally suffered from being identified exclusively with affect, feelings, sensuality, and community, Hispanic women have suffered doubly from this distorting and dehumanizing identification, for they have been denied their intellect, and thus their full humanity, not only as Hispanics, but also as women. If U.S. Hispanic theologians are to avoid assimilating the same bourgeois, sentimentalized sense of community and aesthetics that permeates the dominant culture, our attempts to articulate the rationality of grounding theology in praxis, as communal and aesthetic, must look first to the experience of women, who have both maintained alive the communal and aesthetic sensibilities of our people and yet suffered from the demands of a romanticized community, aesthetics, and popular religiosity.[43]

U.S. Hispanic Theology as Theology

Insofar as praxis, as communal and aesthetic, is also rational, it implies not only the possibility and obligation of ethical-political action, but also the possibility and obligation of rational discourse. If reflection is intrinsic to praxis, then rational discourse is intrinsic to intersubjective action.[44] For U.S. Hispanic theologians—indeed, for all theologians—this means that our theological enterprise, whether as professionals, Christians, or, simply, human beings, is intrinsic to our praxis as U.S. Hispanics. To argue that our theology must be grounded in the praxis of our communities is, thus, to insist that the wisdom of those communities be brought into critical dialogue with the larger society. Again, if U.S. Hispanics fail to engage the larger dialogue, we reinforce the dominant culture's suspicion that we have failed to do so because we cannot do so—that we lack the rational capacity. As U.S. Hispanic theologians, we must be willing to engage the dominant theological paradigms in order, precisely, to critique them. To fail to do so would be to fail to ground theology in praxis— understood now not as opposed to reason but as grounding, and thus embracing, reason dialectically, or critically.[45]

Our claims on the theological establishment are not pastoral but theological: the admission of U.S. Hispanics into the broader theological dialogue is important, not because such inclusion would be the Christian thing to do (though that is also true), but because it would be the theologically and intellectually responsible thing to do. If the inherently communal character of historical praxis implies the obligation to engage in dialogue, it likewise implies the possibility of common understanding and interpretation.[46] To marginalize some voices, such as those of U.S. Hispanics, by excluding them from the possibility of rational discourse is to undermine our common enterprise of understanding and interpretation.

This is the danger of categorizing our theology as "U.S. Hispanic theology." Too often so-called contextual theologies are dismissed as irrelevant to the larger, presumably noncontextual and hence universal, theological enterprise. U.S. Hispanic theology is then perceived as important for U.S. Hispanics, feminist theology for women, African American theology for African Americans, and so on, but none of these is considered important for the task of those who do white, male, Anglo American theology. Thus, for example, a university with no Hispanic students is not likely to hire a U.S. Hispanic theologian, since the assumption is that, in that context, he or she would have no one with whom to speak, no one who would be interested in listening, and no one who would have anything to learn from the theologian. The terms *U.S. Hispanic theology* and *U.S. Hispanic theologian* are appropriate only if we are clear that these are but shorthand ways of saying that a U.S. Hispanic theologian is a theologian who does theology from a self-consciously U.S. Hispanic perspective rather than from an unconsciously Anglo American perspective.

The ontological priority of community revealed in U.S. Hispanic praxis suggests, as we have seen, that all of us are particular manifestations of an organic whole before we are individual entities: community—ultimately, the entire human community—is mediated by the particularity of individual identity. This fact anticipates, as we have also seen, both the possibility of ethical-political action and the possibility of rational discourse. The ontological priority of community implies that the theological reflection of U.S. Hispanics is important, not only because there happen to be Hispanics in our churches, our seminaries, or our universities, but also because, inasmuch as every culture and every individual is a unique and particular manifestation of the whole human community, the theology of Hispanics has significance for the whole theological community. It is by being self-consciously faithful to the particularity of our own experience as U.S. Hispanics that we are faithful to the larger human community. Consequently, it is by being faithful to our identity as U.S. Hispanic theologians that we are faithful to the larger theological community.

Notes

1. Many of the questions raised and ideas articulated in this article were initially set forth in a paper I presented at the 1991 annual convention of the Catholic Theological Society of America, held in Atlanta. "Theology as Intellectually Vital Inquiry: The Challenge of/to U.S. Hispanic Theologians," appears in the *Proceedings of Catholic Theological Society of America* 46 (1991): 58–69. These

represent, in turn, a development of the reflections on theory and praxis proffered in my 1990 presidential address to the Academy of Catholic Hispanic Theologians of the United States, and in my essay "U.S. Hispanic Theology and the Challenge of Pluralism," *Frontiers of a United States Hispanic Theology,* ed. Allan Figueroa Deck (Maryknoll, N.Y.: Orbis Books, 1992).

2. See, e.g., Hans-Georg Gadamer, "Hermeneutics and Social Science," *Cultural Hermeneutics* 2 (1975): 307–16; Jürgen Habermas, *The Theory of Communicative Action* (Boston: Beacon Press, 1984); Richard Bernstein, *Beyond Objectivism and Relativism: Science, Hermeneutics, and Praxis* (Philadelphia: University of Pennsylvania Press, 1985); Matthew Lamb, *Solidarity with Victims* (New York: Crossroad, 1982); and Lamb, "Praxis," in *The New Dictionary of Theology,* ed. Joseph Komonchak, Mary Collins, and Dermot Lane (Wilmington, Del.: Michael Glazier, 1988), 784–87.

3. Gadamer, "Hermeneutics and Social Science," 312.

4. Lamb, "Praxis," 785.

5. Ibid.

6. Ibid., 785–86; Goizueta, "Theology as Intellectually Vital Inquiry."

7. See Lamb, "Praxis."

8. In the North American context, see, e.g., Alasdair MacIntyre, *After Virtue: A Study in Moral Theory* (Notre Dame, Ind.: University of Notre Dame Press, 1981) and *Whose Justice? Which Rationality?* (Notre Dame, Ind.: University of Notre Dame Press, 1988).

9. Nicholas Lobkowicz, *Theory and Practice: History of a Concept from Aristotle to Marx* (Notre Dame, Ind.: University of Notre Dame Press, 1967), 9–11. Lobkowicz illustrates this difference by comparing the activity of playing a flute (praxis) with that of building a house (poiesis): "An activity such as building a house would never be considered satisfactory if it did not stop, that is, resulted in a house built and finished. As opposed to this, . . . playing the flute obviously has achieved its end a long time before it stops. In fact, once it has stopped, it is no longer of any value—precisely because it does not aim at a result beyond the mere 'doing' of it" (p. 10). Lamb provides a further illustration: "What Aristotle was on to is the difference drawn, for example, between a house and a home. Productive techniques are needed to make a house. But a home is a doing, a performing, a praxis which is a good in itself when it is achieved; and the achievement of the happiness which is a family home requires much more than management techniques: a home requires virtuous parents and children" ("Praxis," 786).

10. Aristotle, *Politics* 1, 4; 1254; see also his *Nicomachean Ethics* VI, 4.

11. Karl Marx, "Economic and Philosophic Manuscripts of 1844," in *The Marx-Engels Reader,* ed. Robert C. Tucker (New York, W. W. Norton & Co., 1978), 76.

12. Ibid., 73–76.

13. It is only fair to note that, while so-called orthodox Marxism came to interpret Marx in this reductionist manner, there are elements of Marx's thought, especially in his early writings, that would support arguments against such a reductionist interpretation. This fact is alluded to, for example, by Clodovis Boff in his discussion of Marx's notion of praxis in *Theology and Praxis,* 331.

14. Marx, "Economic and Philosophic Manuscripts."

15. Boff, *Theology and Praxis,* 331.

16. Marx, "Economic and Philosophic Manuscripts," 76.

17. Gustavo Gutiérrez, *A Theology of Liberation,* rev. ed. (Maryknoll, N.Y. Orbis Books, 1988), 6.

18. Ibid., xxxiv, 6.

19. Ibid., xxx.

20. I do not mean to set up a simple dichotomy here but merely to suggest different tendencies.

21. One of the most brilliant attempts to perform such a correlation is Boff's *Theology and Praxis.*

22. A number of Latin American liberation theologians have also paid special attention to popular religiosity: see, e.g., Juan Carlos Scannone, "Enfoques teológico-pastorales latinoamericanos de la religiosidad popular," *Stromata* 40 (1985): 33–47; Segundo Galilea, *Religiosidad popular y pastoral* (Madrid: Ediciones Cristiandad, 1979), and "The Theology of Liberation and the Place of Folk Religion," in *What Is Religion? An Inquiry for Christian Theology* (Edinburgh: T. & T. Clark, 1980), 40–45. Yet popular religiosity has not generally attained the methodological significance in the Latin American liberation theology movement as a whole that it has among U.S. Hispanic theologians—at least thus far. A major reason for this difference in emphasis is the centrality of cultural oppression to the experience of Hispanics living in an alien society; the salience of popular religious praxis as an expression of cultural identity is enhanced where the distinctiveness of that identity becomes more visible. While Latin Americans suffer from devastating forms of cultural oppression vis-à-vis the cultures of North America and Europe (often filtered through the cultures of local elites), the distinctiveness of Latin American culture naturally comes to the fore and becomes more visible when transplanted into the United States, thereby increasing the availability of cultural difference as an instrument of marginalization.

23. See, e.g., Elizondo, *Galilean Journey* and *The Future Is Mestizo;* Orlando O. Espín and Sixto J. García, eds., "Lilies of the Field: A Hispanic Theology of Providence and Human Responsibility," *Proceedings of the Catholic Theological Society of America* 44 (1989): 70–90; Orlando O. Espín, "Tradition and Popular Religion: An Understanding of the *Sensus Fidelium,*" in *Frontiers of U.S. Hispanic Theology,* Deck, *The Second Wave,* 113–19.

24. Espín and García. "Lilies of the Field," 76–77.

25. Ibid., 78.

26. Virgilio Elizondo, *La Morenita: Evangelizer of the Americas* (San Antonio: Mexican American Cultural Center, 1980), 8.

27. In *La Morenita,* Elizondo presents a comparison of the Greek notion of education, or *paideia,* and the notion of education prevalent in indigenous communities, where "the most important aspect of education was the integration of the individual, from the very beginning, into the life of the group which would always be a significant part. . . . It was the group, with its living tradition, which had originated with the gods before time existed and which, thus, 'created' the individual and kept him in existence" (p. 16). Indeed, the Spanish word for "to raise" (as in "to raise" children) is *criar,* which comes from the same root as *crear,* to create.

28. Espín and García, "Lilies of the Field," 78.

29. Elizondo, *La Morenita,* 23.

30. Ibid., 75.

31. Ibid., 8–9.

32. This fact is overlooked when popular religiosity, as a mediation of historical praxis, is instrumentalized, or judged according to its usefulness for social transformation. Since popular religiosity does not lead directly to social transformation, it is then deemed inadequate as a tool for social change. The fundamental mistake made here is that of using technological criteria as the basis for judging human praxis.

33. In their discussion of the centrality of aesthetics to Hispanic culture, Isasi-Díaz and Tarango describe how life is liturgized in Hispanic culture: *Hispanic Women,* 100–101. As an alternative to the Cartesian epistemological paradigm, the aesthetic paradigm has played an important role in the history of Latin American philosophy. See, especially, the works of José Vasconcelos, e.g., *Estética,* in *Obras completas,* III (México: Libreros Mexicanos Unidos, 1961), 1111–1711, and *El monismo estético* and *Filosofía estética,* in ibid., IV, 9–92 and 817–954, respectively. For an analysis of the aesthetic dimension of human praxis within the context of German critical theory, see Shierry M. Weber, "Aesthetic Experience and Self-Reflection as Emancipatory Processes: Two Complementary Aspects of Critical Theory," in *On Critical Theory,* ed. John O'Neill (New York: Seabury Press, 1976), 78–103.

34. Elizondo, *La Morenita,* 69.

35. José Juan Arrom, *Certidumbre de América: Estudios de letras, folklore y cultura* (Madrid: Editorial Gredos, 1971), 214 (my translation).

36. Isasi-Díaz and Tarango, *Hispanic Women,* 1.

37. Lamb, "Praxis."

38. The modern Cartesian paradigm reduces reason to theory, and theory to concept, thereby paving the way for postmodernity, which accepts the basic dualistic presuppositions underlying the Cartesian paradigm, to reject not only conceptualism but reason itself.

39. On poststructuralist postmodernism, see Hal Foster, "(Post)Modern Polemics," *New German Critique* 33 (Fall 1984): 67–78; and Mark Kline Taylor. *Remembering Esperanza: A Cultural-Political Theology for North American Praxis* (Maryknoll, N.Y.: Orbis Books, 1990). 23–45.

40. The roots of community are not in feelings, but in ontology, in our very identity or nature as human beings and creatures, which includes but is not reducible to feelings; see my "Theology as Intellectually Vital Inquiry." Isasi-Díaz and Tarango warn against the dangers of sentimentalization; quoting Gloria Durka, they speak of aesthetics as "characterized by feeling *reasoned* and *feeling* reason"; *Hispanic Women,* 100.

41. Ada María Isasi-Díaz, "Toward an Understanding of *Feminismo Hispano* in the U.S.A.," *Women's Consciousness, Women's Conscience,* 55.

42. See note 38 above, Goizueta, "Theology as Intellectually Vital Inquiry." For an example of the significance of social situatedness for theological method, see Kline Taylor, *Remembering Esperanza.*

43. For a discussion of the ambiguous impact that popular religiosity surrounding the symbol of Mary has had on women, see, e.g., Ana Maria Bidegain, "Women and the Theology of Liberation," in *Through Her Eyes: Women's Theology from Latin America,* ed. Elsa Tamez (Maryknoll, N.Y.: Orbis Books, 1989), 15–36. That Mary has nevertheless remained a strong source of empowerment for many Latinas is reflected in some of the interviews conducted by Isasi-Díaz and Tarango with Hispanic women, recounted in *Hispanic Women.* See, e.g., the interview with

Lupe, in which she movingly describes her devotion to Our Lady of Guadalupe (pp. 28–32). The authors observe that all of the interviews reflect the centrality of community and aesthetics to the experience of Latinas. On the importance of women's experience for theological method, see also Elsa Tamez, *Teólogos de la liberación hablan sobre la mujer* (San José, Costa Rica: DEI, 1986); Tamez, ed., *Through Her Eyes:* María Pilar Aquino, ed., *Aportes para una teología desde la mujer* (Madrid: Biblia y Fe, 1988); Aquino, *Nuestro clamor por la vida: Teología latinoamericana desde la perspectiva de la mujer* (San José, Costa Rica: DEI, 1992); and Kline Taylor, *Remembering Esperanza,* esp. 76–149. On the consequences for women of the sentimentalization of community, see Elizabeth Fox-Genovese, *Feminism without Illusions* (Chapel Hill, N.C.: University of North Carolina Press, 1991), 33–54; on the dangers of sentimentalized community more generally, see Michael J. Sandel, *Liberalism and the Limits of Justice* (Cambridge: Cambridge University Press, 1982), 147–54.

44. See Jürgen Habermas, *Legitimation Crisis* (Boston: Beacon Press, 1975); Helmut Peukert, *Science, Action, and Fundamental Theology: Toward a Theology of Communicative Action* (Cambridge, Mass.: MIT Press, 1984), esp. 163–245; Bernstein, *Beyond Objectivism and Relativism,* esp. 171–231; and Sandel, *Liberalism and the Limits of Justice,* 172–73.

45. Our theology would thus be an example of what Lamb refers to as "critical praxis correlation"; see *Solidarity with Victims,* 82–88.

46. See Sandel, *Liberalism and the Limits of Justice,* 147–83, and Habermas, *Legitimation Crisis,* 110.

Annotated Bibliography—Roberto Goizueta

"U.S. Hispanic Theology and the Challenge of Pluralism," in *Frontiers of Hispanic Theology in the United States,* Allan Figueroa Deck, ed. (Maryknoll, New York: Orbis Books, 1992), pp. 1–21.

Throughout his writings, Goizueta develops a unique Latino hermeneutic. This article is an excellent exposé of the quality of his work. He challenges the epistemological bias in theology of the liberal, individualistic, Enlightenment tradition of Western thought that often masquerades as pluralistic ideology. For Goizueta, the Hispanic organic communal world view rooted in the praxis of Hispanic faith communities offers an insightful corrective to this bias and a direction for a polycentric church and the emergence of an authentic pluralism.

"Rediscovering Praxis: The Significance of U.S. Hispanic Experience for Theological Method," in *We Are a People: Initiatives in Hispanic American Theology,* Roberto Goizueta, ed. (Minneapolis: Fortress Press, 1992), pp. 51–77.

Goizueta expertly explores how praxis grounds U.S. Latino theology. He briefly traces the development and use of the term praxis from Aristotle to recent Latin American liberation theologies and claims that U.S. Latino theology's contribution to a fuller understanding of praxis stems from popular religiosity, the historical praxis of U.S. Hispanic communities. To skeptics of the Western epistemological rationalistic mode who would view popular religiosity as a non-rational and unintellectual dimension in theology, he convincingly argues that praxis as communal, aesthetic, and liberative in U.S. Latino theology is a supreme rational endeavor. He concludes that U.S. Latino theology is a praxis-based theology.

We Are a People: Initiatives in Hispanic American Theology (Minneapolis: Fortress Press, 1992)

As a leading U.S. Latino theologian, Goizueta consistently argues that U.S. Latino theologians no longer need to pay the price of losing their cultural identity to enter the theological arena. With this volume, he clearly demonstrates that U.S. Latino theologians can now engage in theological dialogue as contributing partners. He presents six outstanding critical essays that methodologically situate the Christian faith in the historical experience of the U.S. Latino faith communities. Allan Deck stresses the need for an educated Catholic leadership within a diverse cultural setting of Anglo American Catholicism. Fernando Segovia indicates how, from the Hispanic social location, the Bible is a faithful ally in the struggle for liberation. María Pilar Aquino creatively outlines how poor women now affirm their place as rightful subjects of history, society, church and theology. Sixto García offers a fundamental structure of a Hispanic trinitarian theology from the persepctive of popular religiosity. Orlando Espín presents a fresh view of grace from the view of the U.S. Latino cultural context. The reader will encounter in this volume major themes in U.S. Latino theology as well as some of the salient theological voices.

6

Sixto J. García

Sixto García was born in La Habana, Cuba. He began his theological studies at Barry University in Miami, Florida where he earned a masters (MA) in religious studies. From Notre Dame he obtained his second masters in theology (MA) in 1985, and a doctorate (PhD) in 1986 in systematic theology.

As a theology professor, García has taught at St. Vincent de Paul Regional Seminary since 1980 and at Barry University as adjunct professor in the Department of Philosophy and Theology since 1987. He is also a member of the diaconate faculty for the Archdiocese of Miami.

In his writings and teachings, García focuses on systematic and fundamental theology, history of dogma and theology, and New Testament theology and exegesis. He was among the first to raise issues of methodology in U.S. Latino theology. His strong systematic background is evident in his published articles on trinitarian theology, Mary, and popular religion from the U.S. Latino perspective. He is currently working on a text on christology and hermeneutics from the Latino perspective.

García is a member of the Catholic Theological Society of America, the Catholic Biblical Association, North American Patristic Society, The Academy of Catholic Hispanic Theologians of the United States, the Society of Biblical Literature, and the Catholic Historical Association. In 1985 he was awarded the Zahm Research Travel Grant to work at the Bavarian Academy of Science in Munich, Germany, and in 1985 he was awarded the University of Notre Dame John O'Brien Fellowship.

Sixto García is married to Elena Muller García, and they have two children.

St. Vincent de Paul Seminary
10701 South Military Trail
Boynton Beach, Florida 33436-4811
407-732-4424
Fax 407-737-2205

Sources and Loci of Hispanic Theology

Sixto J. García

Introduction: The Hermeneutical Interdependence of Sources and Loci

Preliminary Definitions

The sources available to the theologian doing Hispanic theology, whether present in their traditional form (i.e., Scriptures, Tradition, the liturgy, and human experience) or revealed through other profiles more specific to the Hispanic milieu, can and will always be found only within general or particular spheres of Hispanic culture.

Before we proceed any further, we would like to provide a definition of *culture* that will place the word in a given semantic and hermeneutical context in this essay. *Culture* may be seen as "a system of inherited conceptions expressed in symbolic forms by means of which human beings communicate, perpetuate and develop their knowledge about, and their attitudes toward, life."[1] A similar definition (one of several coming off our own reflection) might be: *Culture* is the organic totality of the symbols, values, literature, and myths through which a given human (political and/ or social) group identifies itself as unique, and (through which) it communicates the different aspects of this identity.[2]

The Organic Relation Between Sources and Loci

Given this perception of culture, it is obvious that the sources and loci of Hispanic theology will always have an intimate relationship. Since the sources can be found only as they "perform" (in Jürgen Habermas' sense of the word) in a given cultural context, that very same cultural context,

"Sources and Loci of Hispanic Theology," *Journal of Hispanic/Latino Theology* 1:1 (November 1993), pp. 22–43.

in its diversity and complexity, will also offer the loci for Hispanic theology, or, at the very least, will point toward them.

Objectors to this notion might argue that such a theory tends to falsely identify the grounds of Hispanic theology with its necessary points of insertion in the history of the Hispanic faith communities (this is not unlike the criticism that Francis S. Fiorenza aims at Karl Rahner's theological method: according to Fiorenza, Rahner confuses the grounds of theology with the grounds of the faith experience—a short-sighted criticism, at best).[3] The problem with this objection is that it fails to see, as far as Hispanic theology is concerned, that *this is precisely the point:* theologians can only do theology from a Hispanic milieu when they become fully aware that the sources and foundations of Hispanic theology can never be divorced from the privileged locations whence they may practice the art and craft of doing theology from the Hispanic perspective. These locations qualify, shape, and condition the identity of the sources for such a theology.

The above may actually be seen as a truism, for those whose pastoral activity within faith communities allows them a privileged view of the Hispanic faith-dynamics. But for people used to building theological systems which emerge in Olympic isolation from given cultural contexts, for those who do not bother to immerse themselves within the complex realities of multifaceted Hispanic culture, these reflections will always come as new, if not foreign, realities.

The Question of Sources for Hispanic Theology

Preliminary Remarks

In the summer of 1988, Professor Orlando Espín and I offered a joint workshop on the sources of Hispanic theology at the forty-third annual convention of the Catholic Theological Society of America.[4] At the time, we offered a Hispanic reformulation of the sources of theology: Hebrew and Christian Scriptures, Tradition, liturgy, and human experience. We attempted to structure a Hispanic-oriented system of retrieval of the main-line Hispanic theological concepts, on the one hand, and a correlation of these concepts with mainline conventional (i.e., non-Hispanic, mostly Euro-American) theology.

At our past ACHTUS meetings we have had the opportunity to continue our ongoing conversation with the shifting profiles of Hispanic theology. This conversation has invited me to rethink, change, and occasionally deepen our perception of the sources, the places, and the methods of Hispanic theological efforts. Developments in contemporary biblical and systematic/theological scholarship, on the one hand, and the new situations emerging within the Hispanic social and political milieu, on the other, demand corresponding developments in Hispanic theology. What we offer in this essay are our reflections and intuitions concerning, very specifically, the sources and places of Hispanic theology as they have developed from this ongoing dialogue.

The Hermeneutics of the Sources for Hispanic Theology

1. The challenge of Scriptural interpretation for Hispanic theology. Scriptural exegesis presents a challenge to the theologian committed to reflecting on the Hispanic faith experiences. As such, we advert to the following realities:

First, we have a very real dissatisfaction with the formulistic application of modern historico-critical interpretation and other formerly or still widely-used methods (redaction-, form-, text-, source-critical analysis, structuralism, and so on). Although these methods still find wide currency among exegetes (and the Hispanic theologian, insofar as he or she engages the Scriptures as a source, must be professionally acquainted with them), there are voices arguing loudly for a "post-critical" (not necessarily meaning, in this context, "non-scientific" or much less, fundamentalist) approach to exegesis.

From a communitary-structural standpoint, the theologian engaged in Hispanic theology faces the issue of the dominant/oppressive consequences of interpretations of Scripture that end in a purely historical assertion, without reflecting, responding, or offering answers to the reader as individual or as a faith community. Are these interpretations a tool of oppression even if only by omission? If such is the case, some may ask, are we really any more "scientific" or responsible in interpreting Scripture than our predecessors in the Christian tradition? Are these methods any better in their accountability to the people of God than approaches from Christian antiquity, ranging from the Alexandrian christological exegesis of the λόγος-σάρξ ("logos-sarx") and its counterpoint, the Antiochene λόγος-ἄνθρωπος ("logos-anthropos"), to the medieval "four senses" of the Bible? Does a reader-response approach necessarily exclude the historico-critical one?

Walter Brueggemann has suggested a recourse to Habermas' three levels of textual interpretation: any meaningful text will offer, first, a literal (historical?) interpretation; second, a moral, individual (existentialist?) meaning; and finally, at its deepest level, a social meaning.[5] Is this a possible answer to the challenges mentioned above?

We offer the following reflections simply as a possible guideline for the use of Scripture as a source for Hispanic theology:

a. We hold, as a foundational belief, that the Scriptures are the Word of God. To even attempt to engage ourselves in a discussion concerning the interpretation of this statement would be to open a can of hermeneutical worms quite peripheral to our discussion. It is legitimate to say, however, that regardless of the different theological contours that different people might draw concerning "Scriptures as Word of God," we hold in common the normative dimension of the Scriptures (the Scriptures are the soul of all theology)[6] for theological reflection on God's self-communication.

b. The witness of the Hebrew Bible and of the New Testament attests to the living, changing, converting force of God's Word (Gen 1:1ff.; Is 55:10–11; Lk 1:37). As living Word, biblical literature conveys much more than just ethical messages. It engages the active dialogue of the reader and his or her cultural symbols, myths, literature, aesthetics, and value-framework.

c. We can affirm in common that, regardless of the different understandings about the Scriptures as Word, it is a living Word: it communicates, it summons, it "listens," it changes, converts, and persuades. And the object of these activities of the Word of God is a living, thinking, culturally-shaped and rooted, dialogical human person.

These three points ought to stand as the foundational criteria for a new hermeneutics of the Scriptures as living, acting, changing, and converting Word. Here we perceive the echo of Martin Heidegger's somewhat shop-worn axiom: "Die Sprache is das Haus des Seins und die Behausung des Menschenwesens" ("Language is the house of being, and the dwelling place of humanity").[7] Furthermore, Heidegger understood λόγος, among other things, as that word or language (action? deed?—reminiscent of the rewording of John 1:1 by Goethe's *Faust:* "In der Anfang war der Tat" ["In the beginning there was the act (deed?)"])[8] which made truth evident, epiphanic. Let us remember that Heidegger explored the etymology of ἀλήθεια ("truth") and discovered its structural and semantic connections with the actions of illuminating and unveiling (*Enthüllen*) truth about Being.[9]

2. *The Tradition as an ambiguous source for Hispanic theology.* In our 1987 workshop and our 1989 joint keynote address at the CTSA annual meetings in Philadelphia and Toronto respectively, Professor Espín and I approached the issue of the Christian Tradition from the perspectives of popular religiosity. The 1989 meeting, more specifically, provided a forum for the study of popular-religious expressions of the faith as a source for Hispanic theology. I will go back to this point later in this essay. Now we are concerned with the issue of defining the Tradition and its value as a source for doing theology in a Hispanic key.

We can and should make a valid distinction between the Great Tradition (generally considered to be the Scriptures, the Latin and Greek writers of the first eight centuries, the Scholastics,[10] and their contemporary heirs), and the traditions. Although writing with a different sense in mind, Yves Congar affirms this perspective in his work by the same title.[11] Here we need not dwell in great detail on the relationship between Scriptures, Tradition, and theology. It should suffice to say that the New Testament (cf. 1 Cor 11:23ff.; 15:1–8; Acts 2:31ff.; Heb 1:1–4, and so on) witnesses to the earliest apostolic kerygma, and as such these Scriptures are the privileged witness of the earliest Tradition. The normative apostolic Tradition, on the other hand (the *regula fidei* of Tertullian, Origen, and the early writers of the Church), provides the privileged context for the earliest interpretation—certainly, for the redaction itself—of the New Testament canonical writings.

The traditions of the local communities were the starting point of the Tradition, considered as an organic whole. The New Testament gives witness to this: the celebration of the Lord's Supper (1 Cor 11:23ff.; 10:17ff.), the earliest two-stage and/or Old Adam-New Adam christologies (Rom 1:1–4; Rom 5:12–21; Phil 2:6–11), and even local sacramental/ liturgical practices, often abandoned at a later stage. See, for example, 1 Cor 15:29: Ἐπεὶ τι ποιήσουσιν οἱ βαπτιζόμενοι ὑπὲρ τῶν νεκρῶν; εἰ ὅλως νεκροὶ οὐκ ἐγείρονται, τί καὶ βαπτίζονται ὑπὲρ αὐτῶν ("Otherwise, what will people accomplish by having themselves baptized for the dead? If the dead are not raised at all, then why are they having themselves baptized for them?"). The use of ὑπὲρ in this text remains ambiguous for many exegetes, but it may allude to a unique practice among the Corinthians, which consisted in either baptizing themselves on behalf of their beloved deceased who had not been initiated, or perhaps being baptized because (of the example of a committed Christian life?) of the dead.

Some may argue that the Corinthians' practice may not be the best example; there are others, mostly, but not exclusively, of a liturgical/ celebratory nature (we will approach this again later in this essay). Jerome Murphy-O'Connor contended, as far back as 1967, that the hymn of Philippians 2:6–11 sang implicitly the ancient Christian perception of Jesus Christ as the New Adam (an early example of *lex orandi, lex credendi* in practice).[12]

The issue arises, once again, of whether the later dominant-cultures' hermeneutics of the Tradition were interpreted unilaterally, resulting in oppression-inducing interpretations. These interpretations ignored the role of popular celebrations in local communities, of which Phil 2:6–11 should be considered a good example (the hymn probably antedates Paul's own redactional adaptations of it by approximately a decade), and even assuming that the community or communities who sang it had what Paul designates as an *episkopos,* a "leader/coordinator," it still retains its identity as a hymn of the people (an integral part of which were the *episkopoi* of New Testament times).

Jürgen Habermas has offered his amply developed theory of oppression through the "accepted" and "democratic" structures that prevail in dominant-culture-controlled societies in the West. Habermas' analysis is quite valuable for two reasons. First, he emphasizes the need of society for the transmission of the symbols, myths, and values which define, organically, a culture. Second, he argues persuasively that the interpretation of these symbols, myths, and values by resource-controlling groups serves to per-

petuate oppressive structures, even those with a democratic profile.[13] This
remains operative, he says, even in those structures where a certain social
class—workers, for instance—or a cultural/racial group—Hispanics or
African Americans, in our case—feels that "things are improving," or
even that those modes of oppression are vanishing. In such situations, a
sociocultural or economic "Tradition" may be transmitted through mis-
leading, oppressive interpretations, resulting from the hermeneutics of the
oppressors. This applies somewhat analogically in the Church. Unilateral
interpretations of the Tradition and the traditions by dominant-culture
groups inevitably will result in:

a. interpretations of the Tradition that ultimately bear little relation with
the original intention or sense of the text or the verbal proclamations;

b. the obliteration of the memory and the transmissions of the traditions
arising within the local communities, eventually rendering (at least in
appearance) those experiences quite meaningless.[14]

The theologian doing theology in a Hispanic key faces the need to
retrieve and reinterpret the traditions, which first requires rethinking the
hermeneutics of the traditions that speak, and listen to, the Hispanic faith
experience. The retrieval demands the following:

a. rigorous command of historical theology and Church history, at least
in its theological dimensions, and the resolve to pursue and trace the
traditions of local communities;

b. and more pertinently, a full command and appreciation of the Hispanic
theologian's own culture, or the culture within which his/her theology
develops. The traditions of the Hispanic faith community which serve as
source of theology in any particular case, are found only within this cultural
milieu. It is only within this culture that the theologian must trace back,
retrieve, reinterpret, and develop the hermeneutics of that specific local
tradition. Later in this essay, we will argue that the literature of the community, as a privileged means of communicating its own cultural identity,
will demand from the theologian the role of the "poet of the community."[15]

*3. Liturgical celebration as source: the tension between official/universal
and local communitary dimensions.* A careful reader of the New Testament
will advert to the liturgical pregnancy of many key theological texts in
the Gospels and, in a particular fashion, in the authentic Pauline and the
deutero-Pauline letters. We have already alluded to Philippians 2:6–11
(not including Paul's own redactional additions); Romans 1:1–4; possibly
Hebrews 1:1–4; 1 Timothy 3:16; the possible doxology in Romans 9:5
(disputed by a number of exegetes); the possible liturgical use of the
kerygmatic text of 1 Corinthians 15:3–8; and so on.

The apparently formulistic use by Paul of παρέδωκα (the aorist of
παραδίδωμι ["hand down," "pass on"]) and παρέλαβον (aorist of παρα-
λάμβανω ["to receive," often of a tradition]) in both 1 Corinthians 11:23
and 1 Corinthians 15:3, points to the relationship between liturgical celebra-

tion, proclamation, and communication of the living tradition: 1 Corinthians 11:23: Ἐγὼ γὰρ παρέλαβον ἀπὸ τοῦ κυρίου, ὃ καὶ παρέδωκα ὑμῖν ... ("What I have received from the Lord, this I have transmitted [handed on] to you"), and 1 Corinthians 15:3: παρέδωκα γὰρ ὑμῖν ἐν πρώτοις, ὃ καὶ παρέλαβον ... ("For I have communicated [handed on] to you, first of all, what I have received"). Paul's account of the words of Jesus over the bread and cup in 1 Corinthians 11:23ff. (par. Luke 22:19ff., similar to Paul and drawn from the so-called Antiochene tradition of the Eucharistic narrative) included the affirmation, ὁσάκις γὰρ ἐὰν ἐσθήτε τὸν ἄρτον τοῦτον καὶ τὸ ποτήριον πίνητε, τὸν θάνατον τοῦ κυρίου καταγγελλέτε ἄχρι οὖ ἔλθη ("For, as often as you eat this bread and drink the cup, you proclaim the death of the Lord until he comes"). As Xavier Léon-Dufour has remarked, Paul regards the celebration of the bread and cup of the Lord as Word, as proclamation, as communication of the Tradition (another example, perhaps, of the Pauline rendering [in anticipation of a fourth-century axiom] of the *lex orandi, lex credendi*).[16]

If we now bring to bear our reflections on Tradition and the traditions, we may argue that local Hispanic communal celebrations have a claim to be legitimate liturgical expressions of the faith of a given particular Hispanic faith community. Although we hold that Scriptures should remain the privileged text for celebration, even in popular religious expressions, we can entertain the suggestions offered by some concerning the inclusion of popular texts. Here we have in mind those texts born within the faith, social, and even political experiences of the Hispanic communities, that is, born within the dynamics of their culture.

This is applicable, of course, to vastly different cultures. Thomas F. O'Meara has recovered the petition once made by the Hindu Catholic bishops to incorporate texts of the *Baghavad Gita* in the Liturgy of the Word. We may see the argument that some might advance concerning the inclusion of the *Popol Vuh,* the Mayan literary masterpiece, so pregnant with rich and suggestive imagery, mystical and mythical symbols of ascent to the realm of the gods, and the yearning of a people to journey along these ascending pathways.[17]

The question of local or popular liturgies becomes, in light of the above, a crucial one. The liturgy, as the public prayer of the Church and of the faith communities it includes, is the mirror where communities see reflected (in prayer, song, and praise) not only their own faith life but also their own human becoming, their experiences of sorrow and oppression, and their yearnings for joy and deliverance. The liturgy of a Hispanic faith community must celebrate these hopes and yearnings as it also tries to metamorphose the experiences of oppression into experiences of redemption.

But the liturgy also points beyond these reflections to the question of the praxis.[18] Paul already critizes the contradiction practiced and lived by the Corinthians who, as they gathered to celebrate the Supper of the Lord,

112 Sixto J. García

discriminated against the poor and the hungry (cf. 1 Cor 11:21, 28–29). For Paul, the κοινωνία ("communion," not "participation" as rendered by some translations) with the bread of blessing was κοινωνία with the body of the Lord (with the person and the community of Jesus Christ), and the κοινωνία with the cup was κοινωνία with the blood of the Lord (1 Cor 10:16: Τὸ ποτήριον τῆς εὐλογίας ὁ εὐλογοῦμεν, οὐχί κοινωνία ἐστὶν τοῦ αἵματος τοῦ Χριστοῦ; τὸν ἄρτον ὃν κλῶμεν, οὐχί κοινωνία τοῦ σώματος τοῦ Χριστοῦ ἐστιν ("the cup of blessing that we bless, is it not communion with the blood of Christ? The bread that we break, is it not communion with the body of Christ?").

Paul warns against partaking of the bread and cup of blessing without discerning (and implicitly, living) the love that the bread and cup were a symbol of: the ultimate, insuperable, total self-surrendering love of Jesus Christ in his death and resurrection (Karl Rahner).[19] It is this paschal reality of the Lord, as lived in true love by the faith communities, that constitutes the true criterion of salvation, of discerning the body and blood of the Lord as sacrament of the Church, itself sacrament of Jesus Christ.[20]

It seems obvious that the external symbols often projected by the established liturgy of the Church, at all levels (multimillion-dollar church buildings, multimillion-dollar parish halls), all of these in parishes that deny access to prayer and worship to migrant workers living in nearby "camps" (to use a mild word) or to minorities sweltering away their summers and their hopes in rat-infested ghettoes and shacks; parishes where the homilist sings and dances his way around a biblical text whenever the words the evangelists place on Jesus' lips constitute a minefield to be avoided (what would happen, otherwise, to the "generous" contributions of the wealthy parishioners, wealth often amassed with the blood and sweat of the oppressed?).

Since the liturgy, as both public prayer of the Church and source of theology, often reflects the voice and the anti-celebration of the oppressor, rather than the trusting hope of the oppressed, the Hispanic theologian will do well to remember Franz Josef van Beeck's remarks on the role of the verb ἐξομολογέω and the noun ἐξομολογέσις (in liturgical and private prayer-usage, meaning "to confess" or "acknowledge," and/or "to praise," and "confession," "acknowledgment," "praise," "thanksgiving").[21] Liturgy becomes a source of theology as it celebrates and expresses the confessed and praiseful faith of a community. On the other hand, an oppressed Hispanic faith community, seeking fulfillment and redemption, demands from its theologians a deep awareness of how and where this confession/praise fits within the social/anthropological reality of the community. But it demands even more. The theologian engaged in dialogue with the liturgical practice of a community as a source for his or her theology must be aware of another element offered by Van Beeck: witnessing. "Witnessing" here refers to the participants and celebrants in a given liturgical celebration, whose life commitments become the very litmus test for the credibility of that which is being celebrated, confessed, and given thanks for. Quoting from his earlier work, *Christ Proclaimed,* Van Beeck says, "If the Christian self-expression is uttered only to praise God it gets isolated from the world and turns into an act of tribal religiosity—an inauthentic, defensive gesture of self-affirmation directed against outsiders and against all questions, and thus an instance of 'historical atavism' unfortunately popular in certain brands of evangelism ancient and modern."[22]

The Hispanic theologian receives here a reminder that ἐξομολογέω (again, "confession" and/or "praise," "thanksgiving"), understood as privatized or communal vertical praise, becomes demonic, a vicious circle where the community of the oppressor celebrates the very opposite of what the Eucharist was meant to celebrate. Those who do theology within the Hispanic cultural reality must develop their theology around the idea that the Christian witness celebrated in the *anamnesis* of the paschal event must be verified, tested. Theologians themselves, to begin with, and the entire Hispanic faith community that engages in celebration, must become witnesses of the faith confessed and celebrated in worship.

Liturgy then becomes a true source of theology as it allows the theologian to reflect on the form and structure of faith confessed and lived, and to reflect historically on the evolution of this faith expression and its liturgical articulations. This in itself becomes an argument for the inclusion of, say, the *Popol Vuh* as a "liturgical" text. But this perspective also demands from the theologian a prophetic commitment: echoing through the centuries the words of Paul, the Hispanic theologian must always cry at opportune and inopportune times, in practical and impractical fashion, always against the oppressor who celebrates the liturgical anti-witness, and remind us that whoever eats the bread or drinks from the cup of blessing without discerning (διακρίνειν) eats his or her own judgment (condemnation = κρίσις); cf. 1 Cor 15:28–29. The oppressor who attempts to worship while disengaged from the cries of the oppressed, the hungry, the unemployed, and the marginalized simply celebrates a liturgy of self-destruction, of scandal, of the demonic side that the Church (as *casta meretrix*) carries with it along the byways of history.

4. Human experience as a source of Hispanic theology. We begin by offering some foundational points of an anthropological-theological nature:

a. The human person stands, by dint of being created, in a situation of grace, offered as the Trinitarian God's own life.

b. Grace as God's life finds concrete form and shape in history, particularly, but far from exclusively, in what theology calls salvation history. Grace finds its referential symbols in covenant, deliverance, promise, and salvation (understood in a number of possible senses, but ultimately, as the fullness and fulfillment, the pleroma, of human experience and reality).

c. Human persons find themselves in an existential situation of openness to Word and grace, proper to them just by dint of being created. This openness, this point of insertion and contact of grace and human transcendence, of human becoming and its graced expression, has been recognized and called by different names in the Christian tradition. It is Augustine's restless heart which will not find tranquility until it rests in God. It is Aquinas's *potentia obedientialis,* rooted in the human capacity to hear the revealed Word. It is Rahner's *supernatural existential,* superseding and reformulating the ancient neo-Scholastic dichotomy between "human nature" and the "supernatural."

The concrete forms of human experience that find expression in the situations of the oppressed provide new hermeneutical keys for Hispanic theology, allowing theologians to read Scriptures and the Tradition in deeper and more socially and communally conscious ways. We have already discussed how liturgical expressions can reflect the concrete situations of Hispanic communities, and argued for the role of witnessing as a test of those celebrations. We have taken similar approaches to Scripture and the Tradition as we discussed their identity as sources for Hispanic theology. In similar fashion, the situation of oppression, the voices of the unvoiced uttering their silent screams against the unbroken circles of discrimination and marginalization, often coming from mainline Church structures, their hopes and unspoken aspirations celebrated in popular liturgies, unveil (in Heideggerian terms) the ἀλήθεια,[23] the (illuminated) truth of the Hispanic faith communities made epiphany in the often broken lives and bodies of their men and women. This truth comes forth pregnant with hermeneutical criteria for reading in new keys the Scriptures, the texts of the Tradition, and the formal liturgical texts of the Church.

Finally, the Hispanic theologian should be aware that this unveiling of existential, communal, and personal truth, read and thought through the human experience of those who make the Hispanic faith communities, does not necessarily proceed in organic, evolving, always-forward-moving fashion. For that matter, the unveiling of scriptural, traditional, and liturgically expressed truth does not proceed that way either. The model advanced and popularized by John Henry Newman in his work *On the Development of Christian Doctrine,*[24] proposed the view of an ever growing theological and doctrinal body of truths, developing in history, in a fashion not unlike the growth of the concentric rings of a tree as they form the tree trunk. Although Newman's model had the merit of restoring theology and doctrine to a historical-dynamic context (following the lead of the Tübingen theologian Johann Adam Möhler [1796–1838], whose key work, *Die Einheit in der Kirche* he read in French translation), it has been superseded, we feel, by the Heidegger-inspired model of the *Enthüllung,* the "veiling and unveiling of truth." As theologians read the symbols and texts that form the totality of their sources, they detect the truth of historico-theological situations becoming alternately clear and obscure.

We could express this reality through a common Spanish proverb: *Dando un pasito hacia adelante y otro hacia atrás.* Sometimes it is a matter of *dar dos pasitos hacia adelante y uno hacia atrás.* Sometimes it is the opposite. Either way, this dialectical understanding of historical and theological experiences summons the theologian to read with discerning eyes the ebb and flow of human experience, individually and in community, and retrieve the hermeneutical keys that such an experience affords the theological endeavor.

Remarks on Some of the Loci of Hispanic Theology

1. Preliminary remarks: Culture as a locus *of Hispanic theology.* Carlos Fuentes has recently focussed his literary discussion on the question of Spanish (from Spain) and Hispanic (from Latin America and Anglo-speaking North America) cultures as ever emerging forces in the social and political *oikomene.*[25] Fuentes explores the Hispanic culture in the United States, its communities and its contributions. Although aware of a multitude of differences, Fuentes is vehement in arguing for continuity of culture as a bridge spanning the differences. The foundational cultural element, of course, is ultimately our common provenance from Spain, often converging in that deepest form of human κοινωνία, the communion of bodies and blood, with Amerindian cultures, and a common language.[26]

How and what, specifically, do Hispanics in the United States, living in the midst of prejudice, misunderstanding, and institutional, as well as armed, violence, contribute to their different social milieux?

First of all, Fuentes tells us, for some who cross the U.S.-Mexico border, "this is not really a border, but a scar." We could add that there are many others scars, found across the Hispanic visage in the United States and running the breadth and length of the experiences borne by the Hispanic social and faith communities.

There are three developments in the Hispanic experience in the United States. First, Fuentes states that Hispanic immigrants coming for the first time into the United States sometimes ask: "Hasn't this always been our land? Am I not coming back to it? Is it not in some way ours?" He adds: "He can taste it, hear its language, sing it in its songs, and pray to its saints. Will this not always be in its bones a Hispanic land?"[27] Fuentes issues a quick caveat: "First we must remember that ours was once an empty continent." Indeed, strictly speaking, not even Amerindians are "native" to this continent. Appropriating a commonly accepted theory, Fuentes reminds us that they came across the Straits of Bering, and in less than a millenium filled the continent, north and south. Second, the Spaniards, the Dutch, the English, and others came. Then, independence was won for Mexico and the other Spanish colonies; and with independence Mexico inherited vast lands across its northern limits. And third was the rape and the shameless, illegal conquest of these Mexican territories, propelled by one of those cultural lies that, disguised as patriotism, drive gullible Euro-Americans to smash this or that pretended enemy for the sake of land, power, or more often, money. In this case, the cultural lie was, of course, the "manifest destiny" of the United States. The climax of this ignominious crime was the Treaty of Guadalupe Hidalgo, signed in 1848, depriving Mexico of its legitimately owned territories.[28] Fuentes continues:

> The Hispanic world did not come to the United States, the United States came to the Hispanic world. It is perhaps an act of poetic justice that now the Hispanic world should return, both to the United States and to part of its ancestral heritage in the Western Hemisphere. . . . They all join to make up the 25 million Hispanics in the United States. . . . Los Angeles is now the second largest Spanish-speaking city in the world, after Mexico City, before Madrid and Barcelona. You can prosper in South Florida even if you speak only Spanish, as the population is predominantly Cuban. San Antonio, integrated by Mexicans, has been a bilingual city for 150 years. By the middle of the coming century, almost half the population of the United States will be Spanish-speaking.[29]

Seminal realities, all of them. Do they have any bearing as *loci* of Hispanic theology? Of course they do, as we shall see later in this essay.

Fuentes probes ever deeper: "This third Hispanic development, that of the United States, is not only an economic and political event; it is above all a cultural event."[30] Indeed, in Fuentes's literary and historical view, something dramatic has taken place, *is* taking place: "A whole civilization with a Hispanic pulse has been created in the U.S. A literature has been born in this country, one that stresses autobiography—the personal narrative, memories of childhood, the family album—as a way of answering the question: What does it mean to be a Chicano, a Mexican American, a Puerto Rican living in Manhattan, a second-generation Cuban American living in exile in Miami?"[31] Fuentes pursues his point yet further: as he surveys the varied literary work of people such as Rodolfo Anaya, Ron Arias, Arturo Islas, Rolando Hinojosa, Sandra Cisneros, and Alberto Rios, he adds: "An art has also been created here. In a violent, even garish way, it joins a tradition going all the way from the caves of Altamira to the graffiti of East Los Angeles."[32] But this is not static, complacent art:

> The beauty and violence of these artists' work not only contribute to the need for contact between cultures that must refuse complacency or submit to injustice in order to come alive to each other. They also assert an identity that deserves to be respected and that must be given shape if it is not visible, or musical beat if it is not audible. And if the other culture, the Euro-American mainstream, denies Hispanic culture a past, then artists of Latin origin must invent, if

necessary, an origin. And they must remember every single link that binds it to them.[33]

But there is another side to injustice, a side which emerges powerfully when Fuentes surveys the contributions of Hispanics to U.S. culture: "At one end of the spectrum are 300,000 Hispanic businessmen prospering in the U.S., and at the other is a nineteen-year-old Euro-American shooting two immigrants to death for the simple reason that he 'hates Mexicans.' If one proudly spouts the statistic that Hispanic-owned businesses generate over $20 billion a year, one can also, far less proudly, report that immigrants are shot at by Euro-Americans with the paint-pellet guns used in mock-warfare games."[34] The list goes on and on.

Fuentes adds unequivocally that the culture of Spanish America "brings its own gifts." When new Hispanic immigrants come to the United States and are asked about their specific gifts, "they speak of religion—not only Catholicism, but something more like a deep sense of the sacred, a recognition that the world is holy, which is probably the oldest and deepest certitude of the Amerindian world. This is also a sensuous, tactile religion, a product of the meeting between the Mediterranean civilization and the Indian world of the Americas."[35] One can easily see the importance of these remarks for the Hispanic theologian. Almost equally important is Fuentes's comment on family respect for the elders. It is respect for experience and continuity, not so much for old age and novelty. In a basically oral culture (a fact that in our view does not detract at all from its rich literature), the old are the ones who remember stories: "One could almost say that when an old man or an old woman dies in the Hispanic world, a whole library dies with that person."[36]

I have chosen Fuentes as a preeminent representative of the historical and philosophical writers who, from the Hispanic vantage point, have offered us cultural and historical analyses of Hispanic experience in the United States. We have seen how this experience includes religious awe and wonder at the sacredness of creation, expressed through a biblical-like wealth of images, symbols, myths, and metaphors, all of which—if we may be forgiven this piece of cultural chauvinism—is sorely missing in those barren expressions proper to the Anglo-Puritan traditions.

2. Story and myth. We have already explored, albeit in passing, the oral-literary tension prevailing in Hispanic culture. The old ones—or the wise ones—of a family or community become storehouses for those stories and myths which make continuity and self-identity possible. Self-identity—and a legitimate pride in it—can only be possible when the "St. Pauls" of our communities will speak (in Spanish or English) what Paul expressed in *koine* Greek: the flow from the παρέδωκα to the παρέλαβων, that is, from "what I have received" to "what I have passed on [handed on] to you." These stories form the privileged vessels for the cultural elements and the faith experience of Hispanic communities.

Stories, however, are not the only source stored in memory and often passed on in writing. Myth-stories are equally important. Quite obviously, we do not understand *myth* here as that narrative that stands as the very opposite of the historical or the real. Ever since Paul Ricoeur, Hans-Georg Gadamer, and others restored their true value to myth-stories, we have become aware of their importance for the theologian (in our case, for the Hispanic theologian) as well as for the historian of culture. The language of myth allows the deeper layers of history, sacredness, celebration, and feeling to surface from the depths of historical evolution, in a way that descriptive, univocal language cannot.

Hispanic theologians often find the deepest, implicit "theo-logical" and spiritual experiences of their community and culture couched in and enriched by the language of storytelling and myth. Indeed, many of the convoluted thoughts of the Teutonic mind (some of which have been liberally quoted in this essay) can be found, with a wealth of depth and expression, within the framework of myth-language. Hispanic theologians thus feel the summons to engage in a very rigorous, scholarly, and imaginative pursuit of the meanings locked in mythical symbol and metaphor.

3. Poetry. We have offered the concept of the Hispanic theologian as a poet in previous papers and presentations at both the CTSA and ACHTUS. Here we would like to probe deeper into our previous theological reflections concerning this point.

First of all, the idea of the theologian as a poet suggested itself to us from Robert Schreiter's excellent analysis, *Constructing Local Theologies.*[37] Schreiter distinguishes the two functions, the poet and the theologian. Although practicing their respective crafts from within their communities of faith, each has a different mission. On further reflection, it occurred to us that we need not make such a distinction. In fact, in the case of Hispanic theologians plying their craft from the loci of Hispanic faith experiences, *we cannot* separate these two functions.

Theologians have to become, or to be, poets of the community for the same reason that they have a privileged—by dint of their training—although not exclusive, mission to exegete and interpret myth, to bring or help bring to the surface the deeper meanings of the faith community's own symbols, metaphors, and images of hope, sorrow, response to oppression, and awe and wonder before the sacredness of everything human, of everything creational, of everything revelational.

Here we turn again to Heidegger's unique analysis of literature and language—more specifically, to the so-called second phase, or *Kehre* ("turn") of Heidegger's philosophy, when he became concerned with language, poetry, and thought. Kant, Hegel, the pre-Socratics, and Plato began to fade somewhat from Heidegger's writings, and there appeared the poets

Friedrich Hölderlin (1770–1843), Johann Wolfgang von Goethe (1749–1832), Rainer Maria Rilke (1875–1926) and Georg Träkl (1887–1914), among others.[38]

The mission (notice we do not speak of "role" here) of the Hispanic theologian as a poet develops its foundations and draws its profile and nature from the following perspectives:

a. First, we should like to emphatically state that, when we speak of the theologian as a poet, we are not advocating a dilution of the theologian's commitment to rigorous, scientific scholarship. We have argued throughout this essay for the very opposite, for theological professionalism and rigor. Methodological soundness and the poetic mission are not mutually exclusive; rather, they complement each other. To be more accurate, they presuppose each other, simply because, within a Hispanic theological context, scientific theological rigor and poetically-expressed theology are organically interwoven. Moreover, within this perspective, scientific theological study (or scholarship) and poetic/theological language reach and extend beyond the common, conventionally understood meanings of these expressions.

b. The human being can be expressed, ultimately, only through the languages of analogy, symbol, and metaphor. Univocal language is found wanting when the theologian wishes to explore, probe, and eventually express the mystery that is the human person. Hölderlin expressed this in his line: ". . . poetically, man dwells . . ." This is quite true of the faith experiences of the Hispanic communities. Hispanic cultures are, as we have remarked following Carlos Fuentes' insights, cultures of verbal as well as of literary expression, cultures of poets and storytellers and, ultimately, cultures whose deepest layers of humanity, whose most intimate "soul" can only be described by the poet.

c. It is fairly easy to anticipate objections to the above. In times of distress, oppression, urgency for action, what is the poet good for? A pastoral activist, a faith community leader, and even a theologian, yes. But a poet (even a theologian-poet)? Heidegger reminds us that this question has been posed by thinkers from Plato (ca. 428–348 B.C.E.) to Hölderlin himself. Hölderlin answers the question within the framework of his Greek mythology-oriented poetry:

> But they are, you say, like the wine-gods' holy priests
> Who fared from land to land in the holy night?[39]

The metaphors of the "wine-gods" and their "holy priests" speak, in Hölderlin's mind, of the realm of the sacred. For Heidegger, they speak of Being. For a Hispanic theologian, they are symbol/metaphors for the endless quest of the poet attempting to express the ineffable mystery of the graced encounter between the God of Jesus Christ and the men and women whose lives, broken and yet filled with hope, sacramentalize such an encounter. A pre-condition for this, however, is the living experience of Hispanic theologians as immersed in their communities. But this goes beyond mere card-carrying or enrollment. What it demands is best expressed by Hans-Georg Gadamer's notion of the *Zugehörigkeit,* the "belonging-ness" of theologians within their communities. *Belonging-ness* expresses the unique situation of the theologian as someone who, acting neither as a superior mind nor as an authoritarian leader, listens, reflects, voices unspoken concerns, and discerns the spirit of the community, as someone who becomes the transparent mirror that allows the light (the "truth") of the community to shine in a true service of loving self-surrender, of total self-kenosis for others, and for the Other that is the community as a living organism.

d. Finally, the Hispanic theologian's mission as the poet of the community faces the challenge of what Rilke called "the Open."[40] The Open (*Das Öffene*) in Rilke's thought is precisely that alternately veiled and unveiled truth we discussed previously. It is, for Rilke, whose image of God oscillates between mild pantheism and anthropomorphism, an abyss of Being or of Nothingness. For the Hispanic theologian, the Open is simply shorthand for mystery, understood the way Karl Rahner expressed it: God as the total, concealed and unconcealed, *absconditus* and *revelatus,* holy mystery of love.[41] This mystery finds its cipher, its key, in the human person. Each one of us is an indecisive, but ever-so-precious spark of the raging flame of love that is the Trinitarian God, the God of Abraham, Isaac, and Jacob, the God of Jesus Christ. In a very particular way, this is true of the men and women constituting the Hispanic people of God, whose (often broken) lives, individual and communal, reflect the kenotic reality of the Crucified One, whose hopes drink deeply from the font of the Risen One. Ultimately, the very scientific and rigorous mission of the Hispanic theologian as a poet is none other than to articulate, in ever new symbols and metaphors, the ultimately theological and poetic reality of the paschal mystery.

4. Concrete forms of oppression. Just as liberation theologians craft their theologies from the "underside of history," from the plight of the concrete, historical communities they belong to and serve, so must the Hispanic theologians serving the faith communities in the United States build their theological reflections on the brokenness of their respective concrete, historical communities. The understanding of a kenotic christology will have a distinctive mark when it is born out of the plight of a migrant-laborer community, where parents have seen their teenage sons shot to death for involuntarily trespassing into the lands of the oppressor, where workers (whose children depend on them for their very lives) are run over and flattened by the trucks of the oppressor, or where Hispanic women are raped by their overlords, perhaps in sight of their children, and forced to bear their burden even when a new life is forming in their wombs.

Here, of course, is where the objection to the Hispanic theologian's mission as a poet might reach a very high coefficient of emotionalism—and hence of irrationality: "What amount of your suggested poetry will help that laborer, that Hispanic woman, that community crushed under the weight of uncollected harvest? It is not poetry they need, but rather liberating action!!"

Our reply to that is: of course we agree! They need liberating action, not baroque words of counterfeit hope! But liberating action is precisely what the Hispanic theologian's role, as the poet of the community, is all about. The fulfillment of the mission of the poet of the community includes prophetic utterances that should by all means avoid the rigidity that so often ambushes and destroys the best-intentioned efforts of theologians. It is, rather, the language of symbol, metaphor, and images, carefully intertwined with the theological insights coming out of the sources (Scriptures, Tradition, liturgy, etc.) that will allow Hispanic theologians to stand as the prophetic theologians and poets of their communities. Any kind of careful reading of the Hebrew text of Second Isaiah will bear this out: cf. Is 41:17ff.; 43:1; 44:1–3. Luis Alonso-Schökel has stressed the literary beauty and genius of the main author of Second Isaiah, truly an example of a fine theological and poetic mind.[42]

Ultimately, Hispanic theologians can only draw a meaningful, theologically sound and yet historically prophetic theology when they, acting as the voices (although certainly not the only ones!), the ears, the discerning eyes, acting, in sum, as the theologians and poets of the community, immerse themselves as members of that community, and internalize its situation. Theologians can only theologize when the destitution and brokenness of the community are also theirs.

5. Mary, the Mother of Jesus Christ. In a paper on Trinitarian theology and Hispanic culture that I presented at the CTSA's annual meeting in 1990, I introduced the theme of the Hispanic theologian as poet of the community. One of the participants, after much discussion back and forth on the role of Mary vis-à-vis the Trinitarian reality of God, suggested that Mary might be considered the poetess of the Trinity. The idea struck me as original, though theologically problematic. At a second stage of reflection that proposal seems to make more sense. In her self-surrender to God's Word, Mary articulates the innermost depths of God's mystery acting in salvation history, though not, to be sure, in a theological, systematic fashion. Rather, drawing from the wellsprings of her heart, she plunges into an unknown future that somehow, for the young woman of Nazareth, must have loomed frightful (as all unknown futures are) and yet full of God's love and hope.

Here we run into one of the controversial points concerning the role of Mary and its relevance for Hispanic theology. Is the emphasis on Mary's self-surrender to God's will an image that perpetuates the servility and oppression which have plagued Hispanic culture and even Hispanic theology through the years? It all depends, of course, on what we mean by "self-surrender." A self-surrendering person may act by compulsion, or may act freely out of love, even if this demands a leap into a void. The witness of the New Testament—and here we bring forth Joseph Fitzmyer's fine analysis on Mary in Lucan salvation history[43]—points to a self-surrender in love, and love, understood as *agape,* not only flows from an attitude of freedom, but is also the only source of total freedom in a human person. Karl Rahner has pointed out that we have truly loved, as the gospel demands, only when we have expressed our love neither fearing the risks every act of love entails, nor expecting any reward.[44]

Mary then becomes a locus for Hispanic theology when the theologian sees her within the witness of Scripture and the best Tradition, within liturgical celebration and communitary prayer. But theologians can also read the faith and the free, loving self-surrender of Mary in the lives of the men and women forming their communities of faith. The Second Vatican Council reminded us, in different language, that the Marian presence in Christian prayer must always be christocentric and ecclesiotypical. Christocentric because it always points, like a transparent glass window, to the Crucified and Risen One. Ecclesiotypical because the Church and the Churches are called to do what Mary did: listen to the Word, bear it within herself, give it to others, stand in contradiction at the foot of the crosses where so many of the poor, discriminated, and marginalized hang, suspended between heaven and earth, belonging to neither. This, in a fashion, is also what Hispanic theologians find themselves summoned to do: to walk the pathways of the Lord, studded with crosses which always point to the empty tombs by the wayside, on the long journey toward human fulfillment and redemption.

Concluding Remarks

Hispanic theologians must always discern the sources and the loci, distinguishing one from the other, but never losing sight of their organic interdependence.

As they build, dismantle, and then rebuild their theologies, Hispanic theologians must allow the basic, foundational peace flowing from the paschal event of Jesus to enter their heart, fully aware that even in the midst of contradiction and martyrdom, they are echoing, through analogy, symbol, and metaphor, the Word that liberates, redeems, and fulfills.

Hispanic theologians need not be—in fact, most are not—professional poets or literati; but they must develop the poetic sensibility that allows them to look into the deeper layers of the Hispanic faith experience and articulate both the ugliness of pain and oppression, on the one hand, and the beauty of hope and love, on the other.

Finally, Hispanic theologians must be men and women of deeply committed faith, of firmly rooted hope, of freely given and freely received love, able to integrate the question of the sources and the places of Hispanic theology within the unfathomable mystery of the Trinitarian God, the holy mystery of love, *the* source and locus of our own, liberating paschal event.

Notes

1. Aylward Shorter, *Toward a Theology of Inculturation* (Maryknoll, N.Y.: Orbis Books, 1988) 5. The quotation is taken from Clifford Geertz, *The Interpretation of Cultures* (New York, 1975).

2. Ibid., 5.

3. Francis Schüssler Fiorenza, *Foundational Theology: Jesus and the Church* (New York: Crossroad, 1984) 280–281.

4. Orlando Espín and Sixto García, "The Sources of Hispanic Theology," The Catholic Theological Society of America, *Proceedings of the Forty-third Annual Convention* (1988) 122–25.

5. See this approach in several of Jürgen Habermas' main works: *Theory and Praxis* (Boston: Beacon Press, 1973); *Legitimation Crisis* (Boston: Beacon Press, 1971); *The Theory of Communicative Action* (Boston: Beacon Press, 1984, 1987), 2 vols.

6. Second Vatican Council, *Optatam Totius,* 16; *Dei Verbum,* 24.

7. Martin Heidegger, *Über den Humanismus,* 8th ed. (Frankfurt-am-Main: Vittorio Klostemann) 51.

8. Johann Wolfgang von Goethe, *Faust* (Frankfurt-am-Main: Insel Verlag, 1982) 50.

9. Martin Heidegger, *Sein Und Zeit,* 15th ed. (Tübingen: Max Niemyer Verlag, 1979).

10. Cf. for a discussion on this topic, Yves Congar, *La Tradition et les Traditions* (Paris: Fayard, 1960–63) 2 vols.

11. Ibid.

12. Jerome Murphy-O'Connor, "Christological Anthropology in Philippians II:5–11," *Revue Biblique* 83 (1976) 25–50.

13. Fred Dallmayr, "Critical Theory and Reconciliation," in Don Browning and Francis S. Fiorenza, eds., *Habermas, Modernity and Public Theology* (New York: Crossroad, 1992) 119–51. Cf. also note 5, above.

14. Espín and García, "Sources of Hispanic Theology."

15. Sixto García, "A Hispanic Approach to Trinitarian Theology: The Dynamics of Celebration, Reflection and Praxis," in: *We Are a People: Initiatives in Hispanic-American Theology* (Minneapolis: Augsburg Fortress, 1992) 107–32.

16. 1 Cor 11:23ff.

17. Thomas F. O'Meara, "The Future of Catholicism," Inaugural Installation Lecture as Walter K. Warren Professor of Theology, University of Notre Dame, 1986. Cf. also *Popol Vuh,* trans. Dennis Tedlock (New York: Simon and Schuster, 1985).

18. Franz Josef Van Beeck, S.J., *God Encountered: A Contemporary Catholic Systematic Theology,* Vol. 1: Understanding the Christian Faith (New York: Crossroad, 1988) 208–67.

19. Karl Rahner, *Love of Jesus, Love of Neighbor* (New York: Crossroad, 1988) 47–60, 83–95.

20. 1 Cor 11:29.

21. Van Beeck, *God Encountered,* 211–18.

22. Ibid., 219. The quotation is from Van Beeck's *Christ Proclaimed: Christology as Rhetoric* (New York: Paulist Press, 1979) 328.

23. Martin Heidegger, *An Introduction to Metaphysics* (New Haven: Yale University Press, 1976) 102–5.

24. John Henry Newman, *An Essay on the Development of Christian Doctrine* (Westminster, Md.: Christian Classics, 1968).

25. Carlos Fuentes, *The Buried Mirror: Reflections on Spain and the New World* (Boston: Houghton Mifflin, 1992).

26. Ibid., 341–55.

27. Ibid., 342.

28. Ibid., 343.

29. Ibid., 346.

30. Ibid., 343.

31. Ibid., 342–43.

32. Ibid., 344.

33. Ibid.

34. Ibid., 346.

35. Ibid., 346–47.

36. Ibid., 347.

37. Robert Schreiter, *Constructing Local Theologies* (Maryknoll, N.Y.: Orbis Books, 1985) 18–19.

38. Martin Heidegger, *On the Way to Language* (San Francisco: Harper and Row, 1971). Cf. also Heidegger's *Poetry, Language, Thought* (San Francisco: Harper Colophon Books, 1971).

39. Heidegger, *Poetry, Language, Thought,* 94.

40. Ibid., 106–7.

41. Cf. this designation in many of Rahner's works. A summary treatment is in Rahner's *Grundkurs des Glaubens: Einführung in den Begriffs des Christentums* (Freiburg: Herder, 1976) 54–96.

42. Cf. Luis Alonso Schökel, "Introdución al Segundo Isaías," in: Luis Alonso Schökel and Juan Mateos, *Nueva Biblia Española* (Madrid: Cristiandad, 1986).

43. Joseph Fitzmyer, *Luke the Theologian: Aspects of his Thought* (Mahwah, N.J.: Paulist Press) 57–85.

44. Ibid., 83–85.

7

Ana María Pineda

Ana María Pineda was born in El Salvador, Central America. She is a member of the Sisters of Mercy's Regional Community of Burlingame and the Institute of the Sisters of Mercy of the Americas. She obtained the equivalent of a doctorate in ministry (DMin) at the Jesuit School of Theology at Berkeley, California in 1985, her masters in theology (MA) from the Catholic Theological Union in Chicago in 1987, and in 1991 at the Universidad Pontificia de Salamanca, Spain her doctorate (STD) in pastoral theology.

Like many Latino/a theologians, Pineda has a background both in professional academic life and pastoral ministry. Since 1976, she has worked extensively in Latino ministry as teacher, pastoral associate, and diocesan associate director of Latino ministry. She worked with the *Movimiento Familiar Cristiano, Encuentro conyugales/matrimoniales,* leadership formation programs, and the *Encuentro Nacional de Pastoral Hispano* (1977, 1985). Most of this ministry was in the San Jose and San Francisco, California area. Presently she is assistant professor of pastoral theology and director of Hispanic ministry at the Catholic Theological Union in Chicago.

Pineda has co-edited a book and a journal in theology and published nine articles. She writes on topics of Hispanic identity in the U.S., women from a Latina perspective, and orality in the Latino traditions. Nationally, she is a frequent lecturer on U.S. Latino issues. She is a member of the Academy of Catholic Hispanic Theologians in the United States.

Catholic Theological Union
5401 S. Cornell Avenue
Chicago, Illinois 606115-5698
312-324-8000
Fax 312-423-4360

Pastoral de Conjunto

Ana María Pineda

In many sectors of the Christian world, the anticipation of the year 1992 marks the commemoration of five hundred years of Evangelization in the "New World," recalling for many the expansion of Christianity and the evangelization of the indigenous peoples of that land. This historical event will be commemorated in many different ways. A major site for recounting the significance of that event will be that of Sevilla in Spain. Here stands the *Archivo General de Indias* that contains the massive collection of detailed accounts of the discovery, the colonization and evangelization of America. No doubt the commemoration of 1992 will awaken a renewed interest in the authors of these chronicles, inviting reconsideration of the era and its subsequent contributions to both Christianity and the Western world. This is valid.

There is yet another approach that if taken would further enrich the commemoration of the same event, and that is to somehow give voice to the peoples who were the objects of colonization and evangelization in 1492. Who did they become as a result of history, and what contribution were they able to make to that new venture brought about by the *Conquista?* Information of this nature will not be found in the chronicles of Sevilla; that was not their purpose nor their perspective. One of the sources for such information can be the descendants of that people among us here in the U.S., which would give opportunity for Hispanic Catholics, cultural products of that encounter to speak about the contributions that they are making in today's Church and society. This article will address one such contribution by singling out from among many others the pastoral term *pastoral de conjunto,* a term representative of the historical process of evangelization which has occurred among U.S. Hispanic Catholics since 1972. It marks the genius of U.S. Hispanic catholicism, but how is this so? Where does the term *pastoral de conjunto* come from? What does it

"Pastoral de Conjunto," *New Theology Review* 3:4 (November 1990), pp. 28–34. Reprinted with permission.

mean? How has it affected the understanding of church among Hispanics? What is its contribution to the church and society today?

History of a Concept

Pastoral de Conjunto as a concept is not new. It is rooted in the Gospel imperative of communion and unity. It permeates the Vatican II deliberations as it underscores communion and catholicity. It is explicitly stated in the documents of Medellin and Puebla.

It was Medellin's serious and realistic examination of the situation in Latin America in light of Vatican II that led the Latin American hierarchy to acknowledge the poverty of the masses caused by the existing social and political structures. This grave reality challenged the Latin American church to consider anew the mission of the church to bring all humankind to the fullness of communion of life with God. In order to be faithful to its mission, conversion of persons and structures would be urgent. The common salvific activity of the church needed to be directed in such a way as to bring about the transformation of society and of itself as the family of God. The document of Medellin explained that this could only be accomplished by using an integrated approach to pastoral work. The diverse ministries not only must be at the service of the unity of communion, but in doing so must constitute itself and act in solidarity (CELAM, 1968: #7, 219). Ten years later, the conference held in Puebla addressed in part the experience of conflict occurring in pastoral activity due often to a lack of overall integration, lack of community support, the lack of sufficient preparation for work in the social sphere, or the lack of maturity in dealing with such experiences (CELAM, 1979: #122). In order to avoid such conflict, it was necessary to encourage groups, communities, and movements to work consciously toward a pastoral style that stressed coordination and collaboration. This required that all the persons concerned participate at every level in a reflective process of faith which led to praxis. As a consequence of such reflection, the document of Puebla is able to describe the concept of *pastoral de conjunto* as: "A well-planned pastoral effort is the specific, conscious, deliberate response to the necessities of evangelization. It should be implemented through a process of participation at every level of the communities and persons concerned. They must be taught how to analyze reality, how to reflect on this reality from the standpoint of the Gospel, how to choose the most suitable objectives and means, and how to use them in the most sensible way for the work of evangelization" (CELAM: 1307). Chronologically, however, the Conference held in Puebla in 1979 was preceded by the *II Encuentro Nacional Hispano de Pastoral* in the United States in 1977.

The Term *"Pastoral de Conjunto"*

The term *pastoral de conjunto* took on special significance for U.S. Hispanic Catholics during the process of pastoral assessment initiated by the national convocation of Hispanic lay and religious leaders known as the *Encuentro Nacional Hispano de Pastoral* held in 1972, 1977, and 1985. The *Encuentros* sought to give voice to a disenfranchised sector of the U.S. Catholic church. In doing so, it stressed the importance of each person and of the community at large in living and being church. The process of the *Encuentros* required broad participation by the people, small communities, and small groups; team work; integration of different pastoral areas; a common vision; interrelating among the dioceses, regions, and the national level; openness to the needs of the people and to the universality of the church (NCCB/USCC, 1987: 6). As a consequence of such a challenging process, Hispanics experienced what it meant to live the church as communion. It is within this context that the term *pastoral de conjunto* begins to appear in the documents of the *Encuentro Nacional Hispano de Pastoral*. The search to belong to the church—not only by virtue of their long-standing tradition of faith, but as fully incorporated family members with all of the accompanying rights and responsibilities—had led Hispanic Catholics to appropriate the term *pastoral de conjunto* that had been used in the Medellin documents, but now contextualizing it in the actuality of their experience.

Pastoral de conjunto is a rich and challenging term. Simple translation does not do it justice. Nevertheless, the need to convey its meaning, led to the formulation of a definition as used in the *Hispanic National Pastoral Plan:*

> It is the harmonious coordination of all the elements of the pastoral ministry with the actions of the pastoral ministers and structures in view of a common goal: the Kingdom of God. It is not only a methodology, but the expression of the essence and mission of the Church, which is to be and to make communion. (NCCB/USCC, 1987: 28)

The literal translation which is sometimes offered in English is that of "organized pastoral effort." This definition seems to stress the practical dimension of the term. In order to understand the term in its fullness, it is important to reflect on the goal of *pastoral de conjunto*.

Goal of *Pastoral de Conjunto*

The primary concern of *pastoral de conjunto* in the task of evangelization is not pastoral efficiency. Its primary importance is that it is a methodology that places itself at the service of the Kingdom of God and assists the faithful in its announcement and realization. It invites the people of God to commit themselves actively to continue the work of Jesus by entering into the cultural, religious, and social reality of the people, becoming incarnate in and with the people (NCCB/USCC, 1987: 6). The bringing about of the Kingdom that Jesus proclaimed is ultimately the goal of *pastoral de conjunto.* Everything that this pastoral concept and approach seeks to achieve has value insofar as it facilitates the carrying out of the mission of the Church in making evermore present the Kingdom of God, a Kingdom furthered by the church's relentless preaching and testimony for the need of conversion, the affirmation of the dignity of the human person, and the seeking of ways to eradicate personal sin, oppressive structures, and forms of injustice (NCCB/USCC 1987: 6).

In view of this common goal, pastoral ministers and structures are urged to place all of their efforts and existing resources in responding to this goal. However, this calls all pastoral ministers and structures to enter into communion among themselves; to move away from a posture of individualism and competition to one of harmonious coordination of all that they have at their disposal in order to further the goal—the Kingdom of God. Such action necessitates a conversion of persons and structures, a willingness to live the church as communion by entering into communion with each other. *Pastoral de conjunto* is then not only a methodology used to arrive at the goal, but a methodology to which one can be faithful only if it is grappled with in the context of daily living. To do otherwise is to suggest the erroneous belief that faith and daily life exist as two separate entities.

The Model of Church

As a result of living out the dynamism of *pastoral de conjunto,* the Hispanic people grow into an understanding of what model of Church they desire. This model might be described as one in which everyone feels at home as in a family—where interpersonal relations and fraternal love are the norm and not the exception, a community wherein its members are supported in living their faith and in accepting the need for conversion. Communities of faith are nourished by prayer and made conscious of their responsibilities in society and to those in that society most in need. Such a church questions the injustice in society and accepts its responsibility to change it. The journey of a *Pueblo de Dios en Marcha* fleshes out for U.S. Hispanic Catholics a model of church which is communitarian, evangelizing, and missionary; incarnate in the reality of Hispanic people and open to the diversity of cultures; a promoter and example of justice; active in developing leadership through integral education; leaven for the Kingdom of God in society (NCCB/USCC, 1987: 8). This model of church can be promoted and lived by means of a *pastoral de conjunto.*

Contributions of U.S. Hispanic Catholics

The years following the convocation of the *I Encuentro* in 1972 provided Hispanics the time needed to deepen earlier insights that had resulted from their reflection on their social and pastoral reality. The result was the creation of pastoral concepts and terminology which gave expression to their experience as a people. The articulation of this experience of faith is a valuable contribution offered by Hispanics to the church and society. It is a contribution that integrates the best of Hispanic cultural values with those of the Gospel. This process of pastoral theologizing and implementation shows how cultural values can be placed at the service of the Gospel. It affirms the mystery of the Incarnation, and in doing so upholds the dignity of the human person and the uniqueness with which God blesses each culture. *Pastoral de conjunto* is a concept rooted in Gospel values and in the cultural values that a people espouse as ways of expressing what is most cherished in their relationship to others, to the world and ultimately to God.

The National Catholic Conference of Bishops issued a pastoral letter on December 12, 1983 entitled *The Hispanic Presence: Challenge and Commitment.* In it they indicated that Hispanics exemplify and cherish values central to the service of Church and society (NCCB/USCC, 1987: 3). Among the values listed were those of profound respect for the dignity of each person, reflecting the example of Christ in the Gospels; deep and reverential love for family life, where the entire family discovers its roots, its dignity, and its strength; a marvelous sense of community; loving appreciation for God's gift of life (NCCB/USCC, 1987: 3–4). These values have been nourished by God's Word and the life-giving images of Scripture. The flight into Egypt has special significance for those dispossessed. Jesus' concern for the blind, the lame, the imprisoned, the leper, the Samaritan woman are strong messages of the universality of the Kingdom of God, and the respect owed to all. The constant invitation for unity expressed by God's word—that all may be one—is lived out in the reality of the extended family. The extension of hospitality to the stranger and those in need is readily understood by a people who believe that the concept of family is all-inclusive. The existence of the family relies on its interdependence, and the gifts of each member are put to the service of the common good (1 Cor 12:12). The living out of these cultural values has enabled Hispanics to enflesh their model of church and to create the means to promote it—*pastoral de conjunto*.

Conclusion

In a society fragmented by individualism, competition, consumerism, violence, and blatant disregard for human dignity, the concept and methodology of *pastoral de conjunto* is a contribution that Hispanics make to the church and society. It calls for an interdependence of the faithful, based on genuine respect and regard for all. This requires an explicit affirmation of the concept of cultural pluralism in the Church within a fundamental unity of doctrine (NCCB/USCC, 1987: 2). As a methodology, *pastoral de conjunto* moves the faithful toward communion and universality. It provides a pedagogy that requires continuous dialogue among the faithful as an essential dimension in pastoral planning. While it acknowledges the diversity of ministries within the church, it also underscores the mission of all the baptized to evangelize. The experience of living out *pastoral de conjunto* has shaped a model of church for Hispanics which integrates the best of their cultural values with that of Gospel values. Ultimately, *pastoral de conjunto* signals to a model of church that implicitly recognizes both the sense of the faithful and hierarchical teaching as essential elements in the articulation of the faith (NCCB/USCC, 1983: 13). This in part marks the genius of U.S. Hispanic Catholicism.

References

CELAM
  1968 *Medellin.* Mexico: Libreria Parroquial.
CELAM
  1979 *Puebla.* Mexico: Libreria Parroquial. Eagleson, John & Scharper, Philip (eds.)
NCCB/USCC
  1977 *II Encuentro Nacional Hispano de Pastoral: Conclusions.* Washington: Secretariat for Hispanic Affairs.
NCCB/USCC
  1984 *The Hispanic Presence: Challenge and Commitment.* Washington: USCC.
NCCB/USCC
  1987 *National Pastoral Plan for Hispanic Ministry.* Washington: USCC.

8

Harold J. Recinos

Harold J. Recinos was born of a Puerto Rican mother and Guatemalan father in New York and raised in the South Bronx. He is an ordained United Methodist minister and pastor of a Latino parish on the lower east side of Manhattan, New York. After seven years in the local church, in 1987 he joined the Wesley Seminary faculty.

Professor Recinos received his masters in divinity (MDiv) in 1982 from Union Theological Seminary, a doctorate of ministry (DMin) in parish ministry in 1986 from New York Theological Seminary and a doctorate (PhD) in cultural anthropology in 1993 from the American University in Washington, D.C.

In his writings and lectures, Recinos focuses on the politics of Salvadoran Refugees' popular religion, and on the need for the church and theology to become credible by engaging in solidarity with those suffering on the periphery of life. He was named one of four Latino theologians who initiated a novel paradigm for Latino theology in the U.S. termed "*barrio* theology."

Presently, Recinos is professor of theology, culture and urban ministry at Wesley Theological Seminary in Washington, D.C. He was awarded the first annual Oscar Romero Award by the Liberation Resource Center at Wesley Theological Seminary in 1989, the Recognition Award by the *Escuela Teologica Para Ministerios Hispanos* in 1994, the Southeast Jurisdiction Urban Network Award in 1993, and most recently "*Latino de la Semana*" by the Washington D.C.-based *El Tiempo Latino* in 1994.

Wesley Theological Seminary
4500 Massachusetts Avenue N.W.
Washington, D.C. 20016-5690
202-885-8600

Mission: A Latino Pastoral Theology

Harold Recinos

The church was called into being to continue the mission of Jesus in the context of a world in need of hope and liberation. What is the mission and purpose of the church? How has the church interpreted its mission within the totality of human existence? Whose interests has it served? Have the poor had good news preached to them? Do persons crippled by socially structured oppression walk? Do the blind to human suffering regain sight? Do the deaf to the cries of the little ones hear? Can the church present itself before wretched humanity and claim to have lived out the call of the human being from Nazareth? The foundation upon which these questions rest is the knowledge of God. The Scriptures teach us that true knowledge of God means doing justice to the poor and the oppressed. Nothing is more fundamental to the mission of the church than this "gnosis" and practice of faith. The God of the patriarchs, the exodus, of Mary's Magnificat, and Jesus' empty tomb is not interested in solemn assemblies. Instead, the God who is partisan to the poor's struggle to transform radically the social relations of history in the direction of justice desires a mission concerned with letting ". . . justice roll down like waters, and righteousness like an everflowing stream" (Amos 5:24). God can never be known apart from the practice of justice and love on behalf of those in the underside of history.

The silence of the North American Latino church caused by its over-whelmingly privatized Christianity must be broken. We have been a church made up of the poor, but lacking the social voice that comes from below. That silence leads to the condemnation of history's underside to the wretched suffering of Golgotha. Churches that no longer believe that it is important to examine their liturgies, prayers, worship life, and Christian practice from the perspective of their relationship to the suffering poor are living a false piety—the spirituality of solemn assemblies! The church dare not forget that only a God who suffers can save. Jesus of Nazareth

"Mission: A Latino Pastoral Theology," *Apuntes* 3 (Fall 1992), pp. 115–126. Reprinted with permission.

from Galilee taught followers of the *way* that much. The church must never forget that in Jesus God's word became flesh in the form of a poor human being who lived in Galilee, a geographical area that had little significance even in the time of Solomon. God becomes one of the world's outcasts by virtue of the Galilean incarnation. Virgilio Elizondo, in an important theological reflection on the significance of Galilee for both divine revelation and the mission of the church, said: "One cannot follow the way of the Lord without appreciating the scandalous way of Jesus the Galilean."[1] The church dare not continue to cultivate the Jesus of the unscandalous cross and turn its back on the reality of socially organized suffering in the Latino community. For the church to know God and remain faithful to its missionary vocation it must walk with the poor in the service of justice.

The Latino church in the U.S. has witnessed the emergence of a mission revitalization movement on the horizon of global history that has been defining what it means to walk with the God who suffers with the poor. This mission renewal movement is rooted in the experience of Christians in Latin America, Africa, and Asia. Without doubt history's underside—Latin America, Africa, and Asia—is laying the foundation for Christianity into the next millennium. Today's church universal is captive of a mission renewal movement that requires that the once muted cry of wretched humanity be heard in terms of its salvific message for all. Today, the Latino church on this side of the Río Grande finds itself in the position of listening to new voices, viewing new existential experiences, examining new theological interpretations of the faith tradition, and considering liberationist embodiments of ethical activity. The scandalous way of Jesus the Galilean means that society's "non-persons" determine what is ultimate for the practice of faith.

The North American Latino religious community has evolved quite independently of the liberationist tradition on the other side of the Río Grande. More recently, the hermeneutical revolution of the liberationist tradition institutionalized at Medellín (1968) and Puebla (1979) has begun to shape faith perspectives in some sub-divisions of the North American Latino church. For the most part, our Latino church experience in the context of the States, possessed by the legacy of 19th century North Atlantic missionary theology, has operated out of a hermeneutics of passive submission to white society. The profoundest expression of this fact is to be found in a preponderant pietistic tradition that insists on inspiring an escape from reality into an inner personal faith experience. The Latino church in the U.S. must lose its privatized Christian posture and develop a hermeneutics rooted in its historical experience of oppression and poverty.[2] The poor hold the interpretive key to humanity's relationship to God in Jesus Christ. Through them the Latino church learns that life can be structured in such a way as to reflect the intentions of the gospel for human society and for the individual.

Rediscovering our identity in the existential reality of oppression means understanding that Christian missionary activity today entails action directed toward the structural transformation of society in the direction of God's reign.[3] The Latino church in the U.S. cannot afford to follow the theological criteria of "white society" that keep one personally neutral before history. Latinos in the U.S. religious community must rediscover God and Christ as the liberators of human history on behalf of the poor. Our missiological approach in the world demands understanding rigorous social, economic, political historical, and cultural analysis. The Latino church in the U.S. must devote itself to the God who created people for freedom (Gen 1:26)—not to be dehumanized and crushed daily! Our church must be prepared at any moment to embody the political vocation of ministry and say no to all forms of cultural, political, economic, social, and theological domination that engender wretched existence in the Latino community. The Latino church in the U.S. must both socialize its understanding of the gospel and confront "white society" with God's requirements of justice. Allow me to share this reflection written on another occasion about the mission of the Latino church:

> The Latino church in the U.S. must reflect on its role in North Atlantic society in light of the experience of oppression in white society. It must discover the political import of God's preferential option for the poor. It must serve as a light for others, enabling white society to see the context of the barrio and the human disfigurement it represents.[4]

The cry of humanity caused by human decisions and organized structures requires that the gospel be made credible to society's "non-persons" in the form of prophetically structured ethical engagement. The Latino church in the U.S. is being challenged by its sister church tradition of transformation of the south to take an active and responsible role in the transformation of structured evil in the direction of organized justice and love.[5] Churches that are blind and silent in the face of the human suffering of the poor in the U.S. are being asked to see the great events of history from the perspective of the outcasts; the powerless; rejected humanity; the death-toll from wars in Central America; the junkie on the corner; the homeless family of a shanty-town of an urban ghetto; the unemployment line; the redlight districts of local prostitutes; the AIDS patient's bed; pregnant teenagers; the town prison; the culturally isolated and poor refugee family; the broken home; the high-school dropout. God-in-Jesus Christ viewed history from such a perspective. Bearing witness to God-in-Jesus Christ means taking responsibility for the organization of historical experience in society from the existential reality of those below. The practice of Jesus requires that the church root its identity and action in the experiential context of the poor.

Christ walks the village streets of Central and South America and the barrio alleyways of the U.S. Christ continues to place himself at the service of the reign of God in the struggle of history's forgotten persons for a more humane world. We are reminded today by our brothers and sisters of the Church of the Southern hemisphere that Christ died to give life to the poor and those who stand with them. In the context of North American Latino experience, this means that Jesus eats today at the table of the hungry; Christ spills his blood with the little García girl shot to death by a stray bullet from a drug pusher's gun; the Galilean Lord bears on his arms the needle tracks of those who repeatedly inject themselves with dope; the carpenter from Galilee lies on a hospital bed forgotten by family and friends and eaten away by AIDS; the Word made flesh shivers on cold winter nights with the homeless and rejected refugees living in abandoned buildings, parks, and shanty-towns; and the wounded Son of God weeps with the mothers of the disappeared of both Latin America and *el barrio*. The God who is identified with the poor constitutes the proper subject of adoration for the Latino church in the U.S. If we listen closely to God's word for us today, we hear that the Christian vocation for the Latino church in the U.S. is best understood when the church walks with Christ along unconventional avenues that cut a path to God's reign already present in the poor's struggle for justice and life.

The profound meaning of the word made flesh in a Galilean Jew who himself was a member of an oppressed class and race will become rediscovered once the Latino church rereads its mission and purpose in the world from the perspective of its own experience with oppression, injustice, and poverty. Jesus of Nazareth from Galilee took upon himself the flesh of poverty and historical rejection (Phi 2:5–9) to overcome the things that are. Rereading the mission of the church from the perspective of marginal humanity will enable the church to discover that authentic Christian pastoral activity means participating in God's struggle to right the human condition by enabling trampled humanity to know historical salvation. The mission of the Latino church in the U.S. at the close of the second millennium requires embracing the God of Mary's Magnificat who scattered the proud in the imagination of their hearts, put down the mighty from their places of homicidally structured power, and raised the poor in history to become instruments of divine salvation for all humanity (Lk 1:51–52).

The practice of Jesus made followers critically aware of the structures of systemic oppression operating in Roman-occupied Palestinian society.[6] Our church is required to embody a practice of faith no less capable of making the faith community critically aware of the oppressive structures at the root of Latino suffering. The Latino church in the U.S. must incarnate itself in history as a Christ-centered institution of social criticism and agent of social structural transformation. This means that its leadership must initiate in their respective communities a process of issue identification, consciousness-raising, and leadership development. Connecting the rereading of missionary identity to the process of liberating pedagogy will produce church communities better able to understand that the parenthood of God and the equality of all persons means that social inequality, human injustice, economic exploitation, racism and sexism, "language-ism" or the attempt to absolutize a single linguistic modality, and wretched poverty are scandalous to God.

The Church Reinvented

Latin American base Christian communities have a great deal to teach the Latino church in the U.S. Base communities have helped Christians struggling against oppression in the context of Latin American society define faith beyond strictly private and individual terms. Personal faith is understood in light of the larger social reality in which the poor live. The role of faith is to create a movement for just change that begins from the bottom. Poor Christians in Latin America are restructuring the status quo church in light of a rereading of scripture which recognizes the privilege of the poor and oppressed in the reign of God (I Cor 1:27–28; Mt 25). Base Christian communities have taken the Bible and organized the poor around bible study, worship and community works. Out of this simple faith approach the missional reinvigoration of God's people has been made possible. The base Christian communities constitute a growing social movement that is attempting to restructure both society and the church in the direction of God's reign of justice, love, and community. The social appropriation of Scripture has enabled poor Christians in Latin America to participate in revolutionary processes demanding liberation from structured conditions of oppression.[7]

The Latino church in the U.S. might consider the base Christian community model of church in its attempt to struggle with the question of social justice in the context of the ghetto. The churches' leadership should take pains not to mystify the base community ecclesial model. Many Latino churches in the U.S. have operated out of a model of church organized around Bible study, prayer and community work. The fundamental difference between the barrio and the base Christian experience of Latin American society rests in the experiential framework of *conscientization*. What has been lacking in the *barrio* base Christian experience is the element of critical assessment and active engagement with social reality at a level capable of impacting the structures of "white society." The base Christian community model of church coming out of the context of Latin American society can be utilized to enable the *barrio* poor to reappropriate the basic structure of the biblical story: God identifies with the poor and oppressed by choosing their side, and God participates in their struggle to be liberated from the dehumanizing conditions of ghetto existence. The Christian life is more than a private apolitical existence waiting for ultimate fulfillment in God "up there." It requires confrontation with power in history where the blood of our people is exacted daily to fuel the homicidal structures of capitalism.

Radicalizing the faith perspective of the Latino church in North America means encountering the God of the poor and bearing witness to God's word of liberation in the context of a world structured to promote oppression, alienation and human suffering. Faith must be put back into history. The base Christian communities understand that faithfulness to Jesus of Nazareth means identification with the justice struggles of the poor, marginal, despised persons of color, an underside of society. Jesus' ministry did not focus on society's respectable members. Instead, he went directly to society's outcasts offering them life in abundance and an opportunity to participate in the transformation of their world. Giving the base Christian community model the specifications of the North American Latino community will issue forth in renewed faith insight into the mystery of God. The Latino church on this side of the Río Grande will learn that an authentic proclamation of a God who loves persons includes effective opposition to those forms of society that crush persons each day. God has chosen the wretched of the earth to conduct a liberative process encompassing the rich and poor in a single historical stream not characterized by the concentration of wealth, but its redistribution.[8]

A deep sense of communion between persons characterizes the base community experience.[9] The Bible is discovered in that context in terms of its radicality. Persons are enabled by this reading of Scripture out of their own experience of oppression to feel empowered and emerge subjects of history. A liberation missiology is at the heart of the small grass-roots communities. Social engagement flows from the spiritual conviction that God is an advocate of the poor, that the integrity of faith is measured by our action toward securing the well-being of the marginal, and that economic systems are to be judged in terms of their relation to the poor. The base Christian communities speak directly to the Latino church of North America, challenging it to develop a social, economic, and political analysis by which it can link faith to empowerment. Theology in the context of the barrio must make it clear to the faith community that God's promise of a new heaven runs counter to the dehumanization and social invisibility that mark the existential experience of the ghetto; hence, an important dimension of the mission of the Latino church in the U.S. includes enabling people to discover their own power. Here I recall the words of Virgilio Elizondo:

> An important element of this new power is that it is not power for the sake of personal gain, but power for the sake of all the oppressed, ignored, forgotten, and exploited members of society. The powerless are recouping power, but it is not the power of this world, which works for self-gain, but the power of the gospel, which works for the betterment and liberation of all, especially those in greatest need.[10]

The poor of the base Christian communities have opted against capitalism. The value system that capitalism generates is characterized by a
pattern of social irresponsibility, inhumanity to other persons, and desire
for private gain. These values are contrary to the will of God and the
imperatives of the gospel of Jesus from Nazareth of Galilee. The grass-
roots communities are living out the very faith of our Galilean Lord by
engaging in the prophetic denunciation of a system of political economy
that condemns so many to the violence of Golgotha. Members of the base
Christian communities believe the capitalist system is an incurable disease.
Das Kapital is not the root of this insight; rather, the reading of the biblical
story of God's struggle to right oppression and exploitation in history
constitutes the source of prophetic revelation.

For the Latino church in the U.S. prophetic denunciation of a political
economic system that organizes death for its people is essential. Indeed,
we do well to remember how closely linked to the capitalist system are
the majority of the Latino community's 65 newspapers, 200 radio stations,
and 167 television stations.[11] The Christian Right broadcast system seduces
Latinos in the U.S. into linking their faith to the conservative Right agenda
with no thought about the implications for the *barrio* and the people of Latin
America. Our prophetic denunciation of capitalism includes indicating the
disservice the communication media are rendering to the Latino struggle
for justice. The leadership of the Latino church must seize the freedom
God has provided to it in the pulpit and help persons to see that the
requirements of capitalism and the imperatives of the gospel are incompati-
ble. Only the politics of equality and the economics of justice should fuel
the missionary energy of the Latino church in this land. Our responsibility
involves linking Christian ethical activity in the *barrio* and the village
streets of Latin America to a single focus of prophetic endeavor.[12]

Mission Outlook

Latinos in the context of the U.S. have been marginated from the centers
of social, political, and economic power. "White/Black society" ignores
the fact that about three-fourths of all Mexican Americans, half the Puerto
Rican community, one-fourth of all Cubans, and twenty-percent of the
Central and South American populations were born in the U.S. Moreover,
the Latino community in the U.S. represents one of the fastest growing
groups in America given high birth rates (fifty-percent higher than the
U.S. average) and the flow of immigration. Latinos have a young age
structure with a median age of 26, compared to 32 for non-Latinos.[13] What
stands behind the situation of Latino invisibility in North American society?
The bi-racial structure of North American society has contributed a great
deal to our marginalization and veiled existence. From the time of the
Civil War fought between the North and the South the mind of "white
society" has perceived issues of oppression through black/white lenses.

The Mexican/American War has not commanded a similar response. Latinos have remained largely an invisible community in North America despite the fact that all the territory from Colorado to California once belonged to Mexico. Moreover, "white" and "black" societies have yet to recognize that the North American principles of civil disobedience propounded for modernity by Henry David Thoreau were forged around a Latin American issue—the U.S. expansionist war with Mexico.

History has assigned the Latino church in the U.S. the role of prophetic missionary in the New Macedonia of "white/black society."[14] Latino institutions need to impact "white/black society" in such a way that a more comprehensive understanding will issue forth in the North American mind concerning the existential situation of oppression and the need for liberation: First, the Latino church can help to "de-americanize" the gospel of Jesus of Nazareth so that the good news is prevented from being "comfort for the oppressor" and an "opiate for the oppressed." Second, the Latino church in the U.S. must help itself and "white/black society" understand the relationship between the structured evil dominating both the life of the Latino in the barrio and on the other side of the Río Grande. Third, Latino grass-roots church communities must be empowered to develop a global consciousness that fully questions the U.S. presumed right to create the conditions for big business to "rob" and "exploit." Fourth, the Latino church in the U.S. must participate in the struggle of its brothers and sisters to the south directed toward the dismantlement of the "national security" ideology that justifies human brutalization each day.[15]

Other related dimensions of the political vocation of Latino mission out of the context of the U.S. include ministry to the pain and brokenness of our people in the ghetto. Faith witness in the context of the *barrio* needs to make real for people the God who brings life out of death, and hope out of despair. More than a million refugees from Central America are residing in the U.S. experiencing poverty, cultural isolation, and fear of discovery. The Salvadoran community alone represents about half of the estimated refugee population in the U.S. Most Salvadorans came after 1982, following the escalation of the war in El Salvador, which means that the amnesty clause of the regressive Immigration Reform and Control Act (1986) did very little to improve their situation in the U.S. Less than two-percent of all political asylum petitions filed by a Salvadoran or Guatemalan are granted, due to opposition from the State Department. Granting political asylum to a Central American would be the equivalent of U.S. foreign policy "self-condemnation."

Salvadorans and Guatemalans are bearing witness to the brutalization of humanity occurring in Central America by giving testimony in our *barrio* churches. The Latino church in the U.S. dare not close its ears to the cry of the people of Central America bellowing in the context of the *barrio*. From our Guatemalan brothers and sisters we hear that since the mid-60's, with the support of the U.S. government, the Guatemalan regime has killed more than a hundred thousand civilians. Eighty to one hundred persons disappear each month to this day. The cry of El Salvador reaches the ears of Latino Christians in the *barrio* by way of the voices of five hundred thousand refugees who tell of over seventy thousand deaths in El Salvador since the early-80's. We can remember the words of Archbishop Romero broadcast over the diocesan radio and directed to the soldiers, words ordering the soldiers to stop the repression, and which cost his life: "In the name of God, in the name of our tormented people who have suffered so much and whose laments cry out to heaven, I beseech you, I beg you, I order you, I order you in the name of God, to stop the repression."[16]

The North American Latino church's mission involves advocating the cause of Central American refugees within U.S. society and church denominational structures. Worship services ought to reflect the refugee presence in faith communities. All levels of the church should be engaged in examining the plight of the refugee in the U.S. and the effect the new immigration law is having on them. Local faith communities should network with immigrant and refugee rights organizations to strengthen their advocacy role for changes in U.S. foreign and immigration policy. Latino churches in the context of the *barrio* ought to look seriously at the role of sanctuary and immigration law paralegal training as mission responses.[17] Undoubtedly, understanding the mission of the church in these prophetic terms means entering an arena of history characterized by conflict with conservative forces within the church who would prefer to serve the bully interests of a life-denying status quo. Our role is to adore the God identified with the refugees and their struggle at all costs. Borrowing a phrase from Julia Esquivel's poem, *Thanksgiving Day in the United States,* the U.S. Latino church's role is not to be deceived into worshipping ". . . the Beast in the Bank of America or in others of its temples."[18]

The streets of the *barrio* invite the Latino church to a life of prophetic mission. Signs of despair pervade the streets waiting for the winds of hope and transformation. On the *barrio* streets it is not difficult to tell that between 1979 and 1987 poverty in the Latino community increased ninety-percent. In that period of time, the ranks of the Latino poor grew from 2.9 million to 5.5 million.[19] The latter represent approximately one-fourth of the estimated twenty million Latinos in the U.S. You know it is easy to find the four out of every ten Latino youths who drop out of high school hanging around the street corner at any given time. Some of them are hooked on dope and filled with a sense of futurelessness. Allow me to share this poem inspired by one of these youths and the system of oppression that held him captive on the corner:

Been Waiting

Rudy's been waiting on the corner for his big hit,
he's been waiting now for ten years and the tracks
in his arms where Señora Heroina does come quiets

him for the wait while promising a more complete
destiny someday, he's been waiting for the lover he
dreams of, for bitterness to run away, for a blade
of grass to grow from the crack in the sidewalk that
he stares at in the wait, for Orchard Beach
to be in his pocket so he can reach in for a calm
feel to living; he's been waiting for the welfare
check, for the roaches to take a walk from his one
room where there ain't no food no way.

he's been waiting to kick a jones he doesn't have,
for his mother who long ago said good-bye, for his
country to be born in him, he's been waiting for
Lelo, who left the waiting corner to join the navy
and kick his brothers' asses down in Vieques under
orders just to live, he's been waiting for spring

and summer and fall and forget about winter because
the corner is cold, he's been waiting for the right
time of day or night to think about waiting some more.

Junkies like Rudy have a three times greater risk of contracting the
deadly disease AIDS than do whites. Sadly, most Latino churches in the
barrio have not been conduits of God's love offering hope, friendship,
justice advocacy, and community.

The question of language is another area for the Latino church to develop
a focused pastoral response. Spanish is one of the most strongly maintained
ethnic languages in the U.S.; however, linguistic personality alone can no
longer decide one's legitimate claim to Latino cultural identity. Latinos
are a linguistically diverse people in the context of the U.S. The totality
of one's socio-cultural inheritance must be made part of the identity equa-
tion of Latinos. The church needs to recognize the very definite bilingual
modality of the U.S. Latino community—and even English monolingual
modality! Many Latinos shaped by the *barrio* experience use English,
Spanglish or a bilingual expression to communicate. The church is often
viewed by them as a conservative and historically out of touch institution.
Many of these persons are conscientized members of the Latino community
who focus their justice struggles through civic organizations.[20]

Recently I attended a meeting of Latinos serving in executive positions
within the United Methodist Church. The moderator of the conference
very proudly stated how material is finally being produced in Spanish
by Latinos through one of the communications agencies. Clearly, the
indigenization of theological, biblical, and social ethical study materials
can only be applauded. I wondered, however, about the implicit negation
of the linguistic diversity of the Latino community in the U.S. Many

Latino organic intellectuals writing from the perspective of their respective disciplines do so in English; indeed, a whole school of Nuyarican poets write in English or Spanglish.[21] Their reflection is no less Latino! The language of the North American Latino church ought to reflect the totality of our people's linguistic reality. The church in the U.S. can address the question of language by bringing down the barriers that promote dishonesty concerning the linguistic reality of North American *hispanos.*

The Latino church in the U.S. is invited by the Crucified God in the *barrio* to become the voice of those who suffer because of unjust situations, and have no other avenue of appeal in "white society." Christian missional responsibility requires fully embracing the prophetic role to which God has called the Latino church in matters urgent for our time. The God of private spirituality must be ejected by the Latino church from its life. Spiritual impoverishment comes with the removal of the gospel from that place where it reveals the just and creative Spirit of God—the world and struggles of the poor. Only the God of the scandalous cross who identifies with the struggles of the poor to create a more just and humane society should occupy the faith perspective of the Latino church in the U.S. The wretched suffering of our people, the stench of death pervading the *barrio* and Latin American village streets, requires a church capable of confronting the structured evil of history with God's word of justice and radical historical action.

Again, the Latino church in the *barrio* is already a grass roots community, but it is still searching for the element of conscientization. It should not grow weary of the voices of our Latin American sisters and brothers in the *barrio* who are conscientizing instruments of God. Whatever the Latino church decides about its mission these words of Paul from the letter to the Galatians speak to it: *And let us not grow weary of well-doing, for in due season we shall reap, if we do not lose heart* (Gal 6:9).

Notes

1. Virgilio Elizondo, *Galilean Journey: The Mexican-American Promise* (Maryknoll, New York: Orbis Books, 1983), p. 53.

2. See Orlando Costas, *Christ Outside the Gate* (Maryknoll, New York: Orbis Books, 1982); Ada María Isasi-Díaz and Yolanda Tarango, *Hispanic Women: Prophetic Voice in the Church* (San Francisco: Harper and Row, 1979); Harold Recinos, *Hear the Cry!* (Louisville: Westminster/John Knox Press, 1989); Antonio Stevens-Arroyo, *Prophets Denied Honor: An Anthology on the Hispanic Church in the United States* (Maryknoll, New York: Orbis Books, 1980).

3. Jon Sobrino, *Spirituality and Liberation* (Maryknoll, New York: Orbis Books, 1988), pp. 80–86.

4. Harold Recinos. *Hear the Cry!*, p. 80.

5. See Richard Shaull, *Heralds of a New Reformation* (Maryknoll, New York: Orbis Books, 1984); William Tabb, ed., *Churches in Struggle: Liberation Theolo-*

gies and Social Change in North America (New York: Monthly Review Press, 1986).

6. See Severino Croatto, *Exodus, A Hermeneutics of Freedom* (Maryknoll, New York: Orbis Books, 1981); George Pixley, *God's Kingdom* (Maryknoll, New York: Orbis Books, 1981); Norman Gottwald, ed., *The Bible and Liberation* (Maryknoll, New York: Orbis Books, 1983).

7. See Phillip Berryman, *Religious Roots of Rebellion* (Maryknoll, New York: Orbis Books, 1980); Sergio Torres and John Eagleson, eds., *The Challenge of Basic Christian Communities* (Maryknoll, New York: Orbis Books, 1981).

8. See Jack Nelson-Pallmeyer, *The Politics of Compassion* (Maryknoll, New York: Orbis Books, 1988); Elsa Támez. *The Bible of the Oppressed* (Maryknoll, New York: Orbis Books, 1982); Iglesia guatemalteca en el exilio, *Cristianos: ¿por qué temer a la revolución?*.

9. See Leonardo Boff, *Ecclesiogenesis* (Maryknoll, New York: Orbis Books, 1986). I am very indebted to Boff for drawing my attention to the five salient features he observes operating in the base communities: 1) life is celebrated in the grass-roots communities; 2) the social flows from the religious; 3) capitalism is the root cause of human suffering; 4) network building between the grass-root communities and other justice oriented organizations is essential; and 5) the political vocation of ministry has been rediscovered.

10. *Galilean Journey*, p. 118.

11. Rafael Valdivieso, Cary Davis, "U.S. Hispanics: Challenging Issues for the 1990's" *Population Trends and Public Policy*, No. 17. December 1988, p. 9.

12. See Walter Brueggemann, *The Prophetic Imagination* (Philadelphia: Fortress Press, 1983); Renny Golden, Michael McConnell, *Sanctuary: The New Underground Railroad* (Maryknoll, New York: Orbis Books, 1986); Daniel Rodriguez *La primera evangelización norteamericana en Puerto Rico: 1898–1930* (México: Ediciones Borinquen, 1986).

13. Valdivieso, "U.S. Hispanics," pp. 1–5.

14. For an excellent discussion of the role of persons of color in the North Atlantic world see Costas, *Christ Outside the Gate*.

15. One extremely influential Latino institution is the Mexican American Cultural Center (MACC) in San Antonio, Texas. It was founded in 1971 to fill a need largely neglected by the institutions of learning of the dominant society. The Center's role has been providing theological and pastoral guidelines for the Latino church; and providing courses to Latino and white laity focusing on the Latin American theological experience. The Center contributed greatly to the dissemination of liberation theology in the U.S.

16. Martin Lange, Reinhold Ibacker, eds., *Witnesses of Hope: The Persecution of Christians in Latin America* (Maryknoll, New York: Orbis Books, 1981), pp. 79–80.

17. See: Iglesia Metodista Unida, *Amén al extranjero* (New York: Comité Metodista Unido de Auxilio, 1988).

18. Julia Esquivel, *Threatened with Resurrection* (Illinois: Brethren Press, 1982).

19. Valdivieso, "U.S. Hispanics," p. 8.

20. A number of organizations come to mind in this discussion such as COPS, the United Farm Workers, the National Congress for Puerto Rican Rights, Industrial Areas foundations, and the Mexican and Puerto Rican Legal Defense Funds.

21. Good examples of this type of writing are the works by: Miguel Piñero, Pedro Pietri, Miguel Algarín and Piri Thomas. Also see: David T. Abalos, *Latinos*

in the United States: The Sacred and the Political (Indiana: University of Notre Dame Press, 1986); Rodolfo O. de la Garza, et al., *The Mexican American Experience* (Austin: University of Texas Press, 1985).

Annotated Bibliography—Harold Recinos

Hear the Cry! A Latino Pastor Challenges the Church (Louisville, Kentucky: Westminster/John Knox Press, 1989).

With this important work, Recinos challenges those who present the gospel as purely privatized and otherworldly. He offers a vision for a credible praxis for those engaged in the church's mission of integral salvation. Grounded in his personal faith journey and his experience with a Puerto Rican congregation in the lower east side, Manhattan, the author uses socio-economic analysis and creative theological reflection to propose an incarnate gospel which calls the church to be a transforming agent in society.

Using the best tenets of Latin American liberation theology, the author introduces a new *barrio* theology for North America. He presents a critical reading of the Puerto Rican socio-historical situation characterized by economic oppression, political marginalization, and racial discrimination. He then proposes an interpretation of scripture from this perspective, and concludes that liberation theology and popular religion lead to a recovery of authentic faith expressions. The last chapter, in particular, offers a prophetic vision of a new reformation and re-creation of the church.

9

Orlando O. Espín

Orlando Espín was born in La Habana, Cuba. He began his theological studies at St. Vincent de Paul Regional Seminary in Boynton Beach, Florida where he obtained a masters in divinity (MDiv) in 1971 and a masters in theology (ThM) in 1972. He earned his doctorate (ThD) in systematic and pastoral theology from the Pontifical Catholic University of Rio de Janeiro, Brazil, in 1984.

As professor, Espín has taught in the Dominican Republic at Loyola Polytechnical Institute, in Brazil at St. Ursula University and at the Pontifical Catholic University of Rio de Janeiro. In this country he has been associate professor in the Department of Systematic Theology at St. Vincent de Paul Regional Seminary (1985–1990), scholar in residence at the Catholic Center at the University of Florida (1990–1991), and currently is associate professor in the Department of Theological and Religious Studies and Program of the Latino Studies at the University of San Diego.

In his published works and lectures, Espín has contributed greatly to the study of popular Catholicism, exposing its liberative and evangelical role in the U.S. Latino community. His treatment of the *sensus fidelium,* in relation to popular Catholicism, shows it as an authentic bearer of the church's tradition. In seventeen published articles, he elaborates this topic further in relation to inculturation, grace, and spirituality. His forthcoming book focuses on the theology of tradition and the *sensus fidelium.*

Espín is the founder and editor-in-chief of the *Journal of Hispanic/Latino Theology.* In 1993, he was awarded the "Virgilio Elizondo Award" by the Academy of Catholic Hispanic Theologians of the United States, an association in which he was a founding member and its president in 1992. He is also a member of the Catholic Theological Society of America, the American Society of Missiology, the American Academy of Religion,

Sociedade Brasileira de Teologia e Ciências da Religiao, and the Society
for the Scientific Study of Religion.

Department of Theological and Religious Studies
University of San Diego
5998 Alcalá Park
San Diego CA 92110-2492
619-260-4600

Tradition and Popular Religion

An Understanding of the Sensus Fidelium

Orlando Espín

It is practically impossible to study any Hispanic community in the United States, regardless of disciplinary point of departure or methodology, without encountering popular religion. Whether it be to denigrate it or lament its omnipresence in the Hispanic milieu, or to encourage and defend it as a sign of cultural affirmation, scholars sooner or later have to take a stand vis-à-vis popular religious beliefs, practices, and worldviews.

Popular religion (or "religiosity")[1] is indeed omnipresent in the Hispanic universe. And it is one of the few core elements shared by all Hispanic cultural communities in the country. Variations do exist, depending on the specific cultural history of each of the communities,[2] but some basic structures and symbols seem to appear as constants from coast to coast.

Popular religion has all too frequently been considered an embarrassment to Catholicism. It has been derided as the superstitious result of religious ignorance, a product of syncretism, a vestige of the rural past, and an ideologically[3] manipulated tool in the hands of those who would abuse simple folk. These accusations (and many others) do point to real issues and do express serious concerns. But when popular religion is viewed only or mainly through the prism of these accusations, the result can only be prejudiced and distorted.

Theologians have usually avoided the study of popular religion, preferring to leave the field to anthropologists and other social scientists. Even liberation theologies have tended to downplay popular religion's role in the church.[4] It is no exaggeration to say that, in Catholic theological circles, popular religion is either treated as an example of what should not be, or it is simply ignored as of no value for the serious theological enterprise.

"Tradition and Popular Religion: An Understanding of the *Sensus Fidelium*," *Frontiers of Hispanic Theology in the United States,* Allan Figueroa Deck, ed. (Maryknoll, New York: Orbis Books, 1992), pp. 62–87.

It will be argued in this chapter that popular religion can be theologically understood as a cultural expression of the *sensus fidelium,* with all that this understanding would imply for the theology of tradition in the Roman Catholic context. To this end (and as an extended example) I will show how two core symbols of Hispanic popular religion in fact convey essential contents of Christian tradition. I will also insist that—since these symbols do no more than act as vehicles for the people's "faith-full" intuitions—the broader issue of the *sensus fidelium* must be paid closer attention in theology. I start, however, with more general but pertinent observations on tradition that will help us set the context for our argument.

Tradition and *Sensus Fidelium*

The study of tradition[5] lies within the overall theological discussion of revelation and the development of doctrine, with many ramifications into other theological areas. Though this is not the place for an exhaustive reflection on the meaning, importance and role of tradition in Roman Catholicism, some basic observations must be made on the subject.

In the past some authors considered tradition, together with but distinct from the scriptures, as a "source" of revelation.[6] This "two-fonts theory," however, was discarded as the theology of revelation correctly came to emphasize that Jesus Christ is *the* revelation of God, and that this revelation is not primarily the "communication of doctrinal truths" but rather the outpouring of God's love and self in human history.

The two-fonts theory also failed when the relation between the biblical text and tradition was carefully examined. It is evident that the scriptures have a privileged position as the inspired and normative witness to God's revelation. Tradition is correctly valued as the context within which the biblical texts came to be written and within which the very canon of the scriptures came to be fixed and accepted as inspired.[7] Tradition is also the ecclesial (and sometimes normative) interpretation of the scriptures. The fixed texts of the Bible are proclaimed, explained, applied to life, and correctly interpreted by tradition for every Christian generation. This role of tradition is guided and protected from error by the Spirit of God who also inspired the biblical texts.[8]

Scripture is the normative, written expression of a preceding tradition that proclaims and witnesses to the revelation of God to Israel and in Christ, and from him through the apostolic community for the universal, postapostolic church. Scripture, therefore, communicates all the essential contents (gathered in the biblical canon and received by the church) necessary for complete, true and saving faith. Scripture, which must always be interpreted in the light of the tradition that precedes and accompanies it, is the norm for the church's preaching and faith.[9]

Postapostolic tradition, on the other hand, is essentially interpretation and reception of the one gospel of God, which has found its concrete, written expression in scripture. The common content of scripture and tradition is, simply put, their normative witness to the God revealed in Jesus Christ. The Bible and tradition share the same content in the sense that tradition, *through postapostolic expressions, symbols, and language,* recognizes and confesses (creed), refines correct meaning against falsehood (dogmas), and witnesses to that same truth which scripture communicates *through the language, expressions, and symbols of Israel and the apostolic church.* Scripture has been received and its canon fixed forever, while tradition is necessarily living in and through history.

One could speak of tradition exemplified in the definitions of the great ecumenical councils of antiquity, as expounded by the fathers of the church, and as communicated and witnessed to by the ecclesial magisterium and by theologians throughout history.[10] Tradition is certainly expressed in and through all these means. Theologians studying tradition usually concentrate on *written* conciliar documents, patristic texts, episcopal or papal declarations, and the like. Quite correctly, this written material (as also the text of Scripture) is very carefully examined and the methods of textual interpretation applied to it. Most theologians are aware of the need to properly understand a written document within its linguistic, cultural, political, historical, and doctrinal contexts. Without this careful study, the interpretation of the text could be prejudiced or inaccurate. As a consequence, it can yield wrong conclusions that could mislead other theological research dependent on the proper interpretation of tradition's texts.

Just as important as the written texts of tradition (or, in fact, more important), however, is the *living witness and faith* of the Christian people.[11] This living witness and faith do not seem to be taken as seriously by those who study tradition.[12] It is difficult to limit the object of one's study when it is supposed to be found mainly at the experiential level in every faith community. Cultural differences, diversity of languages, and all sorts of other variations make the actual theological study and interpretation of the life and faith of real Christian people a very difficult task indeed. And to complicate things even further, the object of the study (though expressed through cultural categories, languages, and so forth, that run the gamut of human diversity) is found at the level of *intuition.* It is this "faith-full" intuition that makes real Christian people *sense* that something is true or not vis-à-vis the gospel, or that someone is acting in accordance with the Christian gospel or not, or that something important for Christianity is not being heard.[13] This intuition in turn allows for and encourages a belief and a style of life and prayer that express and witness to the fundamental Christian message: God as revealed in Jesus Christ. This "faith-full" intuition is called the *sensus fidelium* (or *sensus fidei*).[14]

The whole church has received the revelation of God and accepted it in faith. And, as a consequence, the whole church is charged with proclaiming, living, and transmitting the fullness of revelation. Therefore, the necessary task of expressing the contents of scripture and tradition are not and cannot be limited to the ordained ministers of the church. The whole church has this mission, and the Spirit was promised to the whole church for this task.[15] Christian laity, consequently, are indispensable witnesses and bearers of the gospel—as indispensable as the magisterium of the church. Furthermore, because the foundational origin of the *sensus fidelium* is the Holy Spirit, it can be said that this "sense of the faithful" is infallible, preserved by the Spirit from error in matters necessary to revelation.[16] In other words, the "faith-full" intuition (*sensus fidei*) of real Christian lay persons infallibly transmits the contents of tradition, and thus infallibly senses the proper interpretation and application of scripture.

The main problem with the study of the *sensus fidelium* as a necessary component in any adequate reflection on tradition, is, precisely, its being a "sense," an intuition. This sense is never discovered in some kind of pure state. The *sensus fidelium* is *always* expressed through the symbols, language, and culture of the faithful and, therefore, is in need of intense interpretive processes and methods similar to those called for by the written texts of tradition and scripture. Without this careful examination and interpretation of its means of expression, the true "faith-full" intuition of the Christian people could be inadequately understood or even falsified. This is where theology and the magisterium must play their indispensable hermeneutic roles, though, as we shall see, this process is not without its limitations and problems.

The means through which the *sensus fidelium* expresses itself are extremely varied, showing the cultural wealth of the Christian people. Given the global demographics of today's church, the means tend to be what they have been throughout most of Christian history: *oral, experiential, and symbolic.* These expressions also show (because of their origin in human culture) the wound of sinfulness capable of obscuring (but never destroying) the "faith-full" and infallible intuitions of the Christian people. The interpretation and discernment needed in the study of the *sensus fidelium* must, therefore, try to ascertain the authenticity of the intuitions (their coherence and fundamental agreement with the other witnesses of revelation) and the appropriateness of the expressions (their validity as vehicles for the communication of revelation, realizing that no human expression is ever totally transparent to God and the gospel). This process calls for at least three confrontations.

The first of these confrontations must be with the Bible, because whatever claims to be a necessary component of Christian revelation must prove itself to be in fundamental coherence with the scriptures. Although not everything that Christians hold to be truly revealed is expressly stated in the text of scripture,[17] nothing held to be revealed can ever be against scripture or incapable of showing its authentic development from a legitimate interpretation of scripture.

The second confrontation must be with the written texts of tradition. By these I mean conciliar definitions of doctrine (dogmas), the teachings of the fathers of the church, the documents of the magisterium of the church, the history of the development of doctrines, the various theological traditions, and so forth. Throughout twenty centuries of Christian history, the church has reflected on God's revelation, come to a number of fundamental decisions on the proper understanding of some dimensions or elements of that revelation, and has made decisions normative for itself and for all following generations of Christians.[18] Consequently, all intuitions that claim to be "faith-full" (as well as all means of expression of those intuitions) must be in basic agreement with those normative decisions of the church, and must also show some degree of coherence with the general doctrinal and spiritual thrust of the church's history.

The third confrontation must be with the historical and sociological contexts within which these "faith-full" intuitions and their means of expression appear. If a "sense" of the faith is to be discerned as a true or false bearer of tradition, it must be capable of promoting the *results expected* of the Christian message and of Christian living.[19] In the same way, the vehicles through which the intuition of faith expresses itself (given the fact that all these means are cultural, historical, and sociological) must somehow be coherent with Christianity's necessary proclamation and practice of justice, peace, liberation, reconciliation, as indispensable dimensions of a world according to God's will. The expressions of the *sensus fidelium* must facilitate and not hinder the people's participation in the construction of God's reign.[20]

This third confrontation, evidently, will demand of the theologian an awareness of culture and of economic and political reality, as well as awareness of one's hidden (but certainly present) class and ethno-cultural biases and interests, which may blind one to dimensions of revelation present precisely in the "faith-full" intuitions being studied. This latter danger seems most evident among theologians trained in the North Atlantic presupposition that European or Euro-American theologies are the truly profound, systematic, real, and normative theologies, the ones—they claim—which effectively dialogue with the truest and most fundamental issues of human existence.[21] Of course, these North Atlantic theologies presume (often implicitly) that their cultural, political, and economic contexts *define* what is truest and most fundamental for the human race, while considering that definitions from other contexts are either inconsequential or merely tangential to the tasks of their presumed "real" theologies. This third confrontation, obviously, calls on the theologian to become aware of the cultural and ideological limits and biases of the very theological tools employed in the study of the *sensus fidelium*.

If the infallible, "faith-full" intuitions of the Christian people can only be expressed through culturally given means, then it is possible that the *same* intuition could be communicated by different Christian communities through *different* cultural means. It is in this context, and as a consequence of what we have been discussing, that I believe Hispanic popular religion is the culturally possible expression of some fundamental intuitions of the Christian faith. Popular religion is indeed a means for the communication of many Hispanic Christians' *sensus fidei*.

The Roots of Hispanic Evangelization

The Hispanic peoples of the United States have diverse origins, both ethnically and historically. Many of the communities are the result of immigration (some recent and others dating from the nineteenth century), while large numbers of Hispanics were already in present-day U.S. territory when American armies invaded and captured the populations together with their lands.[22] It is important to remember that the Hispanic Catholic Church was well established in today's United States two hundred years before John Carroll was elected first bishop of Baltimore.[23]

Hispanic communities with roots in the northeast, Florida or the Spanish-speaking Caribbean tend to be the result of *mestizaje*[24] between Spaniards and Africans. Those communities with roots in the West and Southwest or in Mexico and Central America tend to be the outcome of *mestizaje* between Spaniards and Native Amerindian populations. In other words, U.S. Hispanics are culturally (and very often racially as well) mestizos at their origin. In fact, it is this very *mestizaje* which precisely distinguishes them from both the Spaniards and the Amerindian and African peoples. It is what binds them together as a people distinct from all other segments of the U.S. population.

The very presence of Amerindian or African elements in all U.S. Hispanic communities points to another important fact which has serious consequences for the subject of this chapter: Hispanic origins are profoundly marked by slavery, plunder, oppression, and suffering. Were it not for the African slave trade, with all its horrors, or for the cruel system of the *encomiendas*[25] (Indian forced-labor), the Hispanic peoples would not have come into existence. True, Hispanics did receive from Spain many elements which provided the offspring of *mestizaje* with a cultural richness they still cherish. Spain's greatest contribution, however, was evangelization.

Christianity came to the Americas at the end of the fifteenth century. In a few decades, numerous dioceses had been established, schools and even more than one university had been opened, parishes and scores of mission stations appeared, and holiness and martyrdom accompanied the entire effort.[26] The missionary efforts of Franciscans, Dominicans, Augustinians, and Jesuits cannot be underestimated. They began the massive evangelization of the continent and were, in general terms, quite successful.[27] So successful, indeed, that today's Catholicism in Latin America and among U.S. Hispanics is very much the direct result of the one proclaimed and planted by the early missionaries.

Historical facts, however, remind us that together with these heroic efforts at evangelization, there were enormous sins of injustice committed. As people of their times, the Spaniards who came to the Americas believed themselves to be superior to all other peoples, and their religion the only one worth professing. The same intransigent attitude that led to devastating wars of religion in Europe became the common attitude of Europeans confronted with Amerindian or African populations and their cultures and religions. The European invasion and conquest of the Americas did not take place for purely humanitarian or Christian reasons. The conquerors came in search of material rewards. Yet they never totally disavowed their specifically religious, even "humane," motives.[28]

The Christianity that was proclaimed in this continent, and that stands at the origin of U.S. Hispanic Catholicism, was the complex result of several distinct, historical elements. First of all, Spain had conquered the last Muslim-held territories in the Iberian peninsula the same year (1492) that Columbus arrived in the Americas. The process of driving the Muslims out of the Iberian peninsula had taken over seven centuries, and had made Muslims and Christians profoundly influence each other's culture. These Christians, who for hundreds of years had fought non-Christians, had developed a style of Christianity that was militant and attracted to the heroic, and was not known for its tolerance of religious or ethnic diversity. National self-definition, indeed, had depended on the conquest and expulsion of those who were different. Not surprisingly the same militant, heroic, and intolerant attitudes were brought to the Americas by the Spaniards and made present in the process of evangelization and colonization.

Another element to keep in mind is the medieval fascination with saints, shrines, relics, images, miracles, and religious storytelling.[29] The Spaniards of the late fifteenth and early sixteenth centuries were still medieval in their approach to religion. Theirs was a Christianity that communicated the gospel by means of graphic symbols (verbal or otherwise).

Though there had been much scholarly and theological learning in Spain's Muslim and Christian lands, this learning seldom filtered down to the majority, rural populations. The united Spain of the sixteenth century, though continuing the tradition of high scholarship, did not go beyond the best medieval models of education.[30] The Christian catechesis available to the rural majority tended to emphasize religious storytelling (often Bible stories or lives of saints) and religious dramas (*auto sacramentales*).[31] The observance of the liturgical seasons and the arrival of occasional itinerant preachers gave the rural poor a necessary sense and knowledge of the fundamentals of Christianity. Social and religious traditions among the people of the villages also communicated some fundamental expectations of Christian living.

I am in no way implying that Iberian Catholicism was free of the very serious limitations of the pre-Reformation church. What I am implying, however, is that in spite of the difficulties, Spanish Catholics were certainly not ignorant of the gospel. In other words, the Catholicism that came to the Americas was one used to catechizing through symbols, stories, and dramas, a Christianity that bore the mark of the European Middle Ages and of Spain's long and recent militant anti-infidel past. And it was also a Christianity that, in spite of misconceptions to the contrary, depended mostly on lay leadership at the local level.

Once the Protestant and Catholic Reformations began,[32] most of Spain's religious efforts in the colonies were devoted to keeping Lutheran and Calvinist ideas out. The Catholic Reformation in the Americas was in practice reduced to the creation of seminaries and schools (mainly for Spaniards or the white *criollo* elite), and to stopping some major abuses.[33] But for most of the population on this side of the Atlantic, the Catholic Reformation meant the affirmation (and thus the *continuation*) of that which was held to be the Catholic tradition of the continent: the Iberian fifteenth- and sixteenth-century Catholicism I have just very briefly summarized.

One last point must be added to this summary. Though many members of religious orders came to the Americas as missionaries, I believe that most of the actual communication of Christianity was done by the lay Spaniards who came to this continent (and these were, by and large, Spain's poor). As time went on, it was done by the Amerindian, African, and mestizo laity who entered the church.

The end result of the combination of elements mentioned in this brief summary of the background of Hispanic evangelization is a type of Catholicism that can be called "popular," because it truly reflects the faith and practice of the majority of people. It does not show the sophistication of the educated elites, and it shows little awareness of the issues brought to center stage of all Christian theology by the Protestant and Catholic Reformations. This popular Catholicism evinced the medieval predilection for the visual, the oral, and the dramatic. It was emphatic about certain dimensions of Christianity that tend to be overlooked or pushed aside by post-Reformation North Atlantic theologies, both Catholic and Protesant.

Bearers of the Christian Gospel: Symbols of Popular Religion

The Christian gospel preached in the Spanish-speaking Americas had been previously "filtered" and interpreted by Spain's peoples. The preached gospel was in turn interpreted, understood, and accepted in faith by these Latin Americans, ancestors of today's U.S. Hispanics. This was as it should have been, since the gospel is either inculturated and thus internalized and allowed to transform a people's worldview from within, or it becomes a foreign, sterile message. And, evidently, in order to inculturate one must interpret, understand, and then accept, allowing oneself (and one's culture and previous worldview) to be challenged by the very gospel one is interpreting, understanding, and accepting. This entire process, leading

from proclamation to acceptance, can only occur by means of symbols
and other cultural categories in order to be a truly human process. Even
under the guidance of the Spirit, the hearer of the Word remains human
and thus bound by all the normal processes of humanness. It is, therefore,
very pertinent to remember here the distinction recalled earlier between the
sensus fidelium as intuition and the various cultural expressions historically
employed to communicate and witness to that "faith-full" intuition. It is
also important to remember that what is the infallible bearer of revelation
is the discerned, intuitive sense of the faith, and not the many symbolic
and historical ways employed as its inculturated expressions.

There are many symbols employed in Hispanic popular Catholicism.
Most of them had their origin in the church's liturgies (including late
medieval Iberian sacramental rites, and the sixteenth-century Pius V—or
Tridentine—eucharistic rite).[34] Other symbols were borrowed from Spanish medieval or mendicant piety, and still more were contributed (with
totally or partially modified meaning) by Amerindian and African peoples.

As can be expected, not all symbols have the same importance within
the popular religious universe. For our purposes, I have chosen two that
appear to be central and organizing symbols in Hispanic popular Catholicism: the crucified Christ and Mary. These two symbols are present in
every Catholic Hispanic community in the United States with very similar
functions and meaning, giving us a religious connecting link amid Hispanic
diversity. Finally, as can also be expected, discussion of these two symbols
can only be done in general strokes that in themselves summarize a much
more detailed study of each of the symbols.

If these two devotions, so central to Hispanic Catholicism, are capable
of communicating true elements of Christian tradition, they may justifiably
be called bearers of the *sensus fidelium*. Furthermore, since these two
devotions are so important, they might offer us an entrance to the gospel
preached in the Spanish-speaking Americas since the late fifteenth century.
I will be devoting more space to the symbol of Our Lady of Guadalupe
than to the crucified Christ, because the latter's link with tradition is so
much more evident.

The Crucified Christ

Hispanics give the iconography[35] of the crucifixion a very realistic
quality. The crucified Jesus is painted or sculpted to appear in horrible
pain. The crown of thorns, the nails, the blood, are all made to communicate
real suffering, real torture, and real death. The dying Jesus, however, is
not represented only as nailed to a cross. The entire passion is expressed
through numerous and well-known sculptures and paintings of the flagella-
tion, of the crowning with thorns, of the descent from the cross. Though
many of these images or paintings may have true artistic value in them-

selves, the religious value is usually conveyed not by beauty itself but by the work's ability to elicit feelings of solidarity and compassion.

The passion is also enacted through religious drama, not within the confines of a theater building or a church, but out in the streets. The *Santo Entierro*,[36] with its *Virgen Dolorosa* and its *Jesús Nazareno,* is one of the oldest traditions of Hispanic Good Friday. Some communities are known to accompany *La Dolorosa* as the procession moves through the streets, comforting her with their *pésames* at the death of her son. Needless to say, Good Friday is very important in the Hispanic liturgical year. There are many other popular devotions to numerous *Cristos* that, in one or another graphic way, portray some scene of the passion story.

The Christ of Hispanic passion symbolism is a tortured, suffering human being. The images leave no room for doubt. This dying Jesus, however, is so special because he is not just another human who suffers unfairly at the hands of evil humans. He is the divine Christ, and that makes his innocent suffering all the more dramatic. He is prayed to as one speaks with a living person, and not merely mourned or remembered as some dead hero of the past. His passion and death express his solidarity with all men and women throughout history who have also innocently suffered at the hands of evildoers. In other words, it seems that Hispanic faith intuitively sensed the true humanness of Jesus, like ours in all things except sinful guilt. It sensed his resurrection as an intuition that he is alive now (and forever). And it also sensed that Jesus' innocent death speaks of compassionate solidarity with suffering men and women. The expressions used to convey these faith intuitions are culturally authentic, though they could conceivably be modified as Hispanic cultures develop and adapt to new contexts in the future.[37] However, is there any doubt as to the truth of the intuitions or their infallible character?

Christian preaching in the Spanish-speaking Americas used the available catechizing tools and cultural symbols to convey the centrality of the cross. It emphasized the entire passion narrative, and not merely the actual death. It underlined Jesus' innocence as well as his compassionate solidarity with all those who suffer. The people understood, they believed and interpreted, and among the results were the inculturated expressions of popular religion mentioned above.

These expressions are not part of the normative tradition of the church. But the faith intuitions behind them most certainly are. Iconography has adequately communicated revelation, with contents authentically coherent with the text of the Bible and with other written documents of tradition. Furthermore, the passion symbols of Hispanic popular Catholicism not only do not hinder the building up of God's reign but, in fact, preach solidarity and compassion as attitudes of the crucified God, also expected from Christians. Thus, when confronted with scripture, other texts of tradition and with socio-historical contexts, the passion symbols of Hispanic popular religion can claim to witness to revelation and, therefore, to communicate the "faith-full" intuitions of the *sensus fidelium.*

Mary

Hispanic popular Catholicism frequently stresses the figure and role of Mary. It is difficult to find, besides the crucified Christ, another more powerful religious symbol. While it is not hard to discover "faith-full" intuitions behind devotions to the dying Jesus, it does appear that Marian beliefs and practices, especially as they are expressed in popular Hispanic contexts, are farthest away from the Christian gospel (and, as a consequence, suspect as bearers of the *sensus fidelium*).

I have chosen to look more closely at only one Marian title and story, because practically every Hispanic cultural community has (at least) one title and story for Mary. These titles and stories (similarly structured accounts of apparitions of the virgin or of discovery of her statue, connected to a confirmatory miracle) are foundations of the Marian devotions of specific cultural communities.[38] The devotion I have chosen to address is the one to Our Lady of Guadalupe, which is probably the most widespread in the U.S. Hispanic universe.

The title *de Guadalupe* is a Spanish mispronunciation (and transference of an older Iberian toponym)[39] of the ancient Nahuatl term *Tecoatlaxope,* which means "she will crush the serpent of stone." The story tells of a recently converted Amerindian called Juan Diego who, in December 1531, saw and was addressed by a Nahuatl-speaking, indigenous woman on the hill of Tepeyac. It also mentions that the woman wanted a temple built on that site and that the Spanish church authorities in sixteenth-century Mexico did not believe him until a miracle occurred.[40]

That is the title and that is the story, but this brief recounting does not communicate the context and symbols understood by Juan Diego, by his conquered fellow Amerindians, or by the Spaniards who had invaded Mexico. It was the context and symbols, not just the historical outline, that created one of the most powerful Marian devotions in the history of the Catholic Church.

The context of early sixteenth-century Mexico pitched a multitude of native peoples against a smaller number of Spanish soldiers, administrators, colonizers, and missionaries. The ancient Mexican religion and most ancient native ways were seen by the Spaniards as unacceptable creations of ignorance, superstition, and demonic powers.[41] Though there were indeed some very forceful defenders of the native populations among the Spaniards (especially among the missionaries), none of the defenders believed that the native religion was worth preserving. The missionary *cronistas* described for posterity the ancient Mexican religious universe that they knew and hoped to be disappearing.[42]

Among the important ancient deities there was a certain Tonantzin, "our mother," as she was called by the Mexican natives.[43] She was frequently said to be pregnant, or to be carrying a small child on her back or arms. When depicted as pregnant, the religious symbol representing the fundamental reconciliation of opposites was placed over her womb. Her sacred place had been precisely on the hill of Tepeyac. She dressed in a particular type of tunic and wore a mantle, and was connected in myth to the serpent-high god. The woman who spoke with Juan Diego (in his native Nahuatl) did so on the hill of Tepeyac, wore that particular style of dress with a mantle, appeared to be pregnant, and had the symbol of the reconciliation of opposites over her womb.

I am in no way implying that Juan Diego saw the goddess Tonantzin, however. Though the similarities are too striking to be dismissed, the differences are also too evident to be ignored. Tonantzin had a large enough mythology stressing her inclination to inflict cruel punishment on her worshipers. The goddess was quite capable of sending all kinds of diseases and disgraces on her people, and often did. She was not, in any sense, a loving parent who could easily symbolize divine tenderness or warm affection. Tonantzin was also, under the title of Cihuacóatl, the wife of the serpent-god.

The woman seen by Juan Diego was very pointedly kind and tender, with no trace of cruelty or anger. Her gestures were explicitly those of peacefulness. And the very title used (*Tecoatlaxope*) clearly indicated opposition to the serpent. These and other religious symbols present in Juan Diego's apparition do not allow us to identify Mary with Tonantzin. How do we explain the similarities and the differences?

Juan Diego, a recent convert to Christianity, interpreted what he believed himself to have experienced and seen through cultural categories available to him. He was now a Christian, but his cultural milieu—of which he remained a part—was still in the process of assimilating the shock of the conquest. As was and is common among many peoples, reality in sixteenth-century Mexico was understood in religious terms. And the conquest, followed by the arrival of Christianity, was a part of Juan Diego's reality that had to be explained, understood, and assimilated in *his people's* religious terms. Many were Christians now, but the traditional Christian religious symbols the natives received from the missionaries were Spanish, foreign to them.[44] Guadalupe seems to be the birth of Christianity's inculturation in colonial Mexico. In other words, precisely *because* Juan Diego claimed to have seen Mary *the way* he did, we can say today that this is a sign that the Christian gospel was in fact announced and accepted in early colonial Mexico, and this in spite of all the betrayals of the gospel that can also be documented.

Mary is seen through religious symbols of motherhood and of the reconciliation of opposites, and for this Tonantzin's symbols were used, but without Tonantzin. Mary is also perceived as opposed to the serpent-

high god, without whom there could be no native Mexican religion. She
is pointedly tender and kind, a behavior not expected of Tonantzin. Juan
Diego's Mary assumes the symbols that are useful for Christianity but
certainly rejects those that could identify her with the old religion or that
appear to at least condone it (and in this the Virgin of Guadalupe followed
a long history of Christian appropriation and use of symbols from newly
converted peoples).[45]

The devotion to Our Lady of Guadalupe, especially among Mexicans
and Mexican-Americans, has remained central throughout the centuries
since Juan Diego's visions. The Guadalupe symbol was immediately
judged to belong to the poor, since the educated and the wealthy had their
Virgin of Remedies. And for over four centuries Guadalupe has belonged
to the vast majority of the people.[46]

The inculturation of Mary through the religious symbols of ancient
Mexicans does not alone justify our calling it an inculturated *Christian*
symbol. Mary herself must in turn be the symbol. Catholic pneumatology
and ecclesiology should have today little difficulty in affirming this role
for Mary.[47] But can we say the same thing of pre- and post-Tridentine
Mexico? Were the Marian symbols of sixteenth-century Mexico capable
of communicating, to the native peoples of that period and place, the
meaning of Christ and his unique role in salvation, as well as other
indispensable contents of the gospel?

To answer these questions one first needs to ask other more fundamental
ones. Can analogy (semantic and cultural, *not* ontological) legitimately
help us speak (in the manner of the semantic, cultural analogy) of God
and his Christ?[48] Could Mary be considered, in that sense, an analogy of
some dimensions or attributes that Christians have discovered—as a gift
of the Spirit—in the one they call God? If Mary can be a semantic, cultural
analogy of the church in Catholic theology, could she be the same in
reference to God? These are issues, it seems to me, at the core of all
mariology. And also at the heart of our questions about sixteenth-century
Mexican popular mariology.

But just as important are other issues about development in the understanding of Christian revelation. Obviously, the core of the gospel (its
most indispensable content, upon which all others rest) is God's self-
revelation and self-donation in Jesus Christ. But it is more than evident
that the complete meaning of this revelation was not fully understood and
explicitated at the beginning of the church. The history of doctrine is clear
proof of development in Christian perception and progressive acceptance
of the revelation of God.[49] What might be *clearly* true or accepted at a
given age or place in church history might not have been so at an earlier
period or at a different place in that same history. This sometimes provokes
a confrontation about a certain understanding of truth or about the way
the truth is being expressed.

Could it be possible that sixteenth-century Mexican natives, recently converted to Christianity, intended to say something very true but (given their particular cultural and sociological context and Spain's style of Catholicism) could only express it through the symbols that surrounded Juan Diego's Marian visions? Could the Virgin of Guadalupe be understood as a step—albeit an extremely important one—in the inculturation of the tradition in Mexican (and later Mexican-American) history? Need all Christian communities share the same synchronized steps and moments in the development of doctrine in order to perceive each other as orthodox?

Is Mary of Guadalupe the cultural, historical expression of "faith-full" intuitions of the *sensus fidelium?* I believe she is and, as a consequence, she is also open to "doctrinal development" that might or might not reaffirm all the Guadalupe-related symbols. All development, it should be understood, must be culturally authentic for those who historically have employed these Marian expressions in order to witness to tradition. Cultural inauthenticity would disqualify as bearer of tradition any development of doctrine or of expression.

If it could be shown that Mary may be perceived as a semantic, cultural (never ontological) analogy of some divine attributes—which is another way of asking if she could be interpreted as a culturally legitimate means to express some content of the Christian gospel—which of these contents would the Virgin of Guadalupe be communicating and witnessing to?

To answer the question we must look at the history of this devotion, and especially at two key aspects of it. First of all, Mary of Guadalupe has always been perceived by the people as a tender mother, always compassionate, accepting, supportive and forgiving. And secondly, she is seen as protector, identified with her people but most specially with the weakest and neediest. She procures justice for the oppressed and takes up their cause.

Is it possible to truthfully refer to the Christian God as tender, compassionate, accepting, supportive, and forgiving? Is it possible to experience God as protector, committed to the liberation and defense of the weak and oppressed?[50] Is God really incarnate ("inculturated," therefore)? Can a Christian also refer to God as "mother," using in private devotion, liturgy, and theology the language and symbols of motherhood as validly as those of fatherhood?[51] But more to our point, must the revelation of these attributes of God be communicated *exclusively* through Jesus? Scripture does *not* allow us to answer this last question affirmatively. Though Jesus Christ is the final and unique revelation of God—*the* revelation in the strict sense of the term—nowhere is it affirmed that only through Christ has God been revealed. As a matter of fact, the exact opposite has been a constant in orthodox Christian tradition.[52] What one must affirm with the tradition is the uniqueness and finality of the revelation in and through Christ, and the impossibility of its being repeated. But these affirmations do not exclude other means of revelation, only that these must never appear to compete with or add something *new* to the fullness of Christ's revelation.

This being the case, we can now ask whether it is impossible to understand that, in a given cultural and historical context, certain contents of revelation may be expressed through Marian symbols? As long as what is expressed through Mary is consonant with the gospel (and it is, as we have just seen), is there any theological difficulty in seeing the truth of the "faithfull" intuitions communicated through the devotion of the Virgin of Guadalupe as cultural *embodiments* of the *sensus fidelium?*

Elements of Christian Tradition

If we tried to briefly explicitate through words (as distinct from devotional symbols) the elements of the tradition (elements of revelation) communicated through these two popular Hispanic devotions, what would we find?[53] From the first of these symbols we discover these "faith-full" intuitions: (1) Jesus' true humanness, (2) his compassionate solidarity with the poor and suffering, (3) his innocent death caused by human sin, and (4) his (implied) resurrection and divinity. Through the Guadalupe devotion we find these other "faith-full" intuitions: (5) God's compassion and solidarity with the oppressed and vanquished, and (6) God's maternal affirmation and protection of the weakest. From both devotional symbols we can retrieve a clear sense that (7) if God and the gospel are to be heard and accepted, they must be inculturated ("incarnated"), as they have been, in the world and through the symbols of the poor and the disregarded (Jesus as a tortured Galilean outsider, and Mary as a member of a conquered race). And finally, (8) implied in both stories we might also discover that a lack of faith and a rejection of the truth and of God results where the symbols of the poor (*and* the poor of the symbols) are rejected.

But could we find the same eight or similar elements present in other Hispanic contexts and in other expressions of popular religion? I believe we can.[54] Even though a complete and thorough theological examination of Hispanic popular religion is yet to be done, the few studies that have appeared and those in progress all seem to confirm this thesis.

Much more important, however, is to question whether these eight affirmations, which may be retrieved from the two core devotions of Hispanic popular religion, are in fact contained in tradition. It is necessary to know if these affirmations (which are linguistic transpositions of symbolized or experienced intuitions of faith) can be said to be an integral part of the Christian gospel. If we brought these affirmations, retrieved from the symbols of the crucified Christ and of the Virgin of Guadalupe, to the threefold confrontation with scripture, with the texts of tradition, and with the socio-historical context (as suggested above), we would have to conclude that within contemporary Roman Catholic theology no one, in good conscience, can deny that the eight faith intuitions are, without doubt, elements of Christian revelation, clearly and universally taught by the magisterium, and more importantly witnessed by the texts of scripture and tradition.

And still, in contemporary theology, as witnessed by seminary, university, and theological center curricula and by bibliographical research, there is an evident reticence in the acceptance of popular religion as a valid field for study and for theological reflection on tradition.

The Limitations of Popular Religion as *Sensus Fidelium*

I have been arguing in favor of the study of popular religion as an authentic bearer of the *sensus fidelium,* and for that purpose I have reviewed the roots of Hispanic popular Catholicism and attempted to interpret and retrieve doctrinal contents from its two main symbols. Given the importance that the Spirit-given "faith-full" sense of the Christian people has for theology (especially in Catholicism), and given the appeals to it at the hour of justifying theological, dogmatic, or even disciplinary statements in the church, it will be important to look a little closer at the fundamental limitations of the expressions of the *sensus fidelium* as transmitted in popular religion. Our discussion, though prompted by and applicable to Hispanic popular Catholicism, will not be limited to it.[55]

All expressions of the "faith-full" intuitions of the Christian people are, of necessity, not equal to the intuitions they communicate. The expressions are *human* means through which the Spirit leads the whole church to a deeper and clearer understanding of revelation. As human means these vehicles of understanding are subject to the same conditioning limitations all things human bear. The limitations I am referring to can be grouped in two categories.

Human, Contextual Limitations

There are those limitations, in the first place, that come from the cultural, socio-political, linguistic, and even economic contexts within which the Christian gospel is proclaimed, understood, and lived.[56] The Spirit-suggested "faith-full" intuitions, when expressed, will evidently employ the means made available through the people's cultural and linguistic codes. But the Christians who communicate their sense of faith will also exhibit in their expressions the privilege or the oppression to which they are subjected in society. Their faith will be *their* response to the gospel, and this means that their history, their struggles, failures, and victories, their social class, will *necessarily* act as vehicles (or as contributors to the vehicles) of God-inspired affirmations of Christian truth. The whole of their social, human reality becomes involved as a filter, offering means of expression to the gospel. But if the Christian people's reality is mainly a wounded and invaded context, the truth that the Spirit stirs within them will then express itself in a wounded and invaded manner. It is certainly the function of the entire church (and more specifically of theologians and of the magisterium) to discern the truth amid its wounded expressions. However, it is crucial that this discernment not be guided by or based on the presupposition that the poor's expressions of faith are of a lesser Christian quality than those of intellectual, ecclesiastical, or political elites. Were this evidently false presupposition to be operative in the discernment, the latter would be vitiated as a vehicle for discerning revelation's truth.[57]

In the universe of popular religion, socio-historical and cultural reality has offered opportunities and also created limitations. The experience of poverty and injustice, for example, seems to have inclined Hispanic religious imagery to symbols and devotions that have explicitly to do with compassion and suffering. The same can be said of the Hispanic emphasis on the extended family and on other social networks. These moved the people to conceive symbols and devotions that stress solidarity, community, and even familylike networks with the living and the dead. Many features of the Hispanic family have been projected into the religious realm.[58]

The active presence of these socio-historical and cultural dimensions among U.S. Hispanics has indeed created adequate vehicles for the *sensus fidelium,* as we have been seeing. But—when not properly understood and received, or when wounded by an unjust reality—their presence could also produce doctrinal exaggerations and deviations. However, the only discernment that can help avoid doctrinal deviation (as I mentioned before) is the threefold confrontation with scripture, the texts of tradition, and with the socio-historical context itself.[59] And, one must add, this discernment must also confront the implied racist or class ideologies (frequently expressed through theological or pastoral categories) of those who either by training or ecclesial function might be conducting the discernment.

Limitations of Any Bearer of the Sensus Fidelium

The second group of limitations facing popular religious expressions of the *sensus fidelium* are those inherent in the very idea and reality of the *sensus fidelium.*

As I have pointed out several times, the *sensus fidelium,* strictly speaking, is not the expressions or vehicles through which it makes itself known. It is the "faith-full" *intuition* of the Christian people, moved by the Spirit, that senses, adheres to, and interprets the Word of God.

It is evident that no intuition may be had or may be expressed in human reality without somehow being mediated. This mediation, as we have seen above, will involve the reality of the ones experiencing the intuition. This is just as true of Hispanic popular religion as it is of the expressions of all the other bearers of the *sensus fidelium* in the church. Even if difficult to discern in actual practice, it is theoretically possible (and even necessary) to affirm that the "faith-full" intuitions of Christians are not coextensive or equal to the expressions they employ as vehicles for the former. However, what is left of the intuition after distinguishing and discerning it from its expression? What is an intuition without some mediation to make it understandable or, indeed, even perceivable even at the preconceptual stage?[60]

Evidently, when discerning the truth behind the expression, we must use some kind of symbolic means in order to understand. But the instant a symbolic code is appealed to as mediation (as expression), is this still considered an intuition in the strict sense of the *sensus fidelium?* Are then the mediating expressions of the *sensus fidelium* also granted the gift of infallibility?[61] The seriousness of these questions should be obvious, since so many culturally given, ideologically tainted, and socially wounded mediations are considered to be vehicles of the intuitions of *sensus fidelium.*

These issues cannot be addressed here, but sooner or later professional theology will have to address them, because the days when the *sensus fidelium* was an academic appendix to studies of tradition seem to be coming to an end. The social sciences and non-European theologies have begun to uncover for us the complex and socio-culturally bound structures and functions of religion and theology (and of the ideological "uses" of tradition).[62] They have also begun to uncover the limitations of *all* bearers of tradition, including the *sensus fidelium* and its popular religious expressions.

An Open-Ended Conclusion

Within the church some seem to be arguing that the faithful need their faith "protected." But if the Christian people's "faith-full" intuitions are infallible, Spirit-given witness to the gospel, it seems rather strange to claim that they are practically defenseless against error. On the other hand, to deride the use of the people's defense as a mere political ploy is not to face the issue directly. Can the people's *sensus fidelium* or its expressions be misled? Why? What is the theologically adequate understanding of the relationship between faith intuition and mediation, given the results of the social sciences? Does the *sensus fidelium* witness to all of revelation? Do *any* of the bearers of tradition ever witness to the whole of revelation?

And even more importantly, do the Christian people *actually* play a role in *today's* transmission of tradition, beyond being paid lip service for their "reception" of truth? What is their actual, real-life role in that transmission in the real-life church? Are they supposed to be mere mouthpieces or mirrors for the expressions of the faith of the intellectually sophisticated (whether these be theologians or bishops)? Do they in fact contribute (what and how) to the ongoing process of deepening the church's understanding of revelation?[63] Obviously, to claim that only the theologians or the bishops really understand revelation and, as a consequence, that only they should speak and express the faith in order to avoid deviations and error is to dismiss the *sensus fidelium* outright, to ignore too many facts in the actual history of the development of doctrine, and especially to come uncomfortably close to disregarding the incarnation of the one who is at the heart of the Christian gospel. There is need for a systematic, historically factual, intellectually honest, and detailed study of the relationship between the bearers of tradition and their indispensable interdependence.

This chapter has not been the place to enter into some of the questions that I have been raising throughout. I have also tried to avoid comparing the limitations and contributions of the *sensus fidelium* with those of the magisterium, theologians, and other bearers of tradition (liturgy, for example). This would have led us too far from our subject. Instead I have insisted on the legitimacy of popular religion as one vehicle for the *sensus fidelium* and, as a consequence, as a valid (and necessary) area of theological reflection.

The presence of limitations in the expressions of popular religion (insofar as they express the contents of tradition) cannot be an acceptable argument against popular religion's role as bearer of tradition. Limitations apparently have not challenged the fundamental legitimacy of the other witnesses to Christian tradition.

Perhaps one contribution Hispanics can make to the North American church is to bear prophetic witness—in the name of God—to those elements of tradition essential to Hispanic faith intuition that are not taken seriously by the Euro-American church, starting with the very legitimacy of popular religion itself.

Notes

1. For a comprehensive review of different approaches to and definitions of popular religion, see O. Espín, "Religiosidad popular: un aporte para su definición y hermenéutica," *Estudios Sociales* 58 (1984), pp. 41–56. Popular religion is not necessarily co-extensive with popular Catholicism in the U.S. Hispanic context. In fact, a number of Hispanic communities in Florida and the Northeast would recognize as theirs religious expressions that are certainly not Catholic (e.g., Santería, etc.). In this chapter I will use "popular religion" as synonymous with "popular Catholicism." In my aforementioned article there is an extensive bibliography on the subject, but it needs to be complemented by P. W. Williams, *Popular Religion in America: Symbolic Change and the Modernization Process in Historical Perspective* (Urbana: University of Illinois Press, 1989).

2. The distinctiveness of each Hispanic (or Latino) community in the U.S.A. is more than evident. The different cultural groups cannot be naively grouped together or thought of as having the same basic history, culture, etc. However, there are some fundamental similarities that allow for valid generalizations. The best example is probably the common structures, function and features of popular Catholicism. The *mestizaje* of all Hispanic cultures is also a binding force. See, for example, R. J. Cortina and A. Moncada, eds., *Hispanos en los Estados Unidos* (Madrid: Ediciones de Cultura Hispánica, 1988).

3. By "ideology" I mean the theoretical (conscious or not) explanation or justification of a held option or position, previously chosen (again, consciously or not) for other reasons which cannot be openly acknowledged. Ideology is created and held by social classes or groups as a tool to promote their interests in the context of their interaction with other social classes or groups. A particular ideology is disseminated in society according to the number, extension, and pervasiveness of the means of socialization (schools, mass media, churches, etc.) available to the social class or group that created the ideology in question. See A. Gramsci, *Il materialismo storico e la filosofia di Benedetto Croce* (Rome: G. Einaudi Editore, 1955), pp. 868–73, 1319–20.

4. See S. Galilea, "The Theology of Liberation and the Place of Folk Religion," *Concilium* 136 (1980), pp. 40–45; and J. C. Scannone, "Enfoques teológico-pastorales latinoamericanos de la religiosidad popular," *Stromata* 40 (1985), pp. 33–47. M. R. Candelaria, *Popular Religion and Liberation: The Dilemma of Liberation Theology* (Albany: State University of New York Press, 1990) presents an interesting and suggestive study of the views of popular religion taken by two highly representative liberation theologians: Juan C. Scannone and Juan L. Segundo.

5. See P. Lengsfeld, "La Tradición en el período constitutivo de la revelación," in J. Feiner and M. Lohrer, eds., *Mysterium Salutis: Manual de teología como historia de la salvación* (Madrid: Ed. Cristiandad, 1974), I, pp. 287–337; J. Feiner, "Revelación e Iglesia. Iglesia y revelación," ibid., I, pp. 559–603; M. Lohrer, "Sujetos de la transmisión de la Tradición," ibid., I, pp. 607–68; K. Rahner and K. Lehmann, "Historicidad de la transmisión," ibid., I, pp. 794–851; K. Rahner and J. Ratzinger, *Revelación y Tradición* (Barcelona: Ed. Herder, 1971); Y. Congar, *Tradition and Traditions* (London: Burns and Oates, 1966); J. Geiselmann, *The Meaning of Tradition* (New York: Herder and Herder, 1966); R. P. C. Hanson, *Tradition in the Early Church* (London: SCM Press, 1962); J. Walgrave, *Unfolding Revelation* (Philadelphia: Westminster, 1972).

6. The "two-fonts theory" seems to have resulted from a misunderstanding of Trent. See P. Lengsfeld, "Tradición y Sagrada Escritura: su relación," in J. Feiner and M. Lohrer, eds., *Mysterium Salutis,* I, pp. 527–35.

7. Ibid, I, pp. 535–55.

8. See the Vatican II *Dei Verbum,* nn. 7–11.

9. See *Dei Verbum,* nn. 9, 12. Also G. O'Collins, "Revelation Past and Present," in R. Latourelle, ed., *Vatican II: Assessment and Perspectives* (New York: Paulist Press, 1988), I, pp. 125–37.

10. It is common in contemporary theology to include other less "ecclesiastical" means as legitimate transmitters of tradition. For example, the arts. See H. U. von Balthasar, "Arte cristiano y predicación," in J. Feiner and M. Lohrer, eds., *Mysterium Salutis,* I, pp. 774–92.

11. I think that the discussion on the relationship between "literality" and "orality" is pertinent to the study of the *sensus fidelium* as distinct from the written texts of tradition. See J. Goody, *The Interface Between the Written and the Oral* (Cambridge: Cambridge University Press, 1987); idem, *The Logic of Writing and the Organization of Society* (Cambridge: Cambridge University Press, 1986); M. Vovelle, *Ideologies and Mentalities* (Chicago: University of Chicago Press, 1990).

12. As will be stated immediately in the main text, the reluctance to study that which is transmitted orally or through popular symbols is partly due to the difficulty

in limiting the object of study. This is why the oral or symbolic communication of tradition (with the exception of the official liturgies) has not received the attention it deserves in theology. And this might have also contributed to the often superficial view of popular religion held by many theologians. In interpreting popular religion one needs to appeal to the interdisciplinary approach, just as it is the accepted procedure in the study of scripture and of the other texts of tradition. Popular religion is a very complex reality that cannot be reduced to any one category such as "devotionalism," and cannot be explained by the simplistic appeal to ignorance or syncretism caused by social conditions of poverty. See O. Espín, "Religiosidad popular," pp. 44–52.

13. As we will see later, popular religion insists on the solidarity and compassion of God, and it emphasizes the reality of the incarnation of the Son and his true humanness. Popular Catholicism expects God's affection and care for humans to be maternal and engaged. It sees Christianity as "familial" and it stresses justice, freedom, and equality as part of God's plan for humankind. Evidently, the texts of the magisterium of the church and of much of Catholic scholarship clearly agree with these emphases of popular religion. But since the agreements are mostly set out in written texts and are all too often watered down in practice, they do not appear as bearers of true tradition in the eyes of very many of those whose sincere faith is expressed through popular Catholicism. The permanence and vigor of Hispanic popular religion for close to five centuries in the United States, in spite of frequent efforts to "educate" or eradicate it, might be partially due to the people's Spirit-led insistence that the fullness of tradition be heeded and *put to practice* (and not just in written texts). Relatively recent events and divisions among Catholic African-Americans hinted at the frightening depth of racism in the U.S. church. Hispanics all across the country are well aware of the prevalence of anti-Hispanic racism and discrimination at the diocesan and (specially) the parish levels, often couched in religious or pastoral language. Justice and equality are paid lip service in chanceries and rectories, but reality tells a different story in most places. Popular Catholicism, it seems, will continue insisting on some gospel values being ignored or pushed aside by so many of the ordained ministers of the North American church.

14. These two expressions are practically equal in their use and meaning in the church. See K. Rahner and K. Lehmann, "Historicidad de la transmisión," in J. Feiner and M. Lohrer, eds., *Mysterium Salutis,* I, p. 843.

15. See the Vatican II *Lumen Gentium,* nn. 3–4, 12.

16. See *Lumen Gentium,* n. 12.

17. See J. Pelikan, *Development of Christian Doctrine* (New Haven: Yale University Press, 1969); G. A. Lindbeck, *The Nature of Doctrine: Religion and Theology in a Postliberal Age* (Philadelphia: Westminster, 1984). Also, *Dei Verbum,* n. 9.

18. See T. Citrini, "Tradición," in L. Pacomio et al., eds. *Diccionario teológico interdisciplinar* (Salamanca: Ed. Sígueme, 1983), IV, pp. 523–42; J.H. Leith, "Creeds," in A. Richardson and J. Bowden, eds., *Westminster Dictionary of Christian Theology* (Philadelphia: Westminster, 1983), pp. 131–32. Also, *Dei Verbum,* n. 8.

19. See Third General Conference of Latin American Bishops (1979), *Puebla Document,* nn. 388, 476, and passim.

20. It seems contradictory to profess belief in the indispensable nature and value of the *sensus fidelium* and then use its intuitive character as a reason to dispense with it in theology or in official church statements. Unfortunately this line of thought appeals to the fear of error in order to justify its mistaken position. Equally contradictory is the admission of the *sensus fidelium* while actually disregarding the people's "faith-full" sense in pastoral practice.

21. See R. Goizueta's chapter in this book.

22. See, for example, M. Sandoval, ed., *Fronteras: A History of the Latin American Church in the United States since 1513* (San Antonio: MACC, 1983); M.V. Gannon, *The Cross in the Sand: The Early Catholic Church in Florida, 1513–1870* (Gainesville: University Presses of Florida, 1965); P. Castañeda Delgado, E. Alexander, and J. Marchena Fernández, eds., *Fuentes para una historia social de la Florida española* (Madrid: Fundación España en USA, 1987); W. Moquin and C. van Doren, eds., *A Documentary History of the Mexican Americans* (New York: Bantam Books, 1972); R. Acuña, *Occupied America: A History of Chicanos* (New York: Harper & Row, 1981).

23. After several failed attempts dating back to 1513, the first permanent (and still functioning) settlement of Spanish Catholics occurred at St. Augustine, Florida, on September 8, 1565. See M.V. Gannon's *The Cross in the Sand* for the history of Hispanic Catholicism in Florida during the entire colonial period and well into the nineteenth century. Missionaries and settlers began penetrating today's American Southwest from Mexico as far back as the 1530s.

24. *Mestizaje* is the condition of being a mestizo, a person of mixed races. During the colonial period, and perhaps still today, persons of exclusive European ancestry looked down on the mestizo as a half-breed. So did the Amerindian or African groups that tried to reject everything from the oppressor. The mestizo among them was a living reminder of the rape and violence that accompanied their condition. Colonial legislation often denied civil rights to mestizos, and the ordained ministry was closed to them. In many places there is still a strong sense of prejudice against these persons of mixed blood. (The mestizo of Spaniard and African is usually called *mulato* in Spanish.) I am using the term *mestizaje* here more in reference to cultural mixing than to biological mixture, though the latter evidently happened and in some places very much so. For a theological and pastoral use of *mestizaje* in the United States, see the works of V. Elizondo: *Galilean Journey: The Mexican-American Promise* (Maryknoll, N.Y.: Orbis Books, 1983) and *The Future is Mestizo* (Bloomington: Meyer Stone Books, 1988).

25. The *encomiendas* were groups of Amerindians "entrusted" (i.e., *encomendados*) to a Spanish settler. The latter was supposed to evangelize them, teach them a trade and some rudimentary arithmetic and writing. In return for these benefits the Amerindians were to show their gratitude by working (for only lodging and food) for the Spaniard. The system was, in fact, a way of theoretically preserving the natives' freedom while in fact subjecting them to slavery. Very few Spanish settlers carried out their commitment to evangelize and teach, while most were eager to put the natives to work in the mines and fields. See translations of some pertinent original documents in H. M. Goodpasture, *Cross and Sword: An Eyewitness History of Christianity in Latin America* (Maryknoll, N.Y.: Orbis Books, 1989). Also B. de Las Casas, *En defensa de los indios. Colección de documentos* (Seville: Editoriales Andaluzas Unidas, 1985); O. K. Uya, *Historia de la esclavitud negra en las Américas y el Caribe* (Buenos Aires: Ed. Claridad, 1989).

26. Besides the work by H. Goodpasture mentioned in the preceding note, see the following: M. Sandoval, ed., *Fronteras* (note 22, above); E. Dussel, *Historia general de la Iglesia en América Latina* (Salamanca: Ed. Sígueme-CEHILA, 1983), vol. 1; L. Lopetegui and F. Zubillaga, *Historia de la Iglesia en la América española. Desde el descubrimiento hasta comienzos del siglo XIX* (Madrid: BAC, 1965), vols. 1 and 2. Florida was the first place, in today's United States, to see Christians martyred. See M.V. Gannon, *Cross in the Sand*, pp. 10–14.

27. See, for example, R. Ricard, *The Spiritual Conquest of Mexico* (Berkeley: University of California Press, 1966). For the lands that now are part of the United States, see, among others, M. Sandoval's *Fronteras* and M. Gannon's *Cross in the Sand*.

28. For translation of the early colonial documents, see H. M. Goodpasture, *Cross and Sword*.

29. See B. Ward, *Miracles and the Medieval Mind* (Philadelphia: University of Pennsylvania Press, 1982); R. and C. Brooke, *Popular Religion in the Middle Ages* (London: Thames and Hudson, 1984).

30. See M. Andrés, *La teología española en el siglo XVI* (Madrid: BAC, 1976), vols. 1–2. As Andrés clearly explains, the contents of Spanish theology and philosophy did develop (remember the Dominican scholars in Salamanca and Alcalá, for example), but the educational methods were still medieval.

31. *Autos de fe* were free dramatizations of Bible scenes, performed in the atrium in front of the church building or, less frequently, inside. The laity acted in these dramatizations, which were often quite elaborate. The *autos de fe* were commonly used in the evangelization of the Americas. For example, see R. Ricard, *The Spiritual Conquest of Mexico*, pp. 194–206. For Spain's popular religion at that time, see W. A. Christian, *Local Religion in Sixteenth-Century Spain* (Princeton: Princeton University Press, 1981); and idem, *Apparitions in Late Medieval and Renaissance Spain* (Princeton: Princeton University Press, 1981).

32. It is usual to refer to the Catholic Church's activities in the sixteenth century (and beyond) as the "Counter-Reformation." I think the "counter" dimension, which was certainly there too, does not fully explain what was actually happening in and through the church. See F. Martín Hernández, *La Iglesia en la historia* (Madrid: Ed. Atenas, 1984), vol. 2, pp. 83–170.

33. See E. Dussel, *Historia de la Iglesia en América Latina* (Mexico: Mundo Negro-Esquila Misional, 1983), pp. 91–115. The *Patronato Real* (i.e., "Royal Patronage") had the colonial church firmly under control. No Tridentine or pontifical document could be executed in any of Spain's territories without the royal *exequatur*. This system, which determined even minutiae of church government and customs, ended either with Latin American independence (though some of the new republics attempted for a while to continue the colonial control of the church) or with incorporation into the United States (as was the case of Florida).

34. See L. Maldonado, *Génesis del catolicismo popular* (Madrid: Ed. Cristiandad, 1979). See also C. Dehne, "Devotion and Devotions," in J. A. Komonchak, M. Collins, and D. A. Lane, eds., *The New Dictionary of Theology* (Wilmington: Michael Glazier, 1987), pp. 283–88.

35. By "iconography" I mean the sculptures, paintings, dramatizations, and stories used in the Hispanic context to graphically communicate or symbolize a biblical scene, a doctrine, or a religious disposition or feeling. It is thus only vaguely related to the Eastern Orthodox meaning of the word.

36. The *Santo Entierro* is a Good Friday public procession wherein statues of a grieving Mary (*La Dolorosa* or sorrowful one) and of a dead Jesus are carried about. Sometimes there are other statues of passion scenes included in the procession, such as one of Jesus being flagellated. The *pésames* are words of sympathy offered to the grieving Mary, and they are either set phrases sanctioned by custom or spontaneous ones. The *Cristos* are either crucifixes or statues of Jesus suffering other torments.

37. There has been some discussion as to the future of Hispanic popular Catholicism in the United States. It is argued that the forces of secularizing modernity will extinguish the need for it and the worldview upon which it depends. It seems to me, however, that indications of the effect of secularization on popular religion (in other cultural areas as well as among Hispanics) do not allow us to forecast its early demise. The symbols might be transformed or reinterpreted, as has already happened in the past, but this would be a sign of health and not of impending death. See Candelaria, *Popular Religion and Liberation*. The *Puebla Document*, nn. 460–49, addresses this issue.

38. For example, the story of the discovery of the statue of Our Lady of Charity (for Cubans and Cuban-Americans) and the legend of the origins of the painting of Our Lady of Altagracia (for Dominicans and Dominican-Americans) have the same function as the one involving Our Lady of Guadalupe. The names, geography, and other details are different, of course, but there seems to be a certain *structure* that is *culturally set* to convey precisely the religious meaning intended and to elicit the desired faith response. See Christian, *Apparitions in Late Medieval and Renaissance Spain*, pp. 10–25, 203–14; and also V. and E. Turner, *Image and Pilgrimage in Christian Culture* (New York: Columbia University Press, 1978).

39. See J. Lafaye, *Quetzalcóatl and Guadalupe: The Formation of Mexican National Consciousness, 1531–1813* (Chicago: University of Chicago Press, 1976), pp. 217–24.

40. See F. J. Perea, *El mundo de Juan Diego* (Mexico: Ed. Diana, 1988); and Lafaye, *Quetzalcóatl and Guadalupe*, pp. 211–300.

41. See Ricard, *The Spiritual Conquest of Mexico*, pp. 35–38.

42. Well-known are the chronicles (i.e., *crónicas*, hence *cronistas*) of the Franciscans Toribio de Benavente (a.k.a. "Motolinfa") and Bernardino de Sahagún, and of the Dominican Bartolomé de Las Casas.

43. See Lafaye, *Quetzalcóatl and Guadalupe*, pp. 211–37. Also L. Sejourne, "La antigua religión mexicana," in C. J. Bleeker and G. Widengren, eds., *Historia Religionum. Manual de historia de las religiones* (Madrid: Ed. Cristiandad, 1973), vol. 1, pp. 645–58.

44. See Ricard, *The Spiritual Conquest of Mexico*, pp. 83–96, 264–83.

45. Brown, *The Cult of the Saints: Its Rise and Function in Latin Christianity* (Chicago: University of Chicago Press, 1981); J. LeGoff, *The Medieval Imagination* (Chicago: University of Chicago Press, 1988); C. Saldanha, *Divine Pedagogy: A Patristic View of Non-Christian Religions* (Rome: Ateneo Salesiano, 1984).

46. Lafaye, *Quetzalcóatl and Guadalupe*, pp. 238–300; Ricard, *The Spiritual Conquest of Mexico*, p. 188. As Lafaye points out, the Virgin of Guadalupe became the symbol of Mexican nationality and independence. Ricard explains the devotion of the Spaniards to Our Lady of Remedies almost as in conscious opposition to the natives' and mestizos' devotion to Our Lady of Guadalupe. In the United

States today César Chávez and his followers have explicitly evoked the symbol of Guadalupe in their struggle for farm workers' rights.

47. From a growing body of literature, see, as examples, L. Boff, *O rosto materno de Deus. Ensaio interdisciplinar sobre o feminino e suas formas religiosas* (Petrópolis: Ed. Vozes, 1979); P. D. Young, *Feminist Theology/Christian Theology. In Search of Method* (Minneapolis: Fortress, 1990).

48. D.B. Burrell, "Analogy," in Komonchak, Collins, and Lane, eds., *The New Dictionary of Theology,* pp. 14–16; idem, *Analogy and Philosophical Language* (New Haven: Yale University Press, 1973); J. S. Martin, *Metaphor and Religious Language* (New York: Oxford University Press, 1986); P. A. Sequeri, "Analogía," in L. Pacomio et al., eds., *Diccionario teológico interdisciplinar,* vol. 1, pp. 400–12.

49. Alszeghy, "The *Sensus Fidei* and the Development of Dogma," in R. Latourelle, ed., *Vatican II: Assessment and Perspectives,* vol. 1, pp. 138–56. See also the works mentioned in note 17, above.

50. The references to the Bible, to texts of tradition and of the magisterium, and to the works of spiritual writers and theologians could be countless. The point is that all agree in affirming this possible way of experiencing and imaging God. Merely as a recent and good example, see M. K. Taylor, *Remembering Esperanza: A Cultural-Political Theology for North American Praxis* (Maryknoll, N.Y.: Orbis Books, 1990).

51. After the contributions of feminist theology, it is very difficult to deny this.

52. It is interesting to remember the church's reaction to the Marcionites' attempt to reject the Hebrew scriptures, because these too were considered a vehicle of God's revelation. It is also pertinent to recall that the church has always believed that, though intimately connected to Christ, the apostles and other authors of the New Testament were inspired when writing their texts. The modern exegetical sciences do not allow us to think that the New Testament authors were literally reporting events or words. See the very nuanced article by G. O'Collins, "Revelation Past and Present," in Latourelle, ed., *Vatican II: Assessment and Perspectives,* vol. 1, pp. 125–37. On Marcionites, see R.B. Eno, "Marcionism," in Komonchak, Collins, and Lane, eds., *The New Dictionary of Theology,* pp. 623–24.

53. For background on a method of retrieval of content from popular religion, see O. Espín and S. García, "Hispanic-American Theology," *Proceedings of the Catholic Theological Society of America,* 42 (1987), pp. 114–19; idem, "The Sources of Hispanic Theology," *Proceedings of the Catholic Theological Society of America,* 43 (1988), pp. 122–25.

54. Each devotion or symbol will have its uniqueness, as can be expected, but a systematic retrieval of contents across cultural communities would yield similar results. As an example of the work done with other symbols, see O. Espín and S. García, "Lilies of the Field: A Hispanic Theology of Providence and Human Responsibility," *Proceedings of the Catholic Theological Society of America,* 44 (1989), pp. 70–90.

55. Given the demographics of present and future Catholic population growth in the U.S.A. and in the world at large, and also given that popular religion is very much present and alive among U.S. Hispanics and in Latin America, Africa, and Asia (where the largest number of Catholics live), one is led to wonder if popular Catholicism is not in fact the *real* faith of the majority of Catholics.

56. Pertinent here is a careful consideration of P. L. Berger and T. Luckmann, *The Social Construction of Reality* (Garden City, N.Y.: Doubleday, 1966). Sugges-

tive also are H. Portelli, *Gramsci y la cuestión religiosa* (Barcelona: Ed. Laia, 1977); P. Bourdieu, *A economia das trocas simbólicas* (Sâo Paulo: Ed. Perspectiva, 1974); R. Ortiz, *A consciencia fragmentada. Ensaios de cultura popular e religiao* (Rio de Janeiro: Ed. Paz e Terra, 1980).

57. The magisterium and the theologians must also look at *their* own stereotypes, their biases and prejudices, perhaps even their own racism. Without a clear awareness of these limitations, bishops and theologians run the risk of blocking within them the voice of the Spirit speaking through the poor. What would result, then, from their discernment if they are deaf to the Spirit?

58. See O. Espín and S. García, "Lilies of the Field: A Hispanic Theology of Providence and Human Responsibility," pp. 76–79; O. Espín, "Hacia una teología de Palma Sola," *Estudios Sociales,* 50 (1980), pp. 53–68; idem, "Religiosidad popular: un aporte para su definición y hermenéutica," pp. 41–56.

59. This also means that there is an urgent need, among the people, for a culturally respectful biblical catechesis, for promoting awareness of and critical reflection on church history and socio-historical reality. This will evidently require a socially "engaged" church to grant this process real credibility.

60. See P. L. Berger and T. Luckmann, *The Social Construction of Reality;* and also S. J. Hekman, *Hermeneutics and the Sociology of Knowledge* (Notre Dame: University of Notre Dame Press, 1986). The sociology of knowledge is a pertinent contributor to this discussion.

61. Do the racism, biases, and prejudices embedded in the mediating code affect the intuition or the perception of the intuition being mediated by the code?

62. Perhaps more theological dialogue should be conducted with the social sciences, especially those that directly deal with studies of culture.

63. The theological answers to these questions might at first appear evident. But it is difficult to have these theological answers actually fit the practices that they, in the first place, are supposed to be describing and explaining. There is a gap here that needs to be addressed.

Annotated Bibliography—Orlando Espín

"Lilies of the Field: A Hispanic Theology of Providence and Human Responsibility" in *Proceedings of the Catholic Theological Society of America* 44 (1989) pp. 77–90.

This article was written with Sixto García and is one of the first to articulate the parameters for a U.S. Latino theology. Through the discussion of providence and human responsibility they propose criteria for a U.S. Latino theology. They conclude that popular religiosity data is a font and source for this emerging theology.

"The Vanquished, Faithful Solidarity and the Marian Symbol: A Hispanic Perspective on Providence," in *On Keeping Providence,* Barbara Doherty and Joan Coultas, eds. (Terre Haute: St. Mary of the Woods College Press, 1991), pp. 84–101.

Espín develops a theology of Providence retrieved from the Latino experience of historical vanquishment as symbolized by the people through their devotion to Mary. Two of these devotions are more closely examined in reference to Providence.

"Trinitarian Monotheism and the Birth of Popular Catholicism: The Case of Sixteen-Century Mexico," *Missiology* 20:2 (1992), pp. 177–204.

The author analyzes the reasons why the proclamation and acceptance of trinitarian monotheism are extremely difficult outside of European cultural milieux. This well documented and complex argument uses the example of evangelization in sixteenth-century Mexico as a case study. This article captures Espín's expert grasp of popular religion, a topic neglected in Western theology.

10

Ada María Isasi-Díaz

Ada María was born in La Habana, Cuba. She earned a masters in medieval history (MA) from State University of New York in 1977, and from Union Theological Seminary a masters in divinity (MDiv) in 1985, a masters in philosophy (MPhil) in 1989, and a doctorate (PhD) in theology (social ethics) in 1990.

For over twenty years, Isasi-Díaz has been involved in a variety of pastoral and professional ministerial experiences. She has been a parish minister, parish religious education coordinator, officer and regional developer for the Women's Ordination Conference, lecturer, and process facilitator for women's reflection groups, and director of program and associate general director for Church Women United. Since 1991 she has been associate professor of theology and ethics at Drew University. She is a well-known activist and leader in women's circles, both in this country and abroad.

In her lectures and writings, Isasi-Díaz has been an ardent advocate of *mujerista* theology. Issues of survival for Latina women are central to her work, which has earned her national recognition as a leading Latina theologian. She has published a significant original work on *mujerista* theology entitled *En La Lucha: A Hispanic Women's Liberation Theology.* She has also co-edited and co-authored three other books, and published some twenty articles on theology from the *mujerista* perspective.

Among Isasi-Díaz's many honors and achievements, two notable recent awards include the Women's Ordination Conference Annual Award for Prophetic Figures (1988) and an honorary degree "Doctor of Laws" from Lynchburg College, Virginia (1993). She is also an active member of the

Academy of Catholic Hispanic Theologians in the United States (ACH-TUS), which awarded her the Virgilio Elizondo Award in 1994.

Drew University
The Theological School
Madison, New Jersey 07940-4061
201-408-3000

Mujerista Theology's Method

A Liberative Praxis, A Way of Life

Ada María Isasi-Díaz

Mujerista theology is a liberative praxis—reflective action that has as its goal the liberation of Hispanic women. *Mujerista* theology reflects upon and articulates the religious understandings and practices of Hispanic women. *Mujerista* theology is a communal theological praxis that endeavors to enable Hispanic women to be agents of our own history, to enhance our moral agency, and to design and participate in actions that are effective in our daily struggle for survival.[1] *Mujerista* theology is a way of life, a living out of a divine call to participate in the unfolding of the kindom of God in a very specific way.[2]

Claiming the lived-experience of Hispanic women as the source of *mujerista* theology calls for a theological method that not only explicitly identifies such experience, but also presents it as unmediatedly as possible. Coupled with this methodological requirement is the commitment of *mujerista* theology to provide a platform for the voices of Hispanic women. Such requirement and commitment have led to the use of qualitative research methods to gather information, and to present it and explore it with integrity.

This article presents a brief exposition of ethnomethodology, a critique of professional social sciences that focuses on the particularities of the persons being investigated. It discusses two qualitative research methods (ethnography and meta-ethnography) used to gather the voices and lived-experiences of Hispanic women. I argue here that Hispanic theologians, committed to the liberation of our peoples, must present in their writings particular voices from the communities in which their theology is rooted. Otherwise, Hispanic theologians run two serious risks. Either they objectify Hispanic grassroot people by talking about "them" and for "them," or they

"*Mujerista* Theology's Method: A Liberative Praxis, A Way of Life," *Listening: Journal of Religion and Culture* 27:1 (Winter 1992), pp. 41–54. Reprinted with permission.

will speak exclusively with their own voices instead of providing a forum for the theological voice of their communities of struggle. Only a theological discourse which serves as a vehicle for the poor and the oppressed to speak for themselves can claim to be liberative praxis.

Ethnomethodology

Ethnomethodology is a critique of professional social sciences initially proposed by Harvard social psychologist, Harold Garfinkel. His primary criticism is that in professional sociology there is no "actor," but rather an ideal type, a dummy. Ethnomethodologists argue that it is difficult to find in sociological studies a real person with a biography and a history. The person to whom the studies keep referring is the creation of the social scientist. The self-understanding and everyday life of that person are absent from consideration. Ethnomethodology, on the other hand, is a theory of everyday life.

The basic presuppositions of ethnomethodology provide a pointed explanation of this "new" discipline that wants to be available for everyone to use in any discipline. The first presupposition is that people have and use "practical rationality," that is, people accomplish everyday life. Second, everyday life is reflexive, that is, it is contextual and self-descriptive, not explanatory. Reflexivity in this context refers to the everyday occurrence of people creating life and holding each other accountable for appropriate participation in it. Reflexivity here has to do with the definition of the situation at hand, with its integrity in itself. The third presupposition is that of indexicality, that is, that social interaction can be indexed and documented. These last two presuppositions are undergirded by an understanding of language—gestures, expressions, symbols, deportments—which create the social world.

Because of the centrality of description to ethnomethodology, the test of whether or not what one has observed corresponds to the self-understanding of the person being described is critical. In the case of the written accounts of *mujerista* theology, the test will be whether Hispanic women can respond to it positively, whether or not they can say, "Yes, this is my life, this is what I understand, this is what I mean."[3]

Ethnography

Mujerista theology recognizes and makes explicit the culture of the community out of which it arises: the Hispanic culture. It is appropriate, therefore, for those of us doing *mujerista* theology to avail ourselves of the techniques and principles of qualitative research, which is concerned with coming to know by "watching people in their own territory and interacting with them in their own language, on their own terms."[4] Furthermore, because qualitative research "involves sustained interaction with the people being studied,"[5] it is a highly appropriate technique for Hispanic theologians, who should be an integral part of the community out of which the theology they are formulating arises. Qualitative research is " 'grounded' in the everyday lives of people,"[6] and looks for explanations of "social or cultural events based upon the perspectives and experiences of the people."[7]

Of the different methods used in qualitative research, ethnography is one particularly well suited to doing *mujerista* theology. Ethnography is used by social sciences to describe and classify cultures. Ethnography is a way of conducting research that has as its foundation "the complex relationship between the researcher and his [sic] informants."[8] Ethnographical principles call for participation of the informants, of those who are being studied, in developing the method used for the study of their culture. Ethnography calls for as little mediation as possible in describing and making known the culture in question.

Using ethnographic principles, *mujerista* theology presents the understandings and opinions of Hispanic women, as much as possible, in their own words. To do this we conduct ethnographic interviews. Ethnographic interviews are much more a conversation, a dialogue, than the standard survey form of questions and answers. In contrast with other kinds of interviews, ethnographic interviews have as their goal "to learn from people, to be taught by them,"[9] instead of just gathering information about them. This learning-from-the-people occurs in the dialogic process that takes place between the researcher and the informants during these interviews. Ethnographic interviews also make it possible to hear many voices instead of hearing only the voices of the leaders of the community. The interviews, therefore, are part of a liberative praxis not only because they provide an opportunity for reflection, but also because they are often a vehicle for Hispanic women to develop their own voice. Without this voice-of-one's-own, Hispanic women are not able to be agents of our own history.[10]

In doing *mujerista* theology I have conducted ethnographic interviews in two different settings. One is in what the women who participated called "retreats," that is, reflection done in community during a weekend. The information gathered during these weekends has proved to be extremely rich. The women spark and challenge each other to become more and more reflective and explicit about their experiences and understandings. These weekends have included celebrations, as well as developing strategies for dealing with problematic circumstances at home, in the workplace, or in the community at large.[11] This is my preferred way of conducting ethnographic studies.

When this process has not been possible because of lack of money and/ or time, the interviews have been conducted individually in the homes of the Hispanic women or wherever they have chosen. In these interviews, as in group interviews, I have freely mixed techniques used for focused interviews, free-story interviews, case studies, and life histories. Because I have an ongoing relationship with most of the Hispanic women whose voices are heard in the studies I have done, they themselves have provided me with extensive information about their life histories and their process of socialization. The fact that I have worked with them, that we have engaged in praxis together, has helped me to comprehend better their religious understandings, and to see how those understandings motivate them and are rooted in their actions.

Given the great variety among Hispanic women, I had to make sure that the group of Hispanic women chosen for this study are generally representative of the total population.[12] Therefore, I have included in the sampling not only Hispanic women I know and have worked with, but also Hispanic women from communities in areas of the United States where I have been only marginally involved. I have interviewed Hispanic women from the three most numerous groups of Hispanics in the United States: Mexican American, Puerto Rican, and Cuban. Those I have worked with in articulating a *mujerista* theology come from different socioeconomic strata and different degrees of formal schooling. They vary in age from the early 30s to the late 60s. Some are deeply involved in the church at the local, regional, and even national level. For others, the church is something at best marginal in their lives.

In order to ensure diversity in the sampling, I asked Hispanics working in different parts of the country, Hispanic women with whom I do not have much in common or whose praxis is very different from mine, to choose persons from their communities for interviews. I have also gathered information from Hispanic women whose point of view differs from mine and, indeed, I have incorporated it if it is not an isolated opinion or experience, and if it contributes to the struggle for liberation.

Beyond the gathering of information through interviews, ethnographers need to include in their cultural research social, economic, and political elements. Knowing about these different factors of culture helps the researcher understand what she is seeing and hearing.[13] They help her develop a critical awareness of the everyday reality of those whose culture is being studied.

Meta-Ethnography

Mujerista theology is shaped by the experience of a great variety of Hispanic women with historical roots in different countries and in different socioeconomic contexts. In order to bring together multiple ethnographic accounts, I use the basic understandings and techniques of meta-ethnography.[14] Meta-ethnography is a way of bringing together and synthesizing ethnographic accounts. The meta-ethnography I use in doing *mujerista* theology does not attempt to aggregate the information gathered in interviews, but rather to interpret it. First, I present the different accounts as they were actually voiced by Hispanic women. I then attempt to bring together the single accounts by pointing out some of their commonalities and differences. This results in what meta-ethnography calls "knowledge synthesis," a synthesis which is both inductive and interpretative.[15]

This knowledge synthesis (or interpretative synthesis) uses an emic approach that is holistic and considers alternatives.[16] As used in *mujerista* theology, an emic approach is one that does not judge the religious understandings and practices of Hispanic women, nor does it try to make them fit into traditional theological frameworks or those articulated by others. In using an emic approach, *mujerista* theology not only is concerned with theological answers but, more importantly, asks theological questions from the perspective of Hispanic women. This emic approach is holistic because it takes into consideration the cultural context of Hispanic women. In other words, it does not present their religious understandings as something apart from their day-to-day living. In fact, in many ways, *mujerista* theology is an accomplishment of everyday life!

Finally, *mujerista* theology takes into consideration alternative interpretations of the understandings and experiences of Hispanic women. There is no desire on the part of *mujerista* theology to present a single voice. On the contrary, we consider differences to be a reality which enriches our theology, helping to keep it vital and viable.

What is the process used in meta-ethnography to arrive at knowledge synthesis? After the information is gathered from different persons throughout a certain period of time, the accounts of that information are read repeatedly, and commonalities and differences are noted. Key ideas and understandings begin to emerge. The next step in the process is that of translating the accounts into one another.

> Translations are especially unique syntheses, because they protect the particular, respect holism, and enable comparison. An adequate translation maintains the central metaphors and/or concepts of each account in their relation to other key metaphors or concepts in that account. It also compares both the metaphors or concepts and their interactions in one account with the metaphors or concepts and their interactions in the other accounts.[17]

In an attempt to avoid reductionism as much as possible, meta-ethnography, instead of combining accounts, uses analogies. For example, meta-ethnography does not posit that "Olivia and Lupe say the same thing or mean the same thing when they say. . . ." Instead, meta-ethnography brings together what the two women say by indicating that "Olivia's experience seems to be similar to Lupe's except that. . . ." Olivia's experience is not incorporated into Lupe's or vice-versa, but one is understood in comparison to the other. The differences between their experiences are not erased but read together; the similarities they suggest create the themes which *mujer-ista* theology has to take into consideration.

The purpose in doing "translations" for *mujerista* theology is to discover the themes that are important to the women, the ones which they feel the strongest, which move them, which motivate them. In *mujerista* theology we refer to these themes as generative words.[18] These generative words emerge from the world of Hispanic women and express the situations they have to grapple with, as well as their understanding of themselves in those situations. These generative words or themes are not only those "with existential meaning, and, therefore, with greatest emotional content, but they also are typical of the people."[19]

Because of the goal of *mujerista* theology and the value it places on community, the process of "translating" differs somewhat from the process used in other meta-ethnographies. The latter place both the similarities and differences found in the various individual accounts into an interpreta-tive order which results in what is called a "lines-of-argument synthesis."[20] "Lines-of-argument-syntheses" have as their goal to interpret what each one of the persons involved is saying. Generative themes, however, have as their goal the liberative praxis of Hispanic women. In the doing of *mujerista* theology, the main interest and ultimate goal is a liberative praxis that uses interpretation but does not stop there. Also different is that the interpretation used in arriving at generative themes in *mujerista* theology is not drawn from what one person says, but rather from the lived-experi-ence which makes up the daily life of Hispanic women as a community.

From the very beginning, the mental constructs and experience of the person conducting the ethnographic investigation and the meta-ethno-graphic analysis play a significant role in the process. But at this point the writer becomes, in a very special way, a key element in the process when she explains, from her own perspective, of course, the similarities and differences. In a way, at this point in the process, the materials gathered are "translated" into the experiences and understandings of the writer, and, it is to be hoped, a reverse process also takes place. This is another reason why writers of Hispanic theologies should be immersed in their communities.

Mujerista Professional Theologians as Insiders

Mujerista professional theologians do theology from within our own communities.[21] Therefore, the understanding of researcher as insider is most appropriate for us. There are three important points to consider in this regard. First, the role of insider corresponds with the understanding that the doing of *mujerista* theology is a liberative praxis—a praxis that contributes to the liberation of the *mujerista* professional theologian as well as to that of her community. In other words, as insiders, *mujerista* professional theologians profit from their doing of theology as does the community with which they work.

Second, one of the characteristics of ethnographic methodology is the dialogic relationship between the researcher and the ones being researched. Dialogue is a horizontal relationship between equals that involves communication and intercommunication Dialogue refers to a "relation of 'empathy' between two 'poles' who are engaged in a joint search,"[22] a joint search for understanding and articulating meaning. The professional theologian/researcher is one pole; the community being researched is the other. The joint search is a valuable strategy in our struggle for liberation as Hispanic women. When the professional theologian is not herself part of the community—that is, not having any vested interest in the liberation of those involved because her liberation is not connected to the liberation of others in the group—the dialogue becomes dishonest, the group being researched is objectified, and theology itself becomes a tool of oppression.[23]

Also, as insiders, *mujerista* professional theologians are able to establish this dialogic relationship much more readily than an outsider could. Very often the research is made possible or enhanced by long-term relationships between the *mujerista* professional theologian and the community, or it becomes the beginning of an ongoing relationship.[24] This has made it possible for me while conducting interviews not only to listen intensely, but also to share my own insights openly.

But I have had to accept the fact that I am both an insider and an outsider in the community of Hispanic women. I have struggled to distinguish what I hold in common with the respondents (because I am a woman and Hispanic) from what is different, i.e., class, age, role, degree of formal education, and so forth.[25] It is important to recognize that identities are always complex and multi-faceted, and, therefore, no researcher is ever totally an insider.

The third consideration has to do with factoring the experience and understanding of a professional theologian/researcher who is more an insider than an outsider. Initially in my research, I tried to listen to everyone but myself. I soon realized that it would be impossible to stay away from my own experience. I realized that whether I wanted to or not, my voice would play a role, and that I needed to listen to it instead of allowing it to operate surreptitiously. I came to understand that I had to pay attention to my own voice, to observe carefully and reflect methodically on my own experience as a Hispanic woman working for many years with my own people. The challenge for me has been, and will always be, not to allow my experience, my understandings, to become a sifter for the experiences and understandings of others. Two things have helped me avoid this. First of all, as an insider and because of the dynamics of liberative praxis, I accept seriously my responsibility to take back to the community, in a way that is meaningful to it and in a way that can be used as a tool for liberation, the understandings gained from the community.[26] If the community fails to recognize itself in the *mujerista* theology that I present, then it is obvious that I have manipulated and changed the voices of Hispanic women instead of providing a platform for them. Second, I am eager to have the informants assess my work. I take very seriously their critique, and I am committed to changing whatever they identify as not coming from them or as misrepresenting them.[27]

What can be done when the professional theologian is less an insider than an outsider? The less the professional theologian is an insider the more she must be immersed in and stand in solidarity with the community. In other words, she must allow herself to be deeply engaged by the community so that she can, as much as possible, come to understand the community from within. The difference between her context and that of the community will not disappear, but at least she may be able to grasp better the perspectives, understandings, and experiences of the community. This will lessen the likelihood of equivocation, and will steer the writer away from erroneous understandings and explanations of the commonalities and differences among Hispanic women.[28]

Reasons for Using Ethnography and Meta-Ethnography in Doing *Mujerista* Theology

Ethnography and meta-ethnography provide understandings and techniques that make it possible to discover, organize, present, and interpret the source of *mujerista* theology: the lived-experience of Hispanic women. The reasons for using ethnography and meta-ethnography, then, are to be found in the reasons we have for placing this lived-experience at the center of our theological task.

Though the expression "lived-experience" might seem tautological to some, in the context of *mujerista* theology it refers not only to what has happened—what a person has endured or made happen—but also to that experience upon which she reflects in order to understand its significance and to value it accordingly.[29] Because of the centrality of religion in the day-to-day life of Hispanic women, our understandings about the divine, and about questions of ultimate meaning, play a very important role in the process of giving significance to and valuing our experience. It is imperative for us, therefore, to comprehend better how religious understandings and practices impact our lives. In order to do this, we need to start from what we know, ourselves, our everyday surroundings and experiences.

In society, the dominant understandings and practices that are considered as having important religious significance, the ones that carry weight and impact societal norms, arise from the experience of the dominant culture, class, race, and gender. Whether or not those of the dominant culture, class, race, and gender actually invest themselves in these understandings and practices, they abide by them, consciously or unconsciously, because they are elements of the structures that keep them in power. By using our lived-experience as the source of theology, Hispanic women start from a place outside those structures, outside the traditional theology which is controlled by the dominant group. This gives us an opportunity to be self-defining, to give fresh answers and, what is most important, to ask new questions.

For us who do *mujerista* theology, it is key to look at the questions being asked in theology.[30] Our task, in general, is not that of answering from a different perspective centuries-old questions. It is not to use what grassroots Hispanic women say to answer old questions. This results in so-called "new" answers, which are most often nothing but reinterpretations of old answers. These "new" answers are old answers with different words and different emphasis, but basically they are answers within the parameters of the old answers. We consciously seek to avoid manipulating what grassroot Hispanic women say to fit the parameters established by traditional questions and "old" answers.

For example, some Hispanic theologians give great importance to Scripture. Their goal is to present Jesus in such a way that the common folk can relate to him. Undoubtedly, the experience of Hispanics also plays a part in the exegetical and interpretative work of these theologians. But in their work the fact that the great majority of Hispanics are not Bible-oriented and that the great majority of Hispanics relate very little to Jesus is never placed up front and center. Instead it is glossed over. This results, therefore, in "new" emphasis on Jesus, but never in new questions about Jesus and/or how Jesus has been used by those with power in the churches and among theologians to oppress and marginalize Hispanic women.[31]

Mujerista theology, on the other hand, using the lived-experience of Hispanic women as its main source, pushes out the old parameters and insists on new questions. In the case of Jesus, for example, we ask why it is that the majority of Hispanic women do not relate to Jesus. What does this mean about their understanding of the divine and the presence of the divine in their lives? *Mujerista* theology, then, because it asks new questions, often becomes a subversive act by enabling Hispanic women to be suspicious about what we have not participated in defining.

A third reason for insisting on the lived-experience of Hispanic women as a source for *mujerista* theology has to do with our struggle for liberation and our sanity. As people who live submerged within a culture which is not ours, we often question our ability to comprehend "reality." In a very real way, as Hispanic women, we have to "go out of our minds" in order to survive physically.[32] You can often hear Hispanic women, especially older women, respond to "that's the way things are done here," with the phrase, *¿En que cabeza cabe eso?*—In what kind of head does that fit? The reality that impacts our daily lives is often incomprehensible to us. What we say does not count; our cultural customs—dance, food, dress—are divorced from us and are commercialized; our values hardly count in society; our language is considered a threat, and millions have voted to have Spanish declared "not an official language"; our social reality is ignored. As a people we continue to slip into poverty, and suffer from the social ills prevalent in the culture of poverty.

By using our lived-experience as the source of *mujerista* theology we are trying to validate our world, our reality, our values. We are trying to reverse the schizophrenia that attacks our lives by insisting that who we are and what we do is revelatory of the divine. We ground our theology on the lived-experience of Hispanic women because it constitutes our common and shared reality. The "common sense" of Hispanic women is not wrong. We can trust it to inform and guide our day-to-day life. *Mujerista* theology wants to affirm the world-view of Hispanic women, shaped as it is by our lived-experience. For it is precisely in our world-view, in our paradigm of social reality, that we find "the categories and concepts through and by which we construct and understand the world."[33] And understanding and constructing our world is a liberative praxis.

Finally, what much of the above implies is that the centrality of the lived-experience of Hispanic women in *mujerista* theology is based on what liberation theologies call the epistemological privilege of the poor and the oppressed. This privilege is not based on the moral or intellectual superiority of the oppressed; it does not mean that Hispanic women personally are better or more innocent or more intelligent or purer in our motivations. No, this epistemological privilege is based on the possibility the oppressed have

to see and to understand what the rich and the powerful cannot see nor understand. It is not that their sight is perfect; it is the place where they are which makes the difference. Power and richness have distortionary effects—they freeze our view of reality. The point of view of the poor, on the other hand, pierced by suffering and attracted by hope, allows them, in their struggles, to conceive another reality. Because the poor suffer the weight of alienation, they can conceive a different project of hope and provide dynamism to a new way of organizing human life *for all.*[34]

The lived-experience of Hispanic women, therefore, provides a new dynamism to theology. It is our lived-experience which allows us to conceive another and a new theological reality, a liberative praxis, which we call *mujerista* theology.

Notes

1. For a more complete description of *Mujerista* theology, see Ada María Isasi-Díaz and Yolanda Tarango, *Hispanic Women: Prophetic Voice in the Church* (San Francisco: Harper and Row, 1988).

2. We do not use kingdom because it is both a sexist and classist term. Our use of kin-dom is an attempt to emphasize the communal aspect of the full establishment of God's presence among us.

3. See Harold Garfinkel, *Studies in Ethnomethodology* (Cambridge, England: Polity Press, 1984) 1–115. See also, Thomas Dale Watts, "Ethnomethodology: A Consideration of Theory and Research," *Cornell Journal of Social Relations* 9 (1973) 99–115.

4. Jerome Kirk and Marc I., Miller, *Reliability and Validity in Qualitative Research,* Qualitative Research Methods, Vol. 1 (Beverly Hills, CA: Sage Publications, 1988) 9.

5. Ibid., 12.

6. George W. Noblit and R. Dwight Hare, *Meta-Ethnography: Synthesizing Qualitative Studies,* Qualitative Research Methods, Vol. 11 (Beverly Hills, CA: Sage Publications, 1988) 12.

7. Ibid.

8. James P. Spradly, *You Owe Yourself a Drunk—An Ethnography of Urban Nomads* (Boston: Little, Brown and Company, 1970) 7.

9. James P. Spradley, *The Ethnographic Interview* (New York: Holt, Rinehart and Winston, 1979) 4.

10. Ethnographic interviews are only one of the tools used by *mujerista* theology. Observation, studies of traditional religious understandings and beliefs, studies in comparative religions—all of these are also tools used by *mujerista* theology.

11. I am referring here to the research I did for *Hispanic Women,* and *"En La Lucha": Elaborating a "Mujerista" Theology* (Minneapolis: Fortress Press, 1993).

12. I never ask the Hispanic women I interview if they are Roman Catholic. However, that is my own faith tradition and the church in which I have worked in different ways for many years. Also, most of the women I have worked with in articulating a *mujerista* theology are Roman Catholic. For an explanation of how some elements of Roman Catholicism have become an intrinsic part of Hispanic culture, see *Hispanic Women.* Most of my work in the decade of the 1980s was in ecumenical settings. This allowed me to come in contact with and learn from Hispanic women who belong to Protestant denominations and also to Pentecostal churches.

13. I have used the basic understanding of ethnography presented by Spradley, and adapted it according to the values I hold as a *mujerista* theologian. See Spradley, *The Ethnographic Interview,* 3–16.

14. Though basically following the understandings and techniques explained in the works quoted in this section, I have also adapted meta-ethnography according to values I hold as a *mujerista* theologian.

15. Noblit and Hare, *Meta-Ethnography,* 16.

16. An emic approach is one that deals with various elements of a culture as they are related to each other rather than describing them in reference to a general classification decided in advance, outside the culture. The "emic" approach can best be understood in reference to the "etic" approach which is a generalized approach working to fit the different elements of a culture into general categories claiming to apply to all cultures. See *Oxford English Dictionary,* 2d ed., s.v. "emic" and "etic."

17. Ibid., 28–29. To avoid confusion I will use quotation marks around the word "translation" when it refers to the process just identified.

18. This is the name given to them by Freire. See Paulo Freire, *La educación como práctica de la libertad* (Madrid: Siglo Veintiuno de España Editores, 1976) 108–113.

19. Ibid., 109.

20. Ibid., 62–64.

21. Professional theologians are one of the kinds of Hispanic women theologians that *mujerista* theology recognizes, takes into consideration, enables and welcomes. *Mujerista* theology also welcomes the grassroot Hispanic woman theologian, who does theology in the simple sharing of what happens in day-to-day life, who is gifted in analyzing and expressing the beliefs which ground her religious practices. A third "kind" of *mujerista* theologian includes those Hispanic women who have some training in religious studies: catechists, pastoral workers, and ordained Hispanic women in Protestant churches.

22. Paulo Freire, *Cultural Action for Freedom* (Cambridge: Harvard Educational Review, 1970) 45.

23. Ibid., 52.

24. This has happened to me repeatedly with the women I interviewed. I knew most of them before the inteview, and I have continued to be their friend. Two of those whom I met for the first time during the research for the book have kept in contact with me, and we have become friends.

25. Elizabeth Jameson, "Introduction," in *Insider/Outsider Relationships with Informants,* Working Paper No. 13 (University of Arizona: Southwest Institute for Research on Women, 1982) 3.

26. Elizabeth Jameson, "May and Me" in *Insider/Outsider Relationships with Informants,* Working Paper No. 13 (University of Arizona: Southwest Institute for Research on Women, 1982) 11.

27. Linda Light and Nancy Kleiber, "Interactive Research in a Feminist Setting: The Vancouver Women's Health Collective," in *Anthropologists at Home in North America* (Cambridge: Cambridge University Press, 1981) 167–184. The authors report that the informants they dealt with demanded that they share their research notes!

28. Ada María Isasi-Díaz, "Solidarity: Love of Neighbor in the 1980s," in *Lift Every Voice: Constructing Christian Theologies from the Underside* (Susan Brooks Thistlethwaite and Mary Potter Engel, eds.; San Francisco: Harper and Row, 1990) 31–40.

29. Following Gramsci, I believe that action has a reflective quality. This assertion is very important for Hispanics because U.S. society tends to disregard our intellectual ability due to a certain lack of formal education. Also following Gramsci, I claim that Hispanic women are organic thinkers, and that *mujerista* theology, which is based on "the principles and problems raised by . . . their practical activity," is organic theology. See Antonio Gramsci, *Prison Notebook* (ed. and trans. Quintin Hoare and Geoffrey Nowell Smith; New York: International Publishers, 1975) 6, 330.

30. As Rosaldo said, "What is needed . . . is not so much data as questions." M. Z. Rosaldo, "The Use and Abuse of Anthropology: Reflections on Feminism and Cross-Cultural Understanding," *Signs* 5 (Spring, 1980) 390.

31. See Virgil Elizondo, *Galilean Journey: The Mexican-American Promise* (Maryknoll, NY: Orbis Books, 1983).

32. The first person I ever heard give this expression the interpretation I present here was Barbara Zanotti, who together with me and four other women participated in a dialogue with United States Bishops on the issue of the ordination of women in the Roman Catholic Church at the beginning of the 1980s.

33. Liz Stanley and Sue Wise, *Breaking Out: Feminist Consciousness and Feminist Research* (London: Routledge & Kegan Paul, 1983) 154. Also, Janet Silman, "In Search of a Liberative Methodology," Unpublished Paper, May 7, 1988.

34. José Míguez Bonino, *"Nuevas Tendencias en Teologia,"* in *Pasos* 9 (1987) 22.

Annotated Bibliography—Ada María Isasi-Díaz

Apuntes for a Hispanic Women's Theology of Liberation, In *Voces: Voices from the Hispanic Church,* Justo González, ed. (Nashville: Abindgon Press, 1992), pp. 24–31.

Latino/a theology claims to do theology in *conjunto* with the faith community it represents. In this article the author outlines the role and task of the theological community from the Latina perspective. The result is a description of Latina theology as cultural—against ethnic prejudice; as feminist—struggling against sexism; as liberation—struggling against classism; and as Christian—grounded on Christian understandings and practices. She sees theology as praxis engaged in the survival of Latina women. The task of doing theology is contextualized in the Latina *mestizaje,* the liberative task of Latinas being agents of their history, and done within the communal organic Latina's perspective.

En La Lucha—In the Struggle: Elaborating a Mujerista Theology (Minneapolis: Fortress Press, 1993).

This important work by a leading Latina theologian is more than simply about feminist issues in theology. Since Isasi-Díaz's work is done from within the real life situations of Latina women's survival issues, her methodological and ethical perspectives attempt to deconstruct the dominant normative understanding for doing theology. The text outlines the social context of Latina women, offers an insightful survey of women's voices, argues for a theological methodology for *mujeristas,* and presents a thematization of Latinas' cultural praxis as their struggle for liberation. Her use of other Latina women's voices and the inclusion of a summary in Spanish to each chapter give the book a truly *mestiza* flavor. The author concludes that Latina women's survival issues (*En la lucha*) is an authentic point of departure for doing theology and that the *mujeristas'* moral praxis in the face of oppression provides a renewed theological legacy of liberation for a new humanity.

"Defining Our *Proyecto Histórico: Mujeristas* Strategies for Liberation," In *Journal of Feminist Studies in Religion* 9: 1–2 (Spring/Fall 1993) pp. 17–28.

This article reads like a Latina manifesto. The author calls for a Latina historical project by setting up strong community organizations that help construct the Latina identity, strengthen them as moral agents, and povide fertile settings for liberative praxis. From the Latina perspective liberation is understood as salvation when women become agents of their own history in the realization of the historical project, the "kin-dom" of God. This is realized from within Latina women's struggle for life. She challenges the reader to make a preferential option for struggling Latina women, challenges Latina women to fight against apathy and fear, and to develop their own models of leadership presently lacking in church structures. While this *proyecto histórico* is not a blueprint for society, she presents a provocative test of how to make theology credible.

11

María Pilar Aquino Vargas

María Pilar Aquino Vargas was born in México. She began her theological studies at the noted Instituto Teológico de Estudios Superiores (ITES) in México where she obtained a licentiate in sacred theology in 1984. She earned her doctorate (STD) in systematic theology from the Universidad Pontificia de Salamanca, Spain, in 1991.

Similar to other Latino/a theologians, Aquino's background includes both pastoral and academic experiences. In San Bernardino, California, she worked with the Department of Evangelization and Catechesis. At Mount St. Mary's College in Los Angeles, she directed the Hispanic Pastoral Ministry Program (1985–1993). Currently she is assistant professor of theological and religious studies at the University of San Diego.

Aquino has published and lectured extensively in the United States and Latin America. Her works bridge the theological discussion between U.S. Latino/a theology and Latin American liberation theologies. Besides her recent book, *Our Cry for Life: Feminist Theology from Latin America* (1993), she has written twenty-one articles and edited a volume on theology from the feminist perspective.

Professionally, she serves on several editorial boards such as the theological journal *Reflexión y Liberación* (Chile), *Journal of Hispanic/Latino Theology,* and *Concilium.* She is a member of the Catholic Theological Society of America, the American Academy of Religion, the Ecumenical Association of Third World Theologians, and the Academy of Catholic Hispanic Theologians in the United States of which she was the president (1993).

University of San Diego
Department of Theological and Religious Studies
5998 Alcalá Park
San Diego, California 92110
619-260-4600

Directions and Foundations of Hispanic/Latino Theology

Toward a Mestiza Theology of Liberation

María Pilar Aquino

A quick look at the theological works produced in the last five years by the members of the Academy of Catholic Hispanic Theologians (ACH-TUS) leads us to recognize that the creative abilities of the Latina Christian communities in North America have been exercised with great vitality.[1] My reflections seek to give an account of the great vitality of our theological task during the most recent past and present. For that purpose, I want to concentrate on three correlative dimensions. The first exposes what, in my opinion, constitutes the very character of our theological task, the second explores the context of the reality that compels the elaboration of this type of theology and not another, and finally, I will end by pointing to some active factors in our theology, from which, I believe, our theologizing derives its present creativity and its dynamic character vis-à-vis the future.

1. ACHTUS: A New Thought for a New World

An unprecedented fact in our midst is the birth of a theological trend that consciously and critically seeks to respond to the faith experience, needs, and liberating ends of the Hispanic/Latino people. This theology, brought about as a collective effort, proposes to articulate systematically our self-understanding as *subjects* and *actors* of faith and history in the circumstances of the present. In this effort the decisive participation of a significant number of Latino theologians highlights today, more than ever, that the critical-prophetic sensitivity of the Christian community is alive despite some signs to the contrary. In many ways we share the conviction

"Directions and Foundations of Hispanic/Latino Theology: Toward a *Mestiza* Theology of Liberation," *Journal of Hispanic/Latino Theology* 1:1 (November 1993), pp. 5–21.

that reality does not show all its possibilities until we make the decision to explore it with imagination and open minds, to bring forth our own expectations in congruence with our own roots. Reality itself, in which often the life of a few is saved at the expense of the death of many, has pushed us to discern the real alternatives that we have in the current context of a capitalistic, patriarchal society.

Although there were those who opened the way, who perceived with lucidity the great potential contained in the multiple socio-religious practices of our people, there were also many suspicions, uncertainties, and fears. No one had the answer, no one knew *what* was, or *how* to produce, a theology capable of satisfactorily interpreting the history, crises, strengths, and possibilities for change that our people had before them. In the United States, until recently, there was no theology capable of credibly expressing the motivations, the values, the meaning of Latino existence and the imperatives that guided our actions for change in the framework of a socio-cultural world different from the androcentric, Euro-American one. No one knew how, until we began to do it.

It was necessary, as V. Elizondo has indicated, to think with our own minds, feel with our own senses, and take in our own hands the challenge to live the radical meaning of our new being, that of the "pueblo mestizo."[2] As a matter of fact, other theologies in the United States asked their own questions and produced their own answers to situations seen as relevant in the framework of their own contexts, but none incorporated into their tasks the aspects inherent to the Latinos' and Latinas' human and Christian existence. Even more importantly, the elaboration of a theology congruent with our people's journey implied the search for our own answers to the ancient philosophical question that has concerned all peoples about their own existence, as V. Elizondo summarizes very well: ". . . others had been telling us who we were. Nobody had bothered to ask us, 'Who are you?' Until now, all kinds of experts had studied us, but no one had even sought to enter into conversation with us so that they might truly understand who we see ourselves to be. This was the very root of our oppression. We were not allowed to be who we were. We were never allowed to simply say: 'I am.' "[3]

In the hope of giving an account of our own humanity, without defining it *a priori* with the categories imposed as normative by those who have dominated the world of knowledge during the last five hundred years, we found ourselves needing to draw its features. With the powerful tools of the word, we are shouting loudly in the public squares what many generations were whispering in this land before the European colonizing expansion. In the recent indigenous theology of the Andean peoples, it is said that "We planted our ideas, we made our ideas germinate (that is, we did theology), for us to know how to survive in the midst of much hunger, to defend ourselves from so much scandal and attacks, to organize ourselves in the midst of so much confusion, to be elated despite so many sorrows, and to dream beyond so much desperation."[4]

In the same way, in our case, theological language is a vital tool for rehabilitating the hope of those who have come before us, filling ourselves with the strength of the perseverance of those who refused to be forgotten. Our theological language needs to continue the struggle against the evils that aim to reduce us to nonexistence, to affirm that our destiny is not the cumulative destruction of earth, persons, and peoples. We want to know who we are so that others may know how *we* say "we are" and not how *they* have said it, and to tell ourselves what kind of world we want and how we wish to share it with the whole of creation.

Even with the ambiguities inherent to any new process, Hispanic/Latino theology is showing its own consistency as a discourse valid and credible not only for our communities but also for others interested in the search for alternatives to the present order. Quite explicitly, the present order is demonstrating its incapacity to guarantee the very existence of humanity and of the planet itself. Accordingly, our theology recognizes the need to support efforts that seek a different social order. Basic to this purpose, Hispanic/Latino theology has consciously joined the debate, now at a world level, over the identity and function both of European patriarchal Christianity and of Roman Catholicism in facing the imperatives posed by our indigenous and *mestizo* peoples, by women, and by native cultures and religions of the continent and the Caribbean. The presentations made by J. Rodríguez, A. Stevens-Arroyo, G. Romero, A. M. Isasi-Díaz, and S. J. García during the ACHTUS Colloquium of 1992[5] illustrate this quite well. We cannot predict the final result of this process, but we can be accountable for the motives leading us and for the directions we wish to follow.

The growing strength of our theology can be appreciated, among other factors, in the appropriation it has made of indigenous, African, and European traits as constitutive dimensions of its being; in the appropriation that Latino communities make of this reflection; in the increasing production and publication of collective and individual works; in the consolidation of La Comunidad of Hispanic American Scholars of Theology and Religion and of the Academy of Catholic Hispanic Theologians of the United States; in the founding of the *Journal of Hispanic/Latino Theology* as well as the success of the journal *Apuntes;* in the growing incorporation of Hispanic/Latino theologians in the plenary sessions, convention workshops, and meetings of professional theological associations such as the Catholic Theological Society of America and the American Academy of Religion; in the growing incorporation of courses on Hispanic/Latino theology in the official curriculum of institutions of higher learning as required subjects; and finally, in the growing participation of Hispanic theologians in social movements and in the processes of pastoral ministry that accompany the faith experience of ecclesial communities.

The theoretical quality of our theological reflection must be sought in its *basic structure* as well as in its *principle of articulation* rather than in the criteria derived from the dominant academic community. This is due to the fact that both basic structure and principle of articulation imply and suppose the reformulation of normative theological rationality. A new theory of critical thought is being developed for Latina communities. As R. Goizueta indicates, ". . . U.S. Hispanic theology is born out of the praxis of Latino communities and, as such, attempts to be a *teología de conjunto.* . . . U.S. Hispanic theology does not reject reason, rather it rejects the dominant culture's conceptualist and instrumentalist models of reason and criteria or reasonableness."[6] This theology, intrinsically rooted in our *mestiza* condition, presents itself as a critical reflection on the lived experience our people have of God in their daily struggles against suffering, oppression, and violence. The *object* of Latino theology is God, but a God discovered within the native worldview of the Latina communities, and named from within their experiences of life and death, word and silence, joy and suffering, liberation and oppression. That is, *Ahí, en la lucha,* ("There, in the struggle") as described by A. Isasi-Díaz.[7] This basic structure determines in a radical way the methodological articulation, the theological content, and the central themes of our theology.

In the same manner, following Goizueta's thinking, this theology constitutes itself by the internal principle of *praxis,* articulated communally, aesthetically, and rationally, as opposed to current theological discourses, some of which are regulated by conceptual and abstract principles that do not take history into account, or reject all rational discourse. This understanding implies at least two things. On the one hand, that Latino theology is formed "from within a self-conscious solidarity with the historical struggles of U.S. Hispanic communities," and on the other hand, that our theology presupposes "not only the possibility and obligation of ethical-political action, but also the possibility and obligation of rational discourse."[8] This principle of praxis, "always understood as liberative praxis,"[9] as A. Isasi-Díaz ably qualifies, allows our theology to assume an attitude of critical vigilance so as not to convert itself into an abstract discourse that, in the end, will only hide the subjectivity of the "alterities" or will impede the struggle against the causes that keep our people in misery.

It is with good reason that while A. Bañuelas identifies our theology as "a subversive and passionate theology,"[10] F. F. Segovia points out that its essential components are "struggle, liberation, and self-determination." These are not understood as separate elements "but rather as thoroughly interrelated and interdependent," since Hispanic/Latino theology is radically rooted "in our own *mestizaje* and *mulatez,* in our own expansive and expanding *raza.*"[11]

In this sense, one can appropriately say that the *subject* of Latino theology is the people. In a collective document elaborated as a result of the First Latin American *Encuentro* on Indigenous Theology held in Mexico City, May 1991, it was acknowledged that

> the theological subjects are persons, communities, and not just vague
> people, but communities on the move, with a project, on the
> march. . . . In the community there are persons, the *Machis* of the
> Mapuche world, the *Sáilas* of the Kuna world, the *Yatiri* and the
> *Pacos* of the Quíchuas and Aymaras. The subject is the community,
> but the community has its representatives, its wise men and wise
> women, its mystics; these are leaders who speak, think, heal, convene,
> point the way forward . . . there are persons who at the moment of
> involving themselves in the theological task rediscover their being
> and their mission in the midst of the people.[12]

Coincidentally, we also emphasize the intrinsic relationship that exists among the community, the "historical project," and the understanding of the Hispanic theologian "as the Thinker, Actor, Poet, and Prophet of the Community,"[13] in the words of S. García. On his part, R. Goizueta, formulates a similar statement: "The theological subject is not the *ego* but the *communio* . . . taking the community as its starting point; though an 'individual,' the theologian does not undertake his or her task *qua* individual, but *qua* member of the community. His or her authenticity is either affirmed or denied by that community."[14]

These assertions, in my view, emphasize the convergence that in fact exists in the emerging theologies, both in terms of method and in the manner they produce knowledge. Therefore, the route taken by Latino theology so far indicates that, in our midst, this new theological current presents itself as a theoretical-practical discourse, necessary to face the vital questions posed by the praxis of the Latino communities in the United States from their own sociocultural framework. These questions are related to the building of an alternative society, an alternative Church, and an alternative culture capable of demonstrating their ability to sustain and promote the life of every person, every community, and every people, and of the foundation for the survival of all creation, earth itself.

From this perspective, our theology is understood to be a liberating theology. We then speak of the *teología mestiza de la liberación,* called to share the methodological and epistemological principles to which all liberating theologies subscribe. Our theological task does not exist because of the desire to create a bridge between Latin American liberation theology and European-American critical thought. Neither does it exist to correct the shortcomings of the Roman Catholic conservative discourse vis-à-vis today's emancipatory movements and social sciences. Rather, our task exists because of the vital need for a coherent formulation of *our own* faith experience based on our *mestiza* condition and as we face an oppressive reality that we seek to overcome, there where the liberating traditions of Christianity and the vision and strategies of the liberating socio-ecclesial movements of today dynamically converge.

2. The Historical Coordinates of Hispanic/Latino Theology

What is the context which gives birth to this type of theology and not another? What is the foundation that gives viability and significance to this theology vis-à-vis the reality of our people? The possible responses to these questions must take into account two elements: on the one hand, the forms adopted by patriarchal capitalism in its current neoliberal version, and on the other, the real conditions in which our communities live (with their heterogeneity, tensions, and unsatisfied desires). Both elements can only be adequately understood in the framework of the so-called *crisis of modern civilization,* or the questioning of modernity as cultural horizon. From what I can perceive in the majority of recently published works, this is the context confronted by Latino theology. I will now emphasize some of the more important factors which have been taken into account in the elaboration of our theological discourse.

From the European viewpoint, historically and symbolically the fifteenth century represents the beginning of "a new era," a new civilization based on an understanding of history as universal history and as unlimited progress supported by the "discoveries" of the so-called new world. Instrumental reason was the privileged tool for this unlimited progress, now applied without any regulation outside itself. Along with this, at least theoretically, the spheres of ethics, aesthetics, and science took different paths. This process was set in motion by the belief that unlimited historical progress, through modern science would take societies to higher levels of civility and humanization.[15] It follows that beginning in 1492, as indicated by M. Villamán, through conquest and colonization the now called "American" continent came to be part of a world culture and of a "civilizing project of universal character represented by modernity," both brought from the outside, from the centers of power.[16] Consequently, as O. Espín points out, "when these lands joined Europe's history, they did so as conquered territories and their peoples as vanquished. And when large contingents of Africans were forced to join Europe's trans-Atlantic world, they did so in chains. . . . Only the Europeans (and their successors), by and large, saw the experience as mainly a positive process."[17]

Although unequally, the most diverse societies began the race toward a project now not only understood as normative for obtaining a humanizing and civilizing human social order, but also as the "sole horizon of future for our peoples," as it was realized in the nations of the North.[18] Although based on different ideologies, liberal capitalism and socialism come to be the two models derived from this vision, and both offered real conditions for the historical and symbolic continuation of the ancestral patriarchal world.[19] Nonetheless, an honest look at the results of this project leads one to recognize, in the words of F. Hinkelammert, that "the culture of modernity, as it has emerged since the sixteenth century, has taken [us] to social crises and catastrophes of such magnitude that the entire model of Western civilization seems to be in crisis."[20]

As M. Villamán sums up, the failure of this project expresses itself in "the ample reproduction of poverty at a world level; the ever increasing human capacity for destruction; the ecological disaster resulting from the models of development based on consumerism and profit; and the ecological impossibility to sustain this dominant model of development."[21] Along with this, there is manifest a systemic deepening of Euro-American colonialism, of racism, sexism, and the massive deterioration of entire peoples whose final destiny is death. Given this picture, F. Hinkelammert finds himself obliged to say that "modernity rides on a self-destructive carousel. . . . It is a carousel of death."[22]

What this process has meant to the Latina communities can be seen in the increasing deterioration of their real-life conditions. Ten years ago, the Roman Catholic bishops stated that "in general, most Hispanics in our country live near or below the poverty level . . . 22.1 percent of Hispanics live below the poverty level, compared with 15 percent of the general population."[23] Although the actual population figures might be between 25 and 30 million, the official figures for 1990 speak of 22.4 million. The statistics of only three years ago indicate that

> 28% of Hispanic individuals live below the poverty level, compared to 32% of blacks and 11% of whites; 23% of Hispanic households are headed by single women, and have a medium income of less than $12,000; 25% of Hispanic couples with children live in poverty, compared to 7% of whites and 14% of blacks. The median earnings for Hispanic men are $14,141 compared to $22,207 for non-Hispanic men; 32% of Hispanics have no health insurance, compared to 13% of whites and 20% of blacks. From 1985 to 1990, the number of uninsured Hispanics increased from 5.59 million to 9.95 million, while the numbers of uninsured whites and blacks decreased.[24]

As far as the academic world is concerned, it is recognized that "Hispanics represent only a small number of faculty members and administrators. They hold 3.3 percent of higher education positions. At the faculty level, women hold 1.2 percent of full-time positions. They are more likely to be instructors than to be assistant, associate or full professors."[25]

With this picture, we really cannot say that in the last ten years, nor even in the last three years, there has been any improvement in the living conditions of the Latino communities. To the contrary, their condition has become more dismal and difficult, resulting in dramatic struggles for their very survival. As pointed out by F. Hinkelammert, "uncontained migrations from the Third World to the developed world, by those excluded from their native lands, are going to subvert existing social systems, demonstrating ever more clearly that we live in one world whose survival is a problem for all of us. This seems to be the vortex into which modernity is falling."[26]

As far as the causes that explain modernity's seeming end, following Villamán's thought,[27] they can be summarized as follows: First, the failure of the predominance of instrumentalist reason that, while organizing all inside corners of human existence, blocks all possibility for discussion of social problems from the ethical-political viewpoint since it reduces these to strictly scientific or technical issues. Second, the irruption of diverse rationalities (e.g., Indigenous/Native American, black, feminist, ecological, etc.) that question the pretensions of universality of modern European-American rationality and affirm the legitimacy of the former. Third, the failure of the notion of the inevitability of progress, and along with that the ecological impossibility of the dominant model to support the world economy. Because of this, such progress needs to be submitted to a permanent ethical-political analysis. Fourth, the questioning of the great narratives together with the great utopias on which the project of modernity is based. The rejection of the validity of those narratives is achieved by questioning their totalitarian tendency. These narratives are merely the manifestation of a domesticating rationality as they presume to establish projects of universal character.

At present, however, modernity's project seeks to restructure itself with a new proposal, which is now presented as a "total solution to history."[28] This is possible thanks to the crises of the so-called real socialisms and the movement in Eastern Europe toward a market economy, with the resulting end of the East-West conflict. Now the North American capitalistic model presents itself as the only world model. The result is that now all social decisions are subordinated to the world capitalistic market; one empire with sole power. Thus the belief that the North American capitalist society can be summarized as democratic, open, and pluralistic. In reality, what results is a closed society, a totalitarian capitalistic order in which, so it is believed, there are no alternatives beyond itself. There are no longer any real bases on which to consider an alternative social order. At last, says F. Hinkelammert, "this means that for the first time the Third World finds itself completely alone,"[29] as does each of the Latino communities which are a part of that world. We have been given a choice: either we submit or we perish.

Thus arises the belief that solutions to current problems can only be sought within the framework of neoliberal thinking. Every other proposal for human development makes no sense. This new offering comes dressed with ethical and anthropological values that supposedly not only give it significance and validity, but also present it as the most reasonable alternative for today's world. Among the ethical values proposed, the following can be stressed:[30] the possibility of concurrence in the market system based on individual freedom to buy and sell; competition and individual benefit based on objective efficiency; the affirmation of the right to unlimited property whose only limit is the individual's ability to obtain goods. This world of values[31] is also presented as reasonable in its theologized form to show the congruence between capitalistic society and Christianity. However, this proposal in fact denies the ethical principles that could organize not only an existence worthy of all humanity, but also the very survival of the earth.

The neoliberal anthropological view claims that the individual is the basis for all social structure, and not just any individual, but one intrinsically competitive.[32] Individuals fulfill themselves as human beings when they exercise their individual liberty to obtain the most benefit possible out of life, being led by a compulsive desire to consumerism. As a consequence, competitiveness becomes the maximum criterion to establish the "success level" in society. Whoever does not compete, whoever does not consume, whoever does not seek profit, or whoever does not participate in the free market, has simply signed his/her death sentence. Such a person or community is expelled from every process that brings about growth and benefit.

The current neoliberal project in effect transforms itself into a source of constant conflict and frustration for a multitude of marginalized social sectors, peoples, races, and cultures. For these, the cultural universe of modernity cannot offer a realistic response to the questions of their own human dignity, because patriarchal capitalistic society denies that possibility. Accumulative exclusion becomes the engine for the current social project. The law of competitiveness in a free market does not recognize a responsibility toward the poor or oppressed. Even more, it declares as inefficient, illusory, and irrational any attempt to recast society to one based on justice, universal solidarity, and the common responsibility for all of creation.

In this manner, if we come to believe in the rationality of the powerful, if we accept the version of reality espoused by those who see salvation in the current situation, then we have nothing to do here. There would be no valid reason to justify the existence of Latino theology. Our theology could never claim that its authenticity comes from the community, as the primary subject of reflection. However, I believe that this is not the case. The very existence of a *mestiza* theology of liberation, even with its unresolved challenges, comes to demonstrate a collective discomfort with respect to modern white, male, Euro-American culture. While the current American system declares any alternative dead, thereby destroying any possibility of reaching those alternatives, the Latina communities in the midst of their oppression continue to envision a world in which we all can live. As long as Latino theology continues to demonstrate its ability to coherently articulate that which can be, convinced of its possibility, then our task finds its worth and meaning.

We must not lose sight of the fact that our reflection takes place within a context of conflict in which growing depredation is accepted as necessary to save the free market. This fact is ever more important because, despite the growth of massive impoverishment—even more visible among women—the current dominant discourse denies any existence of a crisis, since there continues to be growth in the business world.[33] In this context, we must critically analyze the trends of patriarchal capitalism, its institutions, its socio-religious world of values, and its consequences on the daily life of our communities. In this context, in contrast with the models of instrumentalist reason,[34] we must also recover historical reason, expressed as *liberating sentient reason,* as a condition for continuing to envision new ways of living from within our own sociocultural points of reference. Those new ways must be found in the framework of an authentic recognition of what our reality shows about itself, namely that we live in an ever more polycentric reality.[35]

What we must do today finds its ultimate justification in what our people recognize as the ultimate basis of their existence. That basis springs from their experience of God, from what the people recognize as the true face of God under many names: Merciful God, the God of peace and justice, the God of the *barrio,* the God of the poor and oppressed, the God of Jesus the *Mestizo,* the God of grace, the God of *mañana,* the God of Life, and the God who is love.[36] From this ultimate foundation emerges the understanding that we have about our ultimate vocation. This is not what F. Hinkelammert denounces as "the heroism of collective suicide,"[37] but rather life at its fullest for the sake of all creation. This is also the root of our stance before what we have and what we must do in present and future circumstances. Because of this, Latino theology emphasizes the urgency of an enterprise seeking alternatives to the present reality. In this respect, Hinkelammert's reflections shed light on this task as they show that

an alternative cannot come forth except from an affirmation of life vis-à-vis this celebration of death. However, the affirmation of life cannot be a mere romantic declaration. . . . It imposes a reformulation of Western civilization which implies overcoming it. It must reshape that civilization from the starting point of the life of all who have been excluded from life by that very civilization. The affirmation of life, if it is not to be mere phraseology, must, of necessity, start by the affirmation of the life of all the excluded who have been expelled by modernity from their possibility of living: human beings and nature. It deals with the only categoric imperative that this affirmation can halt the holocaust which threatens us. But it can do so only if it becomes a transformer of society, its culture and its institutions, which will make possible a society that sustains life for all.[38]

3. The Dynamics of Our Theological Task

Under this simple rubric I am interested in presenting briefly some key elements that I find in several recent works by Latino theologians. I must make clear that each of these elements bears greater theoretical and methodological complexity and, because of this, I can only here sketch those that identify our task within the context I have been discussing in this article. Eight elements stand out.

A. On Behalf of Life and Liberation

While the project of modernity is based on principles that have brought about death in its various forms to peoples, cultures, and the earth, the *mestiza* theology of liberation affirms that life and liberation are its foundational principles. With F. F. Segovia, we come to the conclusion that our theology

> must be a theology of and for life, a theology with an undifferentiated and fully intertwined realized and future eschatology, an unwavering commitment to the world with a driving vision of a different and better world, and a profound sense of joy in the midst of anguish. . . . Conceived in mixture, it must opt for the immense richness and diversity of life, not overwhelming the other, as it too was overwhelmed, but rather affirming the other as other, as it too struggles for such affirmation and dignity.[39]

B. On the Side of the Poor and Oppressed

Since our theology does not have as its central concern abstract subjects nor does it move in a metaphysical world, as do current neoliberal and conservative theologies, our theological task assumes a clear option for the poor and oppressed.[40] That option implies at least four aspects.[41] First, we assume these populations as the subjects for constructing our theology, since their internal structure is based on the principle of life, primarily manifested in their struggles and hopes, audacity and strength, compassion and deep humanism, *fiesta* and celebration, commitment and prayer. Second, we do not declare ourselves irresponsible vis-à-vis the destiny of the larger population which is considered superfluous by current patriarchal capitalism. Third, our theology includes a critical appropriation of all dimensions deriving from our *mestiza* condition. Fourth, this option contains God's truth and therefore becomes the criterion for interpreting divine revelation and for shaping our daily living, both public and private.

C. A Qualified Reading of History

The true reality of events has been hidden by a history based on myths, written by white men in power. Before this history, Justo González asserts, it behooves us to assume an attitude of alertness, an unveiling function, demythologizing it to the point that the issues of justice can be seen clearly as they truly appear in the reality of history.[42] In this sense, the reading of history by Latino or Latina theologians often seems to be qualified by the awareness of their marginal location there where history is read from the Anglocentric and androcentric viewpoints. This awareness, in fact, has led us to identify and emphasize events, instruments, and subjects that define our own personal and collective being. This self-awareness places us on the path of those who seek to reformulate history and its nature.

D. The Reformulation of Our Own Identity

Reflection on our own identity has proven to be a very fertile field. The concurrence of diverse ethnic, racial, and cultural communities in one socioexistential space grants the bases for our self-understanding as an "original reality." The category of *mestizaje,* used by V. Elizondo and expanded on by others, has served to release the complex richness of a people intrinsically affected by their indigenous, African, and European roots. From this *mestizo* people comes, on the one hand, a sociocultural heterogeneity, and on the other, the sharing of common problems and challenges in a single context of reality. The tension existing between these two factors has forced us to express the identity of the *mestizo* people from the starting point of their multiple socio-symbolic practices, contrary to the thinking of modernity which subsumes all identities through abstract generalizations. Even more important, according to O. Espín, such expression supposes the conscious acceptance of diversity and it implies, at the same time, the recognition that "the *mestizos* have only one culture, that of *mestizaje,* and it is this one culture that allows them to maintain and function within their socially constructed reality and symbolic systems."[43]

E. Social Location: Hermeneutics, Theology, and Scripture

A great amount of work has been done on this area in particular. In the interpretation of the contents of Christian faith as well as of Scripture, the experience of struggle against violence and oppression has been recognized as the common point of departure. Nonetheless, different nuances among such authors can be related to their gender, religious, ethnic, racial, linguistic, and intellectual traditions. In my opinion, there are three areas that merit special mention due to their development and importance. These are: theological method, Hispanic/Latina feminist theology, and popular religiosity as a central source of our theological task. On these areas there are excellent contributions in *Frontiers of Hispanic Theology in the United States* and *We Are a People! Initiatives in Hispanic American Theology.*[44]

F. A Spirituality of Hope in the Struggle

In opposition to those who have closed themselves off to hope, the march of the *mestizo* people is rooted in a spiritual experience that affirms the possibility of a reality radically different from the present order. In this sense, as O. Espín observes, popular religiosity serves as the source of a credible hope, since, "through its complex symbol-making system, [it] seems to have successfully managed to maintain the dream of a solidaristic, caring alternative," at the same time that it delegitimizes the pretended absolute character of the present reality.[45] That spiritual experience is translated as active hope in the struggle for a better world whose central reference point is the vision of the reign of God. The Christian spirituality structured by this reference point, according to J. González, allows us to understand ourselves as "the people of the Reign of God, the *Mañana* People."[46] On the other hand, it allows us to articulate critically the classical tensions between the reign of God and historical structures, faith and political action, present and future, celebration and a commitment to justice.[47]

G. The Relationship between Theology and Pastoral Action

Without a doubt, the recent volume edited by Soledad Galerón, Rosa María Icaza, and Rosendo Urrabazo, *Prophetic Vision: Pastoral Reflections on the National Pastoral Plan for Hispanic Ministry,*[48] very well synthesizes the growing concern for finding the most appropriate ways to increase the relationship between theological reflection and concrete pastoral action. Although V. Elizondo and A. F. Deck have contributed significantly to this field, there are still questions that have not been satisfactorily resolved. In my view, the basic concern is not so much how we address the methodological relation between theology and pastoral ministry, but rather how each of us establishes an active relationship with concrete pastoral projects as trained theologians. This is a challenge still to be met if we are not to construct a discourse fed solely by the academic environment. I am also concerned that pastoral agents in dioceses and parishes ask about access to the written works of Latino theologians. This question, certainly, opens the field to other correlative themes such as the selection of the privileged recipients of our theology, the language in which our work is written, and our own commitment beyond the classroom. All these issues call us to seek creative answers at personal and collective levels.

H. Ecumenism from the Base

Latino theology operates within the framework of a wider process whose purpose has to do with the building of alternative cultures, society, and Church capable of sustaining and promoting the life of each person, community, people, and of the earth. That process has made us generate a new type of ecumenism among those who come from different ecclesial traditions. At the present we can no longer claim a symbiosis between Roman Catholicism and the culture of the Latina communities. We can no longer do it, nor should we. What experience is showing us relates to an increasing tendency toward a strengthening of the ecumenical experience *desde abajo,* "from the base," from the praxis of solidarity with oppressed peoples and sectors that works to bring about a new people without borders. In this area too, we have a wide open future.

4. In Conclusion

I want to emphasize the idea that has accompanied me throughout this article. I believe that the *mestiza* theology of liberation is assuming, responsibly and with audacity, the challenges that current reality casts before the faith experience of our communities. With rigor and seriousness, I believe that this theology, despite all difficulties, also poses a profound critique of the current order, in the hope of overcoming it. In this vein, I would like to appropriate for each of us the great creativity that indigenous theology is showing, throughout the continent and the Caribbean, in its effort to name its own peoples. Each of them recognizes the diversity of the peoples of Anáhuac, Aztlán, Tawantisuyo, Xochitlalpan, Quisqueya, Borinquén, Abya-Yala, Erekusú, etc. In our case, it seems that we still have ahead of us the splendid field of creative imagination in the painful search for our own name. A name that does not assimilate us into the image and vision of the *conquistadores* of yesterday or today, but a name capable of expressing the "radical meaning"[49] of our new being, that of the *mañana* people, the *pueblo mestizo.*

Notes

1. Orlando O. Espín, "Pentecostalism & Popular Catholicism: Preservers of Hispanic Catholic Tradition?" Presidential Address at the Fifth Annual Colloquium of ACHTUS, San Diego, 29 June 1992. Text in: ACHTUS *Newsletter* 4/1 (1993).

2. Virgilio Elizondo, "*Mestizaje* as a Locus of Theological Reflection," in: Allan Figueroa Deck, S.J., ed., *Frontiers of Hispanic Theology in the United States* (New York: Orbis Books, 1992) 114.

3. Ibid., 106.

4. Testimony gathered by Pablo Richard, "La Teología de la Liberación en la nueva coyuntura. Temas y desafíos nuevos para la década de los noventa," *Pasos* 34 (1991) 6.

5. See a summary of these presentations in ACHTUS *Newsletter* 4/1 (1993) 2–5.

6. Roberto S. Goizueta, "U.S. Hispanic Theology and the Challenge of Pluralism," in: Deck, *Frontiers of Hispanic Theology,* 17–18.

7. Ada María Isasi-Díaz, *En la Lucha: A Hispanic Women's Liberation Theology* (Minneapolis: Fortress Press, 1993) chapter 6.

8. Roberto S. Goizueta, "Rediscovering Praxis: The Significance of U.S. Hispanic Experience for Theological Method," in: Roberto S. Goizueta, ed., *We Are a People! Initiatives in Hispanic American Theology* (Minneapolis: Fortress Press, 1992) 51–77.

9. Isasi-Díaz, *En la Lucha.*

10. Arturo Bañuelas, "U.S. Hispanic Theology," in: *Missiology,* XX/2 (1992) 293–95.

11. Fernando F. Segovia, "Two Places and No Place on Which to Stand: Mixture and Otherness in Hispanic American Theology," in: *Listening: Journal of Religion and Culture* 27/1 (1991) 34–35.

12. *Teología India. Primer Encuentro Taller Latinoamericano* (México: (ENAM); Ecuador: ABYA-YALA, 1991) 261–62.

13. Sixto J. García, "A Hispanic Approach to Trinitarian Theology: The Dynamics of Celebration, Reflection, and Praxis," in: Roberto S. Goizueta, ed., *We Are a People!,* 113–17. On the importance of the *Proyecto Histórico in Mujerista* theology, see Isasi-Díaz, *En la Lucha,* chapter 2.

14. Roberto S. Goizueta, "U.S. Hispanic Theology."

15. For a broader treatment on these themes, see the excellent work by Marcos J. Villamán, "Iglesia e Inculturación" (Segunda Parte), in: *CAM Estudios Teológicos* 4:3 (1991) 12.

16. Ibid., 13–14.

17. Orlando O. Espín, "Trinitarian Monotheism and the Birth of Popular Catholicism: The Case of Sixteenth-Century México," in: *Missiology,* 20:2 (1992) 181.

18. Villamán, "Iglesia e Inculturación."

19. See María Pilar Aquino, *Our Cry for Life. Feminist Theology from Latin America* (New York: Orbis Books, 1993) chapter 2.

20. Franz Hinkelammert, "Frente a la cultura de la Post-modernidad: Proyecto político y Utopía," in: *Pasos* 12 (1987) 1.

21. Villamán, "Iglesia e Inculturación," 15.

22. Franz Hinkelammert, "La lógica de la expulsión del mercado capitalista mundial y el proyecto de liberación," in: *Pasos* 3 (1992) 18.

23. National Conference of Catholic Bishops, *The Hispanic Presence. Challenge and Commitment* (Washington: USCC, 1984) 6–7.

24. "Statistics on Hispanics in the United States," in: *Instantes. Hispanic Project Quarterly Newsletter* 1:4 (1992) 4.

25. Sara Nieves-Squires, "Hispanic Women: Making their presence on Campus less tenuous," in: *Many Voices. Mount St. Mary's College, Multicultural Advisory Council* 2:1 (1993) 1.

26. Hinkelammert, "La lógica de la expulsión."

27. Villamán, "Iglesia e Inculturación."

28. Franz Hinkelammert, "¿Capitalismo sin alternativas? Sobre la sociedad que sostiene que no hay alternativas para ella," in: *Pasos* 3–7 (1991) 11.

29. Franz Hinkelammert, "La crisis del Socialismo y el Tercer Mundo," in: *Pasos* 30 (1990) 2.

30. In regard to this, see Villamán, "Iglesia e Inculturación"; also the works by Franz Hinkelammert previously cited; and Juan Guillermo Espinosa, "Economía de mercado y economía social," in: *Reflexión y Liberación, 5:16 (1993) 23–36.*

31. Franz Hinkelammert writes of this as a "schizophrenia of values" before which we must "reject becoming insane while our society declares that which is insane as rational. . . . Whoever allow themselves to be taken in by the attraction to insanity can not but celebrate death in the name of the only alternative to which there is no other," "¿Capitalismo sin alternativas?" 16 and 23.

32. Villamán, "Iglesia e Inculturación," 10–11.

33. Hinkelammert, "La lógica de la expulsión," 12.

34. "U.S. Hispanic theology seeks to uncover the irrationality of what dominant society calls reason," (Goizueta, "U.S. Hispanic Theology," 18).

35. Roberto S. Goizueta, "Nosotros: Toward a U.S. Hispanic Anthropology," in: *Listening: Journal of Religion and Culture,* 27:1 (1991) 65–66.

36. On this subject, see the summary presented by Fernando F. Segovia, "Hispanic American Theology and the Bible: Effective Weapon and Faithful Ally," in: Goizueta, *We are a People!,* 48; see also Ada María Isasi-Díaz, "Praxis: The Heart of Mujerista Theology," in this issue of *JHLT;* Orlando O. Espín, "Grace and Humanness: A Hispanic Perspective," in: Goizueta, *We are a People!,* 133–164.

37. Hinkelammert, "¿Capitalismo sin alternativas?" 16.

38. Hinkelammert, "La lógica de la expulsión," 19.

39. Segovia, "Two Places and No Place," 37.

40. On this option as inherent to pastoral ministry, see Rosendo Urrabazo, "Christian Social Responsibility: An Option for the Poor," in: Soledad Galerón, Rosa María Icaza, and Rosendo Urrabazo, eds., *Prophetic Vision. Pastoral Reflections on the National Pastoral Plan for Hispanic Ministry* (Kansas City: Sheed & Ward, 1992) 297–307.

41. On these matters, see Aquino, *Our Cry for Life,* chapter 6; "Perspectives on a Latina's Feminist Liberation Theology," in: Deck, *Frontiers of U.S. Hispanic Theology,* 24–25; "Doing Theology from the Perspective of Latin American Women," in: Goizueta, *We are a People!,* 95–99; Isasi-Díaz, *En la Lucha,* chapters 1 and 6; Goizueta, "Nosotros," 60; Orlando O. Espín, "The God of the Vanquished: Foundations for a Latino Spirituality," in: *Listening: Journal of Religion and Culture,* 27/1 (1991) 73–76, 82.

42. Justo L. González, *Mañana: Christian Theology from a Hispanic Perspective* (Nashville: Abingdon Press, 1990) 38–41.

43. Orlando O. Espín, "A Multicultural Church?: Theological Reflections From Below," Conference at the Symposium on the Implications of the Multi-Cultural Dimension of the Catholic Church in the United States, Catholic University of America, Washington, D.C., 15–17 April 1993.

44. Both works were cited above.

45. Espín, "The God of the Vanquished," 78–79.

46. González, *Mañana: Christian Theology,* 157–67.

47. Ibid.

48. For references, see note 40.

49. Elizondo, "Mestizaje as a Locus," 114.

Annoted Bibliography—María Pilar Aquino Vargas

Our Cry for Life: Feminist Theology from Latin America (Maryknoll, New York: Orbis Books, 1993).

What is unique about this work is that Aquino begins a bridge-building dialogue among U.S. Latinas and Latin American Latinas. This work is a seriously researched book that ranks Aquino as a first rate Latina theologian. Using the core tenets of feminist and liberation theologies, she offers a corrective to some androcentric positions in these theologies and advocates an alternative methodological premise which calls for women to be active protagonists with full rights in the church and society. She offers scholarly rereading of such issues as christology, spirituality, ecclesiology, Mary, and popular devotions, all in keeping with Latina contributions in fashioning a more dignified relationship between men and women and a liberated life for all.

"The Challenge of Hispanic Women," *Missiology* 20:2 (April 1992), pp. 261–268. The author exposes a new voice in theology, that of poor and oppressed Latina women. This new voice in theology calls for doing theology in contrast to the lingering neocolonial postures of the male-dominated and racist Western world. The result is that Latina women, supported by faith, recover their spiritual strength to create religious and social values that will shape the church and society.

12

Eldín Villafañe

Eldín Villafañe was born in Santa Isabel, Puerto Rico, and raised in New York City. As an ordained minister of the Assemblies of God, he served as executive presbyter of the Spanish East District Council. He earned his masters in missions (MA) from Wheaton Graduate School of Theology in 1970 and his doctorate (PhD) in social ethics from Boston University in 1988.

Most of Villafañe's professional teaching work has been at Gordon-Conwell Theological Seminary. He was assistant professor of Christianity and Society (1976–1982), associate professor of Christian social ethics (1982–1990), founding director of the Center for Urban Ministerial Education (CUME) (1976–1990), and associate dean for urban and multicultural affairs (1990–1993). Since 1990, he has been professor of Christian ethics.

In his writings and lectures, Villafañe focuses on issues of ethics from the Pentecostal perspective, social spirituality, the Pentecostal context for developing evangelism in view of a U.S. Latino theology, urban ministry, and the history of U.S. Hispanic Pentecostalism.

Among the numerous boards and associations Professor Villafañe participates in, a selective few include the Society for Pentecostal Studies, National Board for Bilingual Bicultural Ministries, the American Academy of Religion, Society for Pentecostal Studies, *La Comunidad* of Hispanic American Scholars of Theology and Religion, and the Society for the Scientific Study of Religion. He is also associate editor of *Pneuma: The Journal of the Society for Pentecostal Studies.*

Eldín Villafañe is married to Margarita Lopez, and they have three children.

36-C Burroughs Street
Boston, Massachusetts 02130
617-983-9393

An Evangelical Call to a Social Spirituality

Confronting Evil in Urban Society

Eldín Villafañe

As we enter the 21st century, there is no greater need for evangelicals in the cities than to articulate, both in word and deed, a social spirituality. The twin phenomena of urbanization and globalization, which define the ethos of our great cities, demand no more and no less than an authentically biblical and evangelical spirituality. If the Whole Church is to take the Whole Gospel to the Whole World, it must have a "Wholistic" spirituality.

A spirituality, if it is to be authentic and relevant, should correlate with all of life; for after all the Spirit of the Lord, who leads and empowers, must lead and empower all areas of our life. Spirituality has been defined as "a particular style of approach to union with God,"[1] "a following of Jesus,"[2] "a style of living the life of the Holy Spirit,"[3] or my own personal definition, which synthesizes a trinitarian and moral thrust, "in obedience to God, the following of Jesus in the power of the Spirit." Undergirding these various definitions is a self-understanding of a loving heart yearning, seeking and responding as a whole person, in the obedience of faith, to a loving God.

The history of the spiritualities of the church reflects the spiritual pilgrimage of particular individuals and of particular people, at a particular time and in a particular context. The times we live, the cities we live in, and the Gospel we live by, call us to a spirituality that goes beyond, though yet includes, "a personal transfiguration into the image of Christ."[4]

One can surely make a case for the emergence at distinct periods throughout the church (both Catholic and Protestant) of what can be termed a Wholistic spirituality—covering "the following of Jesus" in *both* personal transformation/piety and social transformation/piety. Yet by and large our contemporary evangelical spirituality has been defined only by the individualistic and personal dimension. This personal transformation into the

"An Evangelical Call to a Social Spirituality: Confronting Evil in Urban Society," *Apuntes* 2 (Summer 1991), pp. 27–38. Reprinted with permission.

image of Christ, by grace, through faith, by means of the Word, prayer, contemplation and the exercise of the "spiritual disciplines," is thus inner-directed and vertical. The missing dimension of social transformation/ piety (which includes social witness, social service and social action, thus, outer-directed and horizontal), as "bona fide" spirituality, has been excluded from an authentically biblical and evangelical definition of spirituality. The call is to redefine and re-appropriate from Scripture and from the rich heritage of the church, a social spirituality that is consistent with the "following of Jesus."

Jesus Christ, the Anointed One (Lk 4:18; Ac 10:38), is the paradigm *par excellence* of this spirituality. Through *the power of the Spirit* the believer is *both,* and I quote "being transformed into his likeness with ever-increasing glory, which comes from the Lord, who is the Spirit" (2 Co 3:18); *and* challenged to follow Him, and I quote, "as the Father has sent me, I am sending you . . . receive the Holy Spirit" (Jn 20:21–22). Thus, the double focus and goal of Christian spirituality has: 1) a vertical focus—the continual transformation into the likeness of Jesus, the resurrected Lord; and 2) a horizontal focus—the following of Jesus, in similar obedience of the Father's missional calling (Lk 4:18–19). Both of these foci and goals can only be carried out in the power of the Spirit, and undergirded by God's love. Both have a vertical and horizontal dimension that interrelates them and dynamically "nourishes" them. "Transformation" needs "following" and "following" needs "transformation." Both have a personal and social dimension that equally interrelates them and dynamically "nourishes" them.

The "vertical-transformation" focus and its interrelationship with the horizontal is noted well in 1 Jn 4:7–13 (NIV):

> . . . let us love one another, for love comes from God. Everyone who loves has been born of God and knows God. Whoever does not love does not know God, because God is love. This is how God showed his love among us: He sent his one and only Son into the world that we might live through him. This is love: not that we loved God, but that he loved us and sent his Son as an atoning sacrifice for our sins . . . Since God so loved us, we also ought to love one another. No one has ever seen God; but *if we love each other, God lives in us and his love is made complete in us.* We know that *we live in him* and *he in us,* because he has given us of *his Spirit.*

The "horizontal-following" focus and its interrelationship with the vertical is noted well by Jesus' missional self-understanding (which should also be ours) in Lk 4:18–19 (NIV):

> The *Spirit of the Lord is on me;* therefore he has *anointed me* to preach good news to the poor. He has sent me to proclaim freedom

for the prisoners and recovery of sight for the blind, to release the oppressed, to proclaim the year of the Lord's favor.

This dynamic and dialectical spirituality is to be "worked out" in a social context. A social context that deeply needs both contemplative and apostolic activity. The brokenness of society (so visible in the *barrios* and ghettos of our cities), the scriptural missional mandate, and the Spirit's love constrains us to feed the hungry, visit the sick and prisoners, shelter the homeless and poor—to express God's love in social concerns. We do this as an expression of faithful obedience and authentic spirituality.

In the later part of this century, through the careful reading and re-reading of Scripture (especially from the context of the "periphery") and the critical utilization of the analytical tools of the social sciences, we have gained a new understanding of our social reality. The concomitant Pentecostal/Charismatic outpouring of the Spirit, also in this century, has brought to many a critical awareness and discernment of the depth and complexity of sin—the "mystery of iniquity."

There is a need to extend the evangelicals' classical understanding of spirituality's struggles with the flesh, the world, and the devil with their *social correlates,* namely—sinful social structures, the "world" (*kosmos*), and "principalities and powers." The Evangelical Church is thus challenged to acknowledge that an authentic and relevant spirituality must be wholistic, responding to both the vertical and horizontal dimensions of life. The inclusion of the social dimension in a *redefinition* of spirituality is the missing ingredient of contemporary evangelical spirituality.

Let me move now to consider elements contributing to a social spirituality. These elements will be presented under four major headings: 1) The Spirit's "Grieving"—Sin: Personal and Social; 2) Mystery of Iniquity: The Texture of Social Existence; 3) The Gospel of the Reign of God; and 4) The Challenge to Confront Structural Sin and Evil.

The Spirit's "Grieving"—Sin: Personal and Social[5]

The spiritual pilgrimage of the believer is a pilgrimage of love. Any true spirituality is ultimately the loving of God and the neighbor as oneself (Mt 19:19)—the integration of the spiritual and the ethical, of worship and service, and of identity and vocation. Love is often easier to acknowledge than to define. What Augustine said of "time" can probably be said of love: "If no one asks me, I know, if I wish to explain it to one that asketh, I know not."[6] In any description love is deeply personal. The love of God in Christ poured out by the Holy Spirit establishes a loving relationship with God that, as with all love affairs, particularly the human response, is subject to the vacillations, void, and vicissitudes of life.

As mere humans in a spiritual pilgrimage of love, we aggrieve the object of our love often. Whether the grieving of that object of love be human or divine (in our immediate understanding of the object), it is ultimately a grieving of the Spirit. The "love of the Spirit" (Ro 15:30) can be grieved.

A careful exegesis of Paul's admonition in Eph 4:5 places the context of the grieving of the Spirit within an ethico-spiritual relationship with others. These attitudes and actions of the believers that "cut" the relationship of love and thus grieve the Holy Spirit are called sin in Scripture. In the biblical revelation sin can be more broadly described as: *disobedience* to the Lordship of God, *injustice* and alienation, and *unbelief* and idolatry.[7] We sin, thus the Spirit is grieved, when we do not imitate God, sacrificially give up ourselves as Christ, and "live a life of love." (Eph 4:30; 5:1–2).

The Apostle Paul clearly teaches that sin is a harsh taskmaster, "for the wages of sin is death" (Ro 6:23a). The predicament of *all* persons is death—separation from God, from others, from themselves, and even from creation. Scripture is quite clear that individual action has marked social implications. It likewise notes that social or corporate action has marked individual implications.[8] Sin, while being deeply personal, is not just individualistic. The person as a *socius* ("person-in-community") is vividly portrayed by Paul's anthropological understanding of "corporate personality" as noted in Ro 5:12: "just as sin entered the world through one man, and death through sin, and in this way death came to all men, because all sinned." Orlando Costas notes, commenting on this verse, that:

> The sin of one man affected all, because "all" were represented already in the one. Therefore guilt and condemnation have passed to all. All are guilty of sin, not just because they personally sin, but because they are part of Adam. Thus sin is both personal and social.[9]

Sin and its work is a reality in all human experience. No area of personal and human history is left untouched by its destructive reality. It is ultimately and radically death/separation from God.

The response to sin and death is the need for the loving initiative of the Spirit of God to convict of sin, righteousness, and judgement (Jn 16: 8–11), based on the equally radical answer of "The Crucified God."[10] Paul speaks eloquently of the multifaceted drama of redemption that deals with sin and death:

> But God, who is rich in mercy, for his great love wherewith he loved us, even when we were dead in sins, hath quickened us together with Christ (by grace ye are saved), and hath raised us up together, and made us sit together in heavenly places in Christ Jesus (Eph 2:4–6, KJV).

The power of sin and death is broken. In the Cross of Christ the believer has the resources to overcome its dominion. My colleague David F. Wells notes that "the world, the flesh and the devil are not invincible competitors but doomed adversaries. In the work on the Cross, Christ conquered them, and through the work of the Spirit, that conquest is brought into our modern world."[11]

It grieves the Spirit when believers manifest the works of sin. Paul in his letter to the Galatians chapter five notes that sin's work in human nature (*sarx,* "the flesh")[12] is the antithesis of the Spirit's fruit. The Spirit's fruit (love, joy, peace, patience, kindness, goodness, faithfulness, gentleness and self-control, Gal 5:22–23) is the believer-lover's attestation of growth in spirituality. The Spirit's fruit are both sign and substance of "transformation" to Christ's image, and moral virtues needed in the following of Him. They are marks of genuine spirituality. The Spirit seeks to restore the fellowship broken by sin and to overcome the separation in a bond of love.

Mystery of Iniquity: The Texture of Social Existence[13]

Article Number 12 of the Lausanne Covenant notes that the church is engaged in spiritual warfare with principalities and powers of evil. It is within the framework of the ongoing cosmic conflict between God and Satan, and the restraining power of the Holy Spirit, that any discussion of sin—particularly in its powerful and mysterious (secret) structural or institutional manifestations—must be set.

Social Reality

From the social sciences, particularly the Sociology of Knowledge, we have learned that the institutions and structures of social life are more than the sum of the individuals that make it up.[14] Society is a dialectical phenomenon that is a human product, as well as producer of the human. Social institutions are basically routinized human patterned norms and behaviors for social living (i.e., family, schools, laws, religion, political and social systems). Some institutions (i.e., family, work, the state . . .) may even be categorized as a "given," as God's "orders of creation," "divine orders" or "structures of creation."[15] Thus, they are seen as God's gracious gifts to human beings for social existence and which, as Emil Brunner reminds us, "even if only in a fragmentary and indirect way, God's will meets us."[16]

All social structures and institutions "have moral values embedded in them. They can be good or evil."[17] To speak of sinful structures and institutions is to speak of structures and institutions that have become distorted, misguided, destructive or oppressive.[18] As such they are in need of liberation—by dismantling, reconstruction, transformation, revolution or "exorcism"—by human and divine power. What is significant to note is that the texture of social existence reveals the presence of institutions and structures that regulate life, that seem to have an objective reality independent of the individual, and thus can become oppressive, sinful or evil. We are all part of this texture of social existence and our spiritual living is impacted by this complex web.[19]

Principalities and Powers

The "powers," as they are often noted in current biblical, theological and ethical discussions,[20] speak to us that: beyond personal sin and evil, beyond social structures embedded with sinful or evil moral designs, beyond sinful and evil systems of values, there exists evil "in the social and political roles of powerful supernatural beings."[21] The texture of social existence is indeed permeated by "the mystery of iniquity." Yet, we must note with my colleague Stephen C. Mott that "these biblical concepts relate to phenomena which can be sociologically described and they extend rather than nullify personal responsibility in society."[22]

Contra Berkhoff and others, Mott posits that these "principalities and powers" are angelic powers, not depersonalized social forces or principles. His careful exegesis of Scripture and pertinent Hellenistic and Jewish apocalyptic literature compels him to "stress this background, not to bring the occult into the understanding of institutional evil, but because it shows the political and social significance of the powers."[23]

Our struggle for an authentic and social spirituality must be cognizant that "our struggle is not against flesh and blood, but against the rulers (*archai*), against the authorities (*exousiai*), against the powers of this dark world (*kosmokratores*)" (Eph 6:12). These are "powers" who rebelled against God, and, as John H. Yoder reminds us, "were part of the good creation of God."[24] Their original power and authority over creation included its social and political life. This authority given by God for providential care has resulted in oppression. They are fallen "powers" with *idolatrous-demonic claims*. Notwithstanding their fallen condition they "cannot fully escape the providential sovereignty of God. He is still able to use them for good."[25] Yoder categorizes the "powers" as religious structures, intellectual structures (-ologies and -isms), moral structures (codes and customs), political structures (the tyrant, the market, the school, the court, race, and nation).[26] The ambivalent status of humanity relative to the "powers," and their manifestations in structures, institutions, and other corporate realities is noted by Yoder under two statements: "we cannot live without them . . . we cannot live with them."[27] Yoder states that:

> There could not be society or history, there could not be man without the existence above him of religious, intellectual, moral and social structures. *We cannot live without them.* These structures are not and never have been a mere sum total of the individuals composing them.

The whole is more than the sum of its parts. And this 'more' is an invisible Power, even though we may not be used to speaking of it in personal or angelic terms. But these structures fail to serve man as they should. They do not enable him to live a genuinely free, human, loving life. They have absolutized themselves and they demand from the individual and society an unconditional loyalty. They harm and enslave man. *We cannot live with them.*[28]

What is most significant to note at this time is that the "powers" have been defeated and carried captive by Christ. "And having disarmed the powers and authorities, he made a public spectable of them, triumphing over them by the cross" (Col 2:15, NIV). The "powers" have been "disarmed" by Christ, we need not absolutize or respond to their idolatrous-demonic claims. This "good news" is part and parcel of our demonstration and proclamation of the Gospel of Jesus Christ.

In concluding this section, it is important to note that:

The existence of an evil order ruled by supernatural beings must either be accepted or rejected on faith, but such reality would not be dissonant with our social experience. Our concern here is not to settle the cosmological question of whether angels and demons should be demythologized but rather to come to terms with social material to which their biblical existence points. . . . The world-order and the evil presence of the powers are never *synonymous* with the concrete forms of social and institutional life. Institutions function both to enslave and to liberate human existence. The powers are always present along with enslavement and death in small or large degree; but their real existence is behind the scenes in a system of hostile values vying for control of the life of the world.[29]

Any and every spirituality to be authentic and relevant must come to terms with personal and social sin and evil. What is most critical for an Evangelical spirituality is to incorporate within its theology and ethics, not to say spirituality, a "deeper" understanding of the "mystery of iniquity." It must realize that sin and evil go beyond the individual; that we are all enmeshed in a social living that is complex, dynamic and dialectical; and that our spirituality, and the very Gospel that we preach, needs to be as big and ubiquitous as sin and evil.[30] We will falter in our spirituality and thus grieve the Spirit if "our struggle with evil" does not "correspond to the geography of evil." We are assured in this struggle that

We are more than conquerors through him who loved us. For I am convinced that neither death nor life, neither angels nor demons, neither the present nor the future, nor any powers, neither height nor depth, nor anything else in all creation, will be able to separate us from the love of God that is in Christ Jesus our Lord (Ro 8: 37–39, NIV).

Gospel of the Reign of God[31]

Eschatology forms the central and essential framework of New Testament theology. The "beginning" of the End, the Reign of God, has broken into our world in the person of Jesus. The message of the New Testament is that God's Royal rule is *already* present in Jesus the Messiah, although it awaits final consummation in the *not yet* of the future. In Jesus Christ we have, in the words of George Eldon Ladd, the "fulfillment without consummation," of the Reign of God.[32]

The "good-news" of the Reign meant that beyond God's governing through creation and providence his special reign or rule had broken into history. It is important to note that "the Greek word *basileia,* which is used for *reign* or *kingdom,* means primarily the *act* of reigning rather than the *place* of reigning; thus in most cases it should be translated as *reign, rule, kingship* or *sovereignty,* rather than its usual English rendering, *kingdom.*"[33]

Jesus Christ himself both proclaimed and embodied the Reign. John Wimber notes that "This explains the two-fold pattern of Christ's ministry, repeated wherever he went: first *proclamation,* then *demonstration.* First he preached repentance and the good news of the Kingdom of God. Then he cast out demons, healed the sick, raised the dead—which proved he was the presence of the Kingdom, the Anointed One."[34]

The Reign of God in Jesus is one of the "spiritual power encounters."[35] Jesus' life and mission were both inaugurated and empowered by the Holy Spirit. David Wells states, "so it is that Jesus' birth, baptism, miracles, teaching, sacrifice, and resurrection are all ascribed to the working of the Holy Spirit."[36] Roger Stronstad can thus speak of Jesus' life and mission as that of the Charismatic Christ. He goes on to state that "Jesus is not only anointed by the Spirit, but He is also Spirit-led, Spirit-filled, and Spirit-empowered."[37] Jesus' mission is one of the Spirit's anointment for "spiritual power encounters."[38]

The powers of the age to come have indeed invaded this age. The "signs and wonders" were and still are a witness to this reality. The Reign of God has come because the "strong man's house" has been invaded by the Charismatic Christ (Mt 12:28). C. René Padilla states that:

> The kingdom of darkness that pertains to this age has been invaded; the "strong man" has been disarmed, conquered, and robbed (Mt 12:29; Lk. 11:22) . . . In other words, the historic mission of Jesus can only be understood in connection with the Kingdom of God. His mission here and now is the manifestation of the Kingdom as

a present reality in his own person and action, in his preaching of the Gospel and in his works of justice and mercy.[39]

The Gospel of the Reign of God is the good news that in the life, death and resurrection of Christ, God's reign is manifested in the physical and historical affairs of people—bound and hindered by demonic forces—now able to experience the Spirit's total liberation.[40] God's salvation in Christ affects the whole person—both spiritual and physical—in his/her concrete historical reality. Nothing is exempt from God's reign. While we live in the *not yet* of complete fulfillment of the Reign of God, that awaits the *parousia* in the future, we nevertheless continue to share in Jesus' mission of liberation through *proclamation* and *demonstration* (See: Jn 20:21).

The early church's experience of the baptism of the Spirit (Ac 2) was interpreted as a continuation of Jesus' mission in the power of the Spirit. "Signs and wonders" attested to their participation in the *now* but *not yet* of the inbreaking of the Reign of God. Joel 2:28, 29, was interpreted as the *end* time promise—"the beginning of the end." The early church saw itself as an eschatological community. The Spirit's outpouring gather in a Royal community, the community of the Spirit.[41] Roger Stronstad states that,

> If we have interpreted Luke's Pentecostal narrative correctly, then the gift of the Spirit is not salvation, but it is for witness and service. In other words, with the transfer of the Spirit to the disciples on the day of Pentecost, they became a charismatic community, heirs to the earlier charismatic ministry of Jesus.[42]

While the church is *not* the Reign of God, yet, as the community of the Spirit—where the Spirit manifests itself in a unique and particular way (Ro 8:23; 1 Cor 6:19; Eph 2:14–18)—it has the purpose to both reflect and witness to the values of the Reign, by the power of the Spirit to the world. Orlando Costas states it in the following way:

> Therefore, the church, which is *not* the Kingdom, is nevertheless its most *visible expression* and its most *faithful interpreter* in our age . . . as the community of believers from all times and places, the church both *embodies* the Kingdom in its life and *witnesses* to its presence and future in its mission.[43]

The church as the community of the Spirit is also engaged in "spiritual power encounters." It struggles with the forces of sin and death, with the demonic powers-that-be, whether individually or institutionally manifested and whether morally, physically or spiritually expressed. The church can depend on the *Parakletos* to bring the charismatic renewal of the church *in* and *for* the world. "Signs and wonders" are thus legitimate expectations in the Spirit's total liberation. Orlando Costas eloquently states the significance of the cosmic and historic "power encounter" in the following:

> The Kingdom is an indication of God's transforming presence in history . . . a symbol of God's transforming power, of his determination to make "all things new" (Rev 21:5). The Kingdom of God stands for a new order of life: the new humanity and the new creation which have become possible through the death and resurrection of Jesus. This new order includes reconciliation with God, neighbor and nature, and, therefore, participation in a new world. It involves freedom from the power of sin and death, and, consequently, the strength to live for God and humanity. It encompasses the hope of a more just and peaceful moral order, and thus it is a call to vital engagement in the historical struggles for justice and peace.[44]

The Challenge to Confront Structural Sin and Evil

The Spirit's power encounter defines the cosmic struggle being waged for God's creation. The tendency of many is to see this struggle too individualistically and not see that spiritual warfare must correspond with the geography of evil—the sinful and evil structures of society. The Evangelical Church must see itself not only as a *locus* for personal liberation, but also as a *locus* for social liberation. We must see that the texture of social living makes no easy distinctions between the personal and the social. The church's mission includes engaging in power encounters with sinful and evil structures.

Our confrontation responds to the nature of the structures themselves. On the one hand, we are aware of their creatureness—they are institutions and structures *by* and *for* humans, although their reality is *sui generis*. On the other hand, we are aware of their possible demonic nature—the "powers." On one level of the struggle, it means that the church must bring to bear, through our witness and labors, the power of the Spirit to break the chains of hate, hostility, and injustice embedded in them by introducing the values of the Reign (i.e., love, justice, fair play) and setting in place a "chain of change"[45] that immediately (thus, radical change-revolution), or gradually (thus, multiple and cumulative amelioration-reformation) humanizes these structures and institutions. On the other level of the struggle, the church must witness to the demonic powers that lie behind the scene, by reminding them of their defeat in Christ and the coming New Age. This witness must be in the power of the Spirit, armed with the "full armor of God" (Eph 6:10–18). Jim Wallis states it well,

> The church demonstrates Christ's victory over the powers by reminding them of their created role as servants, rebuking them in their idolatrous role as rulers, and resisting them in their totalitarian

claims and purposes . . . We are not asked to defeat the powers. That is the work of Christ, which he has already done and will continue to do. Our task is to be witnesses and signs of Christ's victory by simply standing firmly in our faith and belief against the seduction and slavery of the powers.[46]

The proclamation of Christ until He comes and its impact on urban society will be predicated on Evangelicals constructing a theology and ethics of the Spirit that is consistent with Scripture and social reality—a theology of the Spirit that leads to a social spirituality, the missing dimension of Evangelical spirituality.

As an Evangelical pentecostal, I challenge the pentecostal and charismatic churches to go beyond the given theology of the second person of the Trinity, to develop a full-blown *pneumatology*,[47] the basis for an authentic and biblical spirituality. Perhaps, this may be our greatest contribution to the church as it approaches the 21st century. *Maranatha!*

Notes

1. George A. Lane, *Christian Spirituality: An Historical Sketch* (Chicago: Loyola University Press, 1984), p. 2.

2. Gustavo Gutiérrez, *We Drink from our Own Wells: The Spiritual Journey of a People* (Maryknoll, New York: Orbis Books, 1984), p. 1.

3. Frances X. Meehan, *A Contemporary Social Spirituality* (Maryknoll, New York: Orbis Books, 1982), p. 1.

4. Donald G. Bloesch, *The Struggle of Prayer* (Colorado Springs, Colorado: Helmers & Howard, 1988), p. 3.

5. See, Eph 4:30; 5:1–2 (NIV).

6. Augustine, *Confessions,* Bk. II (New York: Random House, 1949), p. 253, quoted in Meehan, *Op. Cit.,* p. 1.

7. See, Orlando Costas, *Christ Outside the Gate: Mission Beyond Christendom* (New York: Orbis Books, 1982), pp. 21–24; cf., Walter Grundmann: *hamartía,* Gerhard Kittel, editor, trans., Geoffrey W. Bromiley, *Theological Dictionary of the New Testament,* Volume I (Grand Rapids, Michigan: Eerdmans Publishing Company, 1964), pp. 267–316.

8. In Scripture there are many cases (i.e., Jos 7; Ro 5:12–21) that illustrate this truth of the interrelatedness of human personality in the web of other persons and actions. For the Hebrew conception of this "corporate personality" see, H. Wheeler Robinson, *Corporate Personality in Ancient Israel* (Philadelphia: Fortress Press, 1964).

9. Costas, *Op. Cit.,* p. 25. Both Paul and Costas implicitly underline in this passage not just the universality of sin but equally its manifestation in corporate personality.

10. See, Jürgen Moltmann, *The Crucified God: The Cross of Christ as the Foundation and Criticism of Christian Theology* (New York: Harper and Row, 1974).

11. David F. Wells, *God the Evangelist: How the Holy Spirit Works to Bring Men and Women to Faith* (Grand Rapids, Michigan: Wm. B. Eerdmans, 1987), p. 67.

12. Richard Lovelace's words are instructive: "The New Testament designates the total organism of sin by the term *sarx* (flesh), referring to the fallen human personality apart from the renewing influence and control of the Holy Spirit. The flesh is always somewhat mysterious to us, particularly in its effect on our minds and its operation in the redeemed personality. The New Testament constantly describes it as something much deeper than the isolated moments of sin which it generates." *Dynamics of Spiritual Life* (Downers Grove, Illinois: Inter-Varsity Press, 1979), pp. 89–90.

13. See, 2 Th 2:7; Cf. "Our struggle with evil must correspond to the geography of evil." Stephen Charles Mott, *Biblical Ethics and Social Change* (New York: Oxford University Press, 1982), p. 16.

14. See especially, Peter L. Berger and Thomas Luckman, *The Social Construction of Reality: A Treatise in the Sociology of Knowledge* (New York: Anchor Books, 1967); Peter L. Berger, *The Sacred Canopy: Elements of a Sociological Theory of Religion* (New York: Anchor Books, 1969).

15. See, Emil Brunner, *The Divine Imperative* (Philadelphia: The Westminster Press, 1937); and Pedro Arana Quiroz, "Ordenes de la creación y responsibilidad cristiana," in C. René Padilla, ed. *Fe cristiana y Latinoamérica hoy* (Buenos Aires, Argentina: Ediciones Certeza, 1974) pp. 169–184.

16. Brunner, *Op. Cit.,* p. 291.

17. Meehan, *Op. Cit.,* p. 9.

18. See Patrick Kerans, *Sinful Social Structures* (New York: Paulist Press, 1974).

19. For an early and provocative treatment that deals with sinful and evil social structures, see Walter Rauschenbusch's chapters, "The Super-personal forces of Evil" and "The Kingdom of Evil," in his *A Theology for the Social Gospel* (New York: The Macmillan Company, 1917), pp. 69–94.

20. See, among others, Hendrikus Berkhoff, *Christ and the Powers* (Scottdale, PA.: Herald Press, 1962); Jacques Ellul, *The Subversion of Christianity* (Grand Rapids, Michigan: Wm. B. Eerdmans Pu. Co. 1987), pp. 174–190; Stephen C. Mott, *Biblical Ethics and Social Change,* pp. 3–21; Jim Wallis, *Agenda for Biblical People* (New York: Harper and Row, 1976), pp. 38–55; Walter Wink, *Naming the Powers: The Language of Powers in the New Testament* (Philadelphia: Fortress Press, 1984) and *Unmasking the Powers: The Invisible Forces that Determine Human Existence* (Philadelphia: Fortress Press, 1986); John H. Yoder, *The Politics of Jesus* (Grand Rapids, Michigan: Wm. B. Eerdmans Pu. Co., 1972), pp. 135–162.

21. Mott, *Op. Cit.,* p. 6.

22. *Ibid.,* p. 4.

23. *Ibid.,* p. 8.

24. Yoder, *Op. Cit.,* p. 143. See, Col 1:15–17.

25. *Ibid.,* p. 144.

26. *Ibid.,* p. 145.

27. *Ibid.,* p. 146.

28. *Ibid.,* pp. 145–146. It is interesting to note that Yoder thinks that traditional theologies have sought to describe and treat this theme under the "orders of creation." He finds them wanting, though, in that they were not able to "affirm

that it is in Christ that these values all find their meaning and coherence," *Ibid.*, pp. 146–147.

29. Mott, *Op. Cit.*, pp. 10, 15.

30. For a provocative and insightful study that integrates theology with the finding of clinical psychology in interpreting certain "non-physical realities," see, Morton Kelsey, *Discernment: A Study in Ecstasy and Evil* (New York: Paulist Press, 1978).

31. See Mat 12:28.

32. George Eldon Ladd, *The Presence of the Future: The Eschatology of Biblical Realism* (Grand Rapids, Michigan: Wm. B. Eerdmans Pu. Co., 1974), pp. 105–121. Among the many other, pertinent works on the Reign of God, see: George Eldon Ladd, *A Theology of the New Testament* (Grand Rapids, Michigan: Wm. B. Eerdmans Pu. Co., 1983); Karl Ludwig Schmidt, *Basileus—Basilikos, TDNT,* Vol. I, pp. 564–593; John Bright, *The Kingdom of God* (Nashville: Abington Press, 1953); Herman Ridderbos, *The Coming of the Kingdom* (Philadelphia: Presbyterian and Reformed, 1962); Amos N. Wilder, "Kerygma, Eschatology and Social Ethics," in W.D. Davies and D. Daube, eds., *The Background of the New Testament and Its Eschatology* (Cambridge: Cambridge University, 1956), pp. 509–536; C. René Padilla, *Misión integral: ensayos sobre el reino y la iglesia* (Grand Rapids, Michigan: Wm. B. Eerdmans Pu. Co., 1986).

33. Mott, *Op. Cit.*, pp. 82–83.

34. John Wimber, *Power Evangelism* (San Francisco: Harper and Row, 1986), p. 6.

35. See: John Wimber, *Op. Cit.;* Roger Stronstad, *The Charismatic Theology of St. Luke* (Peabody, Mass: Hendrickson Publishers, 1984); and David F. Wells, "Spiritual Power Encounters" in David Wells, *Op. Cit.*, pp. 65–91.

36. *Ibid.*, p. 29.

37. *Op. Cit.*, p. 45.

38. "The Spirit of the Lord is on me; therefore he has anointed me to preach good news to the poor. He has sent me to proclaim freedom for the prisoners and recovery of sight for the blind, to release the oppressed, to proclaim the year of the Lord's favor" (Lk 4:18–19, NIV).

39. *Op. Cit.*, p. 182.

40. Mott, *Op. Cit.*, p. 94.

41. See James W. Jones, *The Spirit and the World* (New York: Hawthorne Books, Inc., 1975), pp. 51–76.

42. Stronstad, *Op. Cit.*, p. 62. He defines the term "charismatic" in a functional and dynamic sense. "By 'charismatic' I mean God's gift of His Spirit to His servants, either individually or collectively, to anoint, empower, or inspire them for divine service," *Ibid.*, p. 13. It is thus devoid of soteriological connotations, emphasizing the prophetic and vocational.

43. Orlando Costas, *The Integrity of Mission: The Inner Life and Outreach of the Church* (New York: Harper and Row, 1979), p. 8.

44. *Ibid.*, p. 6.

45. See: Mel King, *Chain of Change: Struggles for Black Community Development* (Boston: South End Press, 1981).

46. *Op. Cit.*, pp. 48–49.

47. See: Eldin Villafañe, *Towards An Hispanic American Pentecostal Social Ethic, With Special Reference to North Eastern United States* (Ann Arbor, Michigan: U.M.I., 1989).

Annotated Bibliography—Eldín Villafañe

Villafañe, Eldín, *The Liberating Spirit:* Toward an Hispanic American Pentecostal Social Ethic (Grand Rapids, Michigan: William B. Eerdmans Publishing Company, 1993).

This work is a provocative study of a social spirituality based on the author's conviction that the church is a community of the Spirit for the world, but not of the world. He develops a Pentecostal social ethic from the distinctive perspective of the U.S. Latino reality and Pentecostalism's self-understanding of ethics. The work is carefully researched and well-written, providing an extraordinarily broad scope for a pneumatological paradigm. He challenges any ethic that lacks political and social implications.

13

Allan Figueroa Deck, S.J.

Allan Figueroa Deck was born in Los Angeles, California. He became a member of the Society of Jesus in 1963 and professed final vows in 1982. He earned a PhD in Latin American Studies at St. Louis University in 1973; an MDiv at the Jesuit School of Theology at Berkeley; and from the Gregorian University in Rome, he earned a licentiate (STL) in 1986 and a doctorate (STD) in 1988, both in the field of missiology.

Some of Deck's pastoral and administrative experiences include positions on the parochial, diocesan, and national levels. Allan was director of Centro Pastoral Guadalupe in Santa Ana, California (1976–1979), and director of Latino Ministry in the diocese of Orange, California (1979–1985). He is president of the National Catholic Council for Hispanic Ministry, which he founded in 1991.

After a few years in parish ministry, Deck returned to teach at the Jesuit School of Theology at Berkeley as adjunct professor of Hispanic ministry (1987–1988), was visiting professor of pastoral studies at Mundelein Seminary (1992), and assistant professor of Hispanic ministry and missiology at the Jesuit School of Theology at Berkeley (1988–1992). Currently he is associate professor of pastoral studies, Chicano studies and theology at Loyola Marymount University in Los Angeles.

Since 1974, Deck has published two books, edited two books, and written forty-three articles. His writings focus on pastoral issues from the U.S. Latino perspective. He was awarded the Virgilio Elizondo Award by the Academy of Catholic Hispanic Theologians in 1992, the Catholic Press Association Award for his book *The Second Wave* in 1989, the Serra International Award in 1987, and the O'Grady Award by the National Conference of Catholic Charities for his article on immigrant issues.

In 1988 Deck co-founded the Academy of Catholic Hispanic Theologians of the United States and became its first president. He is also a member of the Catholic Theological Society of America.

Loyola Marymount University
7101 West 80th Street
Los Angeles, California 90045-266699
310-338-2931
Fax 310-338-2706

The Spirituality of United States Hispanics

An Introductory Essay

Allan Figueroa Deck, SJ

Hispanics now constitute approximately one-third of the United States Catholic population. Within the next twenty to twenty-five years they are projected to become the majority of Roman Catholics in the nation. This sea change has an impact on every area of the church's life. The purpose of this essay is to provide a preliminary sketch of issues relevant to the spiritual life of these Hispanics. This is an effort to clarify the constitutive elements in the articulation of what a spirituality or spiritualities of and for the United States Hispanics might be.[1]

Interest in the question of Hispanic spirituality represents a second moment in the ongoing effort to evangelize the growing Hispanic Catholic communities. Concern for the articulation of a spirituality appropriate for these diverse communities is due perhaps to the growing numbers of active lay ministers and leaders in our parishes and dioceses throughout the nation. Even more notable, however, is the growing number of Hispanics in seminaries and religious formation houses.[2] There is a perceived need to provide opportunities for the deepening of the generous faith commitments of these people. But there is, as well, considerable doubt about the validity of the concepts and approaches being used in spiritual formation, approaches that usually reflect cultural orientations and biases of mainline U.S. Catholics.[3]

This essay is a preliminary effort to outline some of the background issues and themes that may eventually lead to a more coherent and convincing account of the what, why, and wherefore of the spiritual formation of United States Hispanics. It is my hope that persons more qualified than I in the several areas that comprise the discipline of spirituality will contribute to the effort to give substance and form to a new branch in this field.

"The Spirituality of United States Hispanics: An Introductory Essay," *U.S. Catholic Historian* 9:1–2 (Winter 1990), pp. 137–46. Reprinted with permission.

Clarifying Some Preliminary Issues

There are three issues that need to be addressed from the outset: (1) Who are these United States Hispanics? (2) Are Latin American efforts to articulate Christian spirituality relevant to our concerns here in the United States; and, if so, how relevant? (3) Given the multifaceted history of spiritualities in the church over the ages, what is the perspective taken by this writer and how is it justified?

Who Are the Hispanics?

Most of the literature on Hispanics points to the inadequacy of the umbrella term "Hispanic" or "Latino" for discussing groups that are so diverse in terms of cultural background, social class, national origin, and level of acculturation to mainline United States society. Consequently one must take generalizations about Hispanics with caution. Any generalized understanding must be complemented by more detailed analysis of the particular group one is dealing with. The most salient points in common among this vast and diverse group are the Spanish language and their particular brand of Catholicism produced beginning in the sixteenth century in the Americas. For the purpose of dividing the Hispanic communities into more workable groupings, one might conceive of them in terms of five historical and geographical divisions: (1) Those whose origins are to be found in Middle America, especially Mexico; (2) Central Americans; (3) The Caribbean peoples (Cubans, Puerto Ricans and Dominicans); (4) The Andean peoples and (5) the Borderlands peoples of the American Southwest and California.[4] Each one of these groups exhibits distinctive qualities and histories. It is true that persons of Mexican origin continue to account for more than 60% of the total Hispanic population of the United States. But there are considerable numbers of Puerto Ricans, Cubans, Dominicans, and an ever-growing Central American cohort.

In addition to the data regarding the cultural and national origins of these people, information about social class status is essential. As Father Joseph Fitzpatrick, S.J., has argued, the working-class status of the vast majority of United States Hispanics is a fact with broad implications for them in their interaction with the North American church and society.

The Relevance of Latin American Approaches

In the past twenty years the church in Latin America has emerged as a powerful force in the production of serious theological reflection for the entire Christian world. The originality and relevance of that reflection, especially the theology of liberation and spiritualities of liberation cannot be denied. The relevance of these important ecclesial trends for understanding the realities of United States Hispanics, however, is somewhat limited.

Both those groups that have remained in the United States for a generation and those who recently immigrated have generally moved into another lifeworld, one powerfully influenced by the North American milieu. Most of the studies of acculturation rates concur in the fact that Hispanic groups, like all others who have come to the United States, are assimilating.[5] I say this not because I applaud everything that this adaptation implies, but simply because it appears to be a fact. That assimilation, it is true, is not identical with that of previous Catholic ethnic groups, however, in that the Spanish language is being retained more and Hispanic customs and values are affirmed and perhaps maintained more in today's pluralistic cultural environment than was the case fifty years ago.

The point is that we are speaking about *United States* Hispanics, not Mexicans in Mexico or Puerto Ricans in Puerto Rico. We are dealing, therefore, with a population whose experience of socio-political and economic oppression is different from that of their countries of origin. We are speaking about a people who tend to adopt the North American middle-class attitude toward poverty or are well on the way to adopting it. Poverty in the United States is not the reality of the mainstream, but that of a minority (albeit growing in recent times). The norm for most North Americans as well as for growing numbers of United States Hispanics is the middle-class way of life. Psychologically, United States Hispanics do not relate as well to references to themselves as poor, even though they frequently do fit the statistical definition of the poverty level.[6] Consequently, Latin American references to the poor and a spirituality forged from the perspective of the popular masses and their legitimate struggles for revolutionary change can seem strangely out of place and somewhat off target for the United States Hispanics. This is not to say that serious attention ought not be given to the copious reflections coming out of Latin America. Rather, the point I am trying to make is that one cannot impose the Latin American frame of reference on the United States experience without doing violence to the actual situation. There has been in my judgment an unhealthy, unconscious dependence on Latin American theologians impeding the original reflections of United States Hispanics.

What General Perspective toward Spirituality Is Being Taken?

The third background consideration has to do with the way spirituality is conceptualized. In this essay I wish to speak of spirituality as encompassing all those ways in which the Christian faithful pursue and deepen their life of faith in Christ within Christian community.[7] The initial impulse for such a journey was given with the gift of life at conception and explicitated in baptism. The persistent tendency to identify Christian spirituality and vocation with the specific call to religious life and priesthood is a source of much confusion. The tendency to identify spirituality with priesthood and religious life is especially confusing with respect to the

Hispanic communities: (1) because it fails to take the emphases of Vatican II seriously by downplaying the universal call to holiness rooted in baptism and (2) it creates a barrier for the understanding of Hispanic spirituality which is that of seemingly ordinary lay people, frequently poor and marginal with respect to church and society.[8] The fundamental expression of that spirituality is popular devotion, not the refined asceticism, profound mysticism, or elaborate spiritualities of great writers, mystics, or saints. The spirituality of Hispanics that I wish to discuss here is not an elitist affair. On the contrary, it is part and parcel of the religious culture of Latin American peoples. It is my conviction that the difficulty many religious leaders have in accepting and appreciating the popular religious culture of Hispanics is the root of our failure to discover what the *people's* spirituality really is. The resistance to local popular manifestations of faith has a long history in most world religions, not just Catholicism.[9]

The perspective taken here, then, is ethnographic. By that I mean that I do not impose some preconceived official idea of what spirituality is upon the people, but rather discover those gestures, customs, symbols and traits of the people expressive of their faith in God. The task of elaborating a spirituality of and for United States Hispanics, therefore, requires that the student suspend his or her expectations. It requires that sense of awe and contemplation in the face of the mystery of God present in those who are very "other." Rationalistic ideas, rigid orthodoxies, prejudices of modernity, of culture and social class are profound obstacles in the attainment of that balance and serenity required in the student of Hispanic spirituality. For whatever that spirituality may be, it is not presently understood, appreciated, or fostered by the majority of leaders and thinkers in the North American Church. The task before us, then, takes us into new realms that have barely found expression in official or learned texts.

Now I wish to turn to several issues which I believe will help us understand better the nature of the task and the difficulties to be expected in moving forward in this effort.

Toward an Inculturated Spirituality

One of the fundamental issues that faces us has to do with the changes that took place after the Second Vatican Council. In the pre-Vatican II period there existed a kind of clearly defined Catholic ethos that was characterized by a certain level of resistance to the trends of modernity and secular life. Priests and religious were generally introduced into a kind of subculture from the very beginning of their formation. The seminary or the formation house was frequently out in "the middle of nowhere." A dress code was rigorously enforced. A new clerical, ecclesiastical language was in vogue. The code of conduct was clear and unambiguous.

The burden of spiritual formation in the pre-Vatican II context, then, was simpler in the sense that there really existed a kind of universal

Catholic subculture of which the Latin language was a powerful vehicle of expression. The issue was not adapting our approach or understanding of spirituality to the candidates, but rather getting the candidates to conform to this seemingly timeless pattern of life whether priestly or religious. The orientation was generally more deductive than inductive. I think, for example, of my Jesuit novitiate years 1963–65. The rules and expectations were incredibly clear, seemingly etched in granite. The task then was simple—getting those impressionistic, enthusiastic novices to toe the line. If so, they would get first vows; if not, they would be dismissed.

Life became more complicated after Vatican II. For one thing it now became necessary to engage the candidates' culture just as the church universal was proclaiming its desire to engage the world in dialogue instead of standing off from it. Today the word inculturation is on everyone's lips. Twenty years ago it did not exist. My point, then, is that a shift took place in our approach to formation as well as in our understanding of spirituality and holiness. We began to see the inadequacy of our pre-packaged concepts and approaches. We began to abandon the symbols and gestures that expressed the values of post-Tridentine Catholicism. There ensued a period of adaptation that is still with us. It became more important than ever to find a way of being Catholic and North American, Catholic and African, Catholic and Asian, and so forth. In the context of seminary and religious formation it became necessary to find a way to be an *American* Catholic religious or priest. As the formation context underwent change it adapted to the prevailing Anglo-American milieu and tended to reduce the elements in that Catholic clerical or religious subculture. One of the consequences of this trend, however, has been very problematic for Hispanics and other non-mainstream groups in the church. For the priesthood and religious life as well as our understanding of spirituality have adapted to the dominant American middle-class ethos. While this is in some ways understandable and even necessary, it has tended to make the priesthood and religious life *less accessible* to Hispanics, not more accessible.

To illustrate my point, consider the situation of North-American women religious. I believe that most would agree that they have moved far along, farther along than men religious and diocesan priests in adapting to the world and North American culture. In doing so, however, they have moved far away from the life world of Hispanic women. Only the most accultu-rated, resourceful Hispanic women are surviving in the ranks of mainstream United States congregations of women. The congregations of women which are attracting Hispanics are frequently those which have not adapted as much to United States culture and have maintained more of the spirit of that traditional Catholic ethos. I say this not to criticize mainstream American women religious, but merely to point out the difficulty.

It seems to me that the *formatores* have struggled with the adaptation of spiritual life, worship, prayer, discipline, academics, community life, and so forth to the dominant middle-class American context. That in itself was and is a major task. Going through a similar task for Hispanics and other non-mainstream groups seems to be asking a great deal, perhaps too much, in terms of resources and energies. That is our dilemma.

Taking the task of inculturation seriously means among other things relativizing our culturally conditioned notions of spirituality. All the good will in the world will not suffice. Inculturation occurs when people become sensitively aware of their own culture, its values and disvalues, when they relativize their absolutes and see Christian faith as incarnated in flesh and blood in a diversity of ways that may be puzzling or appear threatening at first.

Popular Religiosity: A Key Question

I have already alluded to the Central importance of *religiosidad popular.* The resistance educated Catholic leaders, whether clerical or lay, have shown to popular religious expressions has been deep and extensive. That incomprehension is about as great among liberal, progressive mainstream American Catholic priests and religious as among conservatives who may be a little more understanding in regard to popular religion since they are still rooted in that older Catholic ethos with its rich symbolic, sacramental, and mariological orientation.

Neither with the laity nor with priestly and religious candidates has the deeply embedded popular religious orientation of the people been fostered as something foundational. Popular religion, if accepted at all, remains at the level of folklore. It is something quaint, a remnant of bygone times, but hardly the foundation upon which a life of union with God in Christ can be built. It is pushed aside and in its place we give our Hispanic students formation in other, more official, sophisticated, or academically legitimate spiritualities. An adequate preparation for spiritual direction of Hispanics requires, nevertheless, exposure to the trends in popular devotion and religion among the various Hispanic groups. This popular religion is rooted in three areas: Meso or Middle America, the Caribbean and the Andean highlands. The first and second areas account for the vast majority of popular religious trends among U.S. Hispanics. The first area has to do with the islands of the Caribbean and the religions brought by the slaves from Africa. This is the basis for the growing and influential Afro-American religion called *santeria.* The second takes us back to the dramatic world of pre-Columbian religions.

Another issue that arises in the context of the study of Hispanic popular religion is the relationship between these beliefs and customs and the empowerment of the people. Antonio Gramsci, the Italian Marxist thinker, wrote extensively about the religion of the lower classes and how it represents a powerful instrument of resistance to oppression and a force for change.[10] In terms of spirituality the question is: to what extent does the substitution of more privatized, individualistic, and modern approaches to spirituality for popular religion affect the sense of solidarity and community that is of the essence of the popular religious expressions and ideas? Similarly the question can be asked regarding how prevailing official approaches to spirituality might affect the identity of Hispanics and their ability to identify with the socio-economic and political struggles of *their* people. To the extent that popular religious notions are eliminated and in their place more rational and privatized approaches substituted, does the Hispanic move away from his or her people? Does the standard spiritual formation of United States Catholics, especially religious and priests, make it harder to live in community and remain identified with the poor?

It would be a mistake to think of this religiosity as exclusively the pristine religion of Hispanics in Mexico or Puerto Rico. It is important for us to acknowledge, as Segundo Galilea has pointed out, that popular religion in Latin America and most certainly in the United States exists in a secondary form as a result of the rapid urbanization and modernizing trends all over the world.[11] Consequently, it is important that we seek insights into the peculiar secondary forms of religiosity that take root in the United States among Hispanics. One example might be the disappearance of many of the standard practices of religiosity among United States Hispanics but the persistence of certain practices. A case in point is devotion to Our Lady of Guadalupe among Chicanos or their fascination with the *quinceañera,* the fifteenth birthday coming-out celebration for young ladies.

One especially important chapter in the understanding of Hispanic popular religion has to do with Mariology. Most experts concur on the central role of Marian devotion among the Latin Americans as well as United States Hispanics. The current lack of interest in Marian themes and the effort to rethink these matters in a feminist perspective in the United States runs contrary to the experience of United States Hispanics who relate to the topic of Mary in a profoundly different way from mainstream Catholics. To get at the core of Hispanic popular religion is to enter into the unifying, Marian framework for the Catholic Christianity of Hispanics. This fact makes the elaboration of Mary's role in spiritual formation, prayer, and community worship all the more crucial. Gonzales Dorado's book, *Desde la Maria Conquistadora Hasta la Maria Libertadora,* is an especially helpful treatment of the point of contact and divergence between popular Mariology and official Mariology in the context of the people's struggles for fuller life socially, economically, politically, and, of course, spiritually.[12] Popular Mariology is an excellent place to start in the effort to get underneath the people's religion and spiritualities.

Conclusion

This article has only touched the surface of an admittedly complex field. There is a great need to engage spiritual directors and writers on Christian spirituality in the United States context with the issues raised in this rather general and merely suggestive article. It is hoped that future studies will contribute to the synthesis *waiting to be made* between the trends in spirituality over the last few centuries in the modern European and North Atlantic worlds with Third World spiritualities whose existence and general contours are only now becoming obvious to us. The need to serve Hispanics in the United States creates an unprecedented opportunity to enter into dialogue with traditions and cultures that have been marginal in the past.

This writer has noted the goodwill and openness with which committed educated Catholics approach the religions of Asia. There is a deep respect for traditions that are very different from the mainline official forms of Catholic Christianity. Yet there is no similar goodwill and openness with respect to the Hispanic peoples' religion. We must ask ourselves why there is such a strong orientation to reject the religion of our Hispanic confreres and find little that is positive in it, while finding all manner of insight and profundity in the religion of strangers? There is a disturbing lack of consistency here, a disordered charity.

Spiritual directors and *formatores* need to go beyond the categories and concerns of their profession, since rarely do they reflect the rich and varied experiences of Hispanics and other Third World peoples. On the other hand, Hispanics stand to benefit by articulating their experiences of God and the quest for God's reign in terms of the rich, inter-disciplinary and sophisticated categories and concerns of Western spirituality.

Notes

1. See Allan Figueroa Deck, S. J., *The Second Wave: Hispanic Ministry and the Evangelization of Cultures* (Mahwah, NJ., 1989).

2. The CARA Seminary Forum regularly provides data on trends in seminary population including ethnic trends. The recent Autumn and Winter 1989 issue (Vol. 16, No. 3–4) provides data and commentary on changes and developments in religious formation institutions. It is published by Center for Applied Research in the Apostolate in Washington, D.C. It documents the growing number of Hispanics in U.S. seminaries.

3. This is one of the conclusions of "In My Father's House," the most extensive dialogue ever undertaken on the subject of Hispanic vocations to the priesthood and religious life in the United States. See "In My Father's House," Conclusions. Bishops Committee on Priestly Life and Formation. USCC. Washington D.C., 1988.

4. There is no single textbook available as an introduction to these diverse regional histories and realities. The Borderlands theme is important in the understanding of the Mexican American or Chicano as well as the Hispanos of New Mexico and Southern Colorado and the Tejanos of Texas.

5. This was the conclusion of several recent studies; for instance, see Walker O'Connor's *Mexican Americans in Comparative Perspective* (Washington, D.C., 1985) p. 360. A similar conclusion about the integrationist trends among California Hispanics is drawn by Kevin F. McCarthy and R. Burciaga Valdez in *Current*

234   *Allan Figueroa Deck*

and Future Effects of Mexican Immigration in California (Santa Monica, CA., 1985). Father Joseph Fitzpatrick treats the subject in "Cultural Change or Cultural Continuity: Pluralism and Hispanic Americans," in *Hispanics in New York: Religious, Cultural, and Social Experiences* (Archdiocese of New York, Offices of Pastoral Research, 1982) p. 68.

6. This is one of the points that Andrew Greeley made in his article "Defection Among Hispanics" in *America* (July 30, 1988): 61. Some Catholic pastoral ministers talk to United States Hispanics as if they were talking to the poor. Psychologically this is a "turnoff" for many U.S. Hispanics. The success of some Protestant groups is in part due to their avoiding this approach according to Greeley.

7. I find Anne E. Carr's definition of spirituality in her book *Transforming Grace* to be most helpful:

In its widest meaning, spirituality can be described as the whole of one's spiritual or religious experience, one's beliefs, convictions, and patterns of thought, one's emotions and behavior in respect to what is ultimate, or to God. Spirituality is holistic, encompassing all one's relationships to all of creation—to the self and to others, to society and nature, to work and leisure—in a fundamentally spiritual or religious orientation. Spirituality is broader than a theology or a set of values precisely because it is so all-encompassing and pervasive. Unlike theology as an explicit pattern of cognitive or intellectual positions, spirituality reaches into one's physical, psychological, and religious depths, touches those surest human feelings and convictions about the way things really are. And while it shapes behavior and attitudes, spirituality is more than a consciously chosen moral code. In a religious perspective, in relation to God, it is one who really is, the deepest self, not entirely accessible to the most thoughtful self-scrutiny and reflection. And in a Christian perspective, as the experience of God's salvation in Christ and the response of individuals and groups to that salvation, spirituality can be understood as the source of both theology and morality. For it is the experience out of which both derive as a human response. At the same time, theology and morality can work back upon spirituality as sources of its criticism and transformation.

If Carr had added a cultural perspective, her lucid definition would be even more complete. See Anne E. Carr. *Transforming Grace* (San Francisco, 1988) pp. 201–02.

8. See Allan Figueroa Deck's "Ministry and Vocations" in *America* (March 14, 1987): 212–14.

9. See Harvey Cox, *Religion in the Secular City* (New York, 1984) Chapter 21, pp. 240–61. "Carnival Faith-People's Religion and Postmodern Theology."

10. Robert J. Schreiter discusses the import of Gramsci's *Quaderni del Carcere* where the relationship of popular religion to social transformation is dealt with in a provocative and original way for the first time. See Schreiter's *Constructing Local Theologies* (Maryknoll, New York, 1985) especially pp. 123, 136, 137, and footnote no. 4 on p. 167.

11. Segundo Galilea, *Pastoral Popular y Urbana* (Bogota, Columbia, 1977) pp. 23–26.

12. See A. Gonzales Dorado. *Desde la Maria Conquistadora a Maria Libertadora* (Bogota, Colombia, 1986).

Annotated Bibliography—Allan Figueroa Deck

Second Wave: Hispanic Ministry and the Evangelization of Cultures (New York: Paulist Press, 1989).

This book earned Allan F. Deck the Paulist Press Publisher's Award for 1990, the first Latino theologian to receive this distinction. The central focus of Deck's work is the evangelization of North American culture in dialogue with the immigrant Latinos facing a modern (postmodern) culture. He suggests eight mutually related pastoral objectives as pastoral responses to help pastoral agents recognize their inherently modern presuppositions when dealing with premodern Hispanics. Failure to recognize this dichotomy, he argues, will serve only to further ideologies of assimilation often masquerading as evangelization among Hispanics.

"Hispanic Theologians and the U.S. Catholic Church," *New Theology Review* 3:4 (November 1990), pp. 22–27.

This article is also important as a first record of the emerging Latino/a voices in theology. The author outlines the theologians' challenges which are cultural, anthropological, socio-economic, and political, in view of life in a dominant Anglo-American milieu. He lists the initial contributions made by this first generation of Latino/a theologians while cautioning them to avoid the pitfalls of elitism.

"At the Crossroads: North American and Hispanic," in *We Are a People! Initiative in Hispanic American Theology,* Roberto Goizueta, ed. (Minneapolis: Fortress Press, 1992), pp. 1–20.

The author articulates the social-historical reality of U.S. Latino Catholics who have been relegated to be outsiders in both church and society due to the lack of understanding of the diverse cultural world views of Anglo American Catholicism and U.S. Latino Catholicism. His solution is to develop intellectual leaders among U.S. Hispanics and a reconsideration of the controversial notion of national parishes for Hispanics.

14

Justo L. González

Justo L. González was born in La Habana, Cuba. His theological studies began at the Seminario Evangélico de Teología in Cuba. From Yale he received a masters in sacred theology (STM) in 1958, a masters in theology (MA) in 1960 and a doctorate in theology (PhD) in 1961.

After his studies, González began teaching at the Evangelical Seminary in Puerto Rico as professor of historical theology (1961–1969) where he was also dean. He was a Yale University research fellow (1968), assistant professor and later associate professor of World Christianity at Emory University, Candler School of Theology, visiting professor of theology at Interdenominational Theological Center (1977–1988), and adjunct professor of theology at Columbia Theological Seminary (1988–1991). At various times, he has also taught at the Seminario Bíblico de San José, Perkins School of Theology, Pacific School of Religion, Oblate School of Theology, and McCormick Theological Seminary.

González is nationally recognized as a prominent Protestant U.S. Latino theologian. He has published extensively and is perhaps most known for his acclaimed three-volume *History of Christian Thought.* He has written some fifty books and over three hundred articles which have been translated into several languages. In the past few years, González's work reflects a decidedly U.S. Latino Protestant perspective on theology. His works call for a new reformation emerging from within a new ecumenical minority perspective and from a new rereading of the Bible "in Spanish." In 1990 he published *Mañana: Christian Theology from a Hispanic Perspective.*

Professionally, González participates in numerous boards and commissions. These include, for example, the Commission on Faith and Order, World Council of Churches, National Council of Churches, Perkins School of Theology, and Presbyterian Church in the U.S. He is editor of *Apuntes,* Director of the Hispanic Summer Program of the Fund for Theological Education, editor of the *Comentario Bíblico Hispanoamericano* (40 volumes), and president of the *Asociación para la Educación Teológica Hispana.*

He is married to the Rev. Dr. Catherine Gunsalus González who is professor of church history as Columbia Theological Seminary.

Hispanic Summer Program
336 Columbia Drive
Decatur, Georgia 30030
404-378-7651

Hispanics in the New Reformation

Justo L. González

The previous chapter sought to place Hispanic experience and theology within the context of some larger events and trends in our time, first in the world at large and then in the church and its theology. We must now focus more directly on Hispanic religious history and our present situation, in order to see how those wider events relate to our own concrete task.

Our Catholic Background

Perhaps the best starting point is the question of how Hispanics view the end of the Constantinian era, and how it affects us and our faith. The Spanish-American Roman Catholic Church is part of the common background of all Hispanics—if not personally, then at least in our ancestry. Most of us were born within that church and still belong to it. Others were Protestants from the time of birth. Many, born Roman Catholics, are now Protestants. Still others have no ecclesiastical connection whatsoever. But still, somewhere in our common background, there stands the Spanish-American Roman Catholic Church.

It is very difficult for Protestants—and even for Roman Catholics—in the United States to have an idea of the changes that have taken place in Latin American Catholicism during our lifetime. You need to have experienced your classmates' crossing themselves when they learned that you were a Protestant. You need to have been invited by the more devout of those classmates to come with them to "hear mass" (people didn't normally take communion; they didn't even "go" to mass—they "heard" mass). You need to have heard a former Catholic seminarian tell of being taken to the garden, being ordered to pull up the carrots and plant them upside down, and being punished when he protested, because he had not learned the meaning of obedience. You need to have seen the bones of the poor, whose relatives could not pay for a plot of holy ground at $300 a yard, piled six feet high in an abandoned building. You need to have seen schools where poor children who received scholarships wore a uniform different from the one worn by those who paid their tuition. You need to have seen bishops and cardinals routinely blessing the works of tyrants, while the people bled to death. Then you would have some idea of the magnitude of the changes that have taken place. Then you would have understood the prejudices of a Protestant student who, four weeks into a course on the history of Christian thought, asked me when we would leave behind all this "Catholic stuff" and begin dealing with "Christian" thought. Then you would be able to begin to understand the astounding and grateful amazement with which I and my generation of Protestants look at the new Catholic Church in Latin America.

And yet, we should not be so astounded. We should not be so astounded, first, for theological reasons. We have always said and believed that unexpected things take place whenever Scripture is read anew and seriously. We are now seeing it happen, and we are discovering and having to confess that our prejudices did not agree with our theology. But second, and this is my main point, we would not have been so astounded had we realized that the apparently monolithic Catholic Church in Latin America had been two churches from the very beginning.

Few North Americans are aware of the degree to which the Catholic Church in Latin America was an arm of the powers of conquest, colonialism, and oppression. Even fewer are aware of the other reality, the underside of that Church, which repeatedly decried and opposed those powers.

Let us look first at the "topside," at the official organization of the Church and the manner in which it served the interests of conquest and colonization. From the very beginning of the conquest, the Spanish crown had over the Church in the colonies the power of "royal patronage," or *Patronato real.* Alexander VI, who apparently did not wish to be bothered with all the new lands to be evangelized when there were so many exciting developments taking place in Italy, issued a series of bulls[1] in which he granted the Spanish crown both political and religious authority over all lands discovered or to be discovered beyond a line of demarcation one hundred leagues west of the Azores, as long as they were reached sailing west and they did not already belong to a Christian ruler. Similar arrangements were already in force for Portuguese discoveries and were adapted to bring the rights of the Portuguese *Padroado* to the same level as the Spanish *Patronato.* By 1501, and probably earlier,[2] the tithes and offerings from the Church in the colonies were administered by the crown, which in turn was responsible for all expenses of the Church in the colonies.[3] When the first episcopal sees were established, Pope Julius II, who scarcely had time for his Italian wars, granted the Spanish crown the "right of presentation," whereby the crown was to "present" before the Holy See the names of those to be appointed as bishops and other high clerics in the colonies.[4] Eventually, the theory would develop, particularly among Spanish jurists, that what the popes had granted the Spanish crown was actually a "vicariate," so that the king was the pope's vicar in the New World.[5]

The attitude of the crown toward the Indians was ambivalent. On the one hand, the entire enterprise of conquest and colonization was based on deriving benefits from Indian labor. There is ample proof that the crown wished the Indians to be Christianized, not only for the benefit of their souls but also for the benefit of Spanish (or Portuguese) rule. On the other hand, the exploitation of the Indians could lead to the establishment of vast estates—practically independent empires—in the New World. Spain's unification had recently been achieved after a prolonged struggle with noble potentates who resisted the authority of the crown. Therefore, in order to prevent similar events in the New World, the Spanish sovereigns often became the defenders of the rights of Indians.[6]

The same ambivalence existed in the Church. Bishops were appointed by the crown, usually not on the basis of their pastoral experience in the New World or their love for their Indian flocks but on the basis of their connections in court.[7] The diocesan clergy ministered mostly to the Spaniards who had settled in towns, and to their Indian servants. Many of these secular or diocesan priests were devout men.[8] However, others were simply priests who had failed in Spain and were looking for a new post. Such clergy had very little idea of the sufferings that the Indians were undergoing in their process of "Christianization." All that they could see were cities arising in the wilderness, churches being built, tithes collected, schools founded, civilization being brought to savages.

There was, however, another church being born in the New World. Its ministers were mostly friars—Franciscans,[9] Dominicans,[10] Jesuits,[11] and Mercedarians[12]—who had vows of poverty and obedience and who therefore were able and ready to work in places and situations in which the secular clergy would not work. Their vows of poverty allowed these missionaries to witness and often also to share the poverty and the suffering of their flocks. Therefore, it was usually the friars who became the defenders of the Indians, protesting against their mistreatment and on occasion organizing and empowering them to take control over their own lives.

The name that is most commonly known in this context is that of Bartolomé de Las Casas, who spent most of his life seeking new and better laws for the protection of the Indians.[13] Unfortunately, one suspects that the reason he is relatively well known to the English-speaking public is that his writings about the mistreatment of the Indians have been used to confirm all the anti-Spanish and anti-Catholic prejudices of such a public. What few realize is that Las Casas, far from being a lone exception in a sea of insensitivity and injustice, was the voice of an entirely different Christianity that was arising.

The names of the founders of this other Christianity are too many even to mention. But a few of the highlights would serve to illustrate the nature of this "other church" being born out of the ministry of the friars among the dispossessed.

The Dominican Antonio de Montesinos was the first to protest against the mistreatment of the Indians, and in particular against the *encomiendas*. This was a system according to which a group of Indians were *encomendados*—entrusted—to a Spaniard in order to be "civilized" and "Christianized." In exchange for such great benefits, the Indians were to work for the Spaniard. Since the *encomendero* had no investment in the Indians entrusted to him, the resultant system was in some ways worse than slavery. In any case, thanks to Montesinos's protests, and his advocacy before the court in Spain, the laws regarding the treatment of Indians were changed in 1512. This was the first of a long series of legal reforms in which the name of Las Casas appears repeatedly, but whose actual application in the New World was in fact limited.

St. Luis Beltrán,[14] the first of the Spanish missionaries to the New World to be canonized, repeatedly rebuked the Spaniards for living off the blood of the Indians. It is said that on one such occasion, when sitting at the table of an *encomendero*, his host took offense at his comments, and that St. Luis silenced his host by taking a tortilla and squeezing blood from it. Whatever the truth may be behind this legend, it does point to the undeniable fact that there was among some of the friars an often unspoken view of the conquest, and of the economic order of the colonies, which saw the entire enterprise as founded on injustice and exploitation.

The Jesuit missionaries in Paraguay have been accused of being paternalistic, when in fact much the opposite is true. In their villages, in which most of the fields and all the animals and tools were held in common, the Indians not only learned how to manage their own lives but also practiced such specialized arts as the building of organs for their churches. It certainly was not paternalism that led the Jesuits to help the Indians, menaced by the encroachment of slave hunters, to turn their smithies into arms factories and to organize themselves into an army.[15]

In Chile the Dominican Gil González de San Nicolás[16] came to the conclusion that the wars against the Indians, whose real cause was the desire to take Indian lands, were unjust, and that therefore people who profited from such wars should not receive absolution. He convinced many of his fellow Dominicans as well as a number of Franciscans. Finally, he was accused of heresy and silenced by the authorities.

This other church also found opportunity to express itself with the coming of black slaves. As in many other parts of the world, ecclesiastical authorities found very little wrong with the institution of slavery. There were among the friars, however, many who disagreed with the authorities. Since there was not much they could do to end the institution, they did all they could to change it and to expose its opposition to the gospel. Most notable in this work was St. Pedro Claver.[17] A Catalonian Jesuit who arrived at Cartagena while still a novice, young Pedro was deeply disturbed by what he saw of the "peculiar institution," of ships whose stench could be detected before they appeared on the horizon, of broken families, broken bodies, and broken lives, and he determined that he would do something about it. When the time came for him to make his final vows, he added a fourth vow to the traditional three of poverty, chastity, and obedience: *Petrus Claver, aethiopum semper servus* (Pedro Claver, forever a slave to blacks). While he was concerned for the evangelization of blacks, and it was for this ministry that he obtained permission from his order, he did much more than that. He personally took care of lepers who had been abandoned by their masters and organized the freed blacks of the city to provide relief for these and other blacks in need. On festival days, this organization provided banquets in which the guests of honor were the lepers and the beggars, many of whom were former slaves whose owners had abandoned them because they had become unable to earn their keep. He knew that he could not attack slavery per se. But he went as far as was prudent, and then a bit. It soon became well known that he would humbly greet the poorest of slaves, and that he would cross the street to avoid greeting a slave owner. He also made it known that in listening to confession he would follow the "gospel order," beginning with the slaves, then the poor, and finally the children. As to the rich and the slave owners, he was sure they could find another confessor who had time for them. Toward the end, bedridden, unable to move, and made to lie in his filth, he thanked God for the opportunity to experience something of what his flock had experienced in the slave ships. Then the white society realized that a saint was about to leave them, and they flocked to his cell is search of relics. When practically nothing was left but his crucifix, he was ordered to relinquish it to a marquis. Then he died, the fad passed, slavery continued, and it took the Roman Church 234 years to acknowledge him a saint.

This was the other church—the church I did not know when my friends crossed themselves; the church that probably even my friends, middle-class as they were, did not know. The most fortunate of its saints, like Pedro Claver, took centuries to be acknowledged. Most others have been forgotten. And perhaps forgotten they should remain, for this is the church of the poor, the anonymous, the unrewarded.

Whatever the case may be, that other church lived on. At various points it came to the fore. In the eighteenth century José Gabriel Túpac Amaru, claiming to be the direct descendant of the royal Incas, led the Indians of upper Peru in revolt against the Spanish. He and his successor, as well as the other leaders of the rebellion, declared themselves to be true Catholics. They were aware that the hierarchy was an instrument of Spanish power. The bishop of Cuzco instructed his priests to remind the Indians of the great "reward that is promised them if they stay away from riots and rebellions, and remain faithful subjects of our Catholic King."[18] In most cities and large towns, the urban clergy, mostly diocesan and either native Spaniards or colonials of Spanish descent, organized the resistance against the rebellion. Several of them took arms against the rebels. On the other hand, many of the village and country priests supported the rebellion. A priest who had left Peru earlier, when the Jesuits were expelled from the Spanish colonies, now appeared in London trying to persuade the English government to send support to the rebels.

The Túpac Amaru rebellion was short-lived and was drowned in blood three years after it began. But a few decades later, now in Mexico, another rebellion broke out. Under the leadership of Fr. Miguel Hidalgo y Costilla and under the flag of the Virgin of Guadalupe, Mexico proclaimed its independence. The time of the end of the Spanish empire had come, and in the struggles that ensued the Church would once again be divided between a hierarchy, mostly foreign or drawn from the native aristocracy that supported the crown, and a lower clergy that often supported the rebels.

I cannot review here that entire development. It is significant, however, that the banner under which Hidalgo and his troops fought was that of the Virgin of Guadalupe.[19] This is symptomatic, for one of the ways—probably the most important way—in which the church of the dispossessed continued its existence was through the popular piety expressed in cults such as that of the Virgin of Guadalupe.

The legend behind this cult is instructive.[20] Briefly put, it is the story of how the Virgin appeared to Juan Diego, a poor and unlearned Indian, and gave him certain instructions to be conveyed to the bishop of Mexico. The bishop would not listen until he was forced by a miracle to admit that the Virgin had indeed appeared to Juan Diego, and that he was to do as the Indian told him. Thus the Virgin of Guadalupe became a symbol of the affirmation of the Indian over against the Spanish, of the unlearned over against the learned, of the oppressed over against the oppressor.

When I was growing up, I was taught to think of such things as the Virgin of Guadalupe as pure superstition. Therefore, I remember how surprised I was at the reaction of a Mexican professor in seminary when one of my classmates made some disparaging remarks about Guadalupe. The professor, who was as Protestant as they come and who often stooped because he was then elderly, drew himself up, looked my friend in the eye, and said: "Young man, in this class you are free to say anything you please. You may say anything about me. You certainly are welcome to say anything you wish about the pope and the priests. But don't you touch my little Virgin!"

At that time, I took this to be an atavism of an old man who had been fed superstition in his mother's milk. But now I know better. What he was saying was that, in spite of all that our North American friends had told us, in spite of the veneer of superstition, in spite of the horrendous things that took place every Sunday morning as people crawled to the shrine of Guadalupe, there was in there a kernel of truth that was very dear to his heart—and all the dearer, since so much of the religiosity that he knew, both Catholic and Protestant, denied it.[21] For generation upon generation of oppressed Indian people, told by word and deed that they were inferior, the Virgin has been a reminder that there is vindication for the Juan Diegos. And that is indeed part of the gospel message, even if it has not always been part of our own message.[22]

So we should not be too surprised by what has taken place in the Catholic Church in Latin America in recent decades: that Juan Diego has come forth, and many of the bishops have finally believed him; that the other Catholic Church, the church of Las Casas and Montesinos and Pedro Claver, has come to the fore, and that it is forcing the entire church catholic to listen to it. Also, we should not be surprised that the struggle goes on; that the Catholic Church in Latin America does not speak with one voice; that for every Archbishop Romero whose primary concern is for the people, there are a host whose primary concern is for the institutional church.

Thus from its very beginning, Spanish-American Roman Catholicism has been torn between a hierarchical church that has generally represented the powerful and stood by them and a more popular church, formed by the masses and led by pastors who have ministered at the very edge of disobedience.

This duality has been part of the experience of Roman Catholicism for most Hispanics, for it has continued long after the end of the colonial period. In the United States southwest, it is typified by Antonio José Martínez, the "cura de Taos." Martínez had prepared for the priesthood both in Mexico and in Spain and had founded Catholic churches in Peñasco, Abiquiú, Santa Fe, Cañada de Santa Cruz, Tomé, Old Messilla, and, finally, Taos. There he built a school, brought in a printing press from old Mexico, started the first newspaper, and developed a reputation as a saint. He did not believe in celibacy and was openly married. His wife was commonly known as "Madre Teodorita" and was widely respected in the community as the priest's companion. They lived at the time of the Mexican-American war and the Civil War. Through all these conflicts, Fr. Martínez guided his flock and kept it together. When New Mexico came under American rule, he was accused of resisting that rule and of abetting an uprising in Taos in which the American governor was killed. Apparently, such accusations, which were never taken to court, were not true. The truth was that Fr. Martínez repeatedly defended his people against the depredations of the newcomers, and that therefore the latter suspected him of hostile intentions.

Fr. Martínez did clash with the newly appointed bishop of Santa Fe, Jean Baptiste Lamy. Lamy, a member of the American hierarchy, was convinced that Spanish Catholicism left much to be desired. He conceived of his task as consisting partly in Americanizing his Hispanic flock. He apparently had little understanding of the problems that this flock was encountering under the new order—he counted Kit Carson among his friends and could never understand why his Hispanic flock objected. He certainly could not accept this married priest who lived openly with his wife and children. When Bishop Lamy insisted that Hispanic priests collect tithes from their parishioners, Martínez refused to do so on the grounds that his flock was already poor enough and that the business of the Church was not to collect money from the poor but rather to give it to them. For a long time, he continued ministering at the edge of obedience. Eventually, he either was excommunicated or resigned, but he refused to give up his church or his ministry. To the people in Taos, he was still their priest, and this was their church. With him went a number of other priests, and they helped him organize an independent Catholic church that was particularly strong in northern New Mexico. To this day, his name is venerated among the older Hispanic stock in New Mexico, stories still circulate of miracles connected with him and his companions, his descendants proudly claim him as an ancestor, and his tomb in Taos is a place of pilgrimage for the few who remember him.[23] At the same time, at the very center of Santa Fe, by the cathedral, stands a statue of Jean Baptiste Lamy.

Hispanics, no matter whether Catholic or Protestant, and no matter whether or not they have heard of Bartolomé de Las Casas or the cura de Taos, have been shaped by this dual Catholicism, a Catholicism that is deeply pained by the tension within itself and that is best epitomized in the common phrase—almost a contradiction for Catholics of other traditions—"soy católico, pero no creo en los curas" (I am a Catholic, but I don't believe in priests). This is not, as is often thought, a blanket anticlericalism, after the fashion of the French Revolution. It is rather a statement that only those priests who live up to their vocation, after the fashion of the "cura de Taos," are believable priests. Authority does not reside in priesthood in the hierarchical sense but rather in Catholicism—in Catholicism understood as the faith of the people and not as the monopoly of the hierarchy.

In a sense, what happened at the assembly of Latin American bishops in Medellín (1968) was that the church of the poor, of Las Casas, Beltrán, and Claver, captured the hierarchy, with the help and inspiration of the Second Vatican Council and Pope John XXIII. What is currently taking place in Latin American Roman Catholicism is a great struggle between that "new church," which is in truth old, and the understanding of the hierarchy and its function derived from the period of the royal *Patronato*.

Hispanic Catholics in the United States have had similar experiences. Until very recently, the hierarchy, even in those regions where most of the Catholic population was Hispanic, was non-Hispanic. While many of the priests, and certainly those who had closer contact with their parishioners, were Hispanic, they knew that the higher echelons of the hierarchy were closed to them. Thus Hispanic Roman Catholics have lived in a church that was sympathetic to their struggles at the local level but that usually ignored them at the national level. To them this was not new. It was rather a repetition of what had usually taken place under the Spanish regime, and then again under the various national governments in Spanish America.

At the local level, some priests followed the lead of the national hierarchy, while others sought ways, again at the very edge of obedience, to respond to the needs of their parishioners. Their task was not simply to preserve the religious traditions of their parishioners, although such traditions were important. Their task was rather to preserve their parishioners' right to exist as themselves, distinct not only from white Protestants but also from white Catholics. To exist, and to make a significant contribution both to society and to the church. To make a contribution, and to enjoy their just share.

What is happening in the Hispanic Roman Catholic Church in the United States is similar to what happened in the Latin American church at Medellín: This church of the poor is making itself heard. In recent years, a number of Hispanics have come to occupy positions of authority in the Church, as bishops or as directors of institutions and programs. When some of the present-day bishops were considering the priesthood, their friends tried to dissuade them, because they were Hispanic and there was no future in the Church for them. Now they are part of the hierarchy.[24] But some of them are a different sort of hierarchy. They are not the heirs of the bishops appointed by the crown but rather of the friars who struggled for justice for their people. In them, a new day is dawning in the Roman Catholic Church, and Catholic Hispanics are very much aware of this.

In 1969 the National Conference of Catholic Bishops established the Division for the Spanish Speaking. In 1970 its Director, Mr. Pablo Sedillo, was appointed. Since that time, the division—now the Secretariat for Hispanic Affairs of both the National Conference of Catholic Bishops and the United States Catholic Conference—has emphasized the need for grassroots involvement of Hispanics in planning for the mission of the Church. The Primer Encuentro Nacional Hispano de Pastoral took place in June of 1972, with approximately 250 participants. The Second Encuentro Nacional Hispano de Pastoral took place in 1977. By this time, however, a new methodology had been developed. In this methodology, the process leading to the Encuentro was at least as important as the Encuentro itself. As the planners stated,

> The process leading to the Second Encuentro should serve to take the historic step from a mass Church to a Church of small ecclesial communities. It would therefore be an occasion for intensifying the creation and the renewal of these small communities throughout the country.[25]

From the beginning, it was stipulated that no one would be allowed to participate in the Encuentro without prior involvement in one of these basic groups. It was also hoped that the result of the process, as well as of the Encuentro itself, would be that in these basic Christian Communities (Comunidades Eclesiales de Base, or CEBs) the conclusions of the Encuentro would take flesh—and perhaps even, as they put it, blood. The theme of the Encuentro was "Evangelization," understood in its widest sense, as implying a continuous process throughout life whereby believers are increasingly closer to Christ and to a full commitment to the gospel. This will result in sharing the message with others, both in word and deed, seeking the transformation of the world.[26]

The preparation for the Third Encuentro involved thousands of CEBs throughout the nation. At every level, flowing through parish, diocese, and CEB, there was ample consultation, study, and reflection. When the 1,150 delegates finally gathered in Washington in August of 1985, there was a growing consensus among Hispanic Catholics as to what their plan of ministry should be. Out of that Third Encuentro came the working document *Pueblo Hispano—Voz Profetica,* which would be used as the basis for preparing a National Pastoral Plan for Hispanic Ministry to be presented before the bishops in 1987.

The report of the Third Encuentro is a vast document covering various aspects of church life, and it is impossible to review it here. However, in order to understand the mood and the dreams of Hispanic Catholics, a few quotations may be in order:

The Word of God gives us strength to denounce the injustices and abuses that we suffer; the marginalization and scorn, the discrimination and exploitation. It is in the Word of God that we, as pilgrim people, find the motivation for our daily Christian commitment.[27]

... We call upon the Christian community (lay people, bishops, deacons, religious priests) to show the world that worldly things and human institutions, through the determination of God the Creator, are also ordered to the salvation of people, and therefore, may contribute to the building up of the body of Christ. That is why as Christians we have the responsibility to work for social justice.[28]

... We also announce a model of Church that is open to the people's needs, placing its buildings at the disposal of the people and recognizing the reality of Hispanics as a poor community. We affirm a model of priesthood that is more in contact with the people it serves, dedicated to persons, not material buildings, and exercising leadership in smaller communities.[29]

The consequence of all this is that there are in the Catholic Hispanic tradition, both in the United States and in Latin America, many who are ready for the end of the Constantinian era. In Latin America, the church of the poor, which has existed through the ages alongside the coopted church of the powerful, continues to live at the edge of obedience, lacking support from sociopolitical structures and usually opposed by them, even to the point of persecution and martyrdom. When the last vestiges of the Constantinian era finally disappear, this church will be ready for the new day, for it is already living in it. In the United States, Hispanic Catholics have learned how to subsist and to worship without the support of either the dominant white Protestant culture or the also dominant white Catholic subculture. As the post-Constantinian era advances, Hispanic Catholics represent that segment of the church which is best prepared to face the new day.

The Protestant Experience

Although all Hispanic-Americans have a Roman Catholic background, many of us are now Protestant. This growing Protestant Hispanic community has two origins, for some were converted in this country, while others were already Protestant at the time of their immigration. Therefore, to understand the Protestant Hispanic community in the United States, it is necessary to look both at Latin America and at this country.

When I look at Protestantism, both in Latin America and among Hispanics in the United States, I am once again surprised (although I am not as surprised by outward events as at myself) at what has happened to me and my views. As I was growing up, and my classmates were crossing themselves upon learning that we were Protestant heretics, my Protestant friends and I drew courage from a book that was quite popular among Latin American Protestants in those days. It was written by an Alsatian Protestant, Frédéric Hoffet, and its title was *Protestant Imperialism*.[30] The main thesis of the book was that Protestantism was conducive to higher culture and better living standards. It compared Protestant and Catholic countries on everything from literacy to illegitimate birth rates. It pointed to the superior technology of Protestant nations. It listed all the social evils and political unrest of Catholic countries. The conclusion, at least at that time, appeared irrefutable: Protestantism was destined to rule the future. Let my classmates cross themselves. We had a clearer vision of the future, a higher hope for our country and our society. And that vision and that hope were being realized at that very moment in the most advanced and progressive countries of the world.

This created a tension or an ambivalence in our view of culture and the society around us. On the one hand, we were profoundly counter-cultural. In order to be a Protestant in Latin America in those days, one had to have a strong Anabaptist streak. "No smoking, no drinking, no dancing" were not mere legalistic prohibitions. They were constant reminders that life around us was corrupt, and that we belonged to a different reality.

Eschatology was very real, not always in the sense of an imminent expectation but rather in the sense that our hope was for a different city.

On the other hand, we were not always clear whether that city was made by human hands or not. As Hoffet seemed to indicate, the holy city was already being built elsewhere, in countries whose religious stance was the same as ours. In short, our countercultural stance was both eschatological and extraterritorial. We judged our society both by the yardstick of the Reign of God and by the yardstick of the North Atlantic.

In the early years of Protestant Christianity in Latin America, this ambiguity did not immediately lead to contradiction. Protestantism entered Latin America as a liberating force. The first Protestant missionary to Latin America, James Thomson, came as the representative both of a new method of public education and of the British and Foreign Bible Society.[31] Almost immediately after political liberation from Spain, Thomson traveled throughout the continent and the Caribbean, announcing intellectual liberation from ignorance and from the obscurantism of the Catholic Church and the Inquisition. As such, he was received joyfully by the political liberators of the continent, Bernardo O'Higgins, José de San Martín, and Simón Bolivar. After all, these early political leaders shared the view that in order to make Latin America truly free, ideals, principles, and even people must be brought in from the North Atlantic.[32] Placing the Bible in the hands of the people and inviting them to examine it freely was a revolutionary act. Protestant worship, where people participated actively, was also an act of empowerment and liberation. The same could be said for the polity of most Protestant churches—and I still remember how I gloated, telling my Catholic schoolmates about my right to vote on matters affecting the life of the church.

Missionary work, however, was only one of the sources of Latin American Protestantism in the nineteenth century. Another source—most important numerically in the southern tip of the continent, in Argentina, Uruguay, Brazil, and Chile—was immigration. Convinced as they were that democracy could only flourish with a people trained for it, the early leaders of these countries—probably not untainted by racist considerations—encouraged immigration from northern Europe. Such immigrants required religious freedom, which had not always been part of the original program of the wars of independence. Once this was granted to the immigrants, it became untenable to deny similar rights to native citizens. Soon, contact between the two communities produced increasing numbers of native Protestants.[33] Also, as the descendants of the immigrants became enculturated and many of them retained the faith of their ancestors, there developed a large Protestant community that was increasingly native.

In other cases, Protestant communities in Latin America grew out of natives who had been in exile in the United States, or who in some other way had been in touch with Protestantism. This was particularly true of Cuba, whose early Protestant communities were the result of missions sent by Cuban exiles in Florida.[34] These exiles had settled mostly in Key West and Tampa, and there many of them had become Protestant. By the third quarter of the nineteenth century, they had their own Cuban pastors, educated in seminaries in the United States. Since at that time the Spanish government was going through a relatively liberal period, some of these communities sent missionaries to Cuba. Others returned from exile and founded churches that later sought connection with one of the major Protestant denominations in the United States. After 1898 the number of returning exiles grew. Among them were a number of pastors, who became the first leaders of the emerging Protestant churches. When the first missionaries were officially sent by the churches in the United States, they found that much of the preliminary work had been done. Meanwhile, in Puerto Rico, in the town of Aguadilla, a community of "believers in the Word" had been founded by a traveler who had obtained a Bible in the Virgin Islands. This community eventually joined the Presbyterian Church.

Finally, a small number of Protestants in Latin America were the result of schisms within the Roman Catholic Church. In Mexico, President Benito Juárez clashed repeatedly with the Roman Catholic hierarchy, which he considered too aristocratic and retrograde. At that time, several priests left the Catholic Church, taking their flocks with them. Juárez himself used to attend services at one of these congregations. Eventually, these congregations joined the Episcopal Church.[35]

The ambivalence of early Protestantism in Latin America also created a duality in our ecclesiology. For all kinds of reasons, and with some exceptions, Latin American Protestantism was in its origins, and to a great extent still is, a church of the poor. It excelled in the education of poor children, in work among peasants, in providing medical assistance in the most forlorn places, in promoting literacy, and most especially in bringing the good news as we understood it to those who seldom heard any good news.

At the same time, however, it was a church whose ideal was so molded by the image of the North Atlantic that it could not really be a church of the poor. Its ideal was the middle-class church in the United States, from which it received so much economic support. The ideology that was thus associated with early Protestantism was that of the nineteenth-century bourgeoisie: education as the means to solve all national problems, government in the hands of the educated, freedom of thought and worship, free enterprise, and the rewards of personal effort. It was thought that the reason for the "backwardness" of our countries was that these ideas, and the education that went with them, were not sufficiently widespread, and that we still carried the ballast of centuries of obscurantism and Catholic authoritarianism. If we could only rid ourselves of that inheritance, our countries would join those of the North Atlantic in their economic and human progress. The poor were temporarily such, until they could become middle class, largely through the agency of the church and through improvement in their moral standards. If poor peasants were simply given education, healthy bodies, and some technical know-how, most of their problems would be solved. With such resources, hard work and clean living was the formula for success. The result was that there are now in every city in Latin America dozens of professionals, business people, and church leaders who were born in conditions of abject poverty and who owe their success to the church. But this view of the reasons for our social problems also meant, at least implicitly, that lack of success was the result of sloth or vice. And therefore the result was also that many of those successful people whom I have just mentioned feel that if they managed to succeed, others could manage just as well.

This was—and to some extent still is—the ideology of the "historic" churches. Methodists, Presbyterians, Episcopalians, and others have made most of their inroads among the middle classes, and usually through education. Since this was a time of economic expansion, which required a trained middle class, Protestant schools and churches often served as means for social climbing—although normally only to the lower echelons of the middle class—and thus the ideology of progress through education and through Protestantism seemed to be confirmed by the thousands of Protestants who could witness to the success they had achieved.

The twentieth century saw the introduction into Latin America of a different sort of Protestantism. This was fundamentalism, whose birth as a self-conscious movement may be dated from the Niagara Falls declaration of 1895. In the early decades of the present century, the debate between fundamentalists and liberals raged in Latin America. By the middle of the century, there were numerous fundamentalist churches on that continent, and significant segments of the "historic" churches followed a similar orientation. This, however, led to very little change in the basic ideology of Latin American Protestantism. The most noticeable of these changes was in the devaluation of education, now suspected of leading to doubt as to the authority of Scripture. Freedom of thought, although discouraged in theological matters, was still theoretically encouraged. And there were few among the fundamentalists who doubted the principles of individual effort, free enterprise, and middle-class notions of success. Although often drawn from the lower classes, fundamentalist Protestants still thought in terms of middle-class goals and ideals.

Then came the enormous Pentecostal wave. The Azusa Street revival in Los Angeles began in 1906, and by 1910 the movement was so strong in Chile that a group of Methodists whose charismatic practices were condemned by the Annual Conference of Chile founded the Methodist Pentecostal Church. This denomination, which at first had only three congregations, soon outgrew its mother church and became one of the major Protestant denominations in Latin America. Similar events have taken place in other parts of the continent, so that by now the characteristic form of Latin American Protestantism is Pentecostalism.

Although its approach to Scripture is similar to that of the fundamentalists, Latin American Pentecostalism is very different from fundamentalism.
The latter is rigid in its structure and leadership, most of which remains
foreign. Indeed, among some fundamentalist missionaries one often
encounters the unspoken and perhaps unconscious assumption that only
American missionaries are capable of safeguarding the true faith, and that
Latin American converts are not entirely trustworthy on that score. For
that reason, although fundamentalist churches have grown, they have not
achieved the incredible success of Pentecostalism. Pentecostals, on the
other hand, offer a mixture of rigidity and flexibility. Their emphasis on the
power and freedom of the Spirit makes all human practices and institutions
provisional. Also, most of the older Pentecostal churches in Latin America
are autochthonous, and not the result of Pentecostal missionary work from
abroad. Many of those that are not autochthonous have become largely
indigenized. Therefore, these older Pentecostal churches are freer to find
their own way in Latin American culture and society.[36]

For these reasons it is very difficult to characterize Latin American
Pentecostalism. While there is in it a measure of escapism, with faith
directed mostly toward a spiritual afterlife, there is also a significant
measure of earthiness that other Protestants often refuse to acknowledge.
Their theology, with the minor changes required by their charismatic
orientation, is the same as that which many fundamentalist missionaries
taught: the literal inspiration of Scripture, the salvation of the soul through
faith in Christ, and the need for lives of purity while one waits for life in
heaven. Their ideology is still the same as that of most Latin American
Protestantism, although their daily life and social circumstances do not fit
that ideology. The majority of them are poor and have learned by experience
that poverty is not simply the result of sloth, vice, or ignorance. What
thus results is a vast community in transition, seeking its way as it moves
forward, with the outcome still in doubt.[37]

In any case, the one common characteristic of most Latin American
Protestantism until recent times has been its strongly anti-Catholic persua-
sion. Since the surrounding culture bears the Catholic imprint at all levels,
this has resulted in an alienation from Latin American culture. In this
alienation, Latin American Protestants have often looked to Protestant
nations, and particularly to the United States, as paradigms of what they
wish their own nations could become. Thus Protestant alienation in Latin
America has usually been not only otherworldly but also foreign oriented.

One of the main sources of Hispanic Protestantism in the United States
has been the migration of Latin American Protestants to this nation. This
migration, often precipitated by political and economic considerations,
was often inspired at a deeper level by the Protestant ideology itself. . . .
Suffice it to say that many such immigrants, finding their hopes ill-founded,
have begun to doubt the ideology behind those hopes and have thus become
a source of self-criticism in North American Protestantism.

But not all Protestant Hispanics in the United States entered the country as Protestants. Many were converted in the United States, through processes similar to those that took place in Latin America. In the nineteenth century, Protestantism appeared to be as the vanguard of progress, while Roman Catholicism, especially under Pius IX, was going through its most authoritarian and reactionary period. After the Mexican-American War, the Roman Catholic hierarchy in the conquered territories was in the hands of the invaders, and generally in their service. Actually, the first Mexican-American bishop was not named until well into the second half of the twentieth century. These circumstances gave rise to anticlerical feelings similar to those which appeared in Latin America at the time of independence. And this in turn opened the way for Protestantism.

Also, the Mexican-American War—as well as the Spanish-American War, which led to the conquest of Puerto Rico—was defended on ideological grounds as partly a religious war against backward and anti-democratic Catholicism. After the conquest, that ideology was used to justify it, and some of the conquered, as is usually the case, came to believe it. Thus Protestantism and the United States were seen by some as the forces of liberation from obscurantism and medievalism. If one wished to be attuned to the future, one had better join these forces, which were proving irresistible and which in any case were seen as positive. Thus while most clung to Roman Catholicism—even to a Roman Catholicism under foreign leadership—as the means to preserve their dignity and authenticity, others saw in Protestantism a way into the future, and into full participation in the nation that they had now unwillingly joined.

This, however, was not all that attracted Hispanics to Protestantism. The great appeal of Protestantism was in Scripture itself, which the Catholic Church had taught us to respect but not to read. For many Hispanics, both in the United States and in Latin America, the experience of hearing the Word for the first time, of being able to study Scripture in new ways, was revolutionary and liberating. After this, they could no longer understand how anyone could remain tied to a church that either forbade or discouraged the reading of Scripture, and they made every conceivable effort to bring other Hispanics to the same realization.

What is happening today is that the scam that held our ambivalence together is tearing apart. The result is the emergence of a new way of being Protestant among Hispanic Americans. From our earlier countercultural and quasi-Anabaptist stance, this new form of being Protestant retains its ability to be sharply critical of the culture and society around it. The difference is that now it is also critical of that other society, that North Atlantic that Hoffet so praised, and that we now know to be part of this old order that is to pass. From the other pole of our earlier ambivalence, we retain the insight that, however imperfectly and however provisionally, Christian life and action in society must conform to Christian values and to the vision of the future for which we hope.

This is not to say that all Protestants feel this way. There are many who still cling to the earlier understanding and still believe that as a greater proportion of the population becomes Protestant, social ills will be automatically solved. Therefore, just as Catholicism and Protestantism are divided in Latin America, so are they among Hispanics in the United States, and along lines parallel to those that cause divisions in Latin America.

A New Ecumenism

Ever since it encountered Protestantism, the Hispanic community lived in religious tension. On the one hand, Catholics felt that Protestants were not only heretics, as the hierarchy told them, but also traitors to their people and their traditions. On the other, Protestants felt that Catholics were not only antibiblical heretics and idolaters but also relics of an age of obscurantism.

The last few decades, however, have seen very significant changes in this situation. The renewal of Roman Catholicism since the time of John XXIII and the Second Vatican Council has been nothing short of miraculous. Even very conservative Protestants have been forced to admit that on the premises of their own theology, they cannot discount what may happen in a church that has begun to read Scripture anew and has set out on a daring pilgrimage of renewed obedience. Emphasis on the role of the laity has also increased participation in the life of the church at the local level, thus giving Hispanics added input into Roman Catholicism. Eventually, the first Mexican-American bishop was consecrated. He and others have not been content with following the patterns set by the earlier white hierarchy, and with their blessing other Hispanic priests have been organizing communities for social action, inquiring into the possibility of a Hispanic theology and in general bringing to the Hispanic Catholic Church the *aggiornamento* that Pope John inspired.

Meanwhile, Hispanic Protestants have also been on pilgrimage. Besides their own experience of injustice and alienation, which contradicted the ideology they had associated with Protestantism, there were other events that opened their eyes to new realities. The civil rights movement was foremost among these. This was basically a struggle of Protestants against Protestants. In that struggle, white Protestantism did not always show itself to be the force for progress and freedom that we had been told it was. Indeed, a strange anomaly appeared: Those whites who were constantly quoting the Bible were also contradicting it in their daily lives, and those who seemed to discount the authority of Scripture often seemed to have a clearer understanding of the biblical demand for love and justice. This has made it very difficult for many in the Hispanic Protestant community to continue being fundamentalist in the traditional sense. The authority of Scripture is still held in high regard by that community. But there is also a growing awareness that there is a certain sort of fundamentalism that is grossly antibiblical. For this reason, many Protestants are seeking ways of interpreting Scripture that, while respecting the authority of the Bible, are different from what we were taught. The net result is that we find ourselves walking along the same path with Roman Catholics.

This new ecumenism has a practical and political side. The civil rights movement has its counterparts in the Hispanic community, and in those counterparts Catholics and Protestants have been drawn together. This is true of those involved in the unionization of farm laborers in California, in community organization in the barrios of San Antonio and Los Angeles, in the struggle for independence in Puerto Rico, and in the search for more political participation in New York and Chicago. In these struggles, Protestant and Catholic Hispanics march arm in arm and are thus learning to undo many of the prejudices that have divided them. It is true that many Hispanics, both Protestant and Catholic, do not participate in these struggles; but for those who do, out of the struggle itself a new ecumenism has been born.

Furthermore, this new ecumenism is not limited to issues of "life and work." It also includes what have traditionally been called matters of "faith and order." Indeed, it is our contention that there can be no division between life and work on the one hand and faith and order on the other, for as we work and live out the gospel we gain new insights into the meaning of our faith and the proper order for the church.

There is a new reformation already in progress. This reformation is arising, like that of the sixteenth century, in the periphery of Christendom—in the Third World and among minorities in the traditional centers of Christianity.

Notes

1. *Inter caetera, Eximiae devotionis,* second *Inter caetera, Piis fidelium,* and *Duum siquidem.* These are to be found in the extensive work by F. J. Hernáez, *Colección de bulas, breves y otros documentos relativos a la iglesia de América y Filipinas,* 2 vols. (Brussels, 1879; Vaduz: Kraus Reprint, 1964). On the background of these bulls, both in Portuguese missions and in the Crusades, see F. Mateos, "Bulas portuguesas y españolas sobre descubrimientos geográficos," *Missionalia Hispanica* 19 (1962), pp. 5–34, 129–68. There has been considerable debate as to the reasons why these bulls were issued and what their original intent and scope were. See M. Giménez Fernández, *Nuevas consideraciones sobre la historia y sentido de las bulas alejandrinas de 1943 referentes a las Indias* (Seville: Anuario de estudios americanos, 1944), and "Todavía más sobre las letras alejandrinas de 1493 referentes a las Indias," *Anales de la Universidad Hispalense* 14 (1953), pp. 241–301. The other main participant in the controversy was V. D. Sierra, "En torno a las bulas alejandrinas de 1493," *Missionalia Hispanica* 10 (1953), pp. 73–122, and "Y nada más sobre las bulas alejandrinas de 1493," *Missionalia Hispanica* 12 (1955), pp. 403–28. On the basis for the bulls on the legal theory of the time, see P. Castañeda, "Las bulas alejandrinas y la extensión del poder indirecto," *Missionalia Hispanica* 28 (1971), pp. 215–48.

2. The year 1501 is the date of Alexander's bull to this effect. Yet the tone of the bull itself, as well as other signs, would seem to indicate that by then this was already established practice. The bull is in Hernáez, *Collección de bulas,* vol. 1, pp. 20–21.

3. At least during the early stages of the conquest, the crown did not profit directly from this arrangement, for two-thirds of such income was used to support the work of the Church, and the rest was employed in works of charity. F. X. Montalbán, *Manual de historia de las misiones* (Bilbao: El Siglo de las Misiones, 1961), pp. 256–58.

4. Bull *Universalis ecclesiae,* 1508, in Hernáez, *Collección de bulas,* vol. 1, pp. 24–25.

5. See A. de Egaña, *La teoría del regio vicariato español en Indias* (Rome: Universitas Gregoriana, 1958). This includes an extensive bibliography on the subject, on pp. xi-xx.

6. This was already apparent in Isabella's oft-quoted words, spoken upon hearing that Columbus had sent to Spain some Indians to sell as slaves: "Who has given the Admiral the right to sell my subjects?" Isabella ordered that any who had bought such Indians must return them to their land of origin, under penalty of death. A. de Herrera y Tordesillas, *Historia general de los hechos de los castellanos en las islas y tierra firme del mar Océano,* 4 vols. (Madrid, 1601), vol. 1, p. 256. Similar attitudes appeared throughout the early decades of the conquest, until Spanish power was firmly entrenched, not only over the Indians but also and especially over the conquistadors and their descendants. This is not to say, however, that moral considerations did not enter into the picture. Isabella herself was personally concerned over the well-being of her Indian subjects—to the point of issuing instructions that they should not bathe so often. And Charles V, partially as a result of the writings of Las Casas and Vitoria, for a time considered abandoning the entire enterprise as morally unjustifiable. However, economic and political considerations prevailed, and the enterprise continued. The classical work on this entire issue is L. Hanke, *The Spanish Struggle for Justice in the Conquest of America* (Philadelphia: University of Pennsylvania Press, 1949). See also L. B. Simpson, *Los conquistadores y el indio americano* (Barcelona: Ediciones Península, 1970).

7. The most remarkable exception is Las Casas, who was made bishop of Chiapas after he had become well known in government circles for his advocacy for the Indians.

8. See C. Bayle, *El clero secular y la evangelización de América* (Madrid: Consejo Superior de Investigaciones Científicas, 1950).

9. The bibliography on the Franciscans in the Spanish colonies is immense. Much of it is listed in or can be traced through Pedro Borges, *Métodos misionales en la cristianización de América* (Madrid: Consejo Superior de Investigaciones Científicas, 1960), pp. 12–13.

10. A. Figueras, "Principios de la expansión dominicana en Indias," *Missionalia Hispanica* 1 (1944), pp. 303–40.

11. F. Mateos, "Antecedentes de la entrada de los jesuitas españoles en las misiones de América," *Missionalia Hispanica* 1 (1944), pp. 106–66, and "Primera expedición de misioneros jesuitas al Perú," *Missionalia Hispanica* 2 (1945), pp. 41–108.

12. J. Castro Seoane, "La expansión de la Merced en la América colonial," *Missionalia Hispanica* 1 (1944), pp. 73–108; 2 (1945), pp. 231–30; J. Castro Seoane, "La Merced en el Perú," *Missionalia Hispanica* 3 (1946), pp. 243–320; 4 (1947), pp. 137–69, 383–401; 7 (1950), pp. 55–80.

13. Lewis Hanke, *Las teorías políticas de Bartolomé de Las Casas* (Buenos Aires: J. Peuser, 1935); Henry Raup Wagner, *The Life and Writings of Bartolomé de Las Casas* (Albuquerque: University of New Mexico Press, 1967); Angel Losada, *Fray Bartolomé de Las Casas a la luz de la moderna crítica histórica* (Madrid: Tecnos, 1970); Juan Friede and Benjamin Keen, *Bartolomé de Las Casas in History: Toward an Understanding of the Man and His Work* (DeKalb, Ill.: Northern Illinois University Press, 1971); Lewis Hanke, *All Mankind Is One: A Study of the Disputation between Bartolomé de Las Casas and Juan Ginés de Sepúlveda in 1550 on the Intellectual and Religious Capacity of the American Indians* (DeKalb, Ill.: Northern Illinois University Press, 1974); Comisión de Estudios de Historia de la Iglesia en Latinoamérica (CEHILA), *Bartolomé de Las Casas (1474–1974) e historia de la iglesia en América Latina* (Barcelona: Terra Nova, 1976); Juan Friede, *Bartolomé de Las Casas, precursor del anticolonialismo: Su lucha y su derrota* (México: Siglo Veintiuno, 1976); Ramón-Jesús Queralto Moreno, *El pensamiento filosófico-político de Bartolomé de Las Casas* (Sevilla: Escuela de Estudios Hispano-Americanos, 1976).

14. Alvaro Sánchez, *El Apóstol del Nuevo Reino: San Luis Beltrán* (Bogotá: Santafé, 1953). At a more popular level: Stephen Clissold, *The Saints of South America* (London: Charles Knight & Co., 1972), pp. 12–29.

15. The most complete history of the Jesuit missions in Paraguay, especially valuable for its collection of primary sources, is Pablo Pastells, *Historia de la Compañia de Jesús en la Provincia del Paraguay,* 8 vols. (Madrid: V. Suárez, 1912–1949). See also M. Mörner, *The Political and Economic Activities of the Jesuits in the La Plata Region: The Hapsburg Era* (Stockholm: Victor Pettersons Bokindustri Artiebolag, 1953); F. Mateos, "La Guerra Guaranítica y las misiones del Paraguay," *Missionalia Hispanica* 8 (1951), pp. 241–316; 9 (1952), pp. 75–121.

16. Antonio de Egaña, *Historia de la Iglesia en América Española: Desde el Descubrimiento hasta comienzos del siglo XIX,* vol. 2, *Hemisferio sur* (Madrid: Biblioteca de Autores Cristianos, 1966), p. 209. Egaña himself is not very sympathetic toward Gil González.

17. Mariano Picón Salas, *Pedro Claver: El santo de los esclavos* (Mexico: Fondo de Cultura Económica, 1949); Angel Valtierra, *Peter Claver: Saint of the Slaves* (London: Burns & Oates, 1960). A brief biography: Clissold, *The Saints,* pp. 173–201.

18. Quoted by Boleslao Lewin, *La rebelión de Túpac Amaru* (Buenos Aires: Sociedad Editora Latino Americana, 1967), p. 503.

19. It is also to be noted that the Virgin of Copacabana played a similar role in some sectors of the Túpac Amaru rebellion.

20. The sources from which the various steps in the legend, as well as the development of the legend itself, may be reconstructed may be found in León Lopetegui and Félix Zubillaga, *Historia de la Iglesia en América española: Desde el descubrimiento hasta comienzos del siglo XIX,* vol. 1, *México. América Central. Antillas* (Madrid: Biblioteca de Autores Cristianos, 1955), pp. 345–54.

21. This is why the Virgin of Guadalupe plays such an important role in Catholic Mexican-American theology. See Andrés Gonzales Guerrero, *A Chicano Theology*

(Maryknoll, N.Y.: Orbis, 1987); Virgilio Elizondo, *La morenita: Evangelizadora de las Américas* (Liguori, Mo.: Liguori Publications, 1981); Eduardo Hoornaert, "La evangelización según la tradición guadalupana," in SELADOC, *Religiosidad popular* (Salamanca: Sígueme, 1976), pp. 260–79.

22. Carlos Rosas, one of the foremost Hispanic hymnologists in the country, a faithful Catholic and choir director in San Antonio, has expressed such feelings in a song that has become quite popular, "El profeta del barrio." After an initial stanza about Jesus preaching in Galilee and the people's response, the chorus says: "Es hijo del carpintero./Profeta no puede ser./Es uno de nuestro barrio./ Profeta no puede ser." (He is the carpenter's son./A prophet he cannot be./He is one of our very own./A prophet he cannot be.) The third, fourth, and fifth stanzas, in a rough translation, say: "The Virgin looked upon Juan Diego with loving eyes; but the bishop was blind and thus he did not believe. What happened to Juan Diego also happens to many now; Juan Diego was not of the clergy, and the bishop did not believe. The wise and the learned misjudge the poor; they look upon them as retarded and try to keep them down."

23. See Dora Ortiz Vásquez, *Enchanted Temples of Taos* (Santa Fe: Rydal Press, 1975). Ms. Ortiz Vásquez is a great-granddaughter of Fr. Martínez.

24. There are at the time of this writing two Hispanic archbishops (San Antonio and Santa Fe), six diocesan bishops (Fresno, Tucson, El Paso, Corpus Christi, Las Cruces, and Pueblo), and eleven auxiliary bishops (Newark, Los Angeles [2], San Diego, Washington, Sacramento, Houston, New York, Chicago, Miami, and Brooklyn). There are a total of 1,954 Hispanic priests in the United States. This does not count Puerto Rico, where the archbishop and the hierarchy are Puerto Ricans. Manuel J. Rodríguez, ed., *Directorio de sacerdotes hispanos en los Estados Unidos de América* (Forest Hills, N.Y.: Herencia española, 1986). Information updated by the Secretariat for Hispanic Affairs.

25. Secretariat for Hispanic Affairs, *Proceedings of the II Encuentro Nacional Hispano de Pastoral* (Washington, D.C.: National Catholic Conference, 1977), p. 25.

26. Ibid., p. 28.

27. Secretariat for Hispanic Affairs, *Pueblo Hispano—Voz Profética* (Washington, D.C.: National Catholic Conference, 1985), p. 77.

28. Ibid., p. 76.

29. Ibid., p. 125.

30. *L'impérialisme protestant: Considérations sur le destin inégal des peuples protestants et catholiques dans le monde actuel* (Paris: Flammarion, 1948).

31. On the life and work of Thomson, see J. C. Varetto, *Diego Thomson* (Buenos Aires: La Aurora, 1918).

32. Bolívar and several of the principal leaders of Latin American independence believed that the traditions of authoritarianism and obscurantism were so ingrained in the entire continent that democracy would only be possible if those traditions were broken. For a time, Bolívar considered the advisability of placing the entire continent under the temporary tutelage of Great Britain. He also hoped that the United States would support his efforts toward a unified and democratic Hispanic America. The policies of the United States to scuttle such attempts at unity at the Panama Congress were a deep disappointment to Bolívar and to many of his generation. In any case, the policy of most of the young republics was to foster immigration from Europe, especially from the North Atlantic, in the hope of

bringing in new industries, opening up land for agriculture, and introducing traditions of democratic government.

33. As far as is known, the first Protestant sermons in Spanish in Argentina and in Uruguay were preached by Scotsman John F. Thomson, a member of the immigrant community. See J. C. Varetto, *El apóstol del Plata: Juan F. Thomson* (Buenos Aires: La Aurora, 1943).

34. I have written a summary of this process for Episcopalians, Presbyterians, and Methodists in *The Development of Christianity in the Latin Caribbean* (Grand Rapids, Mich.: Eerdmans, 1969), pp. 91–95.

35. T. S. Goslin, *Los evangélicos en la América Latina* (Buenos Aires: La Aurora, 1956), pp. 95, 103.

36. For two different and often conflicting evaluations, specifically on the case of Chile, compare Christian Lalive d'Epinay, *El refugio de las masas: Estudio sociológico del protestantismo chileno* (Santiago de Chile: Editorial del Pacífico, 1968), with Emilio Willems, *Followers of the New Faith: Culture Change and the Rise of Protestantism in Brazil and Chile* (Nashville: Vanderbilt University Press, 1967).

37. In more recent years, a new wave of Pentecostalism and fundamentalism has been added. This is closely connected both with the "electronic church" and with the New Right in the United States and has been particularly successful in Mexico and Central America—Guatemala above all. With very significant financial support from elements in the United States that fear the spread of revolutionary sentiments in Central America, the message of this new form of Protestantism is as otherworldly as that of any previous form. The dimension that is now added, however, is that the great apostasy both of Roman Catholicism and of many Protestant bodies is their involvement in matters of this world. While in earlier times the Catholic "heresy" was "popery," now the heresies are liberation theology, Christian Base Communities, and any form of political involvement. On these items, they are virulently anti-Catholic. Given the present situation, particularly in countries such as Guatemala, where death squads have killed hundreds of Catholic lay catechists and Base Community organizers, this is resulting in unprecedented religious and political tensions. These "new" Protestants claim to stay out of politics, but in fact they support the status quo and say and do nothing about the abuses committed against those who seek political and social changes. Thus it is to be feared that if such changes ever come, they will be followed by painful reprisals, and many in the United States who said nothing about the death squads will cry foul.

U. S. Latino/a Theology Bibliography

Abalos, David T. *Latinos in the United States: The Sacred and the Political.* Notre Dame, Indiana: University Press, 1986.

Aquino, María Pilar. *"El culto a María y María en el culto."* *FEM Publicación Feminista* 5, no. 20 (1981-1982): 41–46. México.

————. *Aportes para una teología desde la mujer.* Madrid: Edición Biblia y Fe, 1988.

————. "Doing Theology from the Perspective of Hispanic Women." In *We Are a People! Initiatives in Hispanic American Theology.* Edited by Roberto Goizueta, 79–105. Philadelphia: Fortress Press, 1992.

————. "Perspectives on a Latina's Feminist Liberation Theology." In *Frontiers of Hispanic Theology in the United States.* Edited by Allan Figueroa Deck, 23–40. Maryknoll, New York: Orbis Books, 1992.

————. "The Challenge of Hispanic Women." *Missiology* 20, no. 2 (April 1992): 261–268.

————. "El 'Des-cubrimiento' colectivo de la propia fuerza: Perspectivas teológicas desde las mujeres Latinoamericanas: Redescubrimiento." In *Five Centuries of Hispanic American Christianity 1492–1992 Apuntes* 13, no. 1 (Spring 1993): 86–103.

————. "Directions and Foundations of Hispanic/Latino Theology: Toward a *Mestiza* Theology of Liberation." *Journal of Hispanic/Latino Theology* 1, no. 1 (November 1993): 5–21.

————. *Our Cry for Life: Feminist Theology from Latin America.* Maryknoll, New York: Orbis Books, 1993.

Arrastía, Cecilio. "The Eucharist: Liberation, Community, and Commitment." *Apuntes* 4, no.4 (Winter 1984):75–81.

Aymes, María de La Cruz. *Fe y Cultura.* Mahwah, New Jersey: Paulist Press, 1987.

Bañuelas, Arturo J. "U.S. Hispanic Theology." *Missiology* 20, no. 2 (April 1992): 275–300.

————. "U.S. Hispanic Theology: A Bibliography." *Apuntes* 2, no. 4 (Winter 1991): 93–103.

Barron, Clemente. "On My Mind: Racism and Vocations." *New Theology Review* 3, no. 4 (November 1990): 92–103.

Costas, Orlando. "Hispanic Theology in North America." In *Struggles for Solidarity: Liberation Theologies in Tension.* Edited by Lorina Getz and Ruy Costa, 63–74. Minneapolis: Fortress Press, 1992.

Deck, Allan Figueroa. "Liturgy and Mexican American Culture." *Modern Liturgy* 3, no. 7 (October 1976): 24–26.

————. "A Christian Perspective on the Reality of Illegal Immigration." *Social Thought* (Fall 1978): 39–53.

————. "A Hispanic Perspective on Christian Family Life." *America* 145, no. 20 (19 December 1981): 400–402.

————. *"El Movimiento Hispano y la Iglesia Cátolica de los Estados Unidos."* *Christus* (Marzo 1983): 48–50.

————. "Fundamentalism and the Hispanic Catholic." *America* (26 January 1985): 64–66.

————. "Hispanic Vocations: Light at the End of the Tunnel." *Call to Growth Ministry* 11, no. 2 (Winter 1986): 12–18.

————. "Hispanic Vocations: What Happens Once You've Got Them." *The Priest* 42 (March 1986): 18–22.

————. "Hispanic Ministry Comes of Age." *America* 17 (May 1986): 400–402.

————. "Multicultural Sensitivities." *Human Development* 8, no. 2 (Summer 1987): 32–34.

————. "Proselytism and the Hispanic Catholic: How Long Can We Cry Wolf?" *America* 10 (December 1988): 485–490.

————. *The Second Wave: Hispanic Ministry and The Evangelization of Cultures*. Mahwah, N.J.: Paulist Press, 1989.

————. "The Pastoral Plan, Window of Opportunity." *Origins* 19, no. 12 (17 August 1989): 198–201.

————. "The Hispanic Presence: A Moment of Grace." *The Critic* 45, no. 1 (Fall 1990): 48–59.

————. "Hispanic Theologians and the United States Catholic Church." *New Theology Review* 3, no. 4 (November 1990): 22–27.

————. "The Spirituality of the United States Hispanics: An Introductory Essay." *U.S. Catholic Historian* 9, nos. 1 & 2 (Winter 1990): 137–146.

————. "At the Crossroads: North American and Hispanic." In *We Are a People! Initiatives in Hispanic American Theology*. Edited by Roberto Goizueta, 1–20. Minneapolis: Fortress Press, 1992.

————. "Latino Theology: The Year of the 'Boom'." *Journal of Hispanic/ Latino Theology* 1, no. 2 (February 1994): 51–63.

————. "The Challenge of Evangelical/Pentecostal Christianity to Hispanic Catholicism." In *Hispanic Catholic Culture in the United States: Issues and Concerns*. Edited by Jay Dolan and Allan Figueroa Deck, 409–439. Indiana: University of Notre Dame Press, 1994.

Deck, Allan Figueroa and Jay P. Dolan, editors. *Hispanic Catholic Culture in the United States: Issues and Concerns*. Indiana: University of Notre Dame Press, 1994.

Díaz-Stevens, Ana María. "Latinas and the Church." In *Hispanic Catholic Culture in the United States: Issues and Concerns*. Edited by Jay Dolan and Allan Figueroa Deck, 240–277. Indiana: University of Notre Dame Press, 1994.

Dimas Soberal, José. *La Verdad Sobre Ciertos Ministerios Falsos*. Bayamón, Puerto Rico: Grafar Arte, 1988.

————. *O Ministério Ordenado da Mulher*. Sao Paulo, Brasil: Edicoes Paulinas, 1990.

Elizondo, Virgil P. *"Educación Religiosa para el Mexico-Norteamericano."* *Catequesis Latinoamericana* (1968). México.

————. *Mary: Prophetess and Model of Freedom for Responsibility.* San Antonio: MACC, 1972.

————. *Anthropological and Psychological Characteristics of the Mexican American.* San Antonio: MACC, 1974.

————. "Pastoral Planning for the Spanish Speaking in the United States." In *Colección Mestiza Americana.* San Antonio: MACC, 1975.

————. "A Challenge to Theology: The Situation of Hispanic Americans." In *Proceedings of the Catholic Theological Society of America* 30 (1975): 163–176.

————. *Christianity and Culture.* Indiana: Our Sunday Visitor, 1975.

————. "The San Antonio Experiment." *New Catholic World* 220 (May-June 1976): 117–120.

————. "Our Lady of Guadalupe as Cultural Symbol: The Power of the Powerless." In *Liturgy and Cultural Religious Traditions.* Edited by Power and Schmidt. *Concilium* 120 (1977).

————. *"La Virgen de Guadalupe como símbolo: 'El Poder de los impotentes'."* In *Concilium,* Madrid: Ediciones Cristiandad, 122 (Febrero 1977): 149–160.

————. "Who Is the Catechumen in the Spanish Speaking Community of the U.S.A.?" In *Becoming a Catholic Christian.* New York: Sadlier, 1977.

————. *The Human Quest: A Search for Meaning though Life and Death.* Indiana: Our Sunday Visitor, 1977.

————. *Mestizaje: The Dialectic of Birth and Gospel.* San Antonio: MACC, 1978.

————. "Commentary on John Paul's Opening Address at Puebla." In *Puebla and Beyond.* Maryknoll, New York: Orbis Books, 1979.

————. *La Morenita: Evangelizer of the Americas.* San Antonio: MACC, 1980.

————. "A Bicultural Approach to Religious Education." *The Journal of the Religious Education Association* 76 (May-June 1981): 258–270.

————. "Thou Shalt Not Have Strange Gods Before Me: A Bicultural Approach to Religious Education." *Religious Education* 76, no. 3 (May-June 1981): 258–270.

————. "The Hispanic Church in the USA: A Local Ecclesiology." In *Proceedings of the Catholic Theological Society of America* 36 (1981): 155–170.

————. *Galilean Journey: The Mexican American Promise.* Maryknoll, New York: Orbis Books, 1983.

————. *"Le Métissage comme lieu théologique."* Spiritus 93 (1983). Paris.

————. "Theological and Biblical Foundations for *Comunidades de Base.*" In *Developing Basic Christian Communities.* Chicago: Federation of Priests' Councils, 1983.

————. *Virgen y Madre: Reflexiones bíblicas sobre María de Nazaret.* San Antonio: MACC, 1983.

————. *Quién Eres Tu?* San Antonio: MACC, 1983.

————. "Christian Challenge and the Disadvantaged." *Linacre Quarterly* 51 (August 1983): 242–245.

————. "Stages of Practical Theology." In *Twenty Years of Concilium: Retrospect and Prospect. Concilium* 170 (1983): 20–26.

————. "Religious Education in the United States." In *The Transmission of the Faith to the Next Generation. Concilium* 174 (1984): 100–105.

————. *Different Theologies, Common Responsibility: Babel or Pentecost?* . Edited by C. Geffré, Virgil P. Elizondo, and G. Gutiérrez. *Concilium* 171 (1984).

———. "Conditions and Criteria for Authentic Intercultural Theological Dialogue." In *Different Theologies, Common Responsibility. Concilium* 171 (1984): 5–41.

———. "Mary in the Struggles of the Poor." *The New Catholic World* 229, no. 1374 (November/December 1986): 244–247.

———. *"Mexamerica—Une Galilée des nations."* *Catéchèse* 102 (January 1986). *Rencontre des Cultures* 102. Paris.

———. "Popular Religion as Support of Identity: A Pastoral-Psychological Case-Study Based on the Mexican Experience in the USA." In *Popular Religion. Concilium* 186 (1986) 36–43.

———. "I Forgive, but I Do Not Forget." In *Forgiveness. Concilium* 204 (1986): 87–98.

———. *Option for the Poor, Challenge to the Rich Countries.* Edited by Virgil Elizondo and Leonardo Boff. *Concilium* 187 (1986).

———. "The Ministry of the Church and Contemporary Migration." In *Social Thought: Special Papal Edition.* Washington, D.C., 1987.

———. *The Future is Meztizo: Life Where Cultures Meet.* New York: Meyer-Stone, 1988.

———. *Theologies of the Third World: Commonalities and Differences.* Edited by Virgil P. Elizondo and Leonardo Boff. *Concilium* 199 (1988).

———. "America's Changing Face." *The Tablet* 23 (July 1988). London.

———. "A Paradigm for Cultural Study." *Journal of Catholic Education* 6, no. 3 (1989). Melbourne, Australia.

———. *"Mestizaje* as Locus of Theological Reflection." In *The Future of Liberation Theology.* Edited by Marc Ellis and Otto Maduro, 358–374. Maryknoll, New York: Orbis Books, 1989.

———. "Elements for a Mexican American *Mestizo* Christology." In *Christologies in Encounter,* XV, 2. Voices from the Third World. Sri Lanka, December, 1989.

———. "The New Humanity of the Americas." In *1492–1992: The Voice of the Victims. Concilium* 1990/6: 141–147.

———. "Mary and the Evangelization of the Americas." In *Mary: Woman of Nazareth.* Edited by Doris Donnelly, 146–160. New York: Paulist Press, 1990.

———. *"Mestizaje* as a Locus of Theological Reflection." In *Frontiers of Hispanic Theology in the United States.* Edited by Allan Figueroa Deck, 104–123. Maryknoll, New York: Orbis Books, 1992.

Escamilla, Roberto. "Worship in the Context of Hispanic Culture." *Worship* 51 (July 1977): 290–293.

Espín, Orlando. *"Religiosidad Popular: Un Aporte Para Su Definición y Hermenéutica." Estudios Sociales* XVII, no. 58 (Octubre–Diciembre 1984): 41–56.

———. "The Sources of Hispanic Theology." In *Proceedings of the Catholic Theological Society of America* 43, 122–125. Toronto, 1988.

———. " 'Lilies of the Field': A Hispanic Theology of Providence and Human Responsibility." In *Proceedings of the Catholic Theological Society of America* 44, 70–90. St. Louis, 1989.

———. "The Vanquished, Faithful Solidarity and the Marian Symbol: A Hispanic Perspective on Providence." In *On Keeping Providence.* Edited by Barbara Doherty and Joan Coultas, 84–101. Terre Haute: St. Mary of the Woods College Press, 1991.

————. "God of the Vanquished: Foundations for a Latino Spirituality." *Listening: Journal of Religion and Culture* 27, no. 1 (1992): 70–83.

————. "Trinitarian Monotheism and the Birth of Popular Catholicism: The Case of Sixteenth-Century Mexico." *Missiology* 20, no. 2 (1992): 117–204.

————. "Grace and Humanness: A Hispanic Perspective." In *We Are a People! Initiatives in Hispanic American Theology*. Edited by Roberto Goizueta, 133–164. Minneapolis: Fortress Press, 1992.

————. "Tradition and Popular Religion: An Understanding of the *Sensus Fidelium*." In *Frontiers of Hispanic Theology in the United States*. Edited by Allan F. Deck, 62–87. Maryknoll, New York: Orbis Books, 1992.

————. "Popular Catholicism Among Latinos." In *Hispanic Catholic Culture in the United States: Issues and Concerns*. Edited by Jay Dolan and Allan Figueroa Deck, 308–359. Indiana: Notre Dame University Press, 1994.

————. "Popular Religion as an Epistemology (of Suffering)." *Journal of Hispanic/Latino Theology* 2, no. 2 (November 1994): 55–78.

Espín, Orlando, and Sixto J. García. "Hispanic-American Theology." In *Proceedings of the Catholic Theological Society of America* 42, 114–119. Philadelphia, 1987.

Estévez, Felipe J. *El Perfil Pastoral de Félix Varela*. Miami: Editorial Universal, 1989.

————. *Felix Varela, Letters to Elpidio: A Critical Translation*. New York: Paulist Press, 1989.

Feliciano, Juan G. "Suffering : A Hispanic Epistemology." *Journal of Hispanic/Latino Theology* 2, no. 1 (August 1994): 41–50.

García, Sixto J. "A Hispanic Approach to Trinitarian Theology: The Dynamics of Celebration, Reflection, and Praxis." In *We Are a People! Initiatives in Hispanic American Theology*. Edited by Roberto Goizueta, 107–132. Minneapolis: Fortress Press, 1992.

————. "U.S. Hispanic and Mainstream Trinitarian Theologies." In *Frontiers of Hispanic Theology in the United States*. Edited by Allan Figueroa Deck, 88–103. Maryknoll, New York: Orbis Books, 1992.

————. "Sources and Loci of Hispanic Theology." *Journal of Hispanic/Latino Theology* 1, no. 1 (November 1993): 22–43.

García, Sixto J. and Orlando Espín. "Hispanic-American Theology." In *Proceedings of the Catholic Theological Society of America* 42, 114–119. Philadelphia, 1987.

García-Rivera, Alejandro. "A Contribution to the Dialogue Between Theology and the Natural Sciences." *Journal of Hispanic/Latino Theology* 2, no. 1 (August 1994): 51–59.

————. "San Martíde Porres: *Criatura de Dios*." *Journal of Hispanic/Latino Theology* 2, no. 2 (November 1994): 26–54.

Goizueta, Roberto S. "The History of Suffering as *Locus Theologicus*: Implications for U.S. Hispanic Theology." *Voices from the Third World: Journal of the Ecumenical Association of Third World Theologians* 12 (December 1989): 32–47.

————. "The Church and Hispanics in the United States: From Empowerment to Solidarity." In *That They May Live: Power, Empowerment and Leadership in the Church*. Edited by Michael Downey. New York: Crossroads, 1991.

266   *U.S. Latino/a Theology Bibliography*

_____. "Theology as Intellectually Vital Inquiry: The Challenge of/to U.S. Hispanics." *Proceedings of the Catholic Theological Society of America* 46 (1991): 58–69.

_____. *"Nosotros*: Toward a U.S. Hispanic Anthropology." *Listening: Journal of Religion and Culture* 27 (Winter 1992): 55–69.

_____. "Rediscovering Praxis: The Significance of U.S. Hispanic Experience for Theological Method." In *We Are a People! Initiatives in Hispanic American Theology.* Edited by Roberto Goizueta, 51–77. Minneapolis: Fortress Press, 1992.

_____. "U.S. Hispanic Theology and the Challenge of Pluralism." In *Frontiers of Hispanic Theology in the United States.* Edited by Allan Figueroa Deck, 1–21. Maryknoll, New York: Orbis Books, 1992.

_____. *We Are a People! Initiatives in Hispanic American Theology.* Editor. Minneapolis: Fortress Press, 1992.

_____. "U.S. Hispanic *Mestizaje* and Theological Method." *Concilium* 4 (1993): 21–30.

_____. *"La Raza Cósmica? The Vision of José Vasconcelos." Journal of Hispanic/Latino Theology* 1, no. 2 (February 1994): 5–27.

González, Roberto O., and Michael La Velle. *The Hispanic Catholic in the United States: A Socio-cultural and Religious Profile.* New York: Northeast Catholic Pastoral Center for Hispanics, 1985.

González, Justo L. *Mañana: Christian Theology from a Hispanic Perspective.* Nashville: Abingdon Press, 1990.

_____. *Out of Every Tribe and Nation: Christian Theology at the Ethnic Roundtable.* Nashville: Abingdon Press, 1992.

_____. *Voces: Voices from the Hispanic Church.* Editor. Nashville: Abingdon Press, 1992.

González, Justo L. and Catherine González. *The Liberating Pulpit.* Nashville: Abingdon Press, 1994.

Guerrero, Andrés G. *A Chicano Theology.* Maryknoll, New York: Orbis Books, 1987.

Herrera, Marina. "A Hispanic Catechetical Project." *Dimensions,* April 1979.

_____. "What is Multicultural Catechesis." *Dimensions,* March 1979.

_____. *Methodology and Themes for Hispanic Catechesis.* Department of Education of the USCC, 1979.

_____. "The Hispanic Challenge." *Religious Education* 74, no. 5 (September/October 1979).

_____. "The Religious Education of Hispanics in a Multicultural Church." *New Catholic World* (July/August 1980).

_____. "Catechetics for a Multicultural Society." *Catechist* (April 1980).

_____. "Hispanic Intercultural Ministry Program." *Dimensions* (March/April 1980).

_____. "Parishes in a Multicultural Society." *Parish Ministry* (July/August 1980). Parish Project of the United States Catholic Conference.

_____. "The Multicultural Challenge for Religious Educators." *Dimensions,* (January/February 1980).

_____. "Catechetics for a Multicultural Society." *Catechist* (April 1980).

_____. "Popular Piety as a Parish Resource." *Service* 3 (1981).

————. "Hispanics: How Can the Church Respond to Their Presence?" *Pace* 12 (April and May 1982).

————. "Celebrations for a Multicultural Church." *Momentum, Journal of the National Catholic Educational Association* (February 1983).

————. "Multicultural Adult Catechesis: What Is It and for Whom?" In *Christian Adulthood: A Catechetical Resource*. Washington, D.C.: United States Catholic Conference, 1983.

————. "Toward Multicultural Youth Ministry." *The Journal of Youth Ministry* 1, no. 1 (Spring 1983).

————. *Adult Religious Education for the Hispanic Community*. The National Conference of Diocesan Directors of Religious Education, 1984.

————. "Popular Religiosity and Liturgical Education." *Liturgy* 5, no. 1 (1985).

————. "Religion and Culture in the Hispanic Community as a Context for Religious Education: Impact of Popular Religiosity on U.S. Hispanics." *The Living Light* 21, no. 2 (January 1985).

————. "Mary of Nazareth in Cross-Cultural Perspective." *Pace* (May 1986).

————. "Towards Multicultural Youth Ministry." In *Readings in Youth Ministry*. National Federation of Catholic Youth Ministry, 1986.

————. "Theoretical Foundations for Multicultural Catechesis." In *Faith and Culture: A Multicultural Catechetical Resource*. Department of Education, USCC, 1987.

————. *Pentecost: A Feast for All Peoples. Celebrating the Multicultural/ Multiracial Church*. Edited by Marina Herrera, Thea Bowman, Martin J. Carter and Jaime R. Vidal. National Catholic Conference for Interracial Justice, 1988.

————. "Providence and Histories: One Hispanic's View." *The Proceedings of the Catholic Theology Society of America* 44 (1989): 7–11.

Herrera, Marina and Vidal, Jaime. "Evangelization: Then and Now(?)." *New Theology Review* 3, no. 4 (November 1990): 6–21.

Hinojosa, Gilberto and Jay Dolan. *Mexican Americans and the Catholic Church 1900–1965*. Indiana: University of Notre Dame Press, 1994.

Hinojosa, Juan-Lorenzo. "Culture, Spirituality, and U.S. Hispanics." In *Frontiers of Hispanic Theology in the United States*. Edited by Allan Figueroa Deck, 154–164. Maryknoll, New York: Orbis Books, 1992.

Huitrado-Hizo, Juan José. "Hispanic Popular Religiosity: The Expression of a People Coming to Life." *New Theology Review* 3, no. 4 (November 1990): 43–55.

Icaza, Rosa María. "The Cross in Mexican Popular Piety." *Liturgy* 1, no. 1 (1980): 27–34.

————. "Spirituality of the Mexican American People." *Worship* 63 (1989): 232–246.

————. "Prayer, Worship, and Liturgy in a U.S. Hispanic Key." In *Frontiers of Hispanic Theology in the United States*. Edited by Allan Figueroa Deck, 134–153. Maryknoll, New York: Orbis Books, 1992.

————. *Prophetic Vision: Pastoral Reflections on the National Pastoral Plan for Hispanic Ministry*. Edited by Rosa María Icaza, Soledad Galeron, Rosendo Urrabazo. Kansas City, MO.: Sheed and Ward, 1992.

Isasi-Díaz, Ada María. "Silent Women Will Never Be Heard." *Missiology* 7, no. 3 (July 1979): 295–301.

_____. "The People of God on the Move—Chronicle of a History." In *Prophets Denied Honor*. Edited by Antonio M. Stevens Arroyo, 330–333. Maryknoll, New York: Orbis Books, 1980.

_____. *"La Mujer Hispana: Voz Profetica en la Iglesia de los Estados Unidos."* Pro Mundi Vita (1982). Brussels.

_____. "Toward an Understanding of *Feminismo Hispano* in the USA." In *Women's Consciousness, Women's Conscience*. Edited by Barbara Hilkert Andolsen, Christine Gudorf and Mary D. Pellauer, 51–61. Minneapolis: Winston Press, 1985.

_____. *God's Fierce Whimsy: Christian Feminism and Theological Education*. (The Mud Flower Collective). Edited by Isasi-Díaz et al. New York: Pilgrim Press, 1985.

_____. *"'Apuntes'* for a Hispanic Women's Theology of Liberation." *Apuntes* 5–6 (Fall 1986): 61–71.

_____. "A Hispanic Garden in a Foreign Land." In Inheriting *Our Mothers' Gardens: Feminist Theology in Third World Perspective*. Edited by Isasi-Díaz et al. Philadelphia: Westminster Press, 1988.

_____. "*Mujeristas:* A Name of Our Own." In *The Future of Liberation Theology*. Edited by Marc H. Ellis and Otto Maduro, 410–419. Maryknoll, New York: Orbis Books, 1989.

_____. "*Mujeristas*: A Name of Our Own." *The Christian Century* 106, no. 18 (May 24–31, 1989): 560–562.

_____. "A Platform for Original Voices." *Christianity and Crisis* 49, no. 9 (12 June 1989): 191–192.

_____. "*Mujeristas*: A Name of Our Own." In *Yearning to Breathe Free: Liberation Theologies in the United States*. Edited by Mar Peter-Raoul et al., 121–128. Maryknoll, New York: Orbis Books, 1990.

_____. "The Bible and *Mujerista* Theology." In *Lift Every Voice: Constructing Christian Theologies from the Underside*. Edited by Susan Brooks Thistlethwaite and Mary Brooks Engel, 261–269. San Francisco: Harper & Row, 1990.

_____. "Hispanic Women in America: Starting Points." *Christianity and Crisis* 51 (May 13, 1991): 150–152.

_____. "Hispanic Women in the Roman Catholic Church." In *Women and Church—the Challenge of Ecumenical Solidarity in an Age of Alienation*. Edited by Melanie A. May, 13–17. Grand Rapids: William Eerdmans Publishing, 1991.

_____. *"'Apuntes'* For a Hispanic Women's Theology of Liberation." In *Voces—Voices from the Hispanic Church*. Edited by Justo González, 24–31. Nashville: Abingdon Press, 1992.

_____. "*Mujerista* Theology's Method: A Liberative Praxis, A Way of Life." *Listening: Journal of Religion and Culture* 27, no. 1 (Winter 1992): 41–54.

_____. "*Mujeristas*: Who Are We and What Are We About." *Journal of Feminist Studies in Religion* 8, no. 1 (Spring 1992): 105–109.

_____. *En La Lucha—In The Struggle: A Hispanic Women's Liberation Theology*. Minneapolis: Fortress Press, 1993.

_____. "Defining Our *Projecto Histórico: Mujerista* Strategies for Liberation." *Journal of Feminist Studies in Religion* 9, nos. 1–2 (Spring/Fall 1993): 17–28.

_____. "On the Birthing Stool." In *Women at Worship: Interpretations of North American Diversity*. Edited by Marjorie Procter-Smith and Janet R. Walton, 191–210. Louisville: Westminster: John Knox Press, 1993.

_____. "Praxis: The Heart of *Mujerista* Theology." *Journal of Hispanic/Latino Theology* 1, no. 1 (November 1993): 44–55.

_____. "The Task of Hispanic Women's Liberation Theology—*Mujeristas*: Who We Are and What We Are About." In *Feminist Theology from the Third World*. Edited by Ursula King, 88–102. London: SPCK; Maryknoll, New York, Orbis, 1994.

_____. *Women of God, Women of the People*. Chalice Press, 1995. (Forthcoming)

Isasi-Díaz, Ada María, and Yolanda Tarango. *Hispanic Women: Prophetic Voices in the Church*. San Francisco: Harper & Row, 1988.

Loya, Gloria Inés. "Hispanic Faith and Culture—and U.S.A. Religions." *Review for Religious* 53, no. 3 (May/June 1994): 460–466

_____. "The Hispanic Woman: *Pasionaria* and *Pastora* of the Hispanic Community." In *Frontiers of Hispanic Theology in the United States*. Edited by Allan Figueroa Deck, 124–133. Maryknoll, New York: Orbis Books, 1992.

Martínez, Dolorita. "Basic Christian Communities: A New Model of Church within the United States Hispanic Community." *New Theology Review* 3, no. 4 (November 1990): 35–42.

Paredes, Tito. "Popular Religiosity: A Protestant Perspective." *Missiology* 20, no. 2 (April 1992): 205–220.

Pazmiño, Robert. "Double Dutch: Reflections of an Hispanic North American on Multicultural Religious Education." *Apuntes* 2 (Summer 1988): 27–37.

Pérez, Arturo J. "Baptism in the Hispanic Community." *Emmanuel Magazine* 87, no. 2 (February 1981): 77–86.

_____. "Lent: Conversion Liturgy." *Hosana* 1, no. 1 (Spring 1983).

_____. *Popular Catholicism*. Washington, D.C.: Pastoral Press, 1988.

_____. "Signs of the Times: Toward a Hispanic Rite, *'Quizas'*." *New Theology Review* 3, no. 4 (November 1990): 80–88.

_____. "The History of Hispanic Liturgy Since 1965." In *Hispanic Catholic Culture in the United States: Issues and Concerns*. Edited by Jay Dolan and Allan Figueroa Deck, 360–408. Indiana: Notre Dame Univeristy Press, 1994.

Pérez, Arturo J., Consuelo Covarrubias and Edward Foley, Editors. *Así Es: Stories of Hispanic Spirituality*. Collegeville, Minnesota: Liturgical Press, 1994.

Pineda, Ana María. "Hispanic Identity." *Church Magazine* 4, no. 4 (Winter 1988): 51–55.

_____. "The Hispanic Presence: Hope and Challenge for Catholicity." *New Theology Review* 2, no. 3 (August 1989): 30–36.

_____. "*Pastoral de Conjunto*." *New Theology Review* 3, no. 4 (November 1990): 28–34.

_____. "Evangelization of the 'New World': A New World Perspective." *Missiology* 20, no. 2 (April 1992): 151–161.

_____. "The Challenge of Hispanic Pluralism in a Hispanic Context." *Missiology* 21 (October 1993): 437–442.

Ramírez, Ricardo. "Liturgy from the Mexican American Perspective." *Worship* 51 (July 1977): 293–298.

_____. *Fiesta, Worship and Family: (Essays On Mexican American Perception On Liturgy and Family Life)*. San Antonio, Texas: Mexican American Cultural Center, 1981.

Recinos, Harold J. *Hear the Cry: A Latino Pastor Challenges the Church.* Louis-
ville, Kentucky: Westminster/John Knox Press, 1989.
_____. "Mission: A Latino Pastoral Theology." *Apuntes* 3 (Fall 1992):
115–126.
Riebe-Estrella, Gary. " Underneath Hispanic Vocations." *New Theology Review*
3, no. 4 (November 1990): 72–79.
Rivera Pagán, Luis N. "Discovery and Conquest of America: Myth and Reality."
Apuntes 4 (Winter 1989): 75–92
_____. *"Idolatría nuclear y paz en el mundo: breves reflexiones teológicas."*
Apuntes 4 (Winter 1987): 75–85.
Rodríguez-Holguin, Jeanette. "Hispanics and the Sacred." *Chicago Studies* 29,
no. 2 (August 1990): 137–152.
_____. "Experience as a Resource for Feminist Thought." *Journal of Hispanic/
Latino Theology* 1, no. 1 (November 1993): 68–76.
_____. *Our Lady of Guadalupe: Faith and Empowerment Among Mexican-
American Women.* Austin: University of Texas Press, 1994.
Romero, C. Gilbert. *"Teología de las raices de un Pueblo: Los Penitentes de
Nuevo México."* *Servir* 15 (1979): 609–630. México.
_____. "On Choosing a Symbol System for a Hispanic Theology." *Apuntes*
1, no. 4 (1981): 16–20.
_____. "Self-Affirmation of the Hispanic Church." *The Ecumenist* 23, no. 3
(March/April 1985): 39–42.
_____. *Hispanic Devotional Piety.* Maryknoll, New York: Orbis Books, 1991.
_____. "Tradition and Symbol as Biblical Keys for a U.S. Hispanic Theology."
In *Frontiers of Hispanic Theology in the United States.* Edited by Allan Figueroa
Deck, 41–61. Maryknoll,New York: Orbis Books, 1992.
Rosado, Caleb. "Thoughts on a Puerto Rican Theology of Community." *Apuntes*
1 (Spring 1989): 10–12.
Ruiz, Jean-Pierre. "Beginning to Read the Bible in Spanish: An Initial Assessment."
Journal of Hispanic/Latino Theology 1, no. 2 (February 1994): 28–50.
Sandoval, Moises. *On the Move: A History of the Hispanic Church in the United
States.* Maryknoll, New York: Orbis Books, 1990.
_____. *Fronteras: A History of the Latin American Church in the USA Since
1513.* Editor. San Antonio: Mexican American Cultural Center, 1983.
Segovia, Fernando F. "A New Manifest Destiny: The Emerging Theological Voice
of Hispanic Americans." *Religious Studies Review* 17, no. 2 (April 1991):
102–109.
_____. "Two Places and No Place on Which to Stand: Mixture and Otherness
in Hispanic American Theology." *Listening: Journal of Religion and Culture*
27, no. 1 (1992): 26–40.
_____. "Hispanic American Theology and the Bible: Effective Weapon and
Faithful Ally." In *We Are a People! Initiatives in Hispanic American Theology.*
Edited by Roberto Goizueta, 21–49. Minneapolis: Fortress Press, 1992.
_____. Theological Education and Scholarship as Struggle: The Life of Racial/
Ethnic Minorities in the Profession." *Journal of Hispanic/Latino Theology* 2,
no. 2 (November 1994): 5–25.
Soliván-Román, Samuel. "The Need for a North American Hispanic Theology."
Listening: Journal of Religion and Culture 27, no. 1 (Winter 1992): 17–25.

Sosa, Juan. "*Liturgia Hispana en Los Estados Unidos.*" *Notitiae: Sacra Congregatio Pro Culto Divino* 20 (1984): 688–696.

————. "Renewal and Inculturation." *Liturgy* 9, no. 2 (Winter 1990): 17–23.

Stevens-Arroyo, Anthony. *Prophets Denied Honor: An Anthology on the Hispanic Church.* Maryknoll, New York: Orbis Books, 1980.

————. "The Emergence of a Social Identity Among Latino Catholics: An Appraisal." In *Hispanic Catholic Culture in the United States: Issues and Concerns.* Edited by Jay Dolan and Allan Figueroa Deck, 77–130. Indiana: University of Notre Dame Press, 1994.

————. "The Hispanic Model of Church: A People on the March." *New Catholic World* 223:1336 (July/August 1980): 153–157.

Tarango, Yolanda. "The Hispanic Woman and Her Role in the Church." *New Theology Review* 3, no. 4 (November 1990): 56–61.

U.S. Catholic Bishops' Conference. "*Los Obispos Hablan con la Virgen (Carta Pastoral de los Obispos Hispanos de los Estados Unidos).*" Maryknoll, New York: *Revista* Maryknoll, 1981.

————. "National Pastoral Plan for Hispanic Ministry." *Origins* 17, no. 26 (10 December 1987).

Urrabazo, Rosendo. *Machismo: Mexican American Male Self-concept.* San Antonio: Mexican American Culural Center, 1986.

Vidal, Jaime R. "Popular Religion in the Lands of the Origin of New York's Hispanic Population." In *Hispanics in New York: Religious, Cultural, and Social Experiences* II, 1–48. New York: Office of Pastoral Research of the Archdiocese of New York, 1982.

————. "Popular Religion Among the Hispanics in the General Area of the Archdiocese of Newark." In *Presencia Nueva: A Study of Hispanics in the Archdiocese of Newark*, 235–352. Newark, N.J.: Office of Research and Planning, 1988.

————. "The American Church and the Puerto Rican People." *U.S. Catholic Historian* 9, nos. 1 and 2 (Winter/Spring 1990): 119–135.

Vidal, Jaime and Jay Dolan. *Puerto Rican and Cuban Catholics in the U.S., 1900–1965.* Indiana: University of Notre Dame Press, 1994.

Vidal, Jaime and Marina Herrera. "Evangelization: Five Hundred Years Ago and Now(?)." *New Theology Review* 3, no. 4 (November 1990): 6–21.

Villafañe, Eldin. "An Evangelical Call to a Social Spirituality: Confronting Evil in Urban Society." *Apuntes* 2 (Summer 1991): 27–38.

————. "Socio-Cultural Matrix of Intergenerational Dynamics: An Agenda for the 90's." *Apuntes* 1 (Spring 1992): 13–20.

————. *The Liberating Spirit: Toward an Hispanic American Pentecostal Social Ethic.* Grand Rapids, Michigan: William B. Eerdmans Publishing Company, 1993.

Zapata, Dominga M. "Ministries Among Hispanics in the United States: Development and Challenges." *New Theology Review* 3, no. 1 (November 1990): 62–71.

Index

lez, 60, 236; ministries of, 234,
259n.33; Pentecostalism, 251–52,
259n.37; and Scripture, 35, 255
Puebla document, 127, 134
Pueblo de Dios en Marcha, 129
Pueblo Hispaño—Voz Profetica (Third
Encuentro), 247

Racism, 58, 63, 168n.13, 173n.57, 249
Rahner, Karl, 106, 112, 114, 120, 122
Recinos, Harold J. 132–45
Reign of God. *See* Kingdom of God
Revelation, 161–62, 172n.52
Ricoeur, Paul, 118
The Righteous Empire (Marty), 11
Rilke, Rainer Maria, 119, 120
Romero, Archbishop, 244

Scripture: González's views on, 65;
importance of, 49, 185, 239; interpretation of, 29, 107–108, 151, 203,
212; and oppressed, 23, 130, 133–
34, 137; and popular religion, 111,
122; and Protestantism, 250, 251,
253, 255; reading, 62, 211, 254; as
revelation, 172n.52; on sin, 213;
and tradition, 114, 149–50, 168n.12
*Second Encuentro Nacional Hispano de
Pastoral*, 246, 247
Second Vatican Council: and changes
in church, 245, 254; and laity, 79;
and *pastoral de conjunto*, 127; and
spiritual issues, 49, 122, 129, 230
*The Second Wave: Hispanic Ministry
and the Evangelization of Cultures*
(Deck), 65
Segovia, Fernando F., 28–43, 195, 202
Sensus fidelium: bearers of, 56, 158; and
popular Catholicism, 146, 161, 162;
and theology, 169n.20.
Sin: and church, 218; defined, 212–15,
221n.12; liberation from, 69; and
society, 49, 74, 219–20
Slavery: and culture, 14, 231; and *encomiendas*, 169n.25, 241; and St.
Pedro Claver, 242; and social structures, 216

Social location, 29, 30
Society: and Christianity, 137, 252; and
domination, 15, 138; perceptions
of, 36, 167n.3, 249; structures of, 35,
215; transforming, 24, 25
Soliván-Román, Samuel, 44–52
Spirituality, 229–31, 226–29, 234n.7
Stereotypes: of Hispanics, 31–32, 40,
51; and prejudice, 17–18; and theology, 37, 173n.57
Suffering: and beauty, 93; and church,
76, 143; elimination of, 23–24;
symbols of, 59, 164
Symbols: and identity, 72; linguistic,
162; poetic, 119; in popular religion, 148, 156, 160, 161, 165, 204;
religious, 11, 120, 157; and suffering, 59, 164

Tarango, Yolanda, 67–70, 94
Tecoatlaxope, 158, 159
Teología de conjunto, 69, 70, 73, 84
Teología de Liberación (Gutiérrez), 7
Teología mestiza de la liberación, 196
Tepeyac: and Hispanic identity, 93, 158;
and Hispanic theology, 57, 59, 73;
as sacred place, 159
Thanksgiving Day in the United States
(Esquivel), 141
Third Encuentro, 247
Tonantzin, 159, 160
Tradition: Christian, 23, 66, 162–63,
165, 166; and church, 8, 76–77,
134; of colonialism, 36, 38; and com-
munity, 34, 114; Hispanic, 61, 67;
and Jesus, 20; and liturgy, 79, 111;
and Mary, 122; and modernity, 97;
and oppression, 15, 32; and popular
religion, 149–53, 168n.12,
168n.13; and theology, 37, 78, 108–
10, 181
Transformation: and liberation, 89, 90;
social, 92, 135; spiritual, 46, 138,
210, 211, 219
Treaty of Guadalupe Hidalgo, 116
Tupac Amaru, José Gabriel, 242
Two-font theory, 149